Minorities and Cancer

Lovell A. Jones
Editor

Minorities and Cancer

Springer-Verlag
New York Berlin Heidelberg
London Paris Tokyo

Lovell A. Jones, Ph.D.
Associate Professor and Director
Experimental Gynecology-Endocrinology
Departments of Gynecology, Biochemistry,
and Molecular Biology
University of Texas
M. D. Anderson Cancer Center
Houston, TX 77030, USA

Library of Congress Cataloging-in-Publication Data
Minorities and cancer / Lovell A. Jones, editor.
    p.   cm.
    Includes index.
    1. Cancer−Epidemiology−United States. 2. Minorities−United
States−Diseases. 3. Cancer−Prevention. I. Jones, Lovell A.
    [DNLM: 1. Minority Groups. 2. Neoplasms−ethnology−United
States. 3. Neoplasms−epidemiology−United States. 4. Neoplasms−
prevention & control−United States.   QZ 200 M666]
RA645.C3M56   1989
614.5'999−dc 19
DNLM/DLC
                                                89-5892

Printed on acid-free paper

Typeset by Publishers Service, Bozeman, Montana.
Printed and bound by Edwards Brothers, Ann Arbor, Michigan.
Printed in the United States of America.

9 8 7 6 5 4 3 2 1

ISBN 0-387-96950-0 Springer-Verlag New York Berlin Heidelberg
ISBN 3-540-96950-0 Springer-Verlag Berlin Heidelberg New York

Preface

In 1984, the National Cancer Institute (NCI) set a goal of reducing the cancer mortality rate in the United States by 50% by the year 2000. If the goal is to be reached, special programs will have to be developed for minority communities. Although not an epidemiologist, but as one of the few minority scientists on staff at a major comprehensive center, I felt that I could play a role in attracting attention to what is a major health crisis in minority communities. I dreamed of holding a national conference addressing the cancer needs of minority groups through the presentation of ideas on intervention, applications of cancer prevention and control principles, as well as recent advances in basic and clinical research.

In April 1987, the first Biennial Symposium on Minorities and Cancer was held in Houston to address a major health crisis occurring in minority communities. Its goals were to stimulate discussion of recent advances in basic and clinical research and their application in the prevention and treatment of cancer in minority and economically disadvantaged groups; to provide a forum for scientific exchange among basic and clinical researchers, clinical practitioners, minority communities, and other lay groups interested in this issue; to provide an overview of how best to convey information concerning cancer to the general minority population and the economically disadvantaged; and to provide a working document as the basis for future meetings on this issue.

The symposium attracted approximately 400 participants from a total of 35 states and Puerto Rico. This was the first such meeting of cancer specialists from a variety of disciplines and the lay public to discuss a problem that has needed more attention for a long time. Of particular interest was the fact that this symposium was supported by both the American Cancer Society and the National Cancer Institute. Believed to be the first such event of its kind to be supported by both agencies, it marked the beginning of a working relationship that continues today. The symposium marked an important milestone; it was the focal point of the first presidential resolution designating the third week of April 1987 "National Minority Cancer Awareness Week." It has also marked the establishment of the LaSalle D. Leffall Jr. Award to be awarded to that person whose work aids in promoting the goal of reducing cancer by 50% in minority and economically disadvantaged communities. This award was created in honor of Dr. LaSalle D. Leffall, Jr., chairman of the Department of Surgery at Howard University Hospital and the first Black president of the American Cancer Society.

This book is a continuation of the original dream. It contains articles that focus on the goals of the symposium. Therefore, it is a book for everyone, health care professionals as well as the lay public. To those of you who participated, especially the authors, I salute you for taking the time and making the effort to write your chapters for this important book. I wish to also thank Dr. Susan McCamant-Grigsby, Ms. Roberta P. Verjan, Ms. Louise A. Scrocchi and Mr. Richard Hajek for their general assistance, to all secretaries, especially Ms. Debra Dabbs, who assisted with the symposium and manuscript preparation, and a special thanks to Drs. Richard Hackney, Edith Irby Jones, and Betty Lewis for their support when all seemed hopeless, and to Mary Markell and Lore Feldman for editorial assistance.

Cancer is an equal opportunity disease. It is my hope that this book will become a key resource in attracting attention to this serious health crisis in minority and economically disadvantaged communities.

For dreams to come true, a great deal of work as well as sacrifices have to be made. For one "to save the world," as my wife Marion describes my dreams, Troy, Tamisha, and Marion have had to make tremendous sacrifices. It is to them this book is dedicated.

Lovell A. Jones

Introduction

Every aspect of American society has been affected by racial discrimination and segregation. Cancer has been no exception. The social, medical, and economic impact of cancer on minority populations in the United States constitutes a major health crisis. Drug abuse was primarily an inner-city concern until the problem migrated to suburbia and only then did it become a national priority. Conversely, cancer programs have previously been addressed mostly to suburban America. Fortunately, the impact of cancer on our inner-city minority populations is now becoming a primary concern.

The first Biennial Conference on Cancer in Minority Populations, skillfully conceived and coordinated by Dr. Lovell Jones of The University of Texas M. D. Anderson Cancer Center, has resulted in this publication. It alerts the nation to this crisis and offers seminal corrective measures. Such an edition reviewing cancer among Blacks, Hispanics, Asian and Native Americans is long overdue and is a useful addition to our libraries. These proceedings include recent clinical and research advancements in cancer control, education, minority participation in National Cancer Institute trials, and site-specific cancers. The special considerations and ethnic variations among this subset are revealing as are the nursing problems and lack of prevention programs. The primary care physician and researcher will find practical and visionary information as well as comprehensive ideas for cancer prevention and detection.

This volume offers carefully drafted challenges for the minority academic health centers, National Cancer Institute, and the American Cancer Society. These data confirm again that socioeconomic status is an important factor in cancer diagnosis and treatment, thereby affecting the results in our minority population.

Claude Organ, Jr.

Contents

Section 1
Cancer Incidence in Minority Populations

Section 2
Prevention and Detection Programs: National and Regional Efforts

Section 3
Prevention and Detection Programs: Community-Based Efforts

Section 4
Cancer Research

Section 5
Treatment

Section 6
Support Resources and Provider Roles

Section 7
The Role of Historically Black Colleges and Universities, the Government, and National Health Agencies

Contributors

Osman I. Ahmed, M.D., D.P.H., Director, Epidemiology Unit, Department of Medicine, Meharry Medical College, Nashville, Tennessee 37208

Ki-Moon Bang, Ph.D., Staff Investigator, Division of Epidemiology and Biostatistics, Howard University Cancer Center and College of Medicine, Washington, District of Columbia 20060

Claudia R. Baquet, M.D., M.P.H., Chief, Special Populations Studies Branch, Division of Cancer Prevention and Control, National Cancer Institute, Bethesda, Maryland 20892

Louis J. Bernard, M.D., Dean, School of Medicine, Meharry Medical College, Nashville, Tennessee 37208

Alan Blum, M.D., Assistant Professor, Department of Family Medicine, Baylor College of Medicine, Houston, Texas 77005

John G. Boyce, M.D., Professor, Department of Obstetrics and Gynecology; Director, Division of Gynecologic Oncology, State University of New York-Health Science Center at Brooklyn, Brooklyn, New York 11203

Stanley E. Broadnax, M.D., M.P.H., Commissioner of Health, City of Cincinnati, Cincinnati, Ohio 45229

Robert M. Byers, M.D., Professor, Department of Head and Neck Surgery, University of Texas M. D. Anderson Cancer Center, Houston, Texas 77030

Barbara S. Bynum, B.A., Director, Division of Extramural Activities, National Cancer Institute, Bethesda, Maryland 20892

George B. Cernada, Ph.D., Professor, Division of Public Health, University of Massachusetts at Amherst, Amherst, Massachusetts 01003

Ted T.L. Chen, Ph.D., Professor, Division of Public Health, University of Massachusetts at Amherst, Amherst, Massachusetts 01003

Janice A. Allen Chilton, B.A., M.A., Communications Specialist, Cancer Information Service, Public Education Office, University of Texas M. D. Anderson Cancer Center, Houston, Texas 77030

Linda A. Clayton, M.D., Assistant Professor and Director of Gynecologic Oncology, Department of Obstetrics and Gynecology, Meharry Medical College, Nashville, Tennessee 37208

Neil J. Clendeninn, M.D., Ph.D., Head, Chemotherapy Section, Cancer Therapy Department, Burroughs Wellcome Co., Research Triangle Park, North Carolina 27709

Judith Craven, M.D., M.P.H., Vice President for Minority Affairs, Dean, School of Allied Health Sciences, The University of Texas Science Center, Houston, Texas 77030

William A. Darity, Ph.D., Professor, Division of Public Health, University of Massachusetts at Amherst, Amherst, Massachusetts 01003

Robert L. DeWitty, Jr., M.D., Assistant Professor of Surgery; Chief, Surgical Oncology, Howard University Hospital, Washington, District of Columbia 20060

Isaiah W. Dimery, M.D., Assistant Professor of Medicine, Section of Head and Neck Medical Oncology, Department of Medical Oncology, University of Texas M. D. Anderson Cancer Center, Houston, Texas 77030

Dolores M. Esparza, R.N., M.S., Corporate Director of Nursing, Comprehensive Cancer Centers, Inc., Beverly Hills, California 90210; Director of Nursing, Cedars Sinai Comprehensive Cancer Center, Los Angeles, California 90048

Lemuel A. Evans, Ph.D., Health Scientist Administrator and Director, Comprehensive Minority Biomedical Program, Division of Extramural Activities, National Cancer Institute, Bethesda, Maryland 20892

Rachel G. Fruchter, Ph.D., M.P.H., Associate Professor, Department of Obstetrics and Gynecology, State University of New York-Health Science Center at Brooklyn, Brooklyn, New York 11203

Barry Gause, M.D., Acting Chief, Department of Medical Oncology, Howard University Medical School and Cancer Center, Washington, District of Columbia 20059

Mario O. Gonzalez, M.D., Medical Director and Chief, Radiation Therapy, Rio Grande Cancer Treatment Center, Inc., McAllen, Texas 78501; Assistant Professor of Clinical Radiotherapy, University of Texas Health Science Center, Houston Medical Center, Houston, Texas 77030; Clinical Assistant Professor of Medicine, University of Texas Health Science Center, San Antonio, Texas 78284; Assistant Professor of Clinical Radiotherapy, University of Texas M. D. Anderson Cancer Center, Houston, Texas 77030

Marc T. Goodman, Ph.D., M.P.H., Epidemiologist and Adjunct Assistant Professor of Public Health, University of Hawaii, Honolulu, Hawaii 96813

Walter M. Griffin, M.S., Research Associate, Howard University Cancer Center, Washington, District of Columbia 20060

Joyce A. Guillory, R.N., M.S.N., Assistant Professor of Nursing, Morris Brown College, Atlanta, Georgia 30314

James W. Hampton, M.D., Clinical Professor of Medicine, Department of Medicine, University of Oklahoma College of Medicine; Medical Director, Cancer Center of the Southwest at Baptist Medical Center; Oklahoma City, Oklahoma 73112

Robert E. Hardy, M.D., Director, Cancer Control Research Unit, Meharry Medical College, Nashville, Tennessee 37208

Margaret K. Hargreaves, Ph.D., Director, Diet and Nutrition Program, Cancer Control Research Unit, and Community Coalition for Minority Health, Meharry Medical College, Nashville, Tennessee 37208

Betty Lee Hawks, M.A., Program Director, Minority Health Projects, Office of Minority Health, Public Health Service, Department of Health and Human Services, Washington, District of Columbia 20201

Waun Ki Hong, M.D., Professor and Chief, Head/Neck and Thoracic Medical Oncology, University of Texas M. D. Anderson Cancer Center, Houston, Texas 77030

Daniel Hoskins, Director of Special Group Relations, American Cancer Society, Atlanta, Georgia 30026

Carrie P. Hunter, M.D., Program Director, Community Oncology and Rehabilitation Branch, Division of Cancer Prevention and Control, National Cancer Institute, Bethesda, Maryland 20892-4200

Lovell A. Jones, Ph.D., Associate Professor and Director, Experimental Gynecology-Endocrinology, Departments of Gynecology, Biochemistry and Molecular Biology, University of Texas M. D. Anderson Cancer Center, Houston, Texas 77030

LaSalle D. Leffall, Jr., M.D., Professor and Chairman, Department of Surgery, Howard University College of Medicine, Washington, District of Columbia 20060

Mickey Leland, U.S. Representative, 18th Congressional District of Texas, Houston, Texas 77030

Edith P. Mitchell, M.D., Associate Professor of Medicine, Section of Hematology/Oncology, University of Missouri School of Medicine, Columbia, Missouri 65212

Suresh Mohla, B.Sc., M.Sc., Ph.D., Associate Professor of Oncology and Pharmacology, Howard University Cancer Center, Howard University College of Medicine, Washington, District of Columbia 20060

J. Henry Montes, Program Officer, Henry J. Kaiser Family Foundation, Menlo Park, California 94025

Vandana Narang, Research Assistant, Howard University Cancer Center, Washington, District of Columbia 20060

Guy R. Newell, M.D., Professor of Epidemiology, Department of Cancer Prevention and Control, University of Texas M. D. Anderson Cancer Center, Houston, Texas 77030

Herbert Nickens, M.D., M.A., Vice President for Minority Health, Disease Prevention/Health Promotion, Association of American Medical Colleges, Washington, District of Columbia 20036

Kenneth Olden, Ph.D., Director, Howard University Cancer Center; Professor and Chair, Department of Oncology, Howard University College of Medicine, Washington, District of Columbia 20060

Claude Organ, Jr., M.D., Professor, Department of Surgery, University of California, Davis-East Bay, Oakland, California 94602

Geraldine V. Padilla, Ph.D., Associate Dean for Research and Associate Professor, School of Nursing, University of California, Los Angeles, California 90024-1702

Harris Pastides, Ph.D., Associate Professor, Division of Public Health, University of Massachusetts at Amherst, Amherst, Massachusetts 01003

Lou Pearson, Ed.D., R.N., Health Educator-Coordinator, Community Coalition for Minority Health, Meharry Medical College, Nashville, Tennessee 37208

Blanca A. Perez, M.S.W., C.S.W., Social Worker, University of Texas M. D. Anderson Cancer Center, Houston, Texas 77030

Eddie Reed, M.D., Senior Investigator, Medicine Branch, National Cancer Institute, Bethesda, Maryland 20892

Noma L. Roberson, R.N., Ph.D., Director of Minority Cancer Education Programs, Department of Cancer Control and Epidemiology, Roswell Park Memorial Institute, Buffalo, New York 14263

Robert G. Robinson, Ph.D., Research Associate Member, Fox Chase Cancer Center, Philadelphia, Pennsylvania 19111

Calvin C. Sampson, M.D., Professor, Department of Pathology, Howard University College of Medicine, Washington, District of Columbia 20060

David Satcher, M.D., Ph.D., President, Meharry Medical College, Nashville, Tennessee 37208

Jerrold P. Saxton, M.D., Staff Radiotherapist, Department of Radiation Therapy, The Cleveland Clinic Foundation, Cleveland, Ohio 44106

Kofi A. Semenya, Ph.D., Biostatistician, Cancer Control Research Unit, Meharry Medical College, Nashville, Tennessee 37208

Neela Sheth, M.D., Research Assistant, General Clinical Research Center and Community Coalition for Minority Health, Meharry Medical College, Nashville, Tennessee 37208

Edward Stanek, Ph.D., Assistant Professor, Division of Public Health, University of Massachusetts at Amherst, Amherst, Massachusetts 01003

Robert W. Tuthill, Ph.D., Professor, Division of Public Health, University of Massachusetts at Amherst, Amherst, Massachusetts 01003

Carlos Vallbona, M.D., Professor and Chairman, Department of Community Medicine, Baylor College of Medicine, Houston, Texas 77030

Jan van Eys, Ph.D., M.D., Mosbacher Chair in Pediatrics; Head, Division of Pediatrics, University of Texas M. D. Anderson Cancer Center; Professor and Chairman, Department of Pediatrics, University of Texas School of Medicine at Houston, Houston, Texas 77030

Louise A. Villejo, M.P.H., Director, Patient Education Office, University of Texas M. D. Anderson Cancer Center, Houston, Texas 77030

Andrew C. von Eschenbach, M.D., Professor and Chairman, Department of Urology, University of Texas M. D. Anderson Cancer Center, Houston, Texas 77030

Sandra L. White, Ph.D., Associate Professor, Department of Microbiology and Oncology, Howard University Medical School and Cancer Center, Washington, District of Columbia 20060

Jerome Wilson, Ph.D., Director of Statistics, Consumer Products, R&D Division, Warner-Lambert Company, Morris Plains, New Jersey 02950

Alvin Winder, Ph.D., Professor, Division of Public Health, University of Massachusetts at Amherst, Amherst, Massachusetts 01003

Section 1

Cancer Incidence in Minority Populations

Introduction to Section 1

Lovell A. Jones and Guy R. Newell

Differences in cancer occurrence among different population groups have long been used by cancer researchers to provide clues to the causes of cancer. Differences in mortality and survival have been used as indicators of access to and utilization of medical services. Most studies have focused on international differences; however, intranational differences provide a rich source of information as well.

There are four main racial/ethnic minority groups in the United States – Blacks (11.5% of the total U.S. population), Hispanic Americans (6.4%), Asian/Pacific Islanders (1.6%), and Native Americans. For all cancers combined, Blacks have 10% higher incidence rates than do Whites (non-Hispanic Caucasians), experience 20% higher cancer mortality rates, and have the least favorable survival rates. Hispanic Americans have 25% lower incidence rates and the same survival rates as Whites. In contrast, Native Americans have only half the incidence and only one third the survival. The occurrence of cancer at specific sites shows striking differences among the minority groups as well. Detailed exploration of these differences in occurrence and survival, with some possible explanations for them, is the objective of this book.

Comprising a high proportion of inner-city dwellers, minorities are exposed to a great number of environmental hazards, including pollution, substandard and overcrowded housing, and crime. The major risk factors for the development of cancer may be disproportionately distributed among minority groups as well. There is, for example, a higher prevalence of smoking among Blacks than Whites and their tobacco-related cancer rates are the highest among all minority groups. Diets high in grain products and fiber and low in dairy products are common among Hispanic Americans and this cultural heritage is thought to provide protection against the development of two common cancers, breast and colon. Asian/Pacific Islanders have unique dietary practices, with rice the primary source of calories and relatively high consumption of vegetables, fruits, fish, and shellfish. Traditional medicine men play a strong role in the health practices of Native Americans, which may contribute to their relatively poor survival compared with that of other groups.

Minorities tend to be equated with the underprivileged, although there are exceptions to this generalization. Minorities and the underprivileged share common features generally termed socioeconomic, which include such highly interrelated factors as education, income, occupation, cultural habits, ethnicity, place of residence, and degree of industrialization of their home community or state. These factors, taken collectively, are related to the prevalence of exposure to risk factors that cause cancer and perhaps to genetic composition that determines resistance to these exposures. They also relate to the accessibility and use of medical facilities and to the knowledge, attitudes, and beliefs concerning health and illness.

Knowledge, attitudes, and practices are important in how individuals respond to health situations, in determining availability of health services, and in how individuals seek health services when available. Disparities in knowledge, attitudes, and practices between minorities and nonminorities may explain the longer delay in seeking diagnosis and treatment among minorities, and thus the greater prevalence of more advanced cancers, and poorer survival.

Among the many factors presumed to influence minority health status in the United States today, four social characteristics are believed to be especially significant: demographic profiles, environmental and occupational exposures, nutritional status and dietary practices, and stress and coping patterns. The demographic profiles of Blacks, Hispanics, Asian/Pacific Islanders, and Native Americans differ considerably from those of non-Hispanic Whites. Future attention to the individual socioeconomic components and how they influence specific minority groups would greatly enhance our understanding of cancer in minorities and the underprivileged and our ability to prevent and treat cancer in these groups more effectively.

1. Cancer Incidence and Mortality Differences of Black and White Americans: A Role for Biomarkers

Jerome Wilson

The study of differences in incidence and mortality from cancer in Black and White Americans may provide clues to the etiology of the disease and generate new hypotheses. An identification of differences in environmental and in biological and life-style factors is a starting point for further study aimed at understanding why Black Americans experience the highest overall cancer rate in the United States (Baquet et al. 1986).

During the past 30 years a number of descriptive studies have shown cancer incidence and mortality rates to be higher in Blacks, so this is not a new problem (Pollack and Horm 1980; Devesa and Silverman 1978; Young et al. 1975; Henschke et al. 1973). Despite the knowledge that Black persons and especially Black men have experienced the largest percentage increases in cancer incidence and mortality in recent decades, large gaps remain in our understanding of these differences in cancer rates.

Several epidemiologic paradoxes are readily apparent when one compares cancer incidence, survival, and mortality data for Blacks and Whites in the United States. Although overall cancer rates (incidence and mortality) are higher for Blacks, this is not the case for each cancer site. Some site-specific cancers show much higher rates for Blacks than Whites (lung, prostate, cervix uteri, and others), whereas at other sites the rates are excessively high for Whites and lower for Blacks (bladder, breast, rectum, ovary, and others). For some cancers no significant rate differences exist between Blacks and Whites (among them colon, female lung, and kidney).

The excessive incidence and mortality experienced by Blacks is usually explained by such diffuse variables as lack of access to medical care, socioeconomic status, improvements in case-finding, census underenumeration, smoking, alcohol consumption, diet, negative social behavior, and urban living. To date, however, few analytic studies have been conducted to sort through the subjective and ill-defined variables used to explain findings of descriptive studies. Clearly, part or all of the above factors are related to cancer etiology, but the precise association with increased risk for Blacks has not been examined.

The time has come to move beyond the description of the problem and conduct rigorous analytic studies of Black populations. In this paper I shall focus on selected cancer sites for which Black and White incidence rates show some differences. A second purpose is to explore some of the ways in which we may begin to understand these differences by using new laboratory technology in biochemistry, genetics, and molecular biology, and at the same time improve the design and analysis of epidemiologic studies. The cancers included are those that on a global basis seem to be the most important in terms of high incidence and mortality in Blacks compared with Whites. In some cases importance was judged not on the basis of purely quantitative significance but because of increases in incidence during the past decade or because of the potential value of the disease as a "model" for use in biochemical and genetic epidemiology. A study of Black-White cancer rate differences that incorporates biomarkers has the potential of providing new insights to the etiology of cancer in all humankind.

Data Sources

Cancer incidence data are from the SEER (Surveillance, Epidemiology, and End Results) Program of the National Cancer Institute. The SEER data represent a nonrandom sample of approximately 10% of the U.S. population from 10 different geographic areas (four states, five metropolitan areas, and Puerto Rico). Because the rates for some cancer sites tend to be unstable for single years, and substantial shifts in diagnosis and reporting occur over time, rates were calculated by using the average rates for five years, 1979-1983 (Sondik et al. 1986). Data on cancer incidence are limited to four SEER areas (Atlanta, Georgia; Detroit, Michigan; San Francisco-Oakland; Connecticut) because 92% of the Black cancer cases are derived from these locations.

Mortality data were obtained directly from National Cancer Health Statistics (Vital Statistics in the United States 1950-1982). Population estimates used to calculate mortality rates were taken from data provided by the U.S. Census Bureau.

Incidence and Mortality Differences for Selected Cancers

Incidence and mortality rate differences for selected cancers in U.S. Blacks and Whites are summarized in Tables 1 and 2, along with highlights of the major etiologic features.

Esophagus

The incidence of cancer of the esophagus (Table 1) is four times higher in Black than in White men, and Blacks of both genders are two times more likely to die from cancer of the esophagus than are their White counterparts. The major risk

TABLE 1. Comparison of Black-White cancer rates by site

Cancer site	Incidence Black-White[a]		Mortality Black-White[a]	
	Men	Women	Men	Women
Esophagus (150)[b]	19.9–5.0 (14.9)[c]	3.6–1.5 (2.1)	15.8–4.6 (11.3)	4.0–1.2 (2.8)
Stomach (151)	22.6–11.6 (11.0)	7.9–5.1 (2.8)	14.7–7.4 (7.3)	6.4–3.5 (2.9)
Colon (153)	41.7–39.8 (1.9)	35.8–31.7 (4.1)	21.4–21.2 (0.2)	17.7–15.6 (2.1)
Rectum (154)	15.0–18.8 (−3.8)	9.6–11.6 (−2.0)	4.3–4.4 (−0.1)	2.8–2.5 (0.3)
Pancreas (157)	17.0–10.8 (6.2)	11.6–7.7 (3.9)	13.9–10.3 (3.6)	9.5–6.8 (2.7)
Larynx (161)	12.2–8.5 (3.7)	2.2–1.6 (0.6)	4.7–2.6 (2.1)	0.8–0.4 (0.4)
Lung (162)	122.5–81.4 (41.1)	32.0–30.7 (1.3)	94.4–70.3 (24.1)	22.0–22.0 (0)
Prostate (185)	124.4–78.0 (46.4)		44.6–21.2 (23.4)	
Breast (174)		75.1–88.3 (−13.2)		26.9–26.6 (−0.3)
Cervix uteri (180)		18.1–8.3 (9.8)		8.4–3.0 (5.4)
Corpus uteri (182)		14.2–24.7 (−10.5)		6.4–3.8 (2.6)
Multiple myeloma (203)	10.7–4.2 (6.5)	7.2–2.9 (4.3)	6.5–3.0 (3.5)	4.3–2.0 (2.3)

[a] Incidence and mortality rates are calculated by using the average of the last five years' rates (1979–1983). Rates per 100,000 (SEER).
[b] Numbers are code of International Classification of Diseases for Oncology (ICDO).
[c] Incidence and mortality rate differences (Black rate−White rate).

factors implicated in the development of esophageal cancer are alcohol, tobacco, and dietary deficiencies (Keller 1980; Pottern et al. 1981; Fraumeni and Blot 1977; Tuyns et al. 1977; Day and Munoz 1982).

Some data suggest that decreased consumption of fruits and vegetables places one at increased risk for developing cancer of the esophagus. In a study of death certificates (Pottern et al. 1981) an association was found between dietary deficiencies and cancer of the esophagus; but, because of the limitations associated with such a study, this finding needs to be examined in an incident case-control study. Currently there is no evidence of familial aggregation of this cancer. However, family studies may be warranted. The factors discussed in the literature include urban living, poverty, socioeconomic status, and life-style, but it is difficult to be specific about etiologic mechanisms because many of these risk factors are difficult to quantify.

TABLE 2. Etiologic factors in Black-White differences in cancer rates, by site

Cancer site	Cigarettes	Alcohol	Diet	Occupation	Familial aggregation	Other risk factors	Other diseases
Esophagus (150)[a]	Increased risk	Increased risk; may interact with cigarettes	Reduced intake of fruits, vegetables	Work as brewers, bartenders, waitresses	Not known	Radiation, urban living	Plummer-Vinson syndrome
Stomach (151)	Weak association	Weak association	Smoked fish, pickled vegetables, low consumption of fresh fruit	Work in asbestos, coal mine, farm, fishing industries	3x	Blood group A	Pernicious anemia 5x, gastritis 3x
Colon (153)	No association	Possible association with beer	High intake of dietary fat, carbohydrates	Work in asbestos shoe, machine industries	Close relatives	Age, ethnic background, urban environment	Familial polyposis, ulcerative colitis, Crohn's disease
Rectum (154)	No association	Possible association with beer	High intake of fat, carbohydrates	Asbestos workers, shoe workers, machinists	Close relatives	Age, ethnic background, urban living, history of inflammatory bowel disease	Crohn's disease, ulcerative colitis
Pancreas (157)	2x	Suggested association	No clear association has been found; coffee?	Work as chemists, with benzidene and naphthylamine, in coke and gas plants	None known	None known	Diabetes mellitus

Larynx (161)	10x	3x	None known	Work with petroleum, nickel, asbestos, mustard gas, and sulfuric acid	None known	None	None
Lung (162)	10x	No association	Diets low in vitamin A, suggestive	Work with asbestos (among smokers), in uranium mines, as coke oven workers, cooks	Relatives, 2–4x	Air pollution, radon	Tuberculosis, bronchitis
Prostate (185)	No association	No association	Fat intake?	Cadmium exposure, electroplating, rubber workers	Families, 3x	Lead possible, social factors	Benign prostate hypertrophy, possible
Breast (174)	Suggested inverse association	Possible association	Possible association with high-fat diet	None known	3x, possible autosomal dominance	Age at first birth, age at menopause, obesity, low estriol ratio and long-term use of exogenous estrogens	Fibrocystic disease, colon cancer

Continued

TABLE 2. *Continued*

Cancer site	Cigarettes	Alcohol	Diet	Occupation	Familial aggregation	Other risk factors	Other diseases
Cervix uteri (180)	Moderate association	No association	None known	Prostitution	No association	Early age at first intercourse, number of sexual partners, herpes and papilloma viruses	Venereal diseases
Corpus uteri (182)	Unknown	Unknown	Excess calories	Unknown	Families, 5x	Obesity and age at menopause, direct parity (strong inverse) long-term use of diethylstilbestrol, use of sequential contraceptives	Breast cancer, hypertension, diabetes
Multiple myeloma (203)	No association	No association	Not known	Farmers, wood and leather workers (metal, plastics, rubber, petroleum, asbestos, possible?)	Possible	Chronic antigenic stimulation	Systemic lupus erythematosus, chronic connective tissue disorder, scleroderma, rheumatoid arthritis, chronic dermatitis

[a]Numbers are code of International Classification of Diseases for Oncology (ICDO).

Stomach

During the last decade, the incidence of stomach cancer has declined for Black and White men and White women but increased for Black women (Sondik et al. 1986). The incidence of this cancer is two to three times higher in Black males than in the other three race-gender groups (Black females, White males, White females), and mortality rates follow a similar pattern. The most important risk factors seem to be related to diet and occupation. Table 2 summarizes what is known about these and other risk factors (Nomura 1982; Billington and Sidney 1956; Correa 1981).

Although dietary factors have been shown to be the strongest risk indicators in the etiology of stomach cancer, not all studies have been consistent, possibly because we cannot collect and specifically define the components of diet related to stomach cancer. Since familial clustering has been observed with this cancer, the dietary factors may be related to genetic markers. Stomach cancer is in some ways an ideal focus for biochemical and genetic epidemiologic research.

Colon

For colon cancer, the third most frequently diagnosed cancer in this country, the incidence is only slightly higher among Blacks than Whites. Nevertheless, Black men experience the highest incidence among the four race-gender groups. Mortality rates are higher for men than women, and they are the same for Black and White men. Black women die at a slightly higher rate from colon cancer compared with White women (Schottenfeld and Winawer 1982).

As the data in Table 1 show, colon cancer rates are similar between Blacks and Whites and rectal cancer rates are higher in Whites than in Blacks, although the etiological factors are believed to be similar for both cancers.

In some studies, researchers have found an association between risk of colon cancer and high-fat, low-fiber diets, whereas others have not demonstrated this. Obviously, generalities like "high fat" and "low fiber" without more specific information lead to confusion. Fats are not all the same; some may well be protective while others are harmful, as demonstrated by the epidemiology of cardiovascular disease. The same is true for fiber, a category that includes soluble and insoluble components. The insoluble fiber is believed to offer some protection from colon cancer. It is this absence of specificity that may explain why some studies have associated colon cancer with dietary fat and fiber and others have not.

Colon cancer seems to cluster in families, but it is unclear whether this familial aggregation is the result of common environmental or genetic backgrounds. If genes are involved, it is important to identify these genes with some degree of specificity. The gaps and contradictions in our knowledge of colon cancer epidemiology warrant detailed genetic and biochemical epidemiologic studies using prospective cohort and case-control nested family study designs (Wilson et al. 1988).

Rectum

For cancer of the rectum, the incidence is higher in Whites than in Blacks. White men have the highest incidence, followed by Black men, White women, and Black women (Table 1). The etiologic features are similar to those of colon cancer, and yet the White-Black reversal in incidence of this cancer is intriguing as a research and clinical question.

Pancreas

Incidence and mortality rates for pancreatic cancer in Blacks and Whites by gender are also compared in Table 1, and they show that the rates are higher for Blacks than Whites and for men than women. The strongest risk factors shown to date are cigarettes and certain occupational exposures (Table 2) (Mack 1982; Mancuso and Sterling 1974; Williams and Horm 1977; Wynder 1973, 1975).

This cancer is poorly understood, mainly because a majority of patients survive only briefly after diagnosis. Dietary factors have been suggested but not well sorted out. Coffee drinking has been implicated in this cancer, but the connection is still an open question (MacMahon et al. 1981; Wynder et al. 1983; Heuch et al. 1983). Some studies have suggested an etiologic role for certain occupations, such as those of chemists, radiologists, and metal workers (Table 2).

Larynx

Cancer of the larynx shows a strong male preponderance in incidence and mortality. The largest burden for this cancer is borne by Black men who have an incidence rate eight times higher than White women, six times higher than Black women, and almost two times higher than White men. Major etiologic factors include cigarettes, alcohol, and certain occupational exposures (Table 2) (Austin 1982; Wynder et al. 1976).

Lung

Both Black and White men have an incidence rate of lung cancer that is more than two times the rate for women. Moreover, Black men have a lung cancer rate four times higher than that of women of both races and almost two times higher than that of White men. The mortality rate follows a similar pattern, Black males having the highest rate. Cigarettes are well established as the major etiologic factor in lung cancer. Other factors include occupational exposures, other respiratory diseases, and having close relatives with the disease (shared common environment) (Table 2) (Fraumeni and Blot 1982; Mancuso 1977; Lloyd 1971). Dietary factors may be involved in the development of lung cancer; diets low in vitamin A and in fruits and vegetables may place one at increased risk of lung cancer. The immune system may be implicated, therefore, since diet and immune function are not independent factors.

Prostate

Prostate cancer incidence and mortality rates are about twofold higher in Black than in White men, and Blacks experience about 46 more cases per 100,000 population than Whites. The etiologic factors are not well established; some of the suggested risk factors are summarized in Table 2 (Greenwald 1982; Levine and Wilchinsky 1979; Kovi et al. 1982; Hutchison 1975; Graham et al. 1983).

In several studies, promiscuity and number of sexual partners have been suggested as reasons for the increased risk of prostate cancer observed in Black men. These explanations have not advanced understanding of the etiology of this cancer. The influences of sexual activity are perhaps surrogates for some other factors still to be identified. The response one gets when asking a man about the number of sexual partners during his lifetime depends on his status in life and his perceptions of his machismo. Recall bias and selective memory weigh heavily in determining the type, quality, and validity of the response to sexual activity-related questions.

Other factors suggested as putative causes of prostate cancer include high-fat diets and chemicals from occupational exposures. The suggestion that cadmium may be a causal agent has some biologic plausibility because this element is capable of displacing zinc (Fox 1976; Underwood 1977), and the highest concentration of zinc in a man's body is in the prostate gland. Understanding the cadmium-zinc relationship in the prostate gland may lead to identifying a mechanism for the cause of prostate cancer. The biologic importance of zinc in the prostate gland is not clearly understood. Zinc is lost from the body as a result of cigarette smoking and by sexual activity; loss of this element without replacement may therefore be related to increased risk of developing cancer.

Prostate cancer seems to cluster in families, which suggests that some genetic markers may contribute to the risk of prostate cancer. This cancer is well suited to a case-control nested family study in which there is an opportunity to sort out familial, environmental, and life-style factors.

Breast

The overall incidence of breast cancer is higher in White women than in Black women. The incidence rate for Black females is 13 cases per 100,000 population, lower than for White females, but mortality rates are the same. Table 2 summarizes the major etiologic factors in this disease (Petrakis et al. 1982; Gray et al. 1980; Leffall 1981; Devesa and Diamond 1980).

When one examines the age-specific rates for breast cancer, Black women under the age of 40 have a slightly higher risk than their White counterparts. This is interesting from the point of view that earlier age at birth of first child generally confers some protection from developing breast cancer, and on average, Black women have their children at a younger age. Some factor seems to override the protection offered by giving birth at an early age, which is a potentially important epidemiologic question.

Alcohol consumption has been suggested as a risk factor in the development of breast cancer. Several recent studies showed that even moderate consumption of alcohol increases the risk for young White women (Willett et al. 1987; Schatzkin et al. 1987). In one study, however, older Black women were found to be at higher risk of breast cancer because of alcohol consumption, but the number of Black women in the study was too small to warrant detailed analysis (Harvey et al. 1987). This type of paradoxical Black-White difference should be the focus of large-scale epidemiologic research.

A diet high in fat has been suggested as a risk factor for breast cancer, but a large follow-up study of nurses by Willett et al. (1987) did not find support for this hypothesis.

Cervix Uteri

Cervical cancer incidence and mortality rates are two times higher in Blacks than Whites (Table 1). Much of what is known about this cancer suggests that behavioral and host factors play an important role in its development (Cramer 1982; Hulka and Redmond 1971; Graham and Schotz 1979).

To date no epidemiologic studies have been conducted among Black women. The focus on age at first intercourse and the number of sexual partners has not helped much in understanding the etiology of this cancer. There is a need for strong analytic studies with biomarkers (including DNA probes, human papillomavirus (HPV), HPV antibodies, and nutritional factors).

No women should die from this cancer, since the Papanicolaou (Pap) test is an effective tool for preventing invasive cervical cancer – provided the population at risk is informed and has unrestricted access to the test. Proper use of the Pap test in high-risk Black women can reduce the incidence of and consequently the mortality rate of invasive cervical cancer.

Corpus Uteri

This cancer has an incidence rate pattern different from that of cervix uteri, that is, about 11 fewer cases per 100,000 population occur in Blacks than Whites. The general etiologic features are presented in Table 2 (Waard 1982).

Why Black women are at lower risk of developing this cancer but, once diagnosed, are at greater risk of dying from it is not clear. One suggestion is that total calorie intake may be related to the development of cancer of the corpus uteri (Nauss et al. 1987).

Multiple Myeloma

Incidence and mortality rates of multiple myeloma are two times higher in Blacks than Whites, the highest incidence and mortality rates being experienced by Black men. The etiologic factors involved in this disease are not well established;

TABLE 3. Future directions for epidemiologic research into Black-White cancer incidence rates

1. Case-control studies, hospital- and population-based
2. Special focus on Black male populations
3. Strengthen biochemical component of epidemiologic research:
    Immunology (T, B, and natural killer cells, immunoglobulin allotypes)
    Human leukocyte antigens
    Somatomedin-C (nutritional status)
    Papillomavirus
    Human T cell lymphotrophic virus type I
    Hormones
    DNA adducts
4. Focus on cancer sites that show greatest Black-White differences

Table 2 shows some of the suggested associations (Blattner 1982; MacMahon and Clark 1956; McPhedran et al. 1972).

Multiple myeloma is not a cancer of high incidence, but its incidence pattern and potential for research in genetic and biochemical epidemiology is of interest. The etiology of this cancer is poorly understood; suggested risks include occupational factors, autoimmune diseases, and diffuse variables such as chronic antigenic stimulation, all of which do little to explain the etiology of multiple myeloma. What does chronic antigenic stimulation mean from the point of view of quantifying disease risk? There is some evidence that genetic factors play a role in the development of this disease. The disease offers an opportunity to study biochemical and genetic epidemiologic influences and to elucidate possible mechanisms in this disease. The D region of the human leukocyte (HLA) system may well provide some explanation in terms of specific genetic associations. Most researchers who attempted to examine the HLA system and multiple myeloma looked at the A, B, and C regions of HLA, which are T cell markers, whereas multiple myeloma is a B cell tumor. Immunoglobulin G and Kappa light chain allotypes are among some of the other genetic markers that may contribute to understanding this cancer (Leech et al. 1983).

Suggestions for Further Research

I shall outline the kinds of studies that should be conducted to further characterize and identify etiologic factors that contribute to the large difference in cancer incidence between Blacks and Whites and to the high rates found in Black men (Table 3).

Descriptive Studies of SEER Data in Conjunction with Non-SEER Hospital Registries

New studies of cancer incidence should be conducted for physical sites that show large Black-White differences and for sites showing increasing incidence among Blacks.

Hospital tumor registry data from non-SEER areas that include large numbers of Blacks should be analyzed and compared with SEER findings, with care taken in the analysis and interpretation of these comparisons.

Pathology slides from selected sites should be obtained for systemic review. These studies would provide accurate data on the specific histologic types of cancer, and it is likely that different histologic types will provide additional insight on rate differences between Blacks and Whites.

Case–Control Studies

Descriptive studies have adequately documented differences in incidence rates of several cancers in Blacks and Whites. Case-control studies designed to explain these observed differences should be conducted. Researchers need to collect data on known and suspected risk factors using well-designed questionnaires, and to collect biologic samples (i.e., white cells, red cells, serum, urine). A good example of this kind of investigation is the population-based case-control study of cancers of the esophagus, prostate, pancreas, and of multiple myeloma currently being conducted by the Environmental Epidemiology Branch of the National Cancer Institute (1986-1989 – Detroit, Atlanta, and New Jersey).

Biochemical and genetic epidemiologic components should be included in case-control studies when possible. These studies need not be restricted to clinically overt disease but should be conducted in healthy populations also. Studies of occult neoplasms could be useful in distinguishing risk factors related to progression of disease. Hulka and Redmond (1971) conducted such a study among Black and White welfare recipients who had atypical Pap smears, to determine who would be most likely to develop outright cervical cancer.

The technology for sophisticated biomarker analysis in the case-control design is available. The next logical step is to pursue aggressively those laboratory assays in which suggested associations have been observed or have a sound biologic basis.

Since Black persons represent a high-risk group for a number of cancers, studies of normal individuals in the highest risk group of Blacks may be useful. A large proportion of members of such a group is destined to develop the cancer in question. A comparison of Blacks and Whites should take into account socioeconomic or occupational differences or both if the cancer under investigation is known to be related to these variables.

Another error of interpretation is to infer that unusual cancer experience (whether high or low) observed in a particular group is a consequence of membership in the group when the reverse is true, that is, the occurrence of cancer (or other disease) predisposes to membership in the group. For example, Blacks have been restricted to certain occupations, and a high mortality rate from cancer or any other disease among Blacks in such occupations does not imply that being Black necessarily carries a special risk. Conversely, entrance to high-hazard occupations may be the reason for a high mortality rate for cancer. Artifactually low mortality can also be produced by selecting ill individuals out of a population subgroup; thus, cancer mortality rates are low in the military not because the military life protects against neoplasia but because affected individuals are usually discharged from service before they die.

If an unusual cancer experience is observed for a population or subgroup, it cannot be assumed that the explanation lies in the characteristic that identifies the subgroup. Many, if not most, of the unfavorable health indicators observed in U.S. Black and Native American populations have their explanation not in the groups' racial identification but in the environmental conditions under which many members of these groups live. The marked differences in cancer rates between Japanese and Caucasians seem largely to be related to life in Japan rather than to being Japanese per se. Studies of migrants have been particularly helpful in separating the effects of racial origin and place of residence on cancer risk (Haenszel and Kurihara, 1968).

Summary

The focus of this paper has been on cancers for which the descriptive data show large differences between U.S. Blacks and Whites, especially during the last decade, 1974-1983 (Sondik et al. 1986). I considered it important to establish a background of incidence differences that could be the basis for conducting well-designed case-control studies with Black populations. Case-control studies of cancer sites showing large differences by race are more likely to yield new information and insight into causal factors in cancer development. The possibility of establishing a clearer understanding of the role of genetics in cancer incidence is a likely by-product of well-focused studies of cancer differences. One example is multiple myeloma, for which there is some evidence that a gene product may help explain the difference in incidence between Blacks and Whites (Leech 1985). Thus, differences in cancer incidence could be a function of host immune capacity. Such susceptibility may, in turn, be modified by genetic, environmental, and life-style factors and exhibit age- and gender-dependent components.

The comparisons show that, of the four race-gender groups, Black men have the highest incidence and mortality rates. The greater differences in incidence rates among the groups are for cancers of the esophagus, stomach, pancreas, lung, prostate, breast, cervix and corpus uteri and multiple myeloma. Possible explanations of differences in rates include cigarette smoking, alcohol consumption, occupational exposures, dietary patterns, and environmental stress.

A majority of all cancer cases in the United States today are believed to be environmentally related, that is, associated in some way with physical surroundings or with personal habits and life-styles. Some environmental causes of cancer are well known. About 20% of all cancers in this country are directly related to the use of tobacco, either alone or in conjunction with excessive consumption of alcohol (Doll and Peto 1981).

A growing body of data indicates, however, that post-World War II production of petrochemical products, as well as changes in life-style and environment (rural to urban and toward a highly stressed existence), account for much of the cancer we see today, especially in industrial centers. Environmental variables that produce greater cancer hazards for the inner-city, low-income Blacks, include chemical substances, air pollution, water pollution, stress, and pesticides.

Stress and stress-related illnesses are examples of socially induced disease. They often result from social rather than physical and psychological factors over which people have varying degrees of control. Unemployment for black men and especially those in the large urban centers of the U.S. is a major source of stress. Because the resulting illnesses often have their origin in social factors beyond the individual's control, they are a major health problem among Blacks.

Given the degree of uncertainty and lack of rigorous etiologic research in the area of cancers among Blacks, it is imperative that studies be conducted in black populations to begin to answer some of the questions. In conducting such studies, a strong biochemical and genetic epidemiology (laboratory) component is important and necessary if knowledge of cancer epidemiology is to continue to advance. The new laboratory technologies in immunology, biochemistry, molecular biology, and genetics will advance our ability to sort out the causal factors associated with cancer development. This approach not only has the potential of clarifying racial differences in cancer incidence, but it may also enrich our knowledge of the causes of cancer for all humankind.

References

Austin DF. Larynx. In: Schottenfeld D, Fraumeni JF, eds. *Cancer Epidemiology and Prevention*. Philadelphia: Saunders, 1982:544–563.

Baquet CR, Ringen A, Pollack ES, et al. *Cancer Among Blacks and Other Minorities: A Statistical Profile*. Bethesda: National Cancer Institute, NIH Publication No. 86-2785, 1986.

Billington BP, Sydney MB. Gastric cancer: relationships between ABO blood groups, sites, and epidemiology. *Lancet* 1956;2:859–862.

Blattner WA. Multiple myeloma and macroglobulinemia. In: Schottenfeld D, Fraumeni JF, eds. *Cancer Epidemiology and Prevention*. Philadelphia: Saunders. 1982:795–813.

Correa P. Gastrointestinal cancer among black populations. In: Mettlin C, Murphy GP, eds. *Cancer Among Black Populations*. New York: Liss, 1981:197–211.

Cramer DW. Uterine cervix. In: Schottenfeld D, Fraumeni JF, eds. *Cancer Epidemiology and Prevention*. Philadelphia: Saunders, 1982:881–897.

Day NE, Munoz N. Esophagus. In: Schottenfeld D, Fraumeni JF, eds. *Cancer Epidemiology and Prevention*. Philadelphia: Saunders, 1982:596–623.

Devesa DS, Diamond EL. Association of breast cancer and cervical cancer incidence with income and education among whites and blacks. *JNCI* 1980;65:515–528.

Devesa SS, Silverman DT. Cancer incidence and mortality trends in the United States: 1935–74. *JNCI* 1978;60:545–571.

Doll R, Peto R. The causes of cancer: Quantitative estimates of avoidable risk of cancer in the United States today. *JNCI* 1981;66:1191–1308.

Fox MRS. Cadmium metabolism: A review of aspects pertinent to evaluating dietary cadmium intake by man. In: Prasad AS, ed. *Trace Elements in Human Health and Disease*, Vol. 2. New York: Academic Press, 1976:401–416.

Fraumeni JF, Blot WJ. Geographic variation in esophageal cancer mortality in the United States. *J Chronic Dis* 1977;30:759–767.

Fraumeni JF, Blot WJ. Lung and pleura. In: Schottenfeld D, Fraumeni JF, eds. *Cancer Epidemiology and Prevention*. Philadelphia: Saunders. 1982:564–582.

Graham S, Haughty B, Marshall J, et al. Diet in the epidemiology of carcinoma of the prostate gland. *JNCI* 1983;20:687–692.

Graham S, Schotz W. Epidemiology of cancer of the cervix in Buffalo, New York. *JNCI* 1979;63:23–27.

Gray GE, Henderson BE, Pike MC. Changing ratio of breast cancer incidence rates with age of black females compared with white females in the United States. *JNCI* 1980;64:461–463.

Greenwald P. Prostate. In: Schottenfeld D, Fraumeni JF, eds. *Cancer Epidemiology and Prevention*. Philadelphia: Saunders, 1982:938–946.

Haenszel W, Kurihara M. Studies of Japanese migrants. I. Mortality from cancer and other diseases among Japanese in the United States. *JNCI* 1968;40:43–68.

Harvey EB, Schairer C, Brinton LA, et al. Alcohol consumption and breast cancer. *JNCI* 1987;78:657–661.

Henschke UK, Leffall LD, Mason CH, et al. Alarming increase of the cancer mortality in the U.S. black population (1950–1967). *Cancer* 1973;31:763–768.

Heuch I, Kvale G, Jacobson BK, et al. Use of alcohol, tobacco and coffee, and risk of pancreatic cancer. *Br J Cancer* 1983:637–643.

Hulka BS, Redmond CK. Factors related to progression of cervical atypias. *Am J Epidemiol* 1971;93:23–32.

Hutchison GB. Etiology and prevention of prostatic cancer. *Cancer Chemother Rep* 1975;59:57–58.

Keller AZ. The epidemiology of esophageal cancer in the West. *Prev Med* 1980;9:607–612.

Kovi J, Jackson MA, Rao MS, et al. Cancer of the prostate and aging: An autopsy study in black men from Washington, D.C. and selected African cities. *Prostate* 1983;3:73–80.

Leech SH, Bryan CF, Elston RC, et al. Genetic studies in multiple myeloma. Association with HLA-CWS. *Cancer* 1983;51:1408–1411.

Leffall LD. Breast cancer in black women. *CA* 1981;31:208–211.

Levine RL, Wilchinsky M. Adenocarcinoma of the prostate: A comparison of the disease in blacks versus whites. *J Urol* 1979;121:761–762.

Lloyd JW. Long-term mortality study of steelworkers. V. Respiratory cancer in coke plant workers. *J Occup Med* 1971;13:53–68.

Mack T. Pancreas. In: Schottenfeld D, Fraumeni JF, eds. *Cancer Epidemiology and Prevention*. Philadelphia: Saunders, 1982:638–667.

MacMahon B, Clark DW. The incidence of multiple myeloma. *J Chron Dis* 1956;4:508–515.

MacMahon B, Yen S, Trichopoulos D, et al. Coffee and cancer of the pancreas. *N Engl J Med* 1981;304:630–633.

Mancuso TF. Lung cancer among black migrants: Interactions of host and occupational environment factors. *J Occup Med* 1977;31:531–532.

Mancuso TF, Sterling TD. Relation to place of birth and migration in cancer mortality in the U.S: A study of Ohio residents (1959–1967). *J Chron Dis* 1974;27:459–474.

McPhedran P, Heath CW Jr, Garcia J. Multiple myeloma incidence in metropolitan Atlanta, Georgia: Racial and seasonal variations. *Blood* 1972;39:866–873.

Nauss KM, Jacobs LR, Newburne PM. Dietary food and fiber: Relationship to caloric intake, body growth, and colon tumorigenesis. *Am J Clin Nutr* 1987;45(suppl):245.

Nomura A. Stomach. In: Schottenfeld D, Fraumeni JF, eds. *Cancer Epidemiology and Prevention*. Philadelphia: Saunders, 1982:624–637.

Petrakis NL, Ernster VL, King MC. Breast. In: Schottenfeld D, Fraumeni JF, eds. *Cancer Epidemiology and Prevention* Philadelphia: Saunders, 1982:855–870.

Pollack ES, Horm JW. Trends in cancer incidence and mortality in the United States, 1969–71. *JNCI* 1980;64:1091–1103.

Pottern LM, Morris LE, Blot WJ, et al. Esophageal cancer among black men in Washington, D.C. I. Alcohol, tobacco, and other risk factors. *JCNI* 1981;67:77–783.

Schatzkin A, Jones DY, Hoover RN, et al. Alcohol consumption and breast cancer in the epidemiologic follow-up study of the First National Health and Nutrition Examination Survey. *N Engl J Med* 1987;316:1169–1173.

Schottenfeld D, Winawer JJ. Large intestine. In: Schottenfeld D, Fraumeni JF, eds. *Cancer Epidemiology and Prevention*. Philadelphia: Saunders, 1982:703–727.

Sondik E, Young JL Jr, Horm JW, et al. *1985 Annual Cancer Statistics Review.* Bethesda, MD: National Cancer Institute, 1986.

Tuyns AJ, Pequiqnot G, Abbatucci JS. Esophageal cancer and alcohol consumption: Importance of type of beverage. *Int J Cancer* 1979;23:443–447.

Underwood EJ. *Trace Elements in Human and Animal Nutrition*, 4th Ed. New York: Academic Press 1977:196–242.

Vital Statistics in the United States, Vol 2. Mortality, Part B. Annual. Rockville, MD: National Center for Health Statistics, 1950–1982, 1977.

Waard FD. Uterine corpus. In: Schottenfeld D, Fraumeni JF, eds. *Cancer Epidemiology and Prevention*. Philadelphia: Saunders, 1982:901–908.

Williams RR, Horm JW. Association of cancer sites with tobacco and alcohol consumption and socioeconomic status of patients: Interview study from the Third National Cancer Survey. *JNCI* 1977;58:525–547.

Willett WC, Stampfer MJ, Colditz GA, et al. Moderate alcohol consumption and risk of breast cancer. *N Engl J Med* 1987;316:1174–1180.

Wilson J, Dunston GM, Bonney GE. Design of case-control nested family studies for genetic epidemiology, 1988. *Genet Epidemiol* (in press)

Wynder EL. An epidemiological evaluation of the causes of cancer of the pancreas. *Cancer Res* 1975;35:2228–2233.

Wynder EL, Covey LS, Maruchi K. Environmental factors in cancer of the larynx. A second look. *Cancer* 1976;38:1591–1601.

Wynder EL, Mabuchi K, Maruchi N, et al. A case control study of cancer of the pancreas. *Cancer* 1983;31:641–648.

Young JL, Devesa SS, Cutler SJ. Incidence of cancer in United States blacks. *Cancer Res* 1975;35:3523–3536.

2. Specific Cancers Affecting Hispanics in the United States

J. Henry Montes

As we examine the health of Hispanics in the U.S., one key point is that Hispanic people are not a homogeneous group in this country but present a number of areas of diversity—different countries of origin, different cultural experiences, different numbers of years in the United States, different socioeconomic backgrounds, different experiences in dealing with the health care systems, different reasons for being in the United States, and different reasons for wanting to stay. Thus, we must bear these complexities in mind when we talk about health issues in relation to Hispanic populations.

Hispanic or Latino—the terms are ethnic and not racial terms. Hispanics are from different races. A prominent NASA astronaut, Dr. Chiang-Diaz, is from Costa Rica and considers himself Latino but of the Asian race.

Another important point is that, generally speaking, Hispanics regard health as the absence of illness and do not necessarily accept the definition of health as a state of well-being that should be maintained.

A third issue is that currently there is a dearth of health data about the Hispanic populations, especially of mortality data, and that is one of the greatest drawbacks in trying to determine the health status of Hispanic people. What data we have are mostly about Mexican-Americans and Puerto Ricans, with very little information about Cuban-Americans and almost none about "other Hispanics." The Hispanic Health and Nutrition Examination Survey (HHANES), which was conducted by the National Center for Health Statistics between 1982 and 1984 (Haynes 1987, preliminary data from the HHANES report to Interagency Committee on Smoking and Health, U.S. Public Health Service), will help shrink this gap by adding significant data related to Mexican-Americans in the Southwest, Puerto Ricans in the New York City area, and Cuban-Americans in Dade County, Florida. Health data about other Hispanics will still be lacking, however, although the HHANES results will give a better sense of the health status of these three Hispanic groups. It is still too early to tell, but the new Immigration Reform Act may result in the gathering of data on Hispanics in the United States that heretofore were inaccessible. Yet there will still be significant numbers of undocumented Hispanics in the U.S. whose health needs may remain unknown.

Demographic Data

Keeping these points in mind, let me introduce a demographic risk profile of
Hispanics in the United States.

Population Numbers

Generally, four major groups of Hispanics are identified for purposes of data collection and analysis. They are Mexican-Americans or Chicanos, the Puerto
Ricans that are not on the island, the Cuban-Americans, and the catch-all
category, "other Hispanics." In a recent census report (U.S. Bureau of the Census,
March 1985), the other-Hispanics category was further divided into Central or
South American and other Spanish. Many of the following demographic data are
from this 1985 report.

The other-Spanish category includes persons from the Dominican Republic,
from Spain, and persons in the Southwest who identify themselves as Spanish-
Americans and trace their roots to the time of the Conquistadores. Many of this
latter group live in New Mexico and the southwestern part of Colorado. According to the 1980 census, about 14.6 million Hispanics live in the United States, not
counting the island of Puerto Rico, which has about 3.3 million inhabitants.

Hispanic populations increased by 61% between the 1970 and 1980 census,
from 9.1 million to 14.6 million. This count may be somewhat artificial in that
the 1980 count was done more accurately by changing the way Hispanics identified themselves and by the extra efforts spent on promoting the 1980 census in
the Hispanic communities. The significant increase in 1980 may be related to this
factor as well as to an actual increase in the number of persons. Between 1980 and
1985 the Hispanic populations experienced another large increase of 16%, from
14.6 to 16.9 million people.

More than 60% of the U.S. Hispanics are Mexican-Americans, along with 15%
Puerto Ricans, 6% Cuban-Americans, and 18% Central or South Americans and
other Spanish. The two last groups include persons from a number of countries
of origin, and thus the groups individually do not have sufficient numbers for
accurate data analyses.

Education

There are, unfortunately, a significant number of undereducated Hispanics in the
U.S. Of Hispanics 25 years old and older, 13.5% have completed five years or less
of school, compared to 2% of non-Hispanics. This is a tremendous problem,
especially with regard to socioeconomic risk factors. The median number of
school years completed by Hispanics is 11.5 years, compared with 12.7 for non-
Hispanics.

In terms of specific populations, the median number of school years completed
by Mexican-Americans is 10.2 years; Puerto Ricans, 11.2 years; Cuban-
Americans, 12.0 years; Central and South Americans and other Spanish, 12.4
years. These compare with 12.7 years for non-Hispanics.

Among Mexican-Americans, 17.1% completed fewer than five years of school; Puerto Ricans, 12.8%; Cuban-Americans, 7.4%; Central and South Americans, 7.2%; other Spanish, 6.0%.

Families

Among Hispanic heads of household, 23% of all families are headed by a woman, compared with 15.7% of non-Hispanic families. If we look closer, however, the Puerto Rican population is comparable to the Black population in the United States in that about 44% of Puerto Rican heads of household are women. In contrast, the Cuban-American female heads of household number about 16%. In aggregating Hispanic data, the resulting number does not always reflect the reality of particular conditions in a particular Hispanic population.

With regard to Hispanic family size, the stereotypical view is that Hispanics have large families, and the data seem to confirm that. Census data indicate that, among all Hispanic families, 14% include six to seven persons or more in their households, compared with about 5% of the non-Hispanic population. But the mean number of persons per family is significantly different between Hispanics, for whom the mean number is 3.88 persons, and non-Hispanics, for whom the mean number is 3.18.

Income

Median family income for Hispanics was $18,833 in 1984, compared with $26,951 for non-Hispanics. Again, the Puerto Rican population stands out in terms of highest risk because of low income. Their median family income of $12,371 is much lower than that of all Hispanics.

Poverty

A large portion of the aggregated Hispanic population lives below the poverty level. Over time, poverty rates for Hispanics have maintained about the same difference in comparison with those of the total U.S. population. In 1972 the Hispanic poverty rate was 22.8%, compared with 11.9% for all others. In 1982 the gap grew wider, with 29.9% of Hispanics in poverty compared with 15% of the total population. And as we noted for 1985, 11.6% of the total population lived in poverty compared with 25.2% of Hispanics, so that again there was and is a tremendous difference in the poverty level.

Occupation

Occupations as possible risk factors in cancer, as well as the work place, are also discussed by others in this volume. In 1984, 29.6% of Hispanic men worked as operators, fabricators, and laborers. Hispanic women, like non-Hispanic women, worked in technical jobs (42.7% compared with 45.9%) but were over-represented in the service occupations (22.3% compared with 17.9%). In 1984 more than 64% of Hispanics 16 years old and older were represented in the civilian labor force, 11.3% being unemployed compared with 7.4% unemployed among non-Hispanics (U.S. Bureau of the Census 1985).

Age

The aggregate Hispanic population has a young median age of 25 years, with more than 36% under 17 years of age, compared to a median age of 31.9 years for the non-Hispanic population, among whom only about 26% are younger than 17. For this median-age number, "non-Hispanic" as used by the Census Bureau includes Blacks and other minorities who have a younger median age. If only non-Hispanic Whites were included in the White population, I believe this age difference would be greater, with Whites having an older median age.

The median age of Hispanics in 1985 by specific subpopulation indicated that Mexican-Americans are the youngest among the groups, with a median age of 23.3 years. This lowers the median age number for the aggregated Hispanic population, since more than 60% of Hispanics are Mexican-Americans in the United States. The next largest group, Puerto Ricans, have a median age of 24.3 years. The Cuban-American population is the oldest group, significantly older, with a median age of 39.1 years.

The "Other Spanish" Group

For the Central and South American and the other-Spanish populations, the median ages are 27.1 years and 29.6 years, respectively. This other-Spanish population is important to keep in mind in relation to cancer because much of the cancer information now available is from the New Mexico Cancer Registry, in which Hispanics tend to be identified as "other Spanish." This other-Spanish group is older, has a higher median income, and is generally quite different from Mexican-Americans.

The demographic data outlined here for the aggregate Hispanic population and its groups point out clearly that health problems will affect different Hispanic groups in different ways, and that these differences must be considered in programs involving this diverse multicultural population.

Risk Factors

The four major health risk factors for U.S. Hispanics, in relation to cancers, are socioeconomic status, smoking, alcohol, and diet and nutrition. Much of the following data is derived from an unpublished work by J. Emilio Carrillo (Carrillo and Torres 1986, presented to the National Coalition of Hispanic Health and Human Services Organizations) regarding Hispanics and these risk factors.

There is ample evidence in the literature to support the relationship between socioeconomic conditions and health. One of the conclusions of a study commissioned by the American Cancer Society was that, although it is difficult to determine a straight cause-effect relationship, much of the medical and sociological literature shows socioeconomic status (SES) to have a strong impact on health (Funch 1985).

Economic Struggle

Under conditions of poverty, low-paying occupations, and little education, Hispanics are forced to struggle to meet basic needs. They are less likely than members of other groups to have health insurance, less able to pay for health care, and they are less likely to have a regular source of care or to participate in prevention programs (Trevino and Moss 1983, 1984).

Socioeconomic status may also influence the process of diagnosis and treatment, that is, when, how, and where Hispanics seek medical care. Data from the National Health Interview Survey, 1978–1980, indicated that about 30% of Mexican-Americans had no health insurance coverage (Trevino and Moss 1983) and had only about 3.7 days of physician visits per year, compared with 4.6 to 4.8 visits per year for other minority groups and the White population (Trevino and Moss 1984).

Rosenwaike and Shai (1986) reported that low-income Puerto Ricans in New York, who have no access to adequate health services, tend to delay the diagnosis, reporting, and treatment of cancer at early stages, thereby reducing their chances of survival.

Smoking

Smoking rates for Mexican-Americans are 43% for men and 24.0% for women. These data are from the Hispanic Health and Nutrition Examination Survey (HHANES) collected from 1982 to 1984. In the past literature about smoking by Hispanics, the belief was that, generally, Hispanics smoked less than others. Perhaps that used to be the case. Recent HHANES data, however, show increases in the prevalence of smoking by Hispanics. The National Health Interview Survey (NHIS) of 1979–1980 showed that 38.7% of Mexican-American men were smoking, so that over a two- to three-year period the number of Mexican-Americans who were smoking had risen about 4%. Smoking among females went up as well; the NHIS data for 1979–1980 showed the smoking prevalence among women to be about 18.3% (Joly 1986, unpublished report).

From a discussion at the March 1987 meeting of the Interagency Committee on Smoking and Health of advertising targeted to minorities, specifically Blacks and Hispanics, it was clear that Hispanics are a favorite target group. This does not argue well for the future health status of Hispanics, especially in terms of mortality from lung cancer. The 1984 HHANES data on the prevalence of smoking among Puerto Rican and Cuban-American males, 20 to 34 years old, show the rates to be 44.7% and 50.1%, respectively. At this same age, 38.6% of Puerto Rican women smoke, as do 29.2% of Cuban women (Haynes 1987, unpublished report).

Although these data from HHANES are preliminary, I believe they give a good sense of potential problems facing Hispanics. This is the first time data about Cubans have been available. The rates are comparable to the smoking rate of Black males in the United States, which is about 51.0% (National Health and Nutrition Examination Survey II, 1976–1980). The data show, furthermore, that younger people are smoking more heavily, which creates even more concern about an increase in cancers in the future.

Alcohol

For the risk factor of alcohol, few data are available for Hispanics. The existing information suggests that Mexican-American males may be the heaviest drinkers among the Hispanic groups. Some studies of drinking patterns indicate that White men tend to reduce their alcohol consumption between their twenties and thirties. Studies of Hispanic men have, however, shown them to maintain steady consumption or to increase heavy drinking patterns into their thirties.

Some limited data on alcohol and its effect on Puerto Ricans in New York have been derived from statistics of mortality from cirrhosis of the liver. The study by Alers (1978) examined how many Puerto Ricans died of cirrhosis and from this information attempted to deduce the nature of that group's drinking problem. From 1968 to 1971, cirrhosis of the liver ranked third as the cause of death among Puerto Ricans in New York City.

No data are available regarding alcohol use by Cuban-Americans, Central and South Americans, and Other Spanish groups.

Diet and Nutrition

Neither is much information available on the dietary and nutritional practices of Hispanics. The 1970 HHANES data indicated that 17% to 25% of Hispanics are anemic (Carrillo and Torres 1986, unpublished). These HHANES data also showed Hispanics to have deficiencies in vitamins C and A. A recent study in New Mexico (Samet et al. 1985) of lung cancer and the protective effects of vitamin A showed Hispanics to have vitamin A deficiencies, although these did not place Hispanics in New Mexico at high risk of lung cancer.

Data from the San Antonio Heart Study and the Laredo project indicate that about 30% of the Mexican-American population, mainly women, are overweight, a proportion two to four times greater than that of Anglo Americans (Stern et al. 1981, 1982, 1983). Moreover, the foods consumed by Hispanics may be risk factors in certain cancers because of high levels of N-nitroso compounds (U.S. Department of Health and Human Services Task Force Report 1985). The HHANES data, when analyzed, may give us the first information on what Hispanics eat and how frequently they eat it. Even with the HHANES data, however, more research is needed concerning the relationship of Hispanics' diet, nutrition, and cancer. As Roberts and Lee (unpublished draft document prepared for Texas Cancer Council, 1986) pointed out, however, the role of diet in the

TABLE 1. Age-adjusted (1970 U.S. Standard) cancer incidence rates per 100,000 by ethnicity and selected sites, SEER 1978–1981.

Cancer site	Whites	New Mexican Hispanics	Puerto Rican Islanders
All sites	335.0	246.2	211.5
Prostate	75.1	76.5	43.4
Stomach	8.0	15.7	17.5
Pancreas	8.9	10.8	5.6
Female breast	85.6	54.1	39.4
Cervix	8.8	17.7	18.1
Oral cavity	11.0	6.8	16.8
Colon and rectum	49.6	25.2	20.1
Lung	50.7	22.9	15.1
Corpus uteri	25.1	11.1	9.2
Bladder	15.4	8.2	8.4

etiology of cancer is difficult to determine because cancer may take 20 to 30 years to manifest itself, and eating patterns may change over time.

Specific Cancers

The incidence data presented in Table 1 are mainly from the National Cancer Institute Surveillance, Epidemiology, and End Results (SEER) Program, and the only SEER sites with data on Hispanics are in New Mexico and Puerto Rico. Currently, SEER data that may contain information on Hispanics are collected in San Francisco/Oakland and the state of New Jersey, but since these data have not been analyzed we do not know what the data bases contain.

According to an unpublished report by J.M. Samet presented in 1984 at the Woodlands Conference, "Chronic Diseases Among Mexican-Americans," esophageal, gallbladder, and liver cancers should be added to the list in Table 1. They are the sites of greatest excess incidence rates for Hispanics in comparison with incidence among Whites. For New Mexican Hispanics and those, mainly Mexican-Americans, who live in the West and Southwest, the incidence rates are higher for cancers of the stomach, pancreas, cervix, gallbladder, and liver than in the White population.

Hispanics in the West and Southwest have a lower incidence of cancers of the oral cavity, colon, rectum, lung, corpus uteri, bladder, and female breast than does the White population. Incidence data from the Los Angeles Cancer Surveillance Program of 1972–1983, from the Colorado Cancer Registry for the Denver area of 1979–1981, from the New Mexico Tumor Registry for 1978–1981, and from the Texas Bureau of Epidemiology on Cancer Incidence in Texas for 1976–1980 reflect, in somewhat different ways, incidence rates for the cancer sites in the Samet (1984, unpublished) report. The distribution of incidence rates among the different data sources is similar for the various cancers, but these data sources collect information differently and do not adhere to the SEER system.

TABLE 2. Comparison of cancer incidence in Hispanic (H) and non-Hispanic (NH) persons for selected sites using data from four locations in the West and Southwest of the U.S.

Cancer site	Los Angeles	New Mexico	Colorado	Texas
In Men				
Gallbladder	H 3 x NH	data not available	H 2 x NH	H 3 x NH
Prostate	H 0.20 x NH	NH 0.10 x H	no difference	H 0.10 x NH
Stomach	H 2 x NH	H 2 x NH	H 2 x NH	H 2.5 x NH
In Women				
Cervix	H 3 x NH	H 2 x NH	H 2 x NH	H 2 x NH
Gallbladder	H 5 x NH	data not available	H 2 x NH	H 5 x NH
Stomach	H 2 x NH	H 3 x NH	H 3 x NH	H 5 x NH

Source: Samet JJ (1984, unpublished report to Woodlands conference, Chronic Diseases Among Mexican-Americans).

High Incidence

As the data in Table 2 indicate, incidence rates of cancer of the stomach, gallbladder, and cervix are two- to fivefold higher in Hispanic than non-Hispanic persons in the four areas enumerated. Only for prostate cancer are the rates nearly the same among Hispanic and non-Hispanic men.

The elevated incidence rate of cervical cancer in Hispanics may reflect early age of first marriage, promiscuity in the husband or male significant other, sexual history, fewer hysterectomies, lack of access to medical care, and low utilization patterns of cervical cancer screening (Samet 1984, unpublished).

Cancer sites for which Hispanic incidence rates are lower than non-Hispanic rates include oral cavity, female breast, colon, rectum, lung, corpus uteri, and bladder.

Except for cervical cancer, the high incidence rates of cancer among Hispanics in the West and Southwest concern cancers of the digestive system. Although dietary carcinogens may have a causal role, specific foods and chemical compounds have not been identified. Specific aspects of the Hispanic diet, what it contains, what it lacks, and how it is prepared, may partly explain these high rates. In addition to diet, the gallbladder cancer rate may be partly attributed to genetic etiology and the American Indian admixture, because an even higher excess of gallbladder cancer is found in American Indians in the West and Southwest (Samet 1984, unpublished report).

Low Incidence

That the rates for some cancer sites—colon and rectum for example (Table 1)— are low for Hispanics may reflect protective factors in some foods such as beans and rice, which are staples of the Hispanic diet. The lower breast cancer rate may reflect protective factors such as early pregnancy and bearing more children; the role of diet and overweight is not clear.

TABLE 3. Age-adjusted (1970 U.S. Standard) mortality rates per 100,000 by ethnicity and selected sites and specific SEER registries, 1978–1981.

Cancer site	Whites	New Mexican Hispanics	Puerto Rican Islanders
All	163.6	149.8	125.3
Colon and rectum	21.6	16.1	10.1
Pancreas	8.4	8.6	5.2
Lung	41.1	31.5	14.5
Female breast	26.6	23.6	12.0
Ovary	8.1	6.6	3.2

For lower rates of uterine cancer (Table 1), protective factors may include a lower proportion of nulliparous women in the population and a lower proportion of women using estrogen after the menopause. A lower incidence of cancers of the buccal cavities, pharynx, and lung (Table 1) may reflect a lower prevalence of pipe and cigar smoking in the Hispanic population and a past history of not very many Hispanics smoking cigarettes (Samet 1984, unpublished report), although this latter point, as I mentioned, is rapidly changing.

Mortality Rates

The SEER mortality data for New Mexican Hispanics and Puerto Rican islanders (Table 3) show that cancer mortality rates are lower in these two populations than for the White population. The mortality situation with regard to Hispanics and cancer is difficult to assess because so few data are available. I avoid relying too much on the New Mexican and Puerto Rican data on Hispanics, not because they are not good data, but because they are not *the* mortality data on Hispanics.

In Texas, cancer mortality rates for Hispanics compared with those for non-Hispanic Whites are higher for Hispanics only for digestive organ cancer sites and cervical cancer (Roberts and Lee 1986, unpublished document). The fact that the incidence rates for cervical cancer are 26.5 per 100,000 population for Hispanics in Texas and 17.7 per 100,000 population for Hispanics in New Mexico is a likely reason for the higher mortality rates. The difference in socioeconomic status between the two populations may be another contributing factor in the higher cancer mortality rates in Texas.

Puerto Ricans

In New York

For Puerto Ricans living in New York City, cancer incidence and mortality data are difficult to come by. Most of the information regarding cancer among Puerto Ricans in New York City is based on mortality data, since little analysis seems to be done based on the New York City Department of Health Cancer Registry (Rosenwaike 1984). Because New Jersey recently joined the SEER program,

TABLE 4. Cancer mortality rates for Puerto Ricans, age-adjusted (per 100,000 population).

Puerto Rican Islanders (1973–1977)[a]				Puerto Rican-Born Residents of New York City (1969–1971)[b]			
Men		Women		Men		Women	
All sites	156	All sites	100	All sites	141	All sites	106
Ten leading sites		Ten leading sites		Selected sites		Selected sites	
Stomach	24	Breast	11	Lung	30	Breast	12
Lung	19	Stomach	11	Stomach	18	Cervix	12
Prostate	19	Lung	8	Esophagus	12	Stomach	11
Esophagus	17	Uterus	7	Pancreas	9	Lung	7
Buccal cavity and pharynx	12	Colon	6	Prostate	9	Colon	7
Colon	7	Esophagus	6	Colon	7	Esophagus	6
Liver	7	Cervix	5	Rectum	4	Ovary	5
Pancreas	6	Liver	5	Urinary bladder	3		
Leukemia	6	Pancreas	4				
Urinary bladder	4	Leukemia	4				

[a] Estimated population: 3.3 million.
Source: Young et al. 1981.
[b] Estimated population: 1.1 million. About 50% of Puerto Rican-born residents in continental U.S. About 7% of Hispanic residents in continental U.S.
Source: Rosenwaike 1984.

I hope that the lack of cancer data regarding the Puerto Rican population in the U.S. will begin to be corrected.

Puerto Rico-born residents of New York City have lower cancer incidence rates than the White population of colorectal, lung, breast, and ovarian cancers, but twofold higher rates of stomach cancer, and threefold higher rates of esophageal and cervical cancer. The mortality rate for esophageal cancer is almost twice as high for male Puerto Rico-born New York City residents than for non-Hispanic Whites, and for stomach cancer it is about 20% higher for both female and male Puerto Rico-born New Yorkers (Table 4) (Rosenwaike 1984).

On the Island

Cancer rates on the island of Puerto Rico show a somewhat similar picture. As the data in Table 1 show, stomach, cervical, and oral cavity cancers are some of the problems of Puerto Ricans on the island as well. Data from the Puerto Rican Cancer Registry for 1950–1983 revealed that the incidence of cancer in Puerto Rican men was 81 per 100,000 and for women it was 103 per 100,000. In 1983, those figures jumped to 207 per 100,000 for men and 180 per 100,000 for women (Marcial 1986, unpublished report to the Sixth Biennial Conference of the National Coalition of Hispanic Health and Human Services Organizations).

A 1983 listing by number of cases of cancer for men (Marcial 1986, unpublished report) showed that prostate cancer was the most common, followed by cancers of lung, stomach, buccal cavity, esophagus, and colon. For women, the most frequently occurring cancers were those of breast, cervix, colon, uterus, and stomach, in that order. In men these cancer rates may be attributed in part to alcohol and tobacco use, since these are the most common major risk factors for the island population. Some characteristics of the cancer incidence were that, in 1983, 58% of all cancers in Puerto Rican men were metastatic, and in Puerto Rican women 54% were metastatic. This may partly explain some survival differences between the Puerto Rican islander and the U.S.-born White population. Thirty percent of Puerto Rican men survived, compared with 39% of White men; 46% of Puerto Rican women survived, compared with 54% of White women (Marcial 1986, unpublished report).

Among Puerto Rican women on the island, the incidence and mortality rates of cancers of the breast, lung, colon, and stomach are increasing; rectal cancer incidence is increasing and mortality is remaining stable; and cervical cancer incidence is increasing and mortality decreasing (Marcial 1986, unpublished report). In general, cancer incidence is increasing among women; however, better screening programs on the island may account for the decrease in incidence of and mortality from carcinoma of the cervix.

For Puerto Rican men on the island, incidence of and mortality from cancers of the prostate, lung, and stomach are increasing; and bladder cancer incidence is increasing without change in mortality. Socioeconomic factors seem to be major contributors to the increased cancer incidence and decreased survival of Puerto Ricans (Marcial 1986, unpublished report).

Other Groups

There were no cancer data for Cuban-Americans and other Hispanics until the 1986 biennial conference of the National Coalition of Hispanic Health and Human Services Organizations, where Edward Trapido (1986, unpublished report) presented some preliminary information gathered from the Florida State Cancer Registry and the Dade County Health Department.

Cancer incidence rates for Cuban-Americans are more similar to those of Whites than of any other Hispanic subgroup—which may be so because Cuban-Americans have the highest socioeconomic status of any Hispanic population.

Cancer incidence rates for Cuban-Americans compared with Whites in Florida indicate that, for men, colorectal and bladder cancer incidence is about the same; the rates of prostate, pancreatic, lung, and stomach cancers are lower among Cuban men; and the incidence of gallbladder cancer is two times higher in Cuban men. Among Cuban-American and White women, the incidence of oral, pancreatic, colorectal, bladder, and breast cancer is equal. Cuban women have a lower rate of lung cancer but higher rates of stomach, gallbladder, and cervical cancers.

Trapido's research also dealt with cancer data for Colombian men and women and Argentinian and Spanish men. Colombian males have a high proportion of prostate and a low proportion of colon, rectal, stomach, and lung cancers, whereas Colombian women have a high proportion of gallbladder and stomach cancers. Argentinian males have a high proportion of cancers of the pharynx and lung and a low proportion of prostate and stomach cancers. Spaniards have a high proportion of prostate and stomach cancers. I cite these disparate data because, the more one examines them, the more one sees that the digestive organs are a main cancer focus in Hispanic populations.

Summary

Incidence rates differ among the Hispanic and the U.S. white population. The data present a paradox, however, because the many risk factors attributed to Hispanics seem to be contradicted by low incidence rates. More research is needed to address this apparent contradiction. Nevertheless, rates of certain cancers are increasing in the Hispanic populations, which may be the result of assimilation, transculturation, more and better education, and longer residence in the U.S. Rates and outcomes of cancer will change with time as Hispanics experience a decrease in cervical and stomach cancers and an increase in lung and colon cancers, which are the current trends accompanying increases in smoking prevalence and other life-style changes.

Hispanics still face barriers to early diagnosis, to high-quality treatment, and to health care support—they need access to interdisciplinary and culturally appropriate care. To reach the Hispanic population one has to communicate with the population. Hispanics must be given the opportunity to recognize their cancer risks and to understand cancer as a basic risk for themselves and their loved ones. The Hispanic population is not easy to reach, but this must be done to reduce the incidence and mortality of this young and growing group. We must think in terms of segments of this population in order to make a difference with regard to targeted treatment and targeted prevention efforts.

References

Alers J. Monograph on *Health of Puerto Ricans in New York City.* New York: Hispanic Research Center, Fordham University, 1978.

Funch DP. *A Report on Cancer Survival in the Economically Disadvantaged.* New York: American Cancer Society Subcommittee on Health Care of Economically Disadvantaged Cancer Patients, July 1985, p. 51.

Rosenwaike I. Cancer mortality among Puerto Rican-born residents of New York City. *Am J Epidemiol* 1984;119:177–185.

Rosenwaike I, Shai D. Trends in cancer mortality among Puerto Rican-born migrants to New York City. *Int J Epidemiol* 1986;15:30–35.

Samet JM, Skipper BJ, Humble CG, et al. Lung cancer risk and vitamin A consumption in New Mexico. *Am Rev Respir Dis* 1985;131:198–202.

Stern M, Gaskill S, Allen C, et al. Cardiovascular risk factors in Mexican Americans in Laredo, Texas. I. Prevalence of overweight and diabetes and distributions of serum lipids. *Am J Epidemiol* 1981;113:546–555.

Stern MP, Gaskill SP, Hazuda HP, et al. Does obesity explain excess prevalence of diabetes among Mexican Americans? Results of the San Antonio Heart Study. *Diabetologia* 1983;24:272–277.

Stern M, Pugh J, Gaskill S, et al. Knowledge, attitudes, and behavior related to obesity and dieting in Mexican Americans and Anglos: The San Antonio Heart Study. *Am J Epidemiol* 1982;115:917–928.

Trevino FM, Moss AJ. *Health, United States, 1983.* Department of Health and Human Services Publication No. (PHS) 84-1232. Washington, DC: US Government Printing Office, 1983.

Trevino FM, Moss AJ. Health indicators for Hispanic, black, and white Americans. *Vital and Health Statistics*, Series 10, No. 148. Department of Health and Human Services Publication No. (PHS) 84-1576. Washington, DC: US Government Printing Office, 1984.

US Bureau of the Census. *Persons of Spanish Origin in the United States* (Advance Report). *Hispanic Link Weekly Report*, March 1985, p. 3.

US Department of Health and Human Services. *The Report of the Secretary's Task Force on Black and Minority Health*, Washington, DC: US Public Health Service, 1985.

Young JL Jr, Percy CL, Asire AJ. *SEER Incidence and Mortality Data: 1973–77. NCI Monogr*, 1981;57–198.

3. Cancer Incidence Among Asian-Americans

Marc T. Goodman

Other chapters in this volume have focused on the *high* rates of cancer among minorities in the United States. In contrast, United States data show that Asian-Americans experience *lower* rates than Blacks and Caucasians for many of the more common malignancies. Epidemiologists, clinicians, nutritionists, and other health professionals may learn much about the etiology of cancer by determining why Asian-Americans have lower incidence rates. Contrasts of ethnic-specific cancer patterns may reveal factors associated with disease causation and disease prevention.

Data are presented for both common and less frequent malignancies to highlight interesting ethnic differences in incidence. Cancer rates for Native Hawaiians, Caucasians, and the three major Asian groups in Hawaii, namely Japanese, Chinese, and Filipinos, are included. Native Hawaiians were added to this discussion because they are a frequently overlooked minority of indigenous Americans. National (U.S.) rates for Caucasians and Blacks as well as Hawaii state data are presented.

All data for cancer incidence were provided by the Surveillance, Epidemiology, and End Results (SEER) Program of the National Cancer Institute for the years 1978 through 1981 (SEER Program 1985). Data concerning dietary and tobacco-smoking patterns for the various ethnic groups were derived from a large cohort study conducted in Hawaii by our group (Kolonel et al. 1981a; Kolonel et al. 1981b). This cohort consists of a representative sample of 41,643 adults who were identified between 1977–1979 through the Hawaii Department of Health. The questionnaire included demographic characteristics, food-consumption data, and alcohol and smoking histories.

General Cancer Patterns

Tables 1 and 2 show annual, age-adjusted incidence rates between 1978 and 1981 for selected cancer sites by ethnic group. Data for Hawaii are compared with data for all SEER areas (excluding Puerto Rico). Japanese, Chinese, and Filipinos

TABLE 1. Age-adjusted (1970 U.S. standard) incidence rates per 100,000 population for males by site and ethnicity, 1978–1981.

Site or type of cancer	Hawaii					All SEER areas (excl. Puerto Rico)	
	Japanese	Chinese	Filipino	Hawaiian	Caucasian	Black	Caucasian
All malignant neoplasms	300	259	235	391	445	488	392
Buccal cavity and pharynx	8	19	11	10	26	23	17
Stomach	41	12	9	48	17	21	12
Colon	43	30	24	21	37	40	39
Rectum	22	17	19	20	18	15	19
Pancreas	9	10	7	9	10	17	11
Larynx	6	3	4	8	11	12	8
Lung and bronchus	47	46	34	101	80	119	81
Melanoma of skin	2	1	1	2	26	1	9
Breast	0	1	0	1	1	1	1
Prostate gland	46	32	52	58	83	120	75
Urinary bladder	11	17	7	11	32	13	27
Kidney and renal pelvis	8	4	4	6	13	9	10
Brain and CNS	2	5	4	4	8	4	7
Hodgkin's disease	1	1	2	1	2	2	3
Non-Hodgkin's lymphomas	9	12	11	10	13	9	12
Leukemias	6	7	5	8	12	11	13

Source: SEER Program 1985

generally have much lower rates of cancer than do Caucasians and Blacks. In an investigation of ethnic-specific cancer patterns in Hawaii, Kolonel (1980) found that among men the occurrence of cancer at four sites — lip, melanoma, prostate, and urinary bladder — was significantly higher among Caucasians than among the other ethnic groups. Among Caucasian women, only the occurrence of melanoma was significantly higher than among the other ethnic groups.

Lung Cancer

Hawaiians and Blacks had the highest rates of lung cancer in the United States between 1978 and 1981, followed by those of Caucasians, Chinese, Filipinos, Japanese, New Mexico Hispanics, Puerto Ricans, and American Indians. Tobacco-smoking patterns are generally acknowledged to be closely related to risk patterns for lung cancer. However, although Caucasian men and women smoke more than do Hawaiians (Table 3), Hawaiians have much higher rates of lung cancer (Kolonel 1979). Hawaiian and Japanese men have comparable cigarette use, yet Hawaiian men have an incidence of lung cancer that is twice

TABLE 2. Age-adjusted (1970 U.S. standard) incidence rates per 100,000 population for females by site and ethnicity, 1978–1981.

Site or type of cancer	Hawaii					All SEER areas (excl. Puerto Rico)	
	Japanese	Chinese	Filipino	Hawaiian	Caucasian	Black	Caucasian
All malignant neoplasms	214	228	192	336	351	290	303
Buccal cavity and pharynx	3	6	9	9	12	8	6
Stomach	19	9	6	21	8	8	5
Colon	27	28	13	15	30	37	32
Rectum	11	8	5	9	9	9	12
Pancreas	6	10	5	11	12	11	7
Larynx	0	0	0	2	2	2	2
Lung and bronchus	14	22	20	39	38	30	28
Melanoma of skin	1	2	1	1	21	1	8
Breast	53	66	39	111	97	72	86
Cervix uteri	8	8	7	14	10	20	9
Corpus uteri	18	23	14	27	29	13	25
Ovary	9	10	10	14	12	10	14
Urinary bladder	5	1	6	6	5	5	7
Kidney and renal pelvis	2	1	0	2	5	4	4
Brain and CNS	2	1	1	3	5	3	5
Hodgkin's disease	0	0	1	1	3	1	2
Non-Hodgkin's lymphomas	7	4	9	7	10	5	9
Leukemias	4	5	3	5	9	7	8

Source: SEER Program 1985

that of the Japanese. A study conducted by our group in Hawaii showed that the odds ratio for lung cancer associated with smoking among women, after adjusting for age and socioeconomic status, was 10 for Hawaiians, 5 for Japanese, and only 2 for Chinese (Hinds et al. 1981). Studies from Hong Kong (Chan et al. 1979) and China (Gao et al. 1985) showed a much greater frequency of non-smoking women among patients with lung cancer. As suggested by Hinds and colleagues (1981), these differences may be genetic (e.g., aryl hydrocarbon hydroxylase activity) or environmental (e.g., dietary vitamin A consumption, passive smoking, excess indoor air pollution).

Urogenital Cancer

Asian-Americans in Hawaii have uniformly lower rates of bladder, kidney, cervix, endometrium, ovary, and prostate cancer than do Caucasians. Differences in the prevalence of tobacco smoking may explain part of the increased risk for

TABLE 3. Age-adjusted percentages of ever cigarette smokers by ethnic group and gender.

	Male	Female
Caucasian	60.8	50.1
Japanese	52.8	26.1
Chinese	36.9	18.5
Filipino	48.0	28.5
Hawaiian	56.5	46.9

Reprinted from Kolonel (1979) with permission of author.

cancers of the bladder, kidney, and perhaps cervix among Caucasians. A greater proportion of Caucasian than of Asian males and females have ever smoked (Table 3), and those who have smoked have tended to do so in greater amounts (Table 4). Furthermore, Caucasian men report a higher consumption of coffee, a beverage that may be associated with an increased risk of bladder cancer, than men of other ethnic groups (Kolonel 1980).

The high rates of cervical cancer among Hawaiians and Blacks in the United States may be a result of factors associated with socioeconomic status, such as sexual practices, hygiene, and access to medical care (Kolonel 1980). It is noteworthy that Filipinos in Hawaii, who are also of low socioeconomic status, have lower rates of cervical and other cancers than Hawaiians. This may be attributable to other cultural (environmental) factors that are yet to be elucidated.

Prostate cancer incidence in Hawaii is highest among Caucasians, followed by that of Hawaiians, Filipinos, Japanese, and Chinese. A recent study by our group (Kolonel et al. 1988) showed that, among men 70 years or older, consumption of

TABLE 4. Age-adjusted percentage distribution of ever cigarette smokers by amount smoked, ethnicity and gender.

	Daily amount smoked (packs)		
	< 1	1	> 1
Male			
Caucasian	50.2	26.7	23.1
Japanese	60.9	25.9	13.2
Chinese	77.1	16.8	6.1
Filipino	73.2	20.3	6.5
Hawaiian	59.0	27.6	13.4
Female			
Caucasian	66.9	23.3	9.8
Japanese	88.7	8.9	2.4
Chinese	93.9	3.2	2.9
Filipino	86.9	11.2	1.9
Hawaiian	73.3	17.6	9.1

Reprinted from Kolonel (1979) with permission of author.

TABLE 5. Age-adjusted (truncated 45 years or older) average daily intakes of selected dietary components for men among five ethnic groups in Hawaii.

	Men				
Nutrient component	Caucasian ($n = 604$)	Japanese ($n = 922$)	Chinese ($n = 200$)	Filipino ($n = 358$)	Hawaiian ($n = 209$)
Total fat (g)	82.3	67.6	70.1	58.1	75.2
Animal fat (g)	52.2	42.7	43.3	40.6	49.6
Saturated fat (g)	29.8	23.4	24.9	21.2	26.7
Unsaturated fat (g)	44.4	37.7	39.1	31.2	40.5
Cholesterol (mg)	367.9	329.6	320.7	330.9	397.0
Protein (g)	69.9	65.6	63.8	61.5	69.0
Carbohydrate (g)	165.2	195.4	176.7	207.1	195.9
Vitamin A (IU)	4080.0	3189.0	3300.0	3249.0	3866.0
Vitamin C (mg)	113.7	101.0	110.6	83.4	123.8

saturated fat was positively associated with the risk of prostate cancer. Recent data from a large population-based cohort study described by Kolonel et al. (1981c), showed that Caucasians consume foods higher in fat and animal protein (Tables 5 and 6) than do members of the other groups studied. Immigrant data, comparing Japanese in Hawaii and Japanese in Fukuoka prefecture in Japan demonstrated a strong, positive correlation between dietary fat and protein intake and the incidence of prostate cancer (Kolonel et al. 1980).

Breast Cancer

The promotional effects of dietary fat on mammary tumor production in rodents are well established (Hopkins and Carroll 1979). Several human ecologic studies have demonstrated a high correlation between breast cancer incidence and mor-

TABLE 6. Age-adjusted (truncated 45 years or older) average daily intakes of selected dietary components for women among five ethnic groups in Hawaii.

	Women				
Nutrient component	Caucasian ($n = 543$)	Japanese ($n = 1102$)	Chinese ($n = 198$)	Filipino ($n = 241$)	Hawaiian ($n = 280$)
Total fat (g)	62.5	52.5	55.9	47.6	58.6
Animal fat (g)	40.7	33.4	37.4	33.3	38.4
Saturated fat (g)	21.9	18.1	19.7	17.2	20.9
Unsaturated fat (g)	34.3	29.6	31.1	25.8	31.9
Cholesterol (mg)	276.0	250.1	267.6	282.7	302.1
Protein (g)	54.2	51.1	53.2	51.2	53.3
Carbohydrate (g)	130.4	150.4	142.8	178.1	152.0
Vitamin A (IU)	3731	2988	3247	3496	3325
Vitamin C (mg)	109.9	107.0	106.3	103.4	104.4

tality and the per capita or individual consumption of dietary fat (Armstrong and Doll 1975; Berg 1975; Kolonel et al. 1981a), animal protein (Armstrong and Doll 1975; Gray et al. 1979), meat (Armstrong and Doll 1975; Correa 1981), and eggs (Armstrong and Doll 1975; Correa 1981). These findings suggest that the large international variations in breast cancer occurrence are a result of differences in the level of consumption of animal fat or protein, or some other risk factor that is highly correlated with the consumption of animal products. On this basis, breast cancer incidence would be expected to be high among Caucasians and Hawaiians whose diets are high in fats and animal protein, and correspondingly lower for Chinese, Japanese, and Filipinos whose consumption of calories from fat is more limited (see Table 6).

Studies have shown that the breast cancer rates for immigrant Asian women shift from the low rates prevailing in their country of origin toward the higher rates experienced in their host country (Haenszel and Kurihara 1968; Buell 1973). For example, women of Japanese ancestry in the United States have a two to three times higher risk of breast cancer than their counterparts in Japan, while the rate for Hawaii-Japanese women is one-half that of Hawaii-Caucasian women (Waterhouse et al. 1982). This finding underscores the role of environmental, as opposed to genetic, factors in the etiology of cancer of the breast. In view of the rapid increase in the incidence of breast cancer in first-generation immigrants, early-life exposure to some carcinogens appears important (Haenszel and Kurihara 1968; Buell 1973).

Obesity has been related to an elevated risk of breast cancer among postmenopausal women (Thomas 1984). In analyzing data from our large cohort study, Kolonel (1980) noted the higher prevalence of obesity among Hawaiian women compared with Japanese, Chinese, and Filipino women. He speculated that the slighter body build and absence of obesity may account, in part, for the low incidence of breast cancer among Asian women. In a subsequent case-control study among Caucasian and Japanese women in Hawaii, however, no association of obesity with postmenopausal breast cancer risk was observed (Kolonel et al. 1986).

Stomach Cancer

Although the incidence of stomach cancer has been declining since 1930 in the United States, the rate of this malignancy is still comparatively high among Japanese and Hawaiians of both genders, Hawaiians having particularly elevated rates. Evidence suggests that diet is an important determinant of stomach cancer development (Howson et al. 1986). A positive association with the disease has been found for rice and carbohydrate (Segi et al. 1957; Modan et al. 1974). Experimental studies have pointed to a role of N-nitroso compounds in the etiology of stomach cancer (Sugimura and Kawachi 1978; Maekawa et al. 1976). The use of smoked or dried and salted fish products has been associated with the development of stomach cancer in Japan (Hirayama 1971) and in Japanese migrants to Hawaii (Haenszel et al. 1972). Pickled vegetable consumption has also been implicated in the risk of stomach cancer in Hawaii (Haenszel et al. 1972) but not Japan (Hirayama 1971). Chinese and Filipino men eat few nitrite-containing meats, and their rates for stomach cancer are also low. Ascorbic acid inhibits the reaction of nitrites and secondary amines to form nitrosamines, and an inverse association has been found between stomach cancer development and the intake of vitamin C in men (Kolonel et al. 1981b). The protective effect of vitamin C does not, however, explain the lower rates of stomach cancer among Chinese and Filipinos (see Table 5). The intake of vitamins A and E may also be inversely associated with the risk of stomach cancer.

Immigrant data provide some interesting clues to the etiology of stomach cancer. United States mainland Caucasians have much lower rates of stomach cancer than Caucasians immigrating to or born in Hawaii, possibly because of the increased consumption of oriental foods (Kolonel et al. 1981b). In turn, Japanese in Japan have much higher rates of stomach cancer than Japanese emigrants to Hawaii (Kolonel et al. 1981b). Furthermore, the fact that Japanese emigrants to Hawaii have a higher stomach cancer incidence than Japanese born in Hawaii suggests the importance of early-life exposures in the etiology of this disease (Haenszel et al. 1972, 1976; Kolonel et al. 1981b). Second-generation immigrants from Japan tend to acquire stomach cancer at rates prevalent in the United States.

Colon Cancer

Besides the stomach, the colon is one of the few sites for which cancer rates are higher among Japanese men than Caucasian and mainland Black men. The colon is also the only cancer site for which Hawaiians (of both genders) are at significantly lower risk compared with Caucasians (Kolonel 1980).

The role of diet in the etiology of colon cancer is the focus of most current research. There is little consensus on the role of dietary fat in the development of this malignancy. Although several epidemiologic and ecologic studies have shown a positive relation for dietary fat and cholesterol and the incidence of colon cancer (McKeown-Eyssen and Bright-See 1984; Miller et al. 1983), others have demonstrated no relation (Enstrom 1975; Potter and McMichael 1986), and there have even been some reports of an inverse relation of cholesterol and colon cancer, especially among men (Stemmermann et al. 1984). The possibility that fiber may modify the risk of colon cancer associated with fat has been suggested by at least two analytic studies (Dales et al. 1979; Manousos et al. 1983).

The dietary fat-colon cancer hypothesis is difficult to reconcile with the ethnic variation in incidence. Hawaiians who have a high-fat diet and Filipinos who consume a low-fat diet (see Table 5) both have relatively low rates of colon cancer. Even though fat consumption is significantly different between first- and second-generation Japanese in Hawaii, their rates of colon cancer incidence are similar. Since most Japanese emigrated to this country as adults, this observation would imply that changes in exposure to certain environmental factors in adulthood (promoters?) may have a major influence on the development of this cancer

(Kolonel et al., 1986). In contrast to Japanese, Filipino immigrants to Hawaii do not experience an immediate increase in the rates of colon cancer, which is perhaps indicative of slower acculturation and adaptation to western life style and diet (Kolonel 1985).

Conclusions

A special report on cancer in poor people by an American Cancer Society subcommittee concluded recently that both cancer incidence and survival are strongly related to socioeconomic status (American Cancer Society 1986) and that ethnic differences in cancer rates largely reflect socioeconomic factors. That mortality rates for cancer of specific sites are particularly high among poor patients is well recognized. However, socioeconomic status is not a risk factor for cancer per se, but a proxy for other real environmental exposures or genetic predispositions that are more prevalent in particular groups in our society. Certain behavioral characteristics such as dietary practice, tobacco use, and occupational exposure are known to be related to cancer incidence and mortality. Thus, Filipinos and Hawaiians, both of lower socioeconomic status in Hawaii, have widely divergent rates for many types of cancer. Ethnicity or race may therefore exert a significant effect on the incidence of cancer that is independent of education, income, or other socioeconomic indicators (American Cancer Society 1986).

During the past decade we have seen major changes in the nutritional habits of large segments of our population. Dietary guidelines have been proposed by the National Cancer Institute as well as the National Heart, Lung, and Blood Institute and others. How will these recommendations filter down to the economically disadvantaged in our society? Although members of the scientific community can prescribe potential remedies for the gap in health status between well-to-do and needy Americans, only public health education can foster the necessary changes in health behavior. Children and adolescents must be shown the dangers of smoking. Parents and educators must teach children about good health behavior, such as proper nutrition, physical activity, and the avoidance of alcohol and illicit drugs. Modifying behavior in our youth must begin with adults. Financial support must be enlisted to provide cancer screening programs for high-risk groups and other secondary prevention measures, such as smoking cessation campaigns. Finally, cancer in minority populations must be recognized at earlier stages to improve prognosis. This can also be accomplished by public education on early signs and symptoms of cancer and by outreach programs for people who do not use and perhaps do not know how to use the health care system. These initiatives must be started by the health care providers to encourage access to medical care. The debate has been heated, and will probably continue to be so, on what the nation must do in our minority communities to effect a 50% reduction in the cancer mortality rate by the year 2000. Perhaps we will come closer to this goal by practicing some of the health habits of Asians in the United States.

Acknowledgment. This research was funded by contract and grant No1-CA-15655 from the National Cancer Institute, U.S. Department of Health and Human Services.

References

American Cancer Society. *Cancer in the Economically Disadvantaged. A Special Report.* Subcommittee on Cancer in the Economically Disadvantaged. New York: American Cancer Society, 1986.

Armstrong B, Doll R. Environmental factors and cancer incidence and mortality in different countries, with special reference to dietary practices. *Int J Cancer* 1975;15:617–631.

Berg JW. Can nutrition explain the pattern of international epidemiology of hormone-dependent cancers? *Cancer Res* 1975;35:3345–3350.

Buell P. Changing incidence of breast cancer in Japanese-American women. *JNCI* 1973;51:1479–1483.

Chan WC, Colbourne MJ, Fung SC, et al. Bronchial cancer in Hong Kong, 1976–1977. *Br J Cancer* 1979;39:182–192.

Correa P. Epidemiological correlations between diet and cancer frequency. *Cancer Res* 1981;41:3685–3690.

Dales LG, Friedman GD, Ury HK, et al. A case-control study of relationships of diet and other traits to colorectal cancer in American blacks. *Am J Epidemiol* 1979;109:132–144.

Enstrom JE. Colorectal cancer and consumption of beef and fat. *Br J Cancer* 1975;32:432–439.

Gao Y-T, Hsu C-W, Blot WJ, et al. A case-control study of lung cancer in Shanghai. *NCI Monograph* 1985;69:11–13.

Gray GE, Pike MC, Henderson BE. Breast cancer incidence and mortality rates in different countries in relation to known risk factors and dietary practices. *Br J Cancer* 1979;39:1–7.

Haenszel W, Kurihara M. Studies of Japanese migrants. I. Mortality from cancer and other diseases among Japanese in the United States. *JNCI* 1968;40:43–68.

Haenszel W, Kurihara M, Locke FB, et al. Stomach cancer in Japan. *JNCI* 1976;56:265–278.

Haenszel W, Kurihara M, Segi M, et al. Stomach cancer among Japanese in Hawaii. *JNCI* 1972;49:969–988.

Hinds MW, Stemmermann GN, Yang H-Y, et al. Differences in lung cancer risk from smoking among Japanese, Chinese, and Hawaiian women in Hawaii. *Int J Cancer* 1981;27:297–302.

Hirayama T. Epidemiology of stomach cancer. *Gann Monograph* 1971;11:3–19.

Hopkins GJ, Carroll KK. Relationship between amount and type of dietary fat in promotion of mammary carcinogenesis induced by 7,12-dimethylbenz[a]anthracene. *JNCI* 1979;62:1009–1012.

Howson CP, Hiyama T, Wynder EL. The decline in gastric cancer: Epidemiology of an unexplained triumph. *Epidemiol Rev* 1986;8:1–27.

Kolonel LN. Smoking and drinking patterns among different ethnic groups in Hawaii. *NCI Monograph* 1979;53:81–87.

Kolonel LN. Cancer patterns of four ethnic groups in Hawaii. *JNCI* 1980;65:1127–1139.

Kolonel LN. Cancer incidence among Filipinos in Hawaii and the Philippines. *NCI Mono-graph* 1985;69:93–98.

Kolonel LN, Hankin JH, Lee J, et al. Nutrient intakes in relation to cancer incidence in Hawaii. *Br J Cancer* 1981c;44:332–339.

Kolonel LN, Hankin JH, Nomura AMY. Multiethnic studies of diet, nutrition and cancer in Hawaii. In: Hayashi Y et al, eds. *Diet, Nutrition and Cancer*, Tokyo: Japan Science Society Press. 1986;29–40.

Kolonel LN, Hankin JH, Nomura AMY, et al. Dietary fat intake and cancer incidence among five ethnic groups in Hawaii. *Cancer Res* 1981a;41:3727–3728.

Kolonel LN, Hinds MW, Hankin JH. Cancer patterns among migrant and native-born Japanese in Hawaii in relation to smoking, drinking, and dietary habits. In: Gelboin HV et al, eds. *Genetic and Environmental Factors in Experimental and Human Cancer*, Tokyo: Japan Science Society Press, 1980;327–340.

Kolonel LN, Nomura AMY, Hirohata T, et al. Association of diet and place of birth with stomach cancer incidence in Hawaii-Japanese and Caucasians. *Am J Clin Nutr* 1981b; 34:2478–2485.

Kolonel LN, Nomura AMY, Lee J, et al. Anthropometric indicators of breast cancer risk in postmenopausal women in Hawaii. *Nutr Cancer* 1986;8:247–256.

Kolonel LN, Yoshizawa CN, Hankin JH. Diet and prostate cancer: A case-control study in Hawaii. *Am J Epidemiol* 1988;127:999–1012.

Maekawa A, Odashima S, Nakadate M. Induction of tumors in the stomach and nervous system of the ACI/N rat by continuous oral administration of 1-methyl-3-acetyl-1-nitroso-urea. *Z Krebsforsch* 1976;86:195–207.

Manousos O, Day NE, Trichopoulos D, et al. Diet and colorectal cancer: A case-control study in Greece. *Int J Cancer* 1983;32:1–5.

McKeown-Eyssen GE, Bright-See E. Dietary factors in colon cancer: International rela-tionships. *Nutr Cancer* 1984;6:160–170.

Miller AB, Howe GR, Jain M, et al. Food items and food groups as risk factors in a case-control study of diet and colo-rectal cancer. *Int J Cancer* 1983;32:155–161.

Modan B, Lubin F, Barell V, et al. The role of starches in the etiology of gastric cancer. *Cancer* 1974;34:2087–2092.

Potter JD, McMichael AJ. Diet and cancer of the colon and rectum. *JNCI* 1986;76: 557–569.

SEER Program. *Cancer Incidence and Mortality in the United States, 1973–81*. Horm JW, Asire AJ, Young JL Jr., et al., eds. Washington DC: NIH Publication No. 85-1837, 1985.

Segi M, Fukushima I, Fujisaku S, et al. An epidemiological study on cancer in Japan: The report of the Committee for Epidemiological Study on Cancer, sponsored by the Minis-try of Welfare and Public Health. *Gann* 1957;48 (suppl):1–62.

Stemmermann GN, Nomura AMY, Heilbrun LK. Dietary fat and the risk of colorectal cancer. *Cancer Res* 1984;44:4633–4637.

Sugimura T, Kawachi T. Experimental stomach carcinogenesis. In: Lipkin M, Good RA, eds. *Gastrointestinal Tract Cancer*. New York: Plenum, 1978:327–341.

Thomas DB. Do hormones cause breast cancer? *Cancer* 1984;53:595–604.

Waterhouse J, Muir C, Shanugaratnam K, et al, eds. *Cancer Incidence in Five Continents*, vol 4. Lyon: International Agency for Research on Cancer, 1982.

4. The Heterogeneity of Cancer in Native American Populations

James W. Hampton

The occurrence of cancer in the Native American population of North America has been studied only sporadically (Skye and Hampton 1976). A number of articles reviewed at the beginning of this century (Levin 1910) stated that American Indians *never* had cancer. In 1932 the excavation of an Indian burial site yielded the skeleton of a pre-Columbian Indian man, and roentgenograms showed destructive lesions identical to those of multiple myeloma (Ritchie and Warren 1932).

In 1917, Hrdlicka observed in a letter to *Science* that American Indians were "disappearing" and that they did not require separate investigation for medical problems because only a few would exist into this century as products of "miscegenation."

We do exist and we are still with you. The credibility of that issue of *Science* is doubtful anyway, since it also contained a review of a book (Buckley 1917) that said unreservedly that cancer was caused by an animal "proteid" and could be cured by giving potassium.

We (Skye and Hampton 1976) reported at the Third International Conference on the Early Detection and Prevention of Cancer a study based on a survey of the then current epidemiological literature and an investigation based on the statistics from the state health department and the university hospitals in Oklahoma. In this study we compared the prevalence of specific cancers in American Indians to that in the total White population. Our work, together with that of Sievers (1962, 1966, 1976), initially indicated the heterogeneity of cancers in Native American populations.

Cancer of the lung (Figure 1) at that time was lower in incidence in American Indians, but the incidence appeared to be increasing. Figure 2 shows that carcinoma of the cervix was clearly higher in Native American women than other women in Oklahoma. The then current and more recent evidence indicates that this cancer has increased in all Native American women (Jordan et al. 1969; Blot et al. 1975; Lanier et al. 1976).

Breast cancer occurred in Native American women but not with the same frequency as in American women as a whole (Figure 3). More recent data indicate

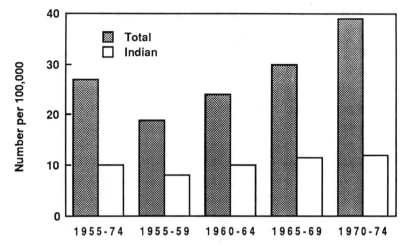

FIGURE 1. Incidence of pulmonary neoplasms as a cause of death in
Oklahoma. Adapted from Skye and Hampton 1976, with permission.

that breast cancer is increasing in Oklahoma Indian women (Sievers and Fisher
1983; Kaufman et al. 1986). Our survey of the literature showed that rates for
specific cancers were extremely high in Native American populations and that
cancers often had an environmental origin.

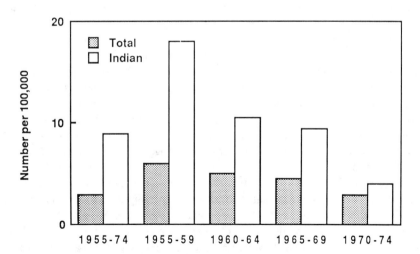

FIGURE 2. Incidence of cervix uteri neoplasms as a cause of death in
Oklahoma. Adapted from Skye and Hampton 1976, with permission.

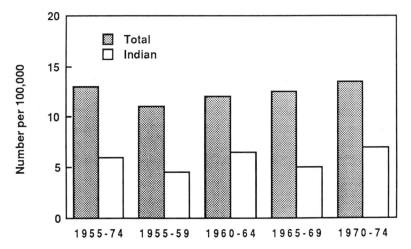

FIGURE 3. Incidence of breast neoplasms as a cause of death in Oklahoma. Adapted from Skye and Hampton 1976, with permission.

Southwestern Indians studied by Sievers (1962, 1966, 1976) clearly had a high incidence of biliary and gastric cancers. In Oklahoma Indians, as in other tribes, cancer of the cervix occurred much more frequently than in their White counterparts (Jordan et al. 1969). Lanier and others reported that Alaskan tribes had cancer of the esophagus but that the incidence may be declining (Blot et al. 1975; Lanier et al. 1976). Woods (1974) also illustrated changing health patterns in the circumpolar regions.

Since our initial article (Skye and Hampton 1976) calling attention to the heterogeneity of cancers both as to type and their uniqueness for Native American populations, a number of relevant observations have been made. Like Lewis Thomas who is a well-known "biology watcher," I have become an "epidemiology watcher" of cancer in Native Americans.

According to the SEER (Surveillance, Epidemiology, and End Results) data, Native Americans in New Mexico and Utah had the lowest cancer incidence among the ethnic groups (Baquet and Ringen 1986), although the Native Americans, as did the Blacks, experienced the least favorable survival rates. Biliary cancer did not appear prominent in these figures, probably because of its low incidence in the total population. As Black et al. reported in 1977, however, gallbladder carcinoma accounted for 8.5% of specific cancer diagnoses by site for American Indian women.

The Sievers group (Sievers 1961; Sievers and Fisher 1983) published their observations about lung cancer in American Indians and later postulated that the heavy cigarette smoking of the Oklahoma Indians had increased their risk of developing this cancer. Samet et al. (1984) observed that, in a predominantly nonsmoking population of Navajo men, the association between uranium mining and lung cancer was statistically significant, which indicated that in this low-risk population lung cancer could be attributed to this hazardous occupation. Many Inuits have become heavy cigarette smokers during the past 20 to 30 years, and Schaefer et al. (1975) reported an increase in lung cancer in this group from 7% of all malignant tumors in 1950–1966 to 25% in 1967–1974.

Sievers and Fisher (1983) also pointed out that American Indians had higher rates of cancer of the gallbladder, kidney, and cervix. These authors described the changing environmental and cultural conditions of Native American populations and urged that attempts to modify behavioral practices and environmental conditions be undertaken by health agencies.

The Indian Health Service has recognized the susceptibility of Native Americans to known carcinogens and has undertaken programs to reduce the incidence of cancers and educate the Native Americans about their risks. Since many Native Americans are not served by the Indian Health Service (Table 1), a registration of cancer incidence should be undertaken for populations outside those boundaries. Tim Taylor (University of Oklahoma, personal communication, 1987) is undertaking such a survey in Oklahoma City to see what portion of the Indian population is served by the private sector and what portion by the urban Indian health clinic.

Data from the Indian Health Service for persons discharged with the diagnosis of malignant neoplasms in 1984, 1985, and 1986 (Table 2) did not show a striking increase in cancer incidence but illustrated the wide divergence of type and frequency of malignant neoplasms reported by the different service areas (Kaufman et al. 1986). When the American Indians' age-adjusted death rates (Table 3) are compared for the year 1981, malignant neoplasms are third for both genders combined and the second leading cause of death of American Indian women.

As programs of the Indian Health Service begin to reduce problems of heart disease and accidents, the incidence of malignant neoplasms should figure more prominently. Other publications have stressed the heterogeneity of cancer in

TABLE 1. Estimated total U.S. Indian population and those served and not served by the Indian Health Service.

State	Estimated total Indian population	Reservation state
Alaska	71,329	Yes
Arizona	169,869	Yes
California	216,070	Partial (142,808)
New Mexico	116,150	Partial (2,581)
North Carolina	69,575	Partial (63,530)
Oklahoma	186,268	Partial (unknown)

Data from the U.S. Department of Human Services, Public Health Service, Indian Health Services Program Statistics Branch.

TABLE 2. Discharges by principal diagnosis: Indian Health Service and contract general hospitals.

Malignant neoplasms	1984	1985	1986
Aberdeen area	219	182	190
Alaska area	272	285	283
Albuquerque area	126	165	86
Bemidji program	51	36	15
Billings area	156	94	79
Nashville program	18	13	15
Navajo area	252	246	218
Oklahoma area	238	207	265
Phoenix area	139	133	164
Portland area	59	50	53
Tucson program	8	10	8

Data from the Office of Planning, Evaluation and Legislation Program Statistics Branch, Indian Health Service, U.S. Department of Health and Human Services.

Native American populations. A recent study (Sorem 1985) of the Zuni and other American Indians again showed the high incidence of carcinoma of the gallbladder and cervix in American Indian women in New Mexico.

Lowenfels et al. (1985) reported a higher incidence of gallstones in South-western Native American women and attempted to interpret this finding as an etiologic factor in biliary cancer. The Alaskan tribes also have a higher incidence of gallbladder cancer (Lanier and Knutson 1986). Nasopharyngeal carcinoma in

TABLE 3. Age-adjusted death rates for American Indians and all U.S. residents, 1981.

	American Indian	U.S.
Both sexes combined		
Diseases of the heart	166.7	195
Accidents/adverse effects	163.3	39.8
Malignant neoplasms	98.4	131.6
Female		
Diseases of the heart	121.5	135.1
Malignant neoplasms	89.4	108.6
Accidents/adverse effects	69.0	20.4
Male		
Accidents/adverse effects	207.8	60.2
Diseases of the heart	219.0	271.2
Malignant neoplasms	109.1	163.7

Data from the Indian Health Services Program Statistics Branch, U.S. Department of Human Services.

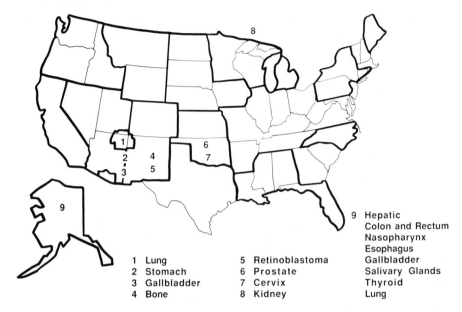

FIGURE 4. Incidence of cancer, by type, in Native Americans served by the Indian Health Service.

Alaskan Indians and Aleuts has been linked to the Epstein-Barr virus (Lanier et al. 1980), and an inspection of the total incidence of age-adjusted annual incidence rates per 100,000 population would indicate a rate of 9.6 for this cancer in Alaskan Native men. These men have a high incidence of liver cancer (hepatitis B in origin), and Alaskan Native women have a high incidence of thyroid cancer. Alaskan Natives also have a high incidence of cancer of the lung, salivary gland, and colon and rectum (Lanier and Knutson 1986).

The heterogeneity of cancer in Native Americans served by the Indian Health Service (Figure 4) clearly indicates the need for enlarging the scope of the SEER data. Duncan et al. (1986) also reported a high incidence of retinoblastoma occurring in children of the Southwestern Indians. And we, in 1984, rewrote the American Cancer Society's seven warning signals for detection of cancer in American Indians according to certain tribal and regional risks and published this in a communication of the National Indian Health Board, a periodical read by most Native Americans (Hampton 1984).

Cancer's Seven Warning Signals

1. Unusual vaginal bleeding or discharge (all Native Americans).
2. Indigestion or difficulty swallowing (Southwestern tribes and Eskimos).
3. Nagging cough or hoarseness (all Native Americans).
4. Change in bowel or bladder habits (Southwestern tribes and Eskimos).

5. A sore that does not heal (all Native Americans).
6. Thickening or lump in the breast or elsewhere (all Native Americans).
7. Obvious change in wart or mole (more in Caucasians but may occur in Native Americans).

With the changing lifestyles of partially assimilated North American Indians, specific campaigns to discourage cigarette smoking should also be undertaken by the federal health agencies.

Diets high in fiber might reduce colorectal cancer incidence in the Alaskan tribes. The Indian Health Service is conducting a hepatitis B vaccination campaign to reduce the incidence of hepatic cancer among those natives.

Intervention to curtail the rise in cancer demands attention to more research involving Native Americans and should include efforts to (1) discourage cigarette smoking, (2) encourage diets high in fiber and low in fat, (3) conduct hepatitis B vaccination programs, (4) use pharmacologic methods to convert bile to the non-lithogenic form, and (5) conduct mass screenings to detect carcinoma of the cervix and to educate the population.

Summary

I express here the concern of members of the Association of American Indian Physicians about the confusing message of nationally published data that tell Native Americans to forget about cancer. Cancer figures significantly as a cause of death in Indian Health Service statistics. There are, furthermore, some unique cancers that are not prominent in overall American statistics but threaten certain Native American tribes. Specific efforts of early detection and prevention should be directed to these population groups, because the high death rate of cancer in Native Americans as suggested by the SEER data might be explained by poor early detection—that is, the population has been ignored, so people have cancer at later stages when it is finally detected—or perhaps by the occurrence of more virulent cancers.

Moreover, the heterogeneity of Native Americans in customs and degree of assimilation needs to be reemphasized. As Native Americans undergo assimilation into the "White society," their risk of cancer grows higher. More studies involving tumor registries are needed to determine cancer frequency in Native Americans.

Members of the Association of American Indian Physicians are particularly concerned about elderly American Indians, whose federal programs were curtailed by the Reagan administration (Gapen 1987). An ancient custom among some of the circumpolar tribes was to set dying, elderly people (with their consent) on an ice floe and push them out to sea (Kjellstrom 1975). The Association of American Indian Physicians is concerned that if medical care to elderly Native Americans continues to be restricted (without their consent) through reduction of federal programs and withdrawing of support to the Indian Health Service, that old and odious custom will have been revived.

References

Baquet C, Ringen K. Surveillance, Epidemiology and End Results (SEER) report, *Cancer Among Blacks and Other Minorities: Statistical Profile*. National Cancer Institute, Division of Cancer Prevention and Control. NIH Publication No. 86-2785, 1986.

Black WC, Key CR, Carmany TB, et al. Carcinoma of the gallbladder in a population of Southwestern American Indians. *Cancer* 1977;39:1267–1279.

Blot WJ, Lanier A, Fraumeni JF, et al. Cancer mortality among Alaska natives, 1960–69. *JNCI* 1975;55:547–554.

Buckley LD. Cancer, its cause and treatment. Book review. *Science* 1917;46:266.

Duncan MH, Wiggins CL, Samet JM, et al. Childhood cancer epidemiology in New Mexico's American Indians, Hispanic whites and non-Hispanic whites, 1970–82. *JNCI* 1986;76:1013–1018.

Gapen B. Panels recommend against Reagan's Indian Health Service budget cuts. *American Medical News* March 13, 1987:13,14.

Hampton JW. Conquering cancer among Indians requires education, lifestyle changes. National Indian Health Board *Health Reporter* 1984;3:10,11.

Hrdlicka A. The vanishing Indian. Letter. *Science* 1917;46:266–267.

Jordan SW, Munsick RA, Stone RJ. Carcinoma of the cervix in American Indian women. *Cancer* 1969;23:1227–1232.

Kaufman SF, D'Angelo AP, Buzzard GP, et al. Trends in utilization of Indian Health Service and contract hospitals FY 1985, 1980 and 1975. Washington, DC: US Department of Health and Human Services, 1986.

Kjellstrom R. Senilicide and invalidicide among the Eskimos. *Folk* 1975;16–17:117–124.

Lanier A, Bender TR, Blot WJ, et al. Cancer incidence in Alaska natives. *Int J Cancer* 1976;18:409–412.

Lanier A, Bender T, Talbot M, et al. Nasopharyngeal carcinoma in Alaskan Eskimos, Indians and Aleuts: A review of cases and study of Epstein-Barr virus, HLA, and environmental risk factors. *Cancer* 1980;46:2100–2106.

Lanier AP, Knutson LR. Cancer in Alaskan natives: A 15-year summary. *Alaska Med* 1986;2:37–41.

Levin I. Cancer among the American Indians and its bearing upon the ethnological distribution of the disease. *Z Krebsforsch* 1910;9:423–425.

Lowenfels AB, Lindstrom CG, Conway MJ, et al. Gallstones and the risk of gallbladder cancer. *JNCI* 1985;75:77–80.

Ritchie WA, Warren SL. The occurrence of multiple bone lesions suggesting myeloma in the skeleton of a pre-Columbian Indian. *Am J Roentgenol* 1932;28:622–628.

Samet JM, Kutvirt DM, Waxweiler RJ, et al. Uranium mining and lung cancer in Navajo men. *N Engl J Med* 1984;310:1481–1484.

Schaefer O, Hildes JA, Medd LM, et al. The changing pattern of neoplastic disease in Canadian Eskimos. *Can Med Assoc J* 1975;112:1399–1403.

Sievers ML. Lung cancer among Indians of the Southwest United States. *Ann Intern Med* 1961;54:912–915.

Sievers ML. The Southwest Indian's burden: Biliary disease. *JAMA* 1962;182:570–572.

Sievers ML. Disease patterns among Southwestern Indians. *Public Health Rep* 1966; 12:1075–1083.

Sievers ML. Cancer of the digestive system among American Indians. *Arizona Medicine* 1976;33:15–20.

Sievers ML, Fisher JR. Cancer in North American Indians: Environment versus heredity. Editorial. *Am J Public Health* 1983;73:485–487.

Skye GE, Hampton JW. A survey of neoplastic disease in Oklahoma North American aborigines. In: *Proceedings of the Third International Symposium on Detection and Prevention of Cancer*, New York, 1976.

Sorem KA. Cancer incidence in the Zuni Indians of New Mexico. *Yale J Biol Med* 1985;58:489–496.

Woods D. Changing health patterns in the circumpolar regions, Part 2. Yellow Knife Symposium. *Can Med Assoc J* 1974;3:457–459.

Section 2

Prevention and Detection Programs:
National and Regional Efforts

Introduction to Section 2

Isaiah W. Dimery

Regional and national programs sponsored by the National Cancer Institute (NCI), which disseminate information and form the basis for a concerted cancer detection, prevention, and treatment strategy, are in place and actively functioning toward reducing cancer morbidity and mortality for minorities. These program initiatives are described in this section.

The Cancer Communication System disseminates information on cancer to the general public, health professionals, and cancer patients and their families through 25 regional offices. The functions of each office include: operation of the Cancer Information Service, which provides a question/answer telephone line to assist in decision making, cancer information and educational projects, and a resource directory of local cancer services.

The Special Populations Studies Branch of the NCI Division of Cancer Prevention and Control has been charged with the identification and elimination of the apparent differences in cancer incidence, mortality, and survival rates of all minority groups compared to the White population by the year 2000. Differences in the incidence of cancers in Blacks may exceed that in Whites by 10%–25% for such sites as breast, uterine cervix, lung, prostate, and gastrointestinal tract, with males being at highest risk. Cancer mortality parallels incidence, generally resulting in an overall lower 5-year survival among Blacks. Known risk factors (tobacco, alcohol, and increased dietary fat), occupational exposure to carcinogenic substances, the effect of various socioeconomic factors including availability of state-of-the-art health care, and possible inherent biologic differences in tumor behavior may all combine to effect the treatability and curability of the disease.

Through NCI-funded projects, in collaboration with predominantly Black medical schools (Charles Drew Medical School in Los Angeles, Calif., Morehouse University in Atlanta, Ga., Meharry Medical College in Nashville, Tenn., and Howard University in Washington, D.C.), avoidable mortality through prevention and cancer awareness is being examined in the minority community. Conducted through Meharry Medical College, an innovative pilot community study focusing on the nutritional behavior of Black populations is reported herein.

The Community Clinical Oncology Program (CCOP) and the Cooperative Group Outreach Program (CGOP), through alignment with comprehensive cancer centers and the NCI, have made it possible to provide patients with the opportunity to be treated with current clinical research protocols in a community setting by their local oncologist. Because more than 80% of cancer patients receive their care in this environment, this mechanism has greatly expanded the number of patients available for experimental clinical trials. Only 7%, however, of CCOP patients were from minority groups. The presence of the low minority enrollment is most likely a direct result of the fact that few minority physicians are enrolled in CCOP.

Only through unrestricted access to programs on the cutting edge of medical progress, both for treatment as well as for prevention, will the potential impact of the resources made available by the NCI be realized through all strata of the population. This chapter gives a detailed, in-depth analysis of these programs.

5. The Cancer Information Service

Janice A. Allen Chilton

Treatment, prevention, and early detection remain important factors in strategies to minimize the racial differences that exist in this country in cancer morbidity and mortality. The general agreement is that these differences exist and persist in minority communities not because of inherent racial differences, but because of other more complex reasons that include a lack of knowledge about cancer and the inaccessibility of accurate cancer information in these communities. There is, however, an information resource, the Cancer Information Service (CIS), that can provide the kind of cancer information that saves lives. It has proved to be a vital force in many cancer control efforts nationwide.

Regional Offices in 31 States

The CIS was created in 1975 in response to a National Cancer Act mandate to "provide and contract for a program to disseminate information on cancer to the general public, to cancer patients and their families and to health professionals."

Today the CIS is a nationwide program with 25 regional offices serving 31 states. Sixteen of these offices have contracts with the National Cancer Institute (NCI) to provide program funding. The remaining offices are funded through a variety of sources including private hospitals and the American Cancer Society.

More than 80% of the population of the United States lives in an area directly served by a regional CIS office. An office at NCI in Bethesda, Maryland, serves the remainder of the country and is staffed after–hours and on weekends. In each office, as in the one in Texas at the University of Texas M. D. Anderson Cancer Center, activities are coordinated through NCI.

All CIS offices must carry out NCI requirements to participate in cancer information and education projects, develop and maintain a resource directory of local cancer services, and operate the service.

CIS office staff members participate in a variety of cancer information and education projects in their service area. In Texas, for example, we operate the M. D. Anderson Cancer Center's CancerWISE Community Speakers Bureau, which has provided information to about 49,000 persons during three years of operation. In New York State, the Roswell Park Memorial Institute CIS staff operates a quit-smoking line, counseling hundreds of smokers each month who call because they want to quit.

Each CIS team develops and maintains a resource directory of cancer-related services available in the area, which may include cancer detection clinics, patient and family support groups, and information about financial aid. Some CIS regional offices serve more than one state, and it is difficult to keep these directories up to date. But the accuracy and currency of these directories enable the CIS to achieve one of its most important objectives, getting people in touch with the health care system as easily and as quickly as possible. In many offices resource directories are being entered in computers to provide even quicker access to the information.

The Telephone Line

A primary component of the CIS is a toll-free telephone information line designed to provide accurate, up-to-date cancer information to the public and to health professionals. In some offices highly trained volunteers provide cancer information to the public.

Each CIS office may be reached by calling one toll-free number, 1-800-4-CANCER, from anywhere in the country. Callers are transferred immediately and automatically—based on their area code—to the office that serves their area of the country. Most telephone lines are operated Monday through Friday, 9 a.m. to 4:30 p.m.

The purpose of the CIS is to give the public easy and rapid access to correct information about cancer. CIS staff members can explain medical terms to a caller and provide emotional support. Information about patient referral to cancer treatment centers is available from each office. As counselors always explain to callers, they are not physicians, but cancer information specialists trained to locate and provide the general information the callers need. Rather than interfering in the doctor-patient relationship, CIS counselors clarify options to help people choose, with their physicians, the best course of action.

The information CIS counselors use to answer questions is augmented daily from many sources, and it includes data from NCI fact sheets and research reports, medical journals, and textbooks. CIS staff members also use an NCI computerized database called PDQ through which they have immediate access to the latest published information on cancer treatment and clinical research.

CIS Evaluation

To ensure that the program meets the needs of the public, the CIS has developed an extensive program evaluation system of internal and external quality control procedures, collection of a common data set from each call, and a user survey of people who called.

Before serving as phone counselors, new staff members and volunteers must participate in a 40- to 45-hour classroom and on-the-job training program. The classes consist of videotapes and lectures on cancer biology and communications techniques presented by experts in these fields. After completing the training program and before going to work, the phone counselors must meet a nationally determined set of criteria and pass a certification examination.

Staff members in the national office also place test calls to each CIS office. Call scenarios are delivered verbatim by telephone to an office and the responses are compared against a set of standards. Staff members at the CIS offices are debriefed after the test call, and problems are discussed immediately. In addition, all regional offices are required to initiate their own test call system and place such calls randomly throughout the year.

To determine public interest in questions concerning cancer, common data are collected nationally for every call to a CIS office. Information recorded on a standard call record form includes type of caller (member of general public, patient, physician, etc.), nature of inquiry, recommendations made to the caller, and some demographics. Information that may directly identify a caller, such as name and address, is destroyed.

The remaining information, collected from more than two million calls in this country since 1976, has been used in local and national program planning and evaluation. These data tell us how well we are supplying cancer information to targeted groups, and from these data we know that minorities do not use our service as often as others. From 1983 to 1985, 87.8% of the callers to the CIS nationally were White, 7.5% were Black, 2.8% were Hispanic, and 1.5% were Asian. In the past six years, the CIS has intensified its efforts to reach minority audiences with cancer messages, running media campaigns geared to minority audiences and recruiting such stars as Aretha Franklin and baseball player Fernando Valenzuela to deliver the message. Several CIS task forces composed of staff members from various regions are developing strategy and programs for reaching minority audiences nationwide.

CIS Caller Data

Data collected between 1983 and 1985 on the type of person who called the CIS is shown in Figure 1. The 20.6% segment of calls from family members and friends of cancer patients reflects the fact that they will sometimes ask questions the patients find too difficult or painful to ask.

About 39% of calls to the CIS concern a specific cancer site, the three most often asked about being breast cancer, cancer of the colon and rectum, and cancer of the lung (Figure 2).

Risk factors comprise 23% of all calls; 80% of those concern tobacco use. The CIS also receives many calls about local organizations and services and physician referrals, which shows that each office must maintain a directory of resources related to cancer. As people began to learn more about the curability of cancer and the role of early detection in prevention of the disease, the CIS began to

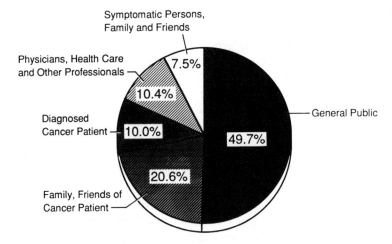

FIGURE 1. Type of caller to the Cancer Information Service, 1983–1985. Represents data from 974,165 calls. *Source*: Project Officer, Cancer Information Service, Health Promotion Sciences Branch, Division of Cancer Prevention and Control, National Cancer Institute.

receive a greater number of requests for information about prevention and screening. Treatment questions range from requests for information concerning treatment options to descriptions of treatment procedures and information about clinical trials (Table 1).

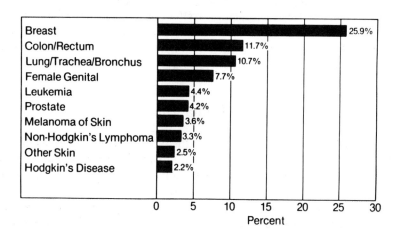

FIGURE 2. Cancer sites and types most frequently asked about, 1983–1985. Represents data from 398,323 calls. *Source*: Project Officer, Cancer Information Service, Health Promotion Sciences Branch, Division of Cancer Prevention and Control, National Cancer Institute.

TABLE 1. Subjects of inquiry in 972,538 calls (1983–1985).

Topics	Percentage
Cancer risk factors	23.2
Local organizations and services; physician referral	20.9
General cancer information	19.4
Primary prevention and screening	17.8
Treatment	15.8
Symptoms and diagnostic tests	8.7
Diet and nutrition	6.5
Continuing care	5.8

Source: Project Officer, Cancer Information Service, Health Promotion Services Branch, Division of Cancer Prevention and Control, National Cancer Institute.

The number of calls has risen over the years from 40,000 calls per year in 1976 to almost 400,000 calls per year in 1986. At the current rate nationally, the CIS is responding to about 33,000 calls each month—more than 1600 inquiries daily (Figure 3).

How Influential Are We?

In 1985, the CIS staff wanted to know how the CIS was serving the public and how the CIS was influencing citizens' health and behavior. In a national survey of more than 7000 callers to the CIS, almost 98% of respondents said they would

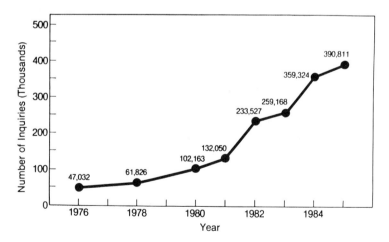

FIGURE 3. Number of inquiries received by the Cancer Information Service, 1976–1984. *Source*: Project Officer, Cancer Information Service, Health Promotion Sciences Branch, Division of Cancer Prevention and Control, National Cancer Institute.

TABLE 2. Action taken after CIS contact (based on 7,006 calls).

Action	Percentage
Read materials that were mailed	82.7
Shared information with at least one other person	58.4
Went to or made appointment with doctor, clinic, or hospital	24.3
Sought more information	18.8
Changed eating habits	16.0
Attempted to stop or reduce smoking	12.0
Learned/practiced self-detection technique	10.4
Contacted community agency/service	5.2

Source: Project Officer, Cancer Information Service, Health Promotion Services Branch, Division of Cancer Prevention and Control, National Cancer Institute.

call the CIS again if they had questions about cancer, and nearly half had already recommended the CIS to others.

During the course of a conversation, many callers to the CIS are encouraged to make some health-related behavioral change. In this survey, when we asked users if they took any health-related action after their call to us, more than 93% reported that they took some sort of action as a result of the information acquired during their call. Their responses concerning specific actions are shown in Table 2.

Comparing the CIS to other sources of cancer information, many respondents indicated that their contact with the CIS was important in their decision to take some sort of action in support of their own health. Nearly all (91%) of the callers said the CIS was very (57.6%) or somewhat (33.9%) important in their decision.

If 58% of respondents actually shared the information given to them by the CIS staff, information provided by CIS counselors to slightly more than 4000 people eventually reached more than 11,000 people, almost three times the number of actual calls. And even if this projection is too optimistic, the number of people reached is still impressive.

As many contributors to this volume have pointed out, members of racial minorities do experience higher morbidity rates for some cancers. This experience leads us to believe that minorities could benefit from knowing techniques of early detection and self-examination for cancer and from better access to information about cancer prevention.

Further, the fact that racial minorities have higher mortality rates for some cancers may indicate that they are not benefiting fully from treatment advances and need more information about warning signals and the importance of seeking care immediately after they experience a symptom of cancer.

Studies have shown consistently that members of racial minorities tend to be less aware of cancer, lack knowledge about the disease, and underestimate the chance of cure once someone has the disease. Such indicators reveal the need for extensive cancer education programs directed at this vital and sizable segment of the population. Myths and misconceptions must be dispelled and confusion reduced.

The Cancer Information Service can help provide information, emotional support, and educational programs. Remember the 1-800-4-CANCER number and share it with others. Our goal is to give everyone access to current, accurate information about cancer.[1]

Acknowledgments. Special thanks to Judith Stein, former project officer for the Cancer Information Service, for her help in preparing this chapter.

---

[1]Anyone who lives in an area not directly served by a CIS office and who wants to know how to establish such an office should write to Cancer Information Service Project Officer, National Institutes of Health, Blair Building, Room 414A, 9000 Rockville Pike, Bethesda, Maryland 20910, or call (301) 427-8656.

6. Cancer Prevention and Control

Claudia R. Baquet, Linda A. Clayton, and Robert G. Robinson

In the United States, cancer is the second leading cause of death, surpassed only by cardiovascular disease. Although cancer affects the general population, the contributors to this volume have shown in specific terms that certain racial and ethnic groups are more severely and disproportionately affected. For all sites combined, Blacks have the highest overall age-adjusted cancer incidence and mortality rates of any population group in the United States (Baquet et al. 1986). Surveillance, Epidemiology, and End Results (SEER) data indicate that the five-year overall survival for Blacks is 12 percentage points below that of Whites (Table 1). A study of cancer rates over several decades indicated that cancer incidence rates for Black Americans increased by 27%, in contrast to 12% for Whites during the same time period, and that cancer mortality rates increased by 40% for Blacks and 10% for Whites (American Cancer Society 1986). Achieving the National Cancer Institute's (NCI) goal of reducing the national cancer mortality rate by 50% by the year 2000 therefore requires intervention research activities directed to specific populations, including groups at high risk for cancer—those with excessive cancer rates and those underserved by cancer control intervention research. Blacks are both at high risk of cancer and underserved.

Blacks comprise about 12% of the United States population and have a disproportionately severe socioeconomic and health experience in comparison to that of Whites (Bureau of Census 1985; Department of Health and Human Services Secretary's Task Force on Black and Minority Health 1985).

Data Sources

Descriptive epidemiologic data on cancer incidence and relative survival are derived from the NCI's SEER—a population-based tumor registry reporting system described in detail elsewhere (Young et al. 1981). Mortality data are derived from the National Center for Health Statistics (NCHS) and the Bureau of the Census.

TABLE 1. Five-year relative survival for selected cancer sites: Black and White differences — SEER Program, 1973–1981.

Primary site	Five-year relative survival (%)		Difference
	Blacks	Whites	
All sites combined	38	50	12
Corpus uteri	57	88	31
Bladder	50	74	24
Breast — female	63	75	12
Rectum	37	49	12
Prostate	59	69	10

Incidence, Mortality and Survival

Blacks have the highest overall age-adjusted incidence rates (1973–1981) of any eight racial/ethnic groups for which data from the SEER Program are available (Baquet et al. 1986). When compared to Whites, Blacks have higher age-adjusted incidence rates for several cancer sites, including breast (in women under 40), cervix uteri, esophagus, lung (in men), prostate, stomach, and for multiple myeloma (Table 2). Between 1973 and 1981, cancer mortality rates increased more for Black men than for any other group.

TABLE 2. Ratio of Black to White age-adjusted (1970 U.S. Standard) cancer incidence and mortality rates by primary site, SEER Program, 1978–1981.

Primary site	Incidence rates	Mortality rates
All sites combined	1.11	1.27
Bladder	0.56	0.97
Breast, female	0.84	0.99
Cervix uteri	2.30	2.75
Colon and rectum	1.00	1.03
Colon	1.10	1.04
Rectum	0.78	1.00
Corpus uteri	0.53	1.69
Esophagus	3.89	3.47
Larynx	1.43	1.92
Lung, male	1.47	1.32
female	1.08	1.00
Multiple myeloma	2.30	2.08
Ovary	0.70	0.79
Pancreas	1.43	1.31
Prostate	1.60	2.09
Stomach	1.72	1.89

TABLE 3. Possible contributing factors.

Risk Factors
Tobacco
Tobacco and ethanol
Diet/nutritional status
Occupation
Knowledge, Attitude, Practices
Stage at Diagnosis and Treatment
Health and Medical Resources
Distribution of state-of-the-art detection, diagnosis, and treatment
Access, availability, utilization of health services
Quality of medical care
Compliance
Other
Immune function
Histologic differences
Socioeconomic status
Co-morbidity
Treatment considerations

Contributing Factors

Factors that may contribute to the excessive cancer experience of Blacks (Table 3) require much more research, definition, and clarification. Some isolated factors have been identified in analytic epidemiologic studies, mainly case-control, cross-sectional surveys, and a limited amount of health services research. But little research has been conducted on the complex interaction, often synergism, of these factors and on the specific cause and effect of many factors that show direct evidence of causing increased cancer risk in Black populations. These factors are further explained in the following categories.

Major Risk Factors/Exposures

Risk factors and exposures are important with respect to cancer incidence because they are conditions (such as smoking patterns or carcinogens in the workplace) which cause or enhance an individual's development of cancer in general or for specific cancers.

Tobacco

Cigarette smoking accounts for the single, major cause of cancer mortality in the United States. Smoking has been clearly defined as the major risk factor for lung cancer and a number of other "tobacco-related" cancers such as lung, cervix uteri, esophagus, oral, and stomach. The overall cancer death rate among smokers is two times greater than for non-smokers. Those classified as heavy smokers (over a pack per day) have a three to four times greater risk. Tobacco accounts for 30% of cancer deaths (Doll and Peto 1976). Blacks have higher prevalence rates for smoking than Whites (Black males 39%, White males 31%) (NHIS 1987); however, Blacks are reported to be lighter smokers (Robinson 1985; Glynn 1984). In addition, Blacks smoke higher tar and nicotine cigarettes more than Whites (Robinson 1985).

Tobacco and Alcohol

The combination of alcohol and tobacco produces an increased risk for certain cancers. This combination is an established and synergistic risk factor for cancers of the head and neck, and esophagus (Keller 1978; Rothman 1980). This risk increases the amount of alcohol consumed and the number of cigarettes smoked.

Occupation

One's occupation may contribute to the development of cancer if there is exposure to certain carcinogenic agents such as certain metals, solvents, dyes, organic and inorganic dusts, pesticides or herbicides. For many historical reasons, Blacks have had higher occupational exposures to hazardous substances compared to Whites. Discriminatory work assignments and the inclusion of Blacks in less skilled jobs resulted in Blacks being placed in more hazardous jobs, including in the steel industry (Lloyd 1971), rubber industry (Monson and Nakano 1976), and chemical industry (Schulte et al. 1985). The greater representation of Blacks in the blue collar workforce, which has higher smoking rates, compounds the cancer risk of these workers.

Diet/Nutritional Factors

The chances of developing cancer may be significantly and profoundly affected by diet. In 1981, Doll and Peto reported that the death rates from all cancer in the United States might be reduced by 30% if practical changes in diet were implemented. Some of the diet components that are thought to affect the development of cancer include: vitamin A, vitamin C, fats, fiber, foods that are cured or smoked, vitamin E and selenium. Anecdotal and survey data suggest that Blacks have high levels of dietary fat consumption—a potentially significant risk factor for breast, colon, and prostate cancers (Hargreaves and Baquet, in press). However, characterization of the diet of Blacks is highly inadequate at this time. Additional anecdotal information suggests that there is high consumption of smoked foods (barbecue), overuse of frying rather than broiling, overcooked vegetables with fat (salt pork or "fat-back") added, and a high intake of foods containing N-nitroso compounds such as sausages. The high rates of obesity in Black females over age 45 compared to Whites (Black females 61%; White female 32%) contributes to breast, colon, and corpus uteri cancers.

Health and Medical Resources

Blacks are over-represented in lower socioeconomic groups. Exactly how this relates to the excesses in cancer rates experienced by Blacks has not been analyzed. Availability, access, quality, continuity and compliance with cancer control services (i.e., screening, detection, and treatment) are affected by social class, employment status, type and extent of medical coverage, and utilization of services. Blacks over utilize emergency rooms and hospital outpatient departments rather than preventive health services facilities (Sparer and Simpson 1985).

Knowledge, Attitudes and Practices

In general, data on the cancer-related knowledge, attitudes and practices of Blacks are limited. It appears that Blacks tend to be less knowledgeable about cancer than Whites (Cardwell and Collier 1981). Blacks tend to underestimate the prevalence of cancer and the significance of the common warning signs for cancer. Blacks tend to be less aware of the benefits of specific cancer screening or self-examination methods (Manfredi et al. 1977). They are reported to be more fatalistic about cancer and are less likely to believe that early detection will make a difference in terms of outcome or that treatment can be effective (Evaax, Inc. 1981). These pessimistic attitudes (seen in Black cancer patients) influence medical care-seeking behavior and could account in part for the delays of 3 to 6 months (Natarajan et al. 1985) in seeking diagnosis and treatment.

Other

Blacks appear to have a higher distribution of biologically more aggressive histologic tumor patterns than Whites for certain cancers such as bladder and corpus uteri (Baquet and Ringen 1986). Histologic patterns can serve as a proxy for biologic behavior of cancer and thus may be related to survival prognosis, and may contribute in part to poorer survival in Black patients for some cancer sites. Little is known about this subject, and the relationship of histologic patterns to differentials in survival requires additional research.

Treatment patterns and response to cancer therapy may differ in Black cancer patients compared to Whites. The high prevalence rates of cardiovascular, pulmonary and vascular renal disease in Blacks may contraindicate the administration of optimal doses of certain chemotherapeutic agents such as adriamycin, bleomycin, and cisplatin due to increased toxicity. This area requires a great deal more research.

Socioeconomic Status (SES)

The marked differences in the cancer experience of Blacks and Whites may be attributed in part to the overrepresentation of the Blacks in the lower SES

TABLE 4. Selected socioeconomic indicators: Black/White comparison.

Socioeconomic indicators	Blacks	Whites
Persons below poverty level (1981)	34%	11%
Unemployment rate (1982)	18%	8%
Median family income (1981)	$13,270	$23,520

Source: U.S. Bureau of the Census, 1985.

categories (Table 4). Socioeconomic status is related to income, educational level, and occupational category. These are related to access and availability of health and medical resources, knowledge of warning signs, and smoking patterns. The exact interaction of SES and cancer is not known. More research is required to specify and define the relationship of SES to cancer incidence and survival.

Cancer Control Science

Cancer control is defined as the reduction of cancer incidence, mortality, and morbidity through an orderly sequence of research on interventions designed to alter cancer rates (Greenwalt and Cullen 1985). The orderly sequence comprises the phases of cancer control science, which is a new and developing scientific discipline concerned with the development, testing, and application of interventions that will ultimately result in an improvement in cancer rates. Cancer control encompasses both primary prevention (incidence rate reduction) and secondary prevention (screening, diagnosis, treatment, and interventions) that will improve survival and mortality rates (Greenwald and Cullen 1985). Research on specific interventions that will improve cancer rates is a critically important approach to reducing the burden of cancer in Black populations. Most previous research on cancer in Blacks has been epidemiologic and largely descriptive or etiologic research that concerned cancer rates or was related to the identification of risk factors for specific cancers. Previous research has not been applied epidemiologic research, that is, cancer control science.

The cancer control research process is viewed as a continuum. It begins with a systematic review of existing data from etiologic research and randomized clinical trials (Phase I), proceeds through methods development (Phase II), then to trials of primary and secondary prevention methods and adoption and diffusion of state-of-the-science treatment (Phase III). After controlled intervention studies demonstrate the effectiveness of intervention methods, studies of defined populations (Phase IV) are conducted to determine potential benefits for target groups.

Like other scientific experiments, cancer control research follows the scientific methods of deriving inferences: formulation and testing of hypotheses, careful observation, methods development, and quantitative analyses. Cancer control science bridges data derived from basic science and epidemiologic research to the utilization and application of research results to well-defined populations and eventually to the general population.

Cancer Control-Related Research Needs

Strong, well-designed studies of cancer control require these preparatory and in-process actions.

Identification and validation of specific interventions with broad application to Black populations. Current cancer prevention and control intervention research supported by NCI to aid in executing this effort are: a) primary prevention which focuses on smoking prevention and cessation, and b) reduction of avoidable mortality by improved access to such services as screening and enhanced delivery of cancer prevention and control services.

Phase I and Phase II cancer control studies. Much of the previous research was done with small numbers of Black persons or with Whites and the results transferred to Blacks without adequate prior validation. Studies with small segments of the Black population have not considered the heterogeneous nature of the population. New studies are especially needed of diet and of cancer-related beliefs and personal priorities. Other significant areas of research include the contribution of occupation to cancer.

Greater involvement in cancer prevention and control research by investigators who have access and are sensitive to the health, social, and cultural needs of Black populations. Critical in this type of research will be the involvement of members of the National Cancer Control Research Network, along with other investigators in the country. The network is composed of physicians and scientists from the Black medical schools, physicians and scientists from majority institutions who are interested in and sensitive to minority population groups, and persons from the private sector, all of whose major purpose is to foster and conduct research targeted to the specific cancer control needs of Black populations.

More clinical research with adequate Black health-provider and patient participation. Needed in all areas of detection and therapy, some of this research must be done immediately to shape national recommendations for screening and detection appropriate to the special needs of Blacks according to available epidemiologic, cultural, and socioeconomic data. Two examples that illustrate the need for developing population-specific screening recommendations are breast cancer screening for high-risk Black women under age 40 and prostate cancer screening for men at risk, in particular Black men, who generally develop more aggressive disease at earlier ages than Whites.

Allocation of resources for cancer prevention and control research and programs by medical, academic, social, legislative, and community-based organizations.

Conclusions

The National Cancer Institute has allocated resources for cancer prevention and control research initiatives targeted to Black populations, recognizing that the national objectives of decreasing overall cancer mortality by 50% by the beginning of the twenty-first century will be severely hindered without a concerted effort to control cancer in the Black population. Cancer prevention and control activities are both hampered and guided by the higher percentage of Blacks than Whites in poverty and by the higher proportion of Blacks who smoke. The health care delivery system will have to be studied to discover methods of overcoming barriers imposed by poverty and cultural differences. We are encouraged by the research community's willingness to grapple with these complex problems. The National Cancer Institute's research initiatives help guide and stimulate these efforts. A major attempt is being made to encourage researchers and institutions interested in focusing on cancer control and prevention research in Black populations. The cooperation of the medical schools whose primary focus is educating Black physicians (The Charles R. Drew Postgraduate Medical School, Howard University Medical School, Meharry Medical College, and Morehouse School of Medicine) has been essential to this effort because access to Black populations is a key element in the overall strategy.

The burden of cancer is disproportionately distributed among Black populations in comparison with the general population. Advances in cancer control science and focused attention on Black populations will help solve the problem. Cancer prevention and control interventions must include:

- Education and cancer awareness programs that focus on laypersons as well as professionals so that positive changes in knowledge, attitudes, and practices will occur.

- Primary prevention programs with special emphasis on smoking and dietary changes.

- Secondary prevention programs with emphasis on increasing screening practices.

- Early detection programs.

- Effective (as well as cost-effective) state-of-the-art treatment modalities.

- Appropriate rehabilitation and surveillance programs.

References

American Cancer Society: Cancer Facts and Figures for Minority Americans, 1986.
Axtell L, Myers M: Contrasts in survival of black and white cancer patients 1960–73. *J Natl Cancer Inst* 1978;60(6):1209–1215.

Baquet C, Ringen K, Pollack E: *Cancer Among Blacks and Other Minorities: A Statistical Profile.* Washington, DC: NIH Publication No. 86-2785, 1986.

Baquet C, Ringen K: Cancer Control in Blacks: Epidemiology and NCI Program Plans. In: *Advances in Cancer Control: Health Care Financing and Research.* New York: Alan R. Liss, Inc., 1986, pp. 215–227.

Bureau of the Census: *America's Black Population, 1970 to 1982: A Statistical View.* U.S. Department of Commerce, Bureau of the Census, 27 pages, 1985.

Cardwell J, Collier W: Racial differences in cancer awareness: What black Americans need to know about cancer. *Urban Health*, October 1981, pp. 29–32.

Devesa S, Diamond E: Socioeconomic and racial differences in lung cancer incidence. *Am J Epidemiol* 1983;118(6):818–831.

DHHS Secretary's Task Force on Black and Minority Health: *Report of the Secretary's Task Force on Black and Minority Health*, Vol. I: Executive Summary. Department of Health and Human Services, Washington, D.C., 1985.

DHHS Secretary's Task Force on Black and Minority Health: *Report of the Secretary's Task Force on Black and Minority Health*, Vol. III: Cancer. Department of Health and Human Services, Washington, D.C., 1986.

Doll R, Peto R: Mortality in relation to smoking: 20 years observation on male British doctors. *Br Med J* 1976;2:1525–1536.

Doll R, Peto R: The causes of cancer: quantitative estimates of avoidable risk of cancer in the United States today. *J Natl Cancer Inst* 1981;66:1193–1308.

Ernster VL et al: Race, socioeconomic status, and prostatic cancer. *Cancer Treat Rep* 1977;61(2):187–191.

Evaxx, Inc: Black Americans' attitudes toward cancer and cancer tests: highlights of a study. *CA* 1981;31(4):212–218.

Funderburk W, Rosero E, Leffall L: Breast lesions in blacks. *Surg Gynecol Obstet* 1972;135:58–60.

Glynn J: Smoking-related cancers and the U.S. black population Conference on Cancer in Black Americans. Tallahassee: Florida A&M University: College of Pharmacy, Nov, 1984.

Goldsmith D, Smith A, McMichael A: A case-control study of prostate cancer within a cohort of rubber and tire workers. *J Occup Med* 1980;22(8):533–541.

Gray G, Henderson B, Pike M: Changing ratio of breast cancer incidence rates with age of black females compared with white females in the United States. *J Natl Cancer Inst* 1980;64(3):461–463.

Greenwald P, Cullen J: The new emphasis in cancer control. *JNCI* 1985;74(3):543–551.

Hargreaves M, Baquet C, Gamshadcahi A: Diet, nutritional status and cancer risk in American blacks. *Nutrition and Cancer* 1989;12:1–28.

Hulka B: Risk factors for cervical cancer. *J Chronic Dis* 1982;35:3–11.

Keller A: Liver cirrhosis, tobacco, alcohol, and cancer among blacks. *J Natl Med Assoc* 1978;70(8):575–580.

Lloyd J: Long-term mortality study of steel workers, V: Respiratory cancer in coke plant workers. *J Occup Med* 1971;13:53–68.

Manfredi C, Warnecke R: Levels and sources of cancer knowledge by demographic characteristics and cancer site. NCI-CA 21954 *Cancer Information Needs in Illinois* and CA 34886 *Cancer Control Science Program: Improving Patient Compliance with Referrals of an Evaluation of Possible Malignancies*, 1978.

Manfredi C, Warnecke R, Graham S, et al: Social psychological correlates of health behavior: Knowledge of breast self-examination techniques among black women. *Soc Sci Med* 1977;11:433–440.

Mettlin C: Nutritional habits of blacks and whites. *Prev Med* 1980;9(5):601–606.

Miller W Jr, Cooper R: Rising lung cancer death rates among black men: The importance of occupation and social class. *J Natl Med Assoc* 1982;74(3):253–258.

Monson R, Nakano K: Mortality among rubber workers: II. Other employees. *Am J Epidemiol* 1976;103(3):297–303.

Myers MH, Hankey BF: *Cancer Patient Survival Experience. Trends in Survival 1960–3 to 1970–3. Comparison of Survival for Black and White Patients. Long-term Effects of Cancer.* Washington, DC: U.S. Department of Health and Human Services, NIH publication no. 80-2148, 1980.

Natarajan N, et al: Race-related differences in breast cancer patients: Results of the 1982 National Survey of breast cancer by the American College of Surgeons. *Cancer* 1985; 56(7):1704–1709.

National Health Interview Survey, 1987.

Robinson R: Strategies for black communities. Proceedings from the Pennsylvania Consensus Conference on Tobacco and Health Priorities. Harrisburg: Commonwealth of Pennsylvania, Department of Health, Oct, pp 80–95, 1985.

Rogers EL, Goldkind L, Goldkind SF: Increasing frequency of esophageal cancer among black male veterans. *Cancer* 1982;49(3):610–617.

Rothman K: The proportion of cancer attributable to alcohol consumption. *Prev Med* 1980;9:174–179.

Schottenfeld D: Alcohol as a co-factor in the etiology of cancer. *Cancer* 1979;43(5):1962–1966.

Schulte P, et al: Risk assessment of a cohort exposed to aromatic amines: Initial results. *J Occup Med* 1985;27(2):115–121.

Sparer G, Simpson N: *Health Services Patterns in U.S. Black and Minority Patients*: Report prepared for the Division of Cancer Prevention and Control, NCI. January, 1985.

Warnecke R, Graham S, Rosenthal S, et al: Social and psychological correlates of smoking among black women. *J Health Soc Behav* 1978;19:397–410.

Warnecke R: "Intervention in black populations." In: Mettlin C, Murphy G (eds.): *Cancer among Black Populations.* New York: Alan R Liss, Inc., 1981, pp. 167–183.

White J, et al: "Cancer among blacks in the U.S.: recognizing the problem." In: Mettlin C, Murphy G (eds): *Cancer among Black Populations.* New York: Alan R Liss, Inc, 1981, pp. 35–53.

Williams R, Horm J: Association of cancer sites with tobacco and alcohol consumption and socioeconomic status of patients: Interview study from the Third National Cancer Survey. *J Natl Cancer Inst* 1977;58(3):525–547.

Wynder E: Dietary habits and cancer epidemiology. *Cancer* 1979;43:1955–1961.

Young J, Percy C, Asire A: Surveillance Epidemiology and End Results: Incidence and mortality data, 1973–1977. *NCI Monogr* 1981;57.

Ziegler R, Morris L, Blot W, et al: Esophageal cancer among black men in Washington, D.C.: II. Role of nutrition. *J Natl Cancer Inst* 1981;67(6):1199–1206.

7. Nutrition and Cancer Risk: Assessment and Preventive Program Strategies for Black Americans

Margaret K. Hargreaves, Osman I. Ahmed, Kofi A. Semenya, Lou Pearson, Neela Sheth, Robert E. Hardy, and Louis J. Bernard

Life-style and environment may account for the development of 82% of all cancers (Weisburger 1979), and up to 70% of all cancer deaths may be attributed to diet and nutrition (Doll and Peto 1981). In addition, food choices as well as the type, quality, and mode of cooking may play an important role in the etiology of cancers of the gastrointestinal tract and endocrine organs (Weisburger 1979). Though the specific role of diet and nutrition has not been elucidated, their importance in causing cancer is suggested by an increasing body of epidemiological and experimental evidence (Newell 1983; Kerr 1984; Hargreaves et al. 1989). Conceivably, therefore, individuals could decrease cancer risk by an improvement in diet and life-style (Newell 1983; Kerr 1984).

Some dietary guidelines have been developed to lower cancer risk (Palmer 1986), but these guidelines do not have the unanimous support of the scientific community (Palmer 1986; Pariza 1984), and they have never been tested for their effectiveness in cancer prevention and control (Balducci et al. 1986). Smoking cessation campaigns, based on the well-established relationship between smoking and cancer, have successfully led to a decline in lung cancer (Horm and Asire 1982; Horm and Kessler 1986). This suggests that similar attempts to modify dietary behavior could have a comparable influence on diet- and nutrition-related cancers. In the absence of an established cause-and-effect relationship, however, criterion variables for quantitating program outcomes must be chosen carefully (Palmer 1986).

National nutrition surveys have shown that Blacks and other minorities are a nutritionally vulnerable, high-risk group in the American population (Centers for Disease Control 1972; National Center for Health Statistics 1979), and Black Americans have higher age-adjusted cancer incidence and mortality rates than any other group in the United States (Baquet et al. 1986; Young et al. 1984). Data from the Surveillance, Epidemiology, and End Results (SEER) Program of the National Cancer Institute (NCI) for 1978–1981 show excesses of 11% and 27% in incidence and mortality, respectively, for Blacks as compared with those figures for Whites (Baquet et al. 1986). The proportion of cancer patients who are diagnosed as having only a local stage of disease is about 10% greater for

Whites than Blacks; moreover, the survival rate for Blacks is less than that of Whites at all stages of the disease (Axtell et al. 1976). It is possible that dietary and nutritional factors are associated with the higher cancer incidence and mortality in Blacks (Hargreaves et al. 1989), so that programs geared to the special dietary and nutritional needs of Blacks could reduce the cancer burden in this population, narrow the gap between Blacks and Whites, and make a definitive contribution to the NCI goal of a 50% reduction in cancer mortality by the year 2000.

The purpose of this report is to describe our efforts to develop, implement, and evaluate a comprehensive, coordinated community program to decrease dietary and nutritional cancer risks in Blacks living in Nashville. To our knowledge, no intervention studies have been reported that have attempted to modify dietary and nutritional cancer risk factors by intensive educational intervention on a large-scale, communitywide basis, and this program could serve as a model for others across the country. Our early developmental work has three facets. The *first* is the rationale for selecting measurement variables to use in screening for dietary and nutritional risk and for measuring the change associated with implementation of the program. The *second* is the rationale for our method of program development, which takes into account the sociological and cultural forces that may foster behavioral change in Blacks. The *third* is a description of our initial intervention strategy to reach Blacks and the target group that expressed an interest in participating in the program.

Rationale for Selection of Measurement/Criterion Variables

In the recent past, a sizable body of literature has developed to support the claim of a specific relationship between diet, nutritional status, and cancer risk (Newell 1983; Kerr 1984; Hargreaves et al. 1989). Epidemiological and experimental studies indicate that diet and nutrition may initiate, promote, or protect against cancer risk (Weisburger 1979; Weisburger et al. 1982; Balducci et al. 1986; Carr 1985; Poirier 1987). Carcinogenesis is a multistage process (Poirier 1987) in which carcinogens enter or form in the body and are metabolized through processes of initiation and promotion. By means of cell differentiation and progression, the tumor grows and develops. These processes are modified by the defensive responses of which the host is capable, and diet and nutritional status are well known to be important in the defensive response. Indeed, diet and nutrition have been determined to be important factors at every stage of tumor development (Poirier 1987).

Dietary and nutritional influences on carcinogenesis (Newell 1983) may occur in many physiological situations, as carcinogens may be ingested with food and drink or occur endogenously through metabolic activation and deactivation mechanisms at various sites throughout the body. Inappropriate nutritional states include overnutrition manifested in obesity, undernutrition manifested in an underweight state or emaciation and deficiencies of vitamins, minerals, or the

TABLE 1. Possible dietary and nutritional cancer inducers and protectors.[a]

Substances	Conditions
Inducers	
Aflatoxins	Obesity
Alcohol	Malnutrition
Nitrosamines	Cellular immune
Fat	deficiency
Amino acid pryolysates	
Sugar carmelization products	
Fatty acid hydroperoxides and cholesterol epoxide	
Ethyl carbamate in wines, fermented foods	
Polycyclic aromatic hydrocarbons	
Protectors	
Vitamins A, E, C	Good nutritional
Selenium, zinc	status
Fiber	
Indoles, aromatic isothiocyanates (cruciferi)[b]	
Flavones (citrus fruits)	
Coumarins (fruits and vegetables)	
Plant sterols (fruits and vegetables)	
Xenobiotics (fruits, vegetables, grains)	

[a] Modified from Carr 1985, and with permission from The American Geriatrics Society. Nutrition, cancer, and aging: An annotated review. I. Diet, carcinogenesis, and aging, by Balducci et al., Journal of the American Geriatrics Society, Vol. 34(2):129, 1986.
[b] Gassy vegetables such as broccoli, cabbage, etc.

immune function. Diet has been proposed to play three roles in carcinogenesis (Balducci et al. 1986) (Table 1): to act as a potential cancer inducer, to cause nutritional conditions associated with increased cancer risk, and to contribute substances with cancer-prevention potential.

Potential Cancer Inducers

Cancer inducers may be either initiators or promoters (Table 1). Although many of these substances have been shown to be powerful carcinogens in experimental animals, their association with cancers in humans has not been proved, and it is difficult to classify them as either initiators or promoters in human beings. Rather, because of their common occurrence in the human diet, these substances have been associated in epidemiological studies with specific cancer types in humans. Besides moderating dosage and exposure to carcinogens, a well-designed diet can modulate the activity of carcinogen-activating or -inhibiting enzymes (Carr 1985).

Aflatoxin, a well-known carcinogen, is produced in peanuts contaminated by a fungus, *Aspergillus flavus*, and is associated with hepatocellular cancer in some human populations (Balducci et al. 1986). Alcohol, proposed to be a cocarcinogen with a function separate from that of initiation and promotion, appears to have synergistic functions with other carcinogenic agents, such as those associated with cigarette smoke. Nitrosamines are carcinogens found preformed in certain foods such as dairy products, fish, and beer, and they may be formed during cooking and digestion of nitrites present in cured and pickled foods. Amino acid pyrolysates are mutagens (potential carcinogens) produced by the action of intense heat and charring in broiled fish and meat. Other mutagens are found in fermented products that contain ethyl carbamate and in sugar caramelization products. Dietary fats may be associated with the formation of free radicals by peroxidation of polyunsaturated fatty acids, with increased prostaglandin synthesis by their increased production of certain bile salts, or with their induction of obesity. Polycyclic aromatic hydrocarbons are released into the air by incomplete combustion of fuels and cover many substances in the food chain (Balducci et al. 1986). In humans, alcohol, the nitrosamines, and fermented products are associated with head, neck and gastric cancers; amino acid pyrolysates are associated with a number of cancers, especially gastric cancer; and fat is associated with colon and the hormone-sensitive cancers (Hargreaves et al. 1989).

Nutritional Conditions Associated with Increased Cancer Risk

Both obesity and the various deficiency states constitute conditions potentially favorable for cancer growth (Balducci et al. 1986; Poirier 1987). In animals, obesity is associated with the occurrence of spontaneous or induced neoplasms, which seems to be lower when food is restricted, thereby prolonging survival. In humans, obesity is associated with cancers of the endometrium, breast, colon, and ovary (Hargreaves et al. 1989). The association of the hormone-sensitive cancers with obesity may be related to an increased conversion of adrenal androgens into estrogens in adipose tissue. In humans, cellular immune deficiency, a possible outcome of protein-calorie malnutrition and zinc deficiency, may facilitate the development of head, neck, and gastric cancers (Hargreaves et al. 1989).

Substances with Cancer-Preventive Potential

Vitamins A, C, and E, selenium, zinc, and fiber are believed to have cancer-preventive potential in humans, but here again the evidence is circumstantial (Balducci et al. 1986). The mechanism of action is believed to be related to these substances' known biochemical action. Reports from three cohort studies indicated that fruits and vegetables in the human diet protect against many types of cancers (Hirayama 1985, 1986; Kuratsune et al. 1986; Colditz et al. 1985). Other substances with cancer-preventive potential include food substances that are not currently classified as nutrients but that induce carcinogen-detoxifying enzymes (Carr 1985): indoles in gas-producing vegetables and flavones in citrus fruits, which alter microsomal mixed-function oxidases; coumarins in fruits and vegeta-

TABLE 2. National diet and nutrition guidelines for the prevention of cancer risk.[a]

Specific recommendations	Supporting agencies
Maintain appropriate weight	NCI, NRC, USDA
Modify dietary fat	ACS, NCI, NRC, USDA
Total amount	ACS, NCI, NRC, USDA
P/S ratio	USDA
Emphasize fruits and vegetables	
All	ACS, NCI, NRC, USDA
Cruciferi	ACS, NCI, NRC
Emphasize complex carbohydrates	
Whole grains	ACS, NCI, NRC, USDA
Fiber	ACS, NCI, USDA
Drink no or moderate amounts of	
alcohol	ACS, NCI, NRC, USDA
Careful food preparation	
Decrease cured, smoked, pickled	
foods	ACS, NCI, NRC
Avoid frying, high temperatures	NCI
Limit salt	USDA
Reduce food additives, contaminants	ACS, NCI, NRC, USDA
Select a balanced diet	ACS, NCI, NRC, USDA

Abbreviations: ACS, American Cancer Society; NCI, National Cancer Institute; NRC, National Research Council; USDA, United States Department of Agriculture; P/S, polyunsaturated/saturated fatty acids.
[a] Modified from Palmer 1986, with permission.

bles and aromatic isothiocyanates in cruciferi, which induce glutathione-s-transferase activity; plant sterols that occur widely in fruits and vegetables; and xenobiotics that are foreign compounds with no nutrient value in fruits, vegetables, and grains and are excreted from the body. This argues for the use of foodstuffs rather than nutrient supplementation alone in cancer-preventive regimens. In humans, a deficiency of vitamins A and C has been associated with lung and cervical cancers, a deficiency of zinc with pancreatic cancer, of selenium with oral cancer, and fiber with colon cancer (Hargreaves et al. 1989).

Dietary Guidelines

In recognition that there is sufficient evidence for a dietary and nutritional relationship with cancer, guidelines have been developed by a number of national agencies (Palmer 1986) (Table 2). Similar guidelines have been developed in Japan and some European countries (Palmer 1986).

Diet, Nutritional Status, and Cancer Risk in American Blacks

Case-control studies suggest that the same dietary and nutritional factors are associated with specific cancers in Blacks and Whites (Hargreaves et al. 1989).

In an attempt to discover the relationship of diet and nutritional status to the high incidence and mortality rates of American Blacks as a whole, we compared Black-White data from diet and nutritional status surveys in the U.S. (Centers for Disease Control 1972; National Center for Health Statistics 1979). Our review indicated that, compared with Whites, Blacks eat more animal fat, less fiber, and fewer fruits and vegetables; their nutritional status is lower with respect to thiamine, riboflavin, vitamins A and C, and iron and higher with respect to obesity in women and underweight in men. Given the established relationship of these dietary and nutritional factors to cancer risk, it is apparent that the poor eating habits and nutritional status of American Blacks are a national problem that could contribute to higher incidence and mortality rates from cancer.

Selection of Criterion/Measurement Variables

Emphasis on the dietary guidelines described earlier should therefore help to decrease the cancer risk of American Blacks. Program emphasis would be on eating less fat, more fiber, more fruits and vegetables, altering food preparation methods, and improving overall food selection. Alcohol should be consumed in moderation or not at all. Furthermore, a balanced dietary caloric intake, offset by adequate caloric expenditure from exercise, would decrease obesity and underweight.

These dietary guidelines are remarkably similar to those for preventing and alleviating cardiovascular disease and hypertension, conditions for which assessment standards already exist. For promotion of dietary guidelines in the community setting, screening tests must be objective, accurate, and capable of offering immediate feedback. Assessment of ideal weight according to the Metropolitan Life Insurance tables or Health and Nutrition Examination Survey (HANES) epidemiologic standards are readily available (Jensen et al. 1983), although the limitations of these standards are well known (Khosha and Lowe 1967; Revicki and Israel 1986). Alternatively, anthropometric measures may be taken to assess percentage of body fat or lean body mass, but the maintenance of consistent technique is difficult in large-scale community studies. Fortunately, new bioelectrical impedance technology is available, which permits the assessment of body fat with great repeatability in minutes.

Self-reports of dietary intake are also unsatisfactory. In the cardiovascular intervention studies (Lipid Research Clinics Program 1984), serum cholesterol proved to be a reliable index of long-term dietary intake of animal fats. Cholesterol was also implicated more certainly as an important risk factor in cancers of the breast and colon, based on its contribution to increased bile acid formation and steroid production (Reddy 1979; Malhotra 1982; Goldin and Gorbach 1979). The availability, in the community setting, of a whole-blood dry chemistry analyzer (Reflotron) with the capacity to screen for serum cholesterol within three minutes provided us with a quick, objective measure of this variable. Although the techniques are available, no objective measures of fiber intake or alcohol consumption could be done for these studies.

Rationale for Intervention Strategies to Reduce Cancer Risk in Black Americans

Blacks appear to delay seeking health care in the traditional health care system (Bailey 1987), preferring to rely on family, friends (Warnecke 1981), perhaps even spiritualists and healers (Mathews 1987), during periods of economic and emotional stress. These unique value systems, together with the expense of medical care, may have prevented Blacks from wider use of the health care system (Bice et al. 1972; Colombo et al. 1969; Goering and Coe 1969; Montiero 1973; Neighbors and Jackson 1987).

Little is known about what Black Americans know and believe about cancer or what they do to prevent or treat it. According to a survey by the American Cancer Society (EVAXX 1980), Blacks seem to be less knowledgeable than Whites about cancer but interested in knowing more about it; more fatalistic than Whites about getting cancer; to believe that cancer affects Whites more than Blacks; and to receive care at a later disease stage than Whites.

In contrast, more is known about what Black Americans know, believe, and do about hypertension. Two national surveys (U.S. Department of Health and Human Services 1973, 1981) on the knowledge and attitudes of Americans about high blood pressure indicated that community intervention programs successfully increased Americans' awareness of the consequences of high blood pressure. In the second survey, however, only a small number of normotensive and hypertensive Blacks (9% and 21%, respectively), reported positive feelings about their health, an awareness of being hypertensive (5%), and an increased compliance with prescribed treatment. In general, Blacks were less compliant than Whites (Haines and Ward 1981).

These data indicate that different loci of control are operating in Blacks, and therefore different health promotion strategies should be used to reach them. Eliminating barriers to care-seeking and behavior change will require new, culturally sensitive approaches to information dissemination, health planning, and resource management and may even require the institution of new health policies. Moreover, the knowledge, attitudes, and practices of health professionals will need special attention.

A review of the literature for possible approaches to program development suggested the use of (1) a coalition for planning, provision of services, and resource management (Cavalaris 1980; Wilcox 1983); (2) the Black church as an external locus of control (Askey et al. 1983; Eng et al. 1985); and (3) trained community volunteers for immediate, personal, and continuous intervention (Ross 1981).

The Case for a Coalition

A coalition of community organizations can bring together knowledge, experience, and resources to provide solutions for a life-style project that requires concerted community action but has few resources. Such a coalition can provide immediate services and direction, coordinate the community effort, and engage in strategic planning to improve the quality, quantity, and allocation of resources (Cavalaris 1980). Furthermore, the coalition can use its fund-raising expertise to organize the project, operate it to fulfill local needs, and ensure program survival as long as necessary (Wilcox 1983).

This integrated organization should be "a broad-based part of the community, including doctors, lawyers, ordinary people, professionals, teachers, government workers, the entire broad spectrum of community people; organized for the purpose of carrying out the most efficient and effective campaign possible" (Wilcox 1983). Respected community agencies must be a part of this new structure. Various groups have been formed in association with comprehensive cancer centers, such as regional councils and support groups, and linkages have been made with health departments (Meister 1981; Engstrom 1983; Janerich and Carlton 1983).

The network needs to address development of culture-specific messages aimed at behavior change, bearing in mind that Blacks respond more readily to interpersonal communications from relatives, friends, and opinion leaders (Butler et al. 1983; Warnecke 1981; Ross 1981). In determining the most effective means of communication, novel approaches and multiple channels of communication should be used, but specific targeting of risk groups is required (Butler et al. 1983). Because of fear and pessimism surrounding cancer, intermediate goals such as increasing optimism may be more realistic than radical behavior change (Sciandra 1983). Vana et al. (1981) reported that effective communication contributed significantly to reducing the delay of diagnosing cancer in Blacks.

The Case for the Black Church

The Black church community can have enormous positive influence on the lifestyle choices of its church congregations. Historically, the Black church in America has been an important social institution for Blacks, influencing standards of conduct, serving as a resource for the Black family, and representing stability and continuity through its pastors (Askey et al. 1983). Religious belief seems to be correlated with better health and improved life satisfaction (Eng et al. 1985). The Black church has the capacity, therefore, to build community competence for undertaking and sustaining health solutions. Eng et al. (1985) discussed ways in which the Black church could be integrated as a unit of identity, solution, and practice in promoting the adoption of life-preserving behaviors without constant intervention from professionals. A number of recent reports have recommended the use of the Black church in health prevention activities related to hypertension (Kong et al. 1982; Perry and Williams 1981; Hatch and Jackson 1981; Thomas and Thomas 1985), and in the training of health professionals (Hatch and Lovelace 1980).

The Case for Trained Volunteers in Behavior-Change Programs for Blacks

Examining factors that may influence successful preventive health education of poor persons, Ross (1981) outlined needs that are especially relevant for Blacks. She made a strong case for suitably trained community residents, people who know their community and can establish rapport with the isolated and disinterested residents through familiar personal networks. Being emotionally accepted, these paraprofessionals can encourage other community members' participation and stimulate them to join in designing a health information program. Trained residents can teach others to use the health care system, and they can counter the prevailing belief that outcomes or rewards are the result of luck, chance, fate, or the actions of powerful political entities. Health system professionals should be ready to respond rapidly and sensitively to those encouraged to participate and recognize these new health agents for the contribution they can make to medical services.

Initial Intervention Efforts

The overall goal of our program was to decrease diet- and nutrition-related cancer risk factors. This included a decrease in fat and alcohol consumption, an increase in fiber consumption, and a decrease in obesity. Our philosophy of educational intervention (Hargreaves et al. 1986) led us to believe, however, that a comprehensive educational approach that addressed other cancer risk factors or major health risk factors of concern would be more appealing to participants and more effective in the long run. Therefore, smoking and high blood pressure were included as risk factors that should receive attention in an effective, comprehensive intervention program for Blacks.

Two major organizational steps brought us nearer to our goal of reaching Blacks and included (1) establishment of a network of interested organizations whose members provided expertise and resources to ensure the program's success and (2) development of an education program that would be acceptable to Blacks at different socioeconomic levels. According to the latter, the program was to be held in Black churches in Nashville, with existing educational materials modified to make them appropriate for Blacks, and community volunteers selected and trained to participate in a personalized intervention program. The third major step was the evaluation of the success of the network in meeting its objectives and the effectiveness of the program in changing behaviors.

To begin work on the first objective, organizations that had agreed to participate in the coalition were invited to attend two day-long workshops in which members discussed plans with project staff at Meharry Medical College and two consultants who were discussion leaders. At these workshops, decisions were made concerning the design of the program intervention and its details and the manner of interaction between coalition members. A description of these follows.

The Community Coalition for Minority Health

Founding member organizations were those providing community services to reduce the influence of life-style factors important in cancer risk and whose staff members were interested in participating in the program—the American Cancer Society, American Lung Association, American Red Cross, Metro Government and Health Fair, Inc., a national agency stimulating the conduct of health fairs in many locations across the country. The Interdenominational Ministerial Fellowship was invited to participate to provide liaison between the coalition and the Black churches and did so. The American Heart Association was invited to participate (and did so) because of its experience in decreasing cardiovascular risk through a variety of effective programs, because certain risk factors (obesity, cholesterol, and smoking) overlap in cancer and heart disease, and high blood pressure as a risk factor would receive attention. Meharry Medical College was recognized as the coalition leader.

Workshops

The purpose of the two workshops held was to ensure that coalition members understood the nature and scope of the project and how they and their organizations could help to make it work. At the first workshop, health educator Dr. John Hatch of the University of North Carolina at Chapel Hill described his many years of experience with health programming in the Black Baptist Convention for North Carolina. A key point was that differences between Black churches would affect program acceptance and success and that this included the church members' socioeconomic status and the pastors' level of education. These were highly correlated and produced a topology of churches based on size: the wealthier churches tended to be larger and to belong to the established denominations; poorer churches were not only smaller but composed of the more nontraditional and newer denominations. The Church of Christ and Baptist churches were selected because they constituted the greatest number of churches attended by Blacks in Nashville, the Church of Christ being a more recently established denomination.

Then coalition members discussed specific approaches to intervention, agreeing that health fairs held at individual churches were the best way to reach Blacks for screening. Each pastor would appoint a church health coordinator to work with church and coalition members. Blacks found to have one or more risk factors would be encouraged to attend one or more program modules. Coalition members would contribute educational materials and waive fees, if warranted.

At the second workshop Dr. Victor Schoenbach, epidemiologist of the University of North Carolina at Chapel Hill, discussed the benefits and limitations of health risk assessment and described his national program of promoting smoking cessation in Black clients of the North Carolina Mutual Insurance Company. The Nashville program was to follow the model by Hargreaves et al. (1986).

Planning and Management Model

According to this model, program development proceeds in four cycles: "trial and error" or pilot, model demonstration, and institutionalization (Hargreaves et al. 1986). During the pilot cycle, the conceptual program is implemented by trial and error on a small scale; during the model cycle, the developed program is evaluated with a small experimental sample; during the demonstration cycle, the program is then implemented on a large scale with a representative population; and finally, the effective program is put in operation in several organizations. Each program cycle proceeds in four phases—by modeling, program planning in the community, implementation, and evaluation.

Coalition members were encouraged to be actively involved in all of these phases and cycles; some members were expected to be more active than others. Between cycles, coalition members were to receive a written report of the results of the cycle just completed and be invited to discuss program evaluation and to develop new intervention strategies or activities, if necessary. Because of the expected differences between denominations (J. Hatch, personal communication), the pilot cycle began with two experimental and two comparison churches, with one each from the Baptist and Church of Christ denominations. During the experimental and demonstration cycles, the number of churches would be increased.

Health Fairs

Subjective and objective measures of health were gathered at stations set up in a suitable area of the church's facilities. Subjective measures were obtained with a questionnaire that covered general background information; current health status, smoking, dietary, and activity practices; stress; specific health practices (related to the risk factors under consideration); and knowledge, attitudes, and opinions about cancer, hypertension, and cardiovascular disease. Objective measures included blood pressure, serum cholesterol, and body fat (by bioelectrical impedance). A total of 173 persons participated in the health fairs.

Specific criterion variables used to classify individual risk for that variable are shown in Table 3. Individuals were not classified as to overall risk, but each received a summary indicating his or her measure for each risk factor. In addition, the serum cholesterol and bioelectrical impedance tests provided a hardcopy handout for all participants. The latter included suggestions for improving body fat status by diet and exercise. Persons with excessively high blood pressure and cholesterol levels were referred to a physician of their choice for follow-up medical attention.

TABLE 3. Criterion variables for assessment of cancer risk: evaluation standards.

Criterion variables	Standards	
Dietary intake	*Adequate*	
Fiber[a]	Every day	
Fat[b] and Alcohol	Once a week or less	
Blood Cholesterol	*Moderate*	*High*
20–29 Years	200–220 mg/dl	> 220 mg/dl
30–39 Years	221–240 mg/dl	> 240 mg/dl
40+ Years	241–260 mg/dl	> 260 mg/dl
Body Fat Status	*Normal range*	*Normal range*
	Males	Females
0–30 Years	12–18%	20–26%
31–40 Years	13–19%	21–27%
41–50 Years	14–20%	22–28%
51–60 Years	16–20%	22–30%
61+ Years	17–21%	22–31%
Body Weight		
> 10% Under ideal weight	Underweight	
10% Under to 10% over ideal weight	Normal weight	
10% to 19% over ideal weight	Overweight	
> 20% Over ideal weight	Obesity	
Smoking		
< 15 Cigarettes/day	Light	
15–25	Moderate	
>25	Heavy	

[a] Includes contribution from fruits, vegetables, and whole grains.
[b] Includes fried foods.

Program Modules

Participants were invited to sign up for information on blood pressure, smoking cessation, and diet and obesity. Health literature was offered at the comparison churches, and specific education modules were offered at the experimental churches.

The blood pressure module, selected from the American Red Cross' "Low Down on High Blood Pressure," consisted of four sessions. The smoking cessation module was the American Lung Association's "Freedom from Smoking Clinic," and consisted of seven sessions. The diet and obesity module, developed by diet-nutrition consultants at Meharry Medical College, consisted of eight sessions.

Characteristics of the Target Population

Demographic characteristics of the target population are shown in Table 4. Divided according to denomination, the target population showed no statistically significant differences in age, gender, or educational level, but a significant difference was seen in marital status and the participation rate. Participating Baptists included a higher percentage of widowed and a lower percentage of

TABLE 4. Demographic characteristics of target population by church denomination.

Characteristic	Baptist		Church of Christ		Chi-square	P
	No.	%	No.	%		
Age (years)					1.396	0.845
≤ 30	15	19	18	20		
31–40	15	19	17	18		
41–50	11	14	15	16		
51–60	11	14	17	18		
> 60	27	34	25	27		
Total	79	100	92	100		
Gender					0.068	0.694
Male	25	31	26	28		
Female	55	69	66	72		
Total	80	100	92	100		
Education					0.994	0.608
1–8 Years	8	11	6	7		
9–12 Years	31	41	36	40		
> 13 Years	37	49	49	53		
Total	76	100	91	100		
Marital Status					11.328	0.010[a]
Single	21	27	18	20		
Married	29	37	56	62		
Separated/divorced	16	20	12	13		
Widowed	12	15	5	5		
Total	78	100	91	100		
Participation					11.1576	0.0012[a]
Participants	81	10	92	6		
Nonparticipants	719	90	1383	94		
Total	800	100	1475	100		

[a] Significant

married persons, and their rate of participation was higher than that of Church of Christ members.

Among those attending the Health Fair from the two churches, 70% were women; 19% of the participants were younger than 30, 20% were between 31 and 40, 14% between 41 and 50, 17% between 51 and 60, and 31% were over 60 years of age. As to marital status, 23% were single, and 16% were separated or divorced. Eight percent had 1 to 8 years of education, 39% had 9 to 12 years, and 50% had more than 13 years of education. Among Baptist participants, 36% were married and 15% widowed, compared with 61% married and 5% widowed among Church of Christ members. Baptists represented 10% of their church membership, compared with 6% participating from the Church of Christ.

Health risk characteristics of the target population are outlined in Table 5. Among the members of both churches, 20% had a high serum cholesterol level, 70% had a high percentage of body fat, 51% reported a high fat intake, and 54% reported a low fiber intake. Baptists reported a higher rate of alcohol intake than

TABLE 5. Distribution of selected variables among attendants of health fairs by denomination.

	Baptist		Church of Christ			
	No.	%	No.	%	Chi-square	P
Cholesterol (mg/dl)					0.000	1.000
Normal	63	80	73	80		
High	16	20	18	20		
Body fat (%)					0.679	0.410
Normal	24	31	21	24		
High	54	69	67	76		
Fat intake					2.490	0.115
Adequate	42	55	37	41		
High	35	45	53	59		
Fiber intake					1.809	0.179
Adequate	30	38	45	50		
Low	48	62	45	50		
Alcohol intake					8.558	0.003[a]
No	55	70	80	89		
Yes	24	30	10	11		
Smoking					13.195	0.0003[a]
No	51	65	81	89		
Yes	28	35	10	11		

[a] Significant

did Church of Christ members (30% compared with 11%), and a higher rate of smoking (35% compared with 11%).

Conclusions

This report describes three facets of our early work to develop, implement, and evaluate a community program that would decrease dietary and nutritional cancer risks in Blacks living in Nashville. The first facet of the report is the rationale for selecting measurement variables for screening and monitoring behavior change; the second facet includes aspects of program development that take into account sociocultural forces important in fostering behavior change in Blacks; and the third facet is the initial intervention strategy using a coalition of resource organizations for program planning and management, and Black churches as channels of communication. A comprehensive approach to health education was believed to be essential for Blacks, so an emphasis on hypertension and cardiovascular disease was included in the program.

A total of 173 persons participated in health fairs held in four Baptist and Church of Christ churches and represented an 11% participation rate from among the church membership. Subjects provided subjective and objective measures of health. Objective measures included blood pressure, serum cholesterol, and body fat (bioelectrical impedance). Subjective measures, covered by questionnaire, included current health status; smoking, dietary, and activity practices; and knowledge, attitudes, and opinions about cancer, hypertension, and cardiovascular disease.

Subjects at high risk were invited to sign up to participate in the American Red Cross program module "Low Down on High Blood Pressure" (four sessions), the American Lung Association's "Freedom from Smoking Clinic" (seven sessions), and a diet and obesity module developed by Meharry Medical College (eight sessions).

Only baseline data were available at the time this paper was written. Other reports are being prepared for publication elsewhere. Differences in demographic variables by church denomination are reported. No statistically significant differences were observed in the distribution of the following criterion variables by denomination: serum cholesterol, percentage of body fat, fat intake, and fiber intake. There was, however, a significant difference in reported frequency of smoking and alcohol consumption, Church of Christ members showing lower frequencies of smoking and alcohol consumption.

Acknowledgments. We are indebted for the contributions made by the founding coalition members and the consultants to our program. Founding coalition members are Sylvia Ramsey, American Cancer Society; Sarah Marquardt, American Red Cross; Peggy Maguire, American Lung Association; Joan Clayton, formerly of Health Fair, Inc. and now with the YWCA; and the Rev. Dr. John Corey, representing the Interdenominational Ministerial Fellowship. Consultants to the program were Drs. John Hatch and Victor Schoenbach, both of the University of North Carolina, Chapel Hill.

References

Askey DK, Parker D, Alexander D, et al. Clergy as intermediary: An approach to cancer control. *Prog Clin Biol Res* 1980; 130:417–424.

Axtell LM, Asire AJ, Myers MH: *Cancer Patient's Survival*. Report No. 5. Washington, DC: US Department of Health, Education, and Welfare, 1976.

Bailey EJ: Sociocultural factors and health care-seeking behavior among black Americans. *J Natl Med Assoc* 1981; 79:388–392.

Balducci L, Wallace C, Khansur K, et al: Nutrition, cancer, and aging: An annotated review. I. Diet, carcinogenesis, and aging. *J Am Geriatr Soc* 1986; 34:127–136.

Baquet CR, Ringen K, Pollack ES, et al: *Cancer Among Blacks and Other Minorities: Statistical Profiles*. National Cancer Institute Publication No. 86-2785. Washington, DC: US Government Printing Office, 1986.

Bice, TW, Eichorn RL, Fox PD: Socio-economic status and use of physician services: A reconsideration. *Med Care* 1972; 10:261–271.

Butler L, King G, White JE: Communications strategies, cancer information, and black populations: An analysis of longitudinal data. *Prog Clin Biol Res* 1983; 130:171–182.

Carr BI: Chemical carcinogens and inhibitors of carcinogenesis in the human diet. *Cancer* 1985; 55:218–224.

Cavalaris CJ: Statewide organization for cancer control. *Prog Clin Biol Res* 1980; 57: 173–175.

Centers for Disease Control: *Ten State Nutrition Survey 1968–70. Demographic Data.* DHEW Publication No. (HSM) 72–8134. Washington, DC: US Government Printing Office, 1972.

Colditz GA, Branch LG, Lipnick RJ, et al: Increased green and yellow vegetable intake and lowered cancer deaths in an elderly population. *Am J Clin Nutr* 1985; 41:32–36.

Colombo TJ, Saward E, Greenlick MR: The integration of an OEO health program into a prepaid comprehensive group practice plan. *Am J Public Health* 1963; 59:641–650.

Doll R, Peto R: The causes of cancer: Qualitative estimates of avoidable risks of cancer in the United States today. *JNCI* 1981; 66:1191–1308.

Eng E, Hatch J, Callan A: Institutionalizing social support through the church and community. *Health Educ Q* 1985; 12:81–92.

Engstrom PF: Cancer control through a network of community hospitals. *Prog Clin Biol Res* 1983; 130:67–81.

EVAXX, Inc: *A Study of Black Americans' Attitudes towards Cancer and Cancer Tests.* New York: American Cancer Society, 1980.

Goering J, Coe R: Cultural versus situational explanations of the medical behavior of the poor. *Social Science Journal* 1970; 23:309–319.

Goldin BR, Gorbach SL: Microbial factors and nutrition in carcinogenesis. *Adv Nutr Res* 1979; 2:129–148.

Haines CM, Ward GW: Recent trends in public knowledge, attitudes, and reported behavior with respect to high blood pressure. *Public Health Rep* 1981; 96:514–522.

Hargreaves MK, Baquet C, Gamshadzahi A: Diet, nutritional status, and cancer risk in American blacks. *Nutr Cancer* 1989; 12:1–28.

Hargreaves MK, Laitakari JK, Huff F, Rautaharju PM: Changing community health behaviors: A model for development and management. *Health Values* 1986; 10:34–43.

Hatch JW, Jackson C: North Carolina Baptist Church program. *Urban Health* 1981; 10:70–71.

Hatch J, Lovelace KA: Involving the Southern rural church and students of the health professions in health education. *Public Health Rep* 1980; 95:23–25.

Hirayama T: Mortality in Japanese with life-styles similar to Seventh Day Adventists: Strategy for risk reduction. *NCI Monogr* 1985; 69:143–153.

Hirayama T: Nutrition and cancer: A large scale cohort study. *Prog Clin Biol Res* 1986; 206:299–311.

Horm JW, Asire AJ: Change in lung cancer incidence and mortality rates among Americans: 1969–78. *JNCI* 1982; 69:833–837.

Horm JW, Kessler L: Falling rates of lung cancer in men in the United States. *Lancet* 1986; 1:425–426.

Janerich DT, Carlton K: Linking resources: Cancer centers and health departments. *Prog Clin Biol Res* 1983; 130:67–81.

Jensen TG, Englert DM, Dudrick ST: *Nutritional Assessment: A Manual for Practitioners.* Norwalk, CT: Appleton-Century-Crofts, 1983.

Kerr GR: Nutritional counseling for cancer prevention. *Prog Clin Res* 1984; 204:165–189.

Khosha T, Lowe CR: Indices of obesity derived from body weight and height. *Br J Prev Soc Med* 1967; 21:122–128.

Kong BW, Miller JM, Smoot RT: Churches as high blood pressure control centers. *J Natl Med Assoc* 1982; 74:920–923.

Kuratsune M, Ikeda M, Hayashi T: Epidemiologic studies on possible health effects of pyrolysates of foods, with reference to mortality among Japanese Seventh Day Adventists. *Environ Health Perspect* 1986; 67:143–146.

Lipid Research Clinics Program: Lipid research clinics coronary primary prevention trial results. II. The relationship of reduction in incidence of coronary heart disease to cholesterol lowering. *JAMA* 1984; 251:365–374.

Malhotra SL: Fecal urobilinogen levels and pH of stools in population groups with different incidence of cancer of the colon, and their possible role in its etiology. *J R Soc Med* 1982; 75:709–714.

Meister N: Cancer support groups: A community model. *Prog Clin Biol Res* 1981; 53:215–216.

Montiero L: Expense is no object . . . income and physician visits reconsidered. *J Health Soc Behav* 1973; 14:99–114.

National Center for Health Statistics: *National Health Survey (HANES I) Caloric and Selected Nutrient Values for Persons 1–74 Years of Age: First Health and Nutrition Examination Survey. United States 1971–74.* Series 11, No 209. U.S. Department of Health and Human Services Publication No. (PHS) 79–1657. Washington DC: US Government Printing Office, 1979.

Newell G: Nutrition and diet. *Cancer* 1983; 51:2420–2425.

Neighbors HW, Jackson JS: Barriers to medical care among adult blacks: What happens to the uninsured? *J Natl Med Assoc* 1983; 79:489–493.

Palmer S: Dietary considerations for risk reduction. *Cancer* 1986; 58:1949–1953.

Pariza MW: A perspective on diet, nutrition, and cancer. *JAMA* 1984; 251:1455–1458.

Perry EJ, Williams BJ: Memphis TN: The Memphis church-based high blood pressure program. *Urban Health* 1981; 10:70–71.

Poirier LA: Stages in carcinogenesis: Alteration by diet. *Am J Clin Nutr* 1987; 45:185–191.

Reddy BS: Nutrition and colon cancer. *Adv Nutr Res* 1979; 2:199–218.

Revicki DA, Israel RG: Relationship between body mass indices and measures of adiposity. *Am J Public Health* 1986; 76:992–994.

Ross CK: Factors influencing successful preventive health education. *Health Educ Q* 1981; 8:187–208.

Sciandra R: Effective communications in cancer control. *Prog Clin Biol Res* 1983; 121:109–112.

Thomas J, Thomas DJ: High blood pressure control in black Americans: A role for the church in control and prevention. *AME Church Review* 1985; 320:34–37.

US Department of Health and Human Services: *The Public and High Blood Pressure.* DHEW Publication No. (NIH) 73–356. Washington DC: US Government Printing Office, 1973.

US Department of Health and Human Services: *The Public and High Blood Pressure: A Second Look. Six Years Follow-Up Survey of Public Knowledge and Reported Behavior.* NIH Publication No. 81–2118. Washington, DC: US Government Printing Office, 1981.

Vana J, Bedwani R, Mettlin C, et al: Trends in diagnosis and management of breast cancer in the US from the surveys of the American College of Surgeons. *Cancer* 1981; 48:1043–1052.

Warnecke RB: Intervention in black populations. *Prog Clin Biol Res* 1981; 53:167–183.

Weisburger JH: Mechanism of action of diet as a carcinogen. *Cancer* 1979; 43:1987–1995.

Weisburger JH, Reddy BS, Cohen LA, et al: Mechanisms of promotion in carcinogenesis, in Hecker E et al. (eds): *Carcinogenesis*. New York: Raven Press, 1982, pp 175–182.

Wilcox, FJ: The role of organization in cancer control. *Prog Clin Biol Res* 1983; 132A:25–29.

Young JL Jr, Gloeckler RL, Pollack ES: Cancer patient survival among ethnic groups in the US. *JNCI* 1984; 73:341–352.

8. Cancer Control and the Community Oncology Programs: Minority Participation in the National Cancer Institute Clinical Trials Network

Carrie P. Hunter

The goal of the National Cancer Institute (NCI) by the year 2000 is the reduction of cancer mortality by 50% in the American population. The estimate is that this reduction can largely be obtained by implementation of effective programs in smoking, diet, and early detection and the application of existing knowledge in cancer control (Greenwald and Sondik 1986). The process by which this goal will be achieved is, in part, the education, recruitment, and participation of the vast resource of trained community physicians who are available to implement state-of-the-art cancer care and thus take advantage of progress in cancer research.

Nearly 80% of cancer patients are treated in their communities. Other contributors to this volume reviewed the higher incidence and mortality rates and the lower survival rates of selected cancers in minority populations. Central to reducing incidence and mortality rates and improving survival in minority populations is the application of the best available knowledge of prevention, early diagnosis, and treatment. One of the NCI's major efforts has been to design and implement program interventions to assure that patients treated in their communities have access to the same quality of cancer care and the same technologic advances available to patients treated in major centers. The Division of Cancer Prevention and Control (DCPC) supports research in prevention, health promotion, smoking cessation, nutrition, treatment, continuing care, and rehabilitation. Together with the Division of Cancer Treatment, DCPC also supports clinical trials by cooperative groups and cancer centers. Clinical trials research in treatment and cancer control provides community patients and their physicians with access to cancer care, and provides community oncologists with a source of continuing education concerning innovations in diagnostic techniques and treatment applications.

The evolution of NCI's clinical trials program has led to a network of clinical, teaching, and research activities among community hospitals, oncology specialists and allied health providers, cancer centers, and cooperative groups involved in clinical research. Greater involvement in clinical trials research by Black, Hispanic, Asian American, American Indian, and other minority physicians and patients is needed if the advances in clinical research are to be realized by all ethnic groups, and if the results of clinical trials are to be generalizable to the entire population. I shall describe the development of community oncology programs for treatment and cancer control research in community settings, the network of research programs through which greater minority participation is encouraged, and recommendations for what minority physicians and other physicians involved with minority populations can do to increase their involvement in treatment and cancer control research, thus gaining greater access to state-of-the-art cancer care management.

Community Oncology Programs

Community oncology programs are part of a network of NCI-sponsored cancer clinical research initiatives. Thirty years ago, the framework for the present clinical trials program was established with the funding of the first cooperative groups committed to improving therapy for cancer patients. Today, 11 cooperative groups involving several thousand oncologists, more than 465 member institutions, and 675 affiliated institutions are actively engaged in multidisciplinary clinical cancer research.

With the passage of the National Cancer Act in 1971 came increased support of basic and clinical research in cancer etiology, treatment, and cancer control, which allowed the expansion of research opportunities and the improvement of linkages among university and community physicians and their patients. The NCI Cancer Centers Program established during the early 1970s today supports basic and clinical research in 20 comprehensive, 21 clinical, 14 basic science, and two consortial centers. One planning grant for a minority consortial center has been funded.

The Cooperative Group Outreach Program, organized in 1976, was designed to encourage the participation of community oncologists in clinical trials research, thereby increasing the number of cancer patients receiving the best available care. Through the cooperative groups, funding support is provided to physicians in the program for data management of patients entered in clinical trials. To date, the program has supported the participation in clinical research of several hundred community oncologists, their associated nurses and data managers, and other health care professionals from more than 700 hospitals. About 20% of patients in clinical treatment trials are from this community program.

By the early 1980s, it was clear that the NCI's cancer education training program had been successful. Many community hospitals were staffed by university-trained oncologists experienced in clinical trials research. The published reports also showed that the quality of data from community oncologists participating in clinical trials was comparable to that of data from their colleagues in academic centers (Begg et al. 1983a and b; Koretz et al. 1983).

In 1983, the NCI implemented the Community Clinical Oncology Program (CCOP). This cancer-control initiative was designed to increase the involvement of community oncologists in up-to-date cancer care management and expand their and their patients' participation in studies to answer research questions through clinical trials. Sixty-two CCOP organizations in 34 states, consisting of 187 hospital components, 63 physician offices, and 37 group practices, were funded. More than 1,100 community physicians and 300 nurse oncologists/data managers involved in the care of about 100,000 new cancer patients are active participants in CCOP. For access to NCI-approved protocols, the CCOPs established affiliations with up to five research bases (cooperative groups and cancer centers). The Community Clinical Oncology Program led to an expanded network of community oncologists, of clinical researchers in academic institutions, cooperative groups, and cancer centers, and of nurse oncologists and data managers for conducting research in treatment and cancer control (Figure 1).

The CCOP is also a success. It has provided access to treatment trials for community oncologists and their patients. Approximately 20% of all patients on treatment protocols are entered by CCOP physicians. The program has also stimulated many communities to organize their cancer activities, and it has expedited the development of a cancer program in some localities. Although little research was conducted in cancer control during the first three years, the program established a base for extending cancer control research efforts in areas such as smoking cessation, early detection and screening of high-risk populations, chemoprevention, continuing care, rehabilitation, and treatment applications to participating physicians and their patients.

Minority Populations in Clinical Cancer Research

In general, the participation of minority physicians and patients in clinical research is limited, and, as CCOP data indicate, minority cancer patients are underrepresented in clinical trials. A log of new cancer patients for whom particular disease site and stage research protocols are available shows that only 7% of patients seen by CCOP physicians are members of minorities, compared with 13% minority representation in the U.S. Surveillance, Epidemiology, and End Results (SEER) population (Hunter et al. 1987). This ethnic profile probably reflects the patient populations available to the successful CCOP applicants and their institutions. The log data for Black patients show a trend similar to that of Caucasian patients: (a) 40% of Caucasian and 37% of Black patients have a protocol available for site and stage of cancer; (b) more than 50% of patients with a protocol available are clinically eligible for it; and (c) of clinically eligible patients, one-third entered the study. The numbers in the log data for other ethnic groups collected over the 16-month reporting period are too small to establish a trend. Improving the access of minority patients and their physicians to state-of-the-art cancer care through the clinical trials process is a key factor in increasing minority participation in clinical research.

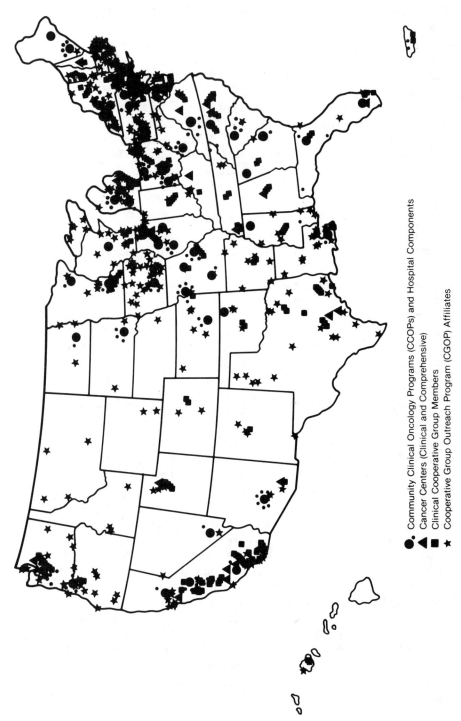

Community Clinical Oncology Programs (CCOPs) and Hospital Components

Cancer Centers (Clinical and Comprehensive)

Clinical Cooperative Group Members

Cooperative Group Outreach Program (CGOP) Affiliates

FIGURE 1. The National Cancer Institute's clinical trials network.

Multiple factors may affect the ability of physicians and minority cancer patients to engage in the best available cancer care:

- awareness by physicians of clinical trials and other treatment options;
- access to participation in clinical trials by minority oncologists and other physicians caring for minority cancer patients, and access of cancer patients to oncology specialists involved in clinical research;
- access of patients to medical facilities with appropriate diagnostic and treatment capabilities;
- availability to physicians of other health care providers to assist in data management and quality control procedures;
- availability of protocols for site and stage of disease of patients;
- availability of supportive care services necessary for optimal continuing care;
- adaptability of the "usual sources of care" for many minority patients (i.e., municipal hospital clinics, health care facilities, and private physician's offices) to become environments that foster clinical research; and
- availability of adequate funding resources to support clinical trials participation.

Why Participate and How to Get Involved

For the oncologist, participation in clinical research is a form of continuing medical education. It allows access to new technical developments in diagnosis, makes available innovative cancer treatments that are ready for scientific testing and application, provides access to investigational drugs, and increases opportunities for an exchange of ideas between community oncologists and researchers. For oncologists with limited opportunities to interact with other oncology specialists because of their practice locations, participation in clinical trials may be an important communication link for maintaining knowledge of advances in cancer research and treatment and therefore is a valuable investment for physicians and their patients.

Community oncologists involved in the care of minority cancer patients and who are interested in participating in the clinical trials process have several options, depending on their research interest, practice situation, health care resources, data management support, and the requirements of the program to which they are applying. Currently, access to participation in clinical trials is provided through several mechanisms (Table 1). The Minority Satellite Supplement Program provides some funding through cooperative groups for linking minority patients and their physicians to clinical research. Oncologists interested in protocol research may apply to and should affiliate with a cooperative group, member institution, CCOP, or regional cancer center in their area.

Participation in clinical research requires a commitment of time and resources. The practicing oncologist, allied health professional, university center, cancer center, and large cancer treatment group need the elements outlined in Table 2 to participate in or operate an effective research program.

TABLE 1. Access to participation in clinical trials

Cooperative Group Outreach Program
Community Clinical Oncology Program
Member institution of cooperative groups
Cancer centers
Minority Satellite Supplement Program

Minority patients and oncologists involved in their care must become involved in the clinical treatment and cancer control research process. Interested investigators are encouraged to take their chances in the funding arena with well-conceived research proposals. Such proposals may be responses to specific calls like the CCOP request for applications or be directed at intermediate funding sources such as the CGOPs through the cooperative groups. By organizing local efforts, by carefully reviewing initiatives that can be conducted with existing community resources, by establishing links to experts in other fields who are not currently in the organization or immediate area, and by establishing links with appropriate facilities and other community groups in developing the research program (e.g., cancer centers are a good source of experts for community programs), an applicant's chances of successful competition in the grants review process will be greatly enhanced. In writing proposals, applicants must state their goals and objectives clearly, describe concisely why the proposal should be conducted in the area or with the designated population, and document the availability of the potential population to be studied, the facilities, and qualifications of personnel.

Details of how the proposed intervention will be conducted and a plan for evaluating the outcome and effectiveness of the research should be described. Applicants preparing grants are encouraged to talk with and obtain guidance from NCI program staff members and experienced researchers in their own communities.

TABLE 2. Basic elements of participation in cancer clinical trials

Environment conductive to research
Patient resources
Nucleus of interested oncologists and other health professionals
  Experienced leadership
  Investigator commitment
Central organizational focus
  Data management system
    Nurse oncologists
    Data managers
  Quality assurance and
  Quality control procedures
Protocol availability
Funding support (institutional, federal, other)
Individual contributions of time and effort

The NCI encourages interested physicians from minority groups and from community programs treating minority patients to become involved in clinical research. Through the implementation of cancer control research in prevention, early detection, effective screening practices, educational awareness of cancer by physicians and patients, and appropriate applications of existing technology and treatment, cancer incidence and mortality will be reduced in minority populations, resulting in improved survival for the entire population served.

References

Begg CB, Carbone PP, Elson PJ, et al: Participation of community hospitals in clinical trials: Analysis of five years of experience in the Eastern Cooperative Oncology Group. *N Engl J Med* 1983a; 306:1076–1080.

Begg CB, Zelen M, Carbone PP, et al: Cooperative groups and community hospitals: Measurement of impact in the community hospitals. *Cancer* 1983b; 52:1760–1767.

Greenwald PG, Sondik E, (eds): *Cancer Control Objectives for the Nation: 1985–2000*, No. 2. Bethesda, MD: National Cancer Institute, 1986.

Hunter CP, Frelick RW, Feldman AR, et al: Selection factors in clinical trials: Results from the Community Clinical Oncology Program physician's patient log. *Cancer Treat Rep* 1987; 71:599–565.

Koretz MM, Jackson PM, Torti FM, et al: A comparison of the quality of participation of community affiliates and that of universities in the Northern California Oncology Group. *J Clin Oncol* 1983; 1:640–644.

Section 3

Prevention and Detection Programs:
Community–Based Efforts

Introduction to Section 3

Lemuel A. Evans

Advances in the early detection, treatment, and cure of cancer in many of its forms has made it the most curable chronic disease. This means little, however, to those who see cancer as a hopeless condition. This perception is most prevalent among members of minority groups, especially Blacks, who are most at risk for the disease. It is now generally recognized that many lives can be saved with current technology for cancer cure and prevention. Various surveys reveal that minority populations' view of cancer is clouded by confusion and skepticism. Difficulties encountered while attempting to communicate information about a complex, highly technical subject are further compounded by the sometimes controversial and inconclusive nature of the information being disseminated. The potential for alienation resulting from unclear or inappropriate messages is great and adds to the many obstacles facing health professionals and others as they attempt to help the public obtain and evaluate messages about the disease.

Cancer detection and prevention programs are important to the dissemination of knowledge about the disease and for the modification of health behavior to control cancer. Consideration of cultural diversity and other factors during planning, implementation, and evaluation of these programs would contribute to knowing how minority individuals and groups perceive cancer, what the differences between minority subpopulations are, and how minority individuals receive information about cancer. It is also important to understand minority group attitudes about cancer and how those attitudes affect their grasp and acceptance of health information. Current attitudes, beliefs, and behavior patterns relating to cancer, along with perceptions of disease susceptibility, must be examined as culturally relevant messages are developed for specific groups. The most credible sources of information for minority populations and who within the population is likely to request information also should be determined.

According to survey findings, especially those from the National Cancer Institute (NCI), much of the public, especially the minority segments, remains inadequately informed about cancer. Many individuals from these groups agree that it seems like everything causes cancer and there is not much a person can do to prevent the disease. Blacks in particular are less likely to believe that the chances of being cured of cancer are better today than ever. Agreement with this statement appears to be affected by income as well as educational level. Blacks, according to an NCI survey, list cancer as the most serious health problem and believe more often than the general public that they are likely to get cancer. Notably, a smaller percentage of Blacks than Whites believe that tobacco, sunshine, and x-rays increase cancer risk. There are significant differences between Blacks' and the general population's knowledge of specific cancer risks, personal health practices, willingness to follow a doctor's advice, and awareness of cancer information sources.

In this section, Dr. Noma Roberson reviews the role of cancer control activities in reducing Black/White differences in cancer mortality and notes that data about the knowledge, beliefs, and behaviors relevant to cancer are limited, as are the number of specific interventions that target Blacks. The challenge to program planners, Dr. Roberson concludes, is how to develop definitive research initiatives related to the design of cancer control interventions for Blacks.

Dr. Stanley Broadnax describes a community approach to promoting anticancer efforts among Blacks that uses a network of local agencies and community organizations in the Cincinnati, Ohio, metropolitan area. Dr. Broadnax concludes that the strength of this effort is its success in attracting peer-group volunteers and in effectively coordinating the resources of funded organizations in targeting the Black community.

Dr. William A. Darity outlines a long-term, community-oriented project that emphasized educational principles and the involvement of community residents. A major objective of the study is to develop community-oriented smoking intervention strategies to motivate smokers in Black communities to stop smoking cigarettes.

Betty Lee Hawks discusses smoking and cancer among Asian and Pacific Islander Americans. She notes that researchers relative lack of interest in the smoking habits of this population may be attributed to an inadequate data base. Current statistics show it is the fastest-growing segment of the U.S. population, a fact that underscores the importance of understanding cancer incidence and mortality in this group. Hawks feels that studies are needed to determine the knowledge, attitudes, and practices of Asian/Pacific Islander groups with respect to smoking-related cancer and tobacco use.

Dr. Alan Blum discusses how cigarette advertisers have slowly changed their focus from upscale publications to downscale ones or other media more likely to gain the attention of Black and ethnic minority readers as well as blue-collar workers, who increasingly constitute the smoking public. Dr. Blum notes that lung cancer, a major consequence of smoking, is principal among the rising preventable causes of death in minority populations.

Our overall challenge lies in convincing Blacks and other minorities that there is a direct relationship between life-style choices and the risk of contracting cancer.

9. Cancer Education Programs

Noma L. Roberson

The disproportionately severe impact of cancer on certain minority groups in the United States, particularly Black Americans, suggests that cancer is a major health problem in these groups that warrants attention. This is suggested by national data that show Black Americans, the largest minority group in the United States, experience the highest overall age-adjusted cancer rates in both incidence and mortality and the lowest survival of any U.S. population group (Baquet and Ringen 1986; Cutler and Young 1979; Garfinkel et al. 1980; Henschke et al. 1973; Myers 1981; SEER 1984).

Recent reports state that the goals and objectives of the National Cancer Institute and the American Cancer Society are to improve cancer rates among minorities over the next few years (Report of Subcommittee for Cancer 1986; Report of Secretary's Task Force 1986). However, an issue of growing importance is the identification of mechanisms by which national goals of reducing cancer incidence and mortality can be translated into programs tailored for defined population groups.

The ultimate utility of carcinogenetic and epidemiologic research rests in the application of knowledge to specific programs of cancer control at the community and individual levels. Application of knowledge may best be applied through cancer education programs. The aim of this paper is to discuss the planning process necessary to tailor cancer education programs that may influence health behavior and thus promote cancer control.

Background

Epidemiologic studies suggest that Black/White differences in cancer mortality rates can be reduced by increased cancer control activities (e.g., cancer education) (Warnecke 1981; White et al. 1981; Windsor et al. 1978). Unfortunately, traditional methods of providing cancer education to the public often have failed to reach Blacks. There is little evidence that interventions designed to improve accessibility and utilization of cancer education programs address the special characteristics of Blacks. In addition, there is little information about knowledge, beliefs, and behaviors relevant to cancer and the planned interventions that target Blacks.

These factors are often overlooked during the planning process. In most cases, national survey data and a few descriptive studies are used to design the intervention. Although national survey data can be useful, they tend to identify a set of generalizable intervention models believed to function effectively in diverse communities. Evidence from several studies (Griffiths 1980; Lynch and Ronis 1982; Rogers and Shoemaker 1971; Ross 1981; Suchman 1965) indicates that if educational programs are tailored to the needs and cultures of specific population groups, they can effectively increase knowledge, change beliefs, and modify health behavior.

Cancer Education

Because the purpose of cancer education is to modify health behavior, it may be an important component of cancer control among Blacks. More specifically, cancer education programs that are planned and tailored for this population are likely to have a significant impact on knowledge, beliefs, and behavior relevant to disease control.

Cancer education programs, like all educational efforts, are designed to affect the perceptions of those who are exposed to them. Before planning cancer education programs, it may be important to define cancer education, know its specific aims, understand how it may influence behavior, and understand how cancer is perceived by the target audience.

According to Wakefield (1975), the aims of cancer education are to educate the public, particularly high-risk groups, about treatable forms of cancer; to provide an environment for motivating people to initiate and maintain preventive health behaviors; to encourage people to undergo tests designed to detect cancer in the early stages; and to assure people that early detection and treatment are beneficial. In essence, the emphasis of cancer education is on modifying behavior.

The complex process by which health behavior is modified through cancer education is not well understood. Health behavior is generally believed, however, to be modified by several related factors that include dissemination of information, personal or face-to-face communication, technical advances, economic conditions, and enactment of regulations and laws (Griffiths 1980).

Social science research indicates that individuals may go through an orderly decision-making process before modifying or adopting a particular behavior. Five distinct stages have been identified for most people in this process (Beal and Klonglon 1976, unpublished report).

In the first, the awareness stage, individuals hear about the new idea but know few details. In the information stage, they develop an interest in and knowledge of the new idea and perhaps see its possible application. At the next step, evaluation, they rehearse the new idea mentally; at the trial stage, they try out the idea and decide whether to use it. Lastly, they adopt the new habit if it has personal benefit. This process may be the key to motivating people to act, once knowledge is disseminated by educational programs.

A wide range of communication and educational methods should be employed systematically in a cancer education program based on what people in the target population currently know, believe, and do about cancer. In this respect, program objectives might be to increase awareness about a subject, alter people's attitudes and involvement, influence their actual behavior or action, or produce a combination of these.

Intervention Targets

The intervention targets may be diverse. Cancer education programs may concern one particular cancer site such as the breast or lung, and they may be directed to a specific segment of the population such as community residents, health center clients, and health professionals for a specific period of time. Or, like the American Cancer Society's continuing education program, the discussions may attract the widest possible audience by emphasizing cancer categories and sites with a high prevention or life-saving potential.

The diversity of intervention targets reflects the multiplicity of intervention levels that should be considered when planning cancer education programs and the difficulty that may be associated with attempting to target such programs. According to Rappaport (1972), program planners should consider at least four levels — individual, small group, organization, and community — in setting up targeted intervention programs. Most planners are familiar with individual and small-group levels, the first being person-centered, the other involving interpersonal communications. Organizational and community levels tend to be more complex. At the organizational level, cancer control strategies include modifying the program for implementation by existing organizations, for example, screening offered by community hospitals. At the fourth level, community institutions, the strategy focuses on social advocacy and alternative settings for health services, for example, church-based screening sites.

Planning a Cancer Education Program

Five elements are believed to be critical to the success of any cancer education program (Cullen 1984; Donaldson 1983; James 1978; Lieberman 1978). First, a committee to plan and supervise the program should include persons who represent the population targeted to be served. Such a committee may have ties to specific groups of an area and provide unique strategies for reaching these people. Besides establishing cancer education goals and deciding on methods of achieving them, the committee should provide means of measuring performance and evaluating results.

The second element believed to be critical to the success of cancer education programs is defining the local cancer problem. Specifically, planners should know cancer incidence and mortality rates by major sites for segments of the population at high risk. The target population's knowledge, beliefs, and health practices in relation to cancer as well as the availability of medical facilities are also important to understand when examining the local cancer problem.

Third, a wide range of health education and communication methods should be used to capitalize on the strength of each. No educational method is effective alone; combination of didactic and two-way communication techniques uses the best assets of each. Mass media communication and personal contact are commonly used in cancer education programs.

Fourth, a procedure or instrument to measure program success is needed. An evaluation of this sort may require both qualitative and quantitative analysis, particularly if programs are community-based. The particular evaluation design will vary, depending on whether the planners want to measure short-term or long-term effects and whether they are dealing with experimentally produced or natural variations (Lieberman 1978). These factors require careful consideration during the planning process, particularly if program success is based on dispersal of a message as well as its effectiveness.

The last element is the need for sufficient funds and manpower to carry out the plans. Basically, the first year of cost is operational, and programs generally are viewed as pilot efforts. During the planning phase, therefore, decisions about funding and manpower will also determine the feasibility of continuing the program after the first year.

A flow chart for planning minority cancer education (Figure 1) is based on my research in a community setting in Buffalo, New York (Roberson 1985). Basic issues in community planning were the identification of types and amount of intervention, lead time to establish programs, length of time to operate programs, eligibility criteria, and evaluation of the cumulative effects and effects of various strategies (Berkanovic et al. 1983; Roberson 1985).

Interacting factors believed to hinder communication among minority groups were identified as language, class, and culture (Sue and Sue 1977; Vontress 1971). Class-based values are important to consider because minorities are disproportionately represented in the lower classes, whose members struggle with day-to-day crises. This experience tends to involve them in tangible, immediate problems and does not favor a conceptual or anticipatory approach to situations. For this reason, members of most racial minorities do best with health education directed toward defined problems they recognize and toward a specific course of action they see as reasonable and possible.

Culture-bound values are used to judge normality and abnormality among various population groups (Sue and Sue 1977). Culture may be viewed as a learned and transmitted blueprint for living that guides a particular group's thoughts and actions (Jones 1972). In Western society, a basic manifestation is the attempt of the dominant group to impose its standards, beliefs, and ways of behaving on the minority group. Thus, minorities are placed under strong pressures to adopt the

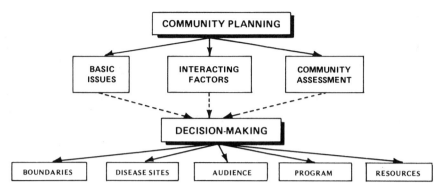

FIGURE 1. Flow chart for planning community-based programs.

ways of the dominant culture; their own ethnicity or cultural heritage is seen as a handicap to be overcome, and to be different is to be deviant. Variables of language, class, and culture are important in planning cancer education when emphasis is on designing programs sensitive to cultural characteristics.

For community assessment, the last area of consideration in the planning process, availability and utilization of health services, is taken into account, as are the social services available to specific population groups. During community assessment program planners learn about the community's attitude to cancer and about community problems and support mechanisms.

Organizing the Program

Investigating basic issues, exploring interacting factors, and conducting a community assessment led to our decisions about geographic boundaries, disease sites, audience, program, and resources. Thus, the Minority Cancer Education Program was conducted in inner-city Buffalo, New York, and targeted to minority groups over 18 years of age. Programs concentrated on breast and lung cancer.

The framework of our cancer education program was based on the interrelationship of several components (Roberson 1987). Cancer education aimed at high-risk minority populations requires effective strategies and communication techniques for channeling cancer detection messages appropriately. Cancer education is believed to be essential to cancer-related knowledge and beliefs that eventually result in a decision to act. When an action is adopted as a health practice, the expected outcome is eventually improved cancer rates.

Our Minority Cancer Education Program involved extensive planning by community leaders and residents representative of their community. Six categories of volunteers made up a network that played significant roles in planning, operating, and evaluating the programs. Two important contributions were the development of culturally sensitive educational materials and assistance with recruiting program participants.

More than 500 community residents participated in the cancer education programs, and we do not know how many people were reached by our intensified media campaign. Our evaluation showed that afterwards the participants had more cancer-related knowledge and that health practices related to prevention or early detection of breast and lung cancer improved.

According to the objectives set for the program, our pilot project was successful as the result of a combination of factors: a human service approach, neighborhood cooperation, program visibility, program identity, and service flexibility (Roberson 1985). Because a great deal of consideration was given to each of these during the planning process, one may be inclined to believe that planning contributed to the program's success.

Summary

Cancer education programs are vehicles necessary to disseminate knowledge and modify health behavior conducive to cancer control. For Black Americans, and members of other minorities, cancer education programs must be properly planned, organized, and evaluated so that cancer rates may be reduced over time. This presents a challenge to program planners in that definitive research is lacking for this area and little is known about the design of cancer control interventions for Blacks. Clearly, future research needs to be concerned with program planning if we expect cancer education efforts to be well-designed and directed effectively to minorities in the United States.

References

Baquet CR, Ringen K: Cancer among black and other minorities: Statistical profiles. National Cancer Institute, Division of Cancer Prevention and Control, NIH Publication No. 80-2785, 1986.

Berkanovic E, Gerber B, Brown H, et al: Some issues concerning community-based chronic disease control programs. In Mettlin C, Murphy GP (eds): *Progress in Cancer Control. IV: Research in the Cancer Center.* New York: Alan R Liss, 1983, pp 271–281.

Cullen JW: The organization of community disease prevention services. *Cancer Detect Prev* 1984;7:225–235.

Cutler SL, Young JL: Cancer incidence and mortality in Black Americans. In *Proceedings of the National Conference on Meeting the Challenge of Cancer among Black Americans.* New York: American Cancer Society, 1979, pp 15–20.

Donaldson WS: Ohio's mortality based system for identification of cancer intervention programs. In Mettlin C, Murphy GP (eds): *Progress in Cancer Control. IV: Research in the Cancer Center.* New York: Alan R Liss, 1983, pp 261–270.

Garfinkel L, Poindexter CE, Silverberg E: Cancer among Black Americans. *CA* 30:39–43.

Griffiths W: Can human behavior be modified? *Cancer* 1980;47:1221–1225.

James W: Overview of methods of public education. In Nieburgs HE (ed): *Prevention and Detection of Cancer.* New York: Marcel Dekker, 1978, pp 2323–2327.

Jones JM: *Prejudice and Racism.* Reading, MA: Addison-Wesley, 1972.

Henschke UK, Leffall LD, Mason CH, et al: Alarming increases of the cancer mortality in the U.S. black population (1950–1967). *Cancer* 1973;31:763–768.

Lieberman S: Methods of evaluating the effectiveness of cancer education programs. In Nieburgs HE (ed): *Prevention and Detection of Cancer.* New York: Marcel Dekker, 1978, pp 2329–2334.

Lynch PD, Ronis DL: Cancer information for blacks: A radio program evaluation. *Prog Clin Biol Res.* New York: Alan R Liss, 1982, pp 399–408.

Myers MH: Survival from cancer by blacks and whites. In Mettin C, Murphy GP (eds): *Cancer Among Black Populations.* New York: Alan R Liss, 1981, pp 151–165.

Rappaport J: *Community Psychology: Values, Research, and Action.* New York: Holt, Rinehart, and Winston, 1977, pp 164–165.

Report of the Subcommittee on Cancer in the Economically Disadvantaged. New York: American Cancer Society, 1986.

Report of the Secretary's Task Force on Black and Minority Health, Vol III, Cancer. Bethesda, MD: U.S. Department of Health and Human Services, 1986.

Roberson NL: *A Cancer Control Intervention for Black Americans in Buffalo, New York: A Case Study.* Doctoral dissertation. New York: State University of New York at Buffalo, 1985.

Roberson NL: A community-based cancer education program. *Union Internationale Contrele Cancer: Technical Report Series. Public Education. VICC:* Geneva, 1987; 80:33–40.

Rogers EM, Shoemaker EF: *Communication of Innovations: A Cross-Cultural Approach.* New York: Free Press, 1971.

Ross CR: Factors influencing successful preventive health education. *Health Educ Q* 1981;8:187–208.

Suchman EA: Social factors in medical deprivation. *Am J Public Health* 1965;55:1725–1733.

Sue DW, Sue D: Barriers to effective cross-cultural counseling. *Journal of Counseling Psychology* 1977;24:420–429.

Surveillance, Epidemiology and End Results, 1980–1981. Washington, DC: Biometry Branch, National Cancer Institute, 1984.

Vontress C: Racial differences: Impediments to rapport. *Journal of Counseling Psychology* 1971;18:7–13.

Wakefield J: Education of the public. In Fraumeni JF (ed): *Persons at High Risk of Cancer,* New York: Academic Press, 1975, pp 415–434.

Warnecke RB: Interventions in black populations. In Mettlin C, Murphy GP (eds): *Cancer Among Black Populations.* New York: Alan R Liss, 1981, pp 167–187.

White JE, Enterline JP, Alam Z, et al: Cancer among blacks in the United States — recognizing the problem. In Mettlin C, Murphy GP (eds): *Cancer Among Black Populations.* New York: Alan R Liss, 1981, pp 35–58.

Windsor RA, Kronefeld JJ, Kilzo J: An evaluation of a community health education program in breast and uterine cancer. Los Angeles: *American Public Health Association,* 1978.

10. Community-Based Cancer Education

Stanley E. Broadnax

Funding Dilemmas

Education and prevention programs targeted to minorities are critically needed. Massive amounts of data support the notions that the environment, life-styles, educational disadvantages, barriers to health care, and economic inequalities have all played a part in the disparities in health status between American minorities and Whites.

For many public and private agencies, particularly those depending on grants and public tax support, these kinds of education, prevention, and early-intervention health programs become victims of budget cuts and get defeated in the priorities battle with direct health service programs. Although health education and prevention are cost-effective health programs, many funding sources give direct health service programs higher priorities.

To illustrate this point I can use the city of Cincinnati. I am the commissioner of health for Cincinnati. We have the largest health department in Ohio, and even though we are the third-largest city, we have a budget of roughly $26 million and a staff of 650 people.

We run a variety of programs. These include traditional public health programs such as environmental services, restaurant inspection, weights and measures, community public health nursing, licensing and inspection of nursing homes and day care centers, and treatment for sexually transmitted diseases. In addition, we participate in and operate a large primary health care network. We have 12 community health centers; six are owned and operated by our department and six by independent nonprofit community governing boards. For the Cincinnati Health Department's network of health centers we have a budget of about $12 million. We provide comprehensive services, obstetrics/gynecology, adult medicine, and pediatrics. Our staff includes social workers and some public health educators; our centers have pharmacies and diagnostic laboratories.

As the director of the Health Department, I am constantly juggling funds, constantly trying to review programs and set priorities. The $26 million budget includes 19 grants, six of which total $6 million.

At the local level, we often find that, when other funding entities look at priorities, they will fund physicians and nurses, and sometimes laboratory technicians and pharmacists, but they start cutting out psychosocial workers, public health educators, and outreach workers. This is nothing new, and I am sure that everyone working in direct service delivery has similar experiences. So when we look at the issue of health education in general, and cancer among minorities in particular, there are many funding hurdles to be overcome.

Finding Alternatives for Funding and Program Development

The governor of Ohio organized a task force on minority health, provided a small amount of money, and established an Office of Minority Health in the Ohio Department of Health. Funds were made available to look at cancer rates in the Black community as a special initiative and to obtain some grants for health promotion and health education. The state officials organized a nice application process; we applied, and they awarded us the whopping sum of $9000—for a community of nearly 35,000 Black persons whom we were supposed to influence with this program. We had to be truly creative and innovative in trying to figure out how we were going to accomplish this feat. We started with the major premise of networking.

Other community organizations were concerned about the problem but were following their own paths, with little coordination and few links between them. Our first strategy was to build a network with the $9000 grant, using part of it to pay for some work on the project by the department's health education workers and a nurse. But most of the work was done as in-kind or donated services. We set the need to contribute staff time as a priority in the health department, and contacted the American Cancer Society's local affiliate, the American Heart Association, the University of Cincinnati's Cancer Control Consortium, Cancer Family Care, which is a United Appeal agency that provides some counseling and support services for cancer patients and their relatives, Romans Psychiatric Institute, Operation PUSH, and the board of education. The Gaines United Methodist Church, a Black church whose minister had a widely known television ministry, also became involved in the network. The church, through its ministry, had done much community service with discussions of critical issues in the Black community. The church leaders were eager to participate. We brought all of these people together, and with that $9000 we generated in-kind services from the other agencies of at least $100,000, not including our donated staff time and talent, and donated supplies and materials.

Program Definition and Implementation

The premise on which we started was that, to make life-style choices or changes, individuals must have information and must realize that a problem exists.

Another premise was that all people tend to adopt health behaviors of their social stratum and that we needed to reach peer leaders. One of our working principles was to involve community leaders with whom people in our target population were familiar and with whom they could identify; this would increase the likelihood of behavioral changes.

We wanted to target cancer education to the Black community to increase knowledge of the disease and promote preventive steps individuals could take to reduce their risks of cancer. In addition, our goals were and are to help individuals understand the importance of early detection and its relation to successful cancer treatment and to dispel the feelings of hopelessness and helplessness that often inhibit early intervention. We wanted to consolidate and share information on the variety of treatments, services, and support activities offered in our community.

We looked at a number of methods of disseminating information; we wanted to go where the people were. We wanted to identify where we would get the largest congregations of folks on a fairly regular basis. This focused our attention on the Black churches, the barber shops, the beauty shops, the schools, and the community health centers. We wanted to use as many approaches as possible. In addition, we explored the use of public service announcements in print and broadcast.

In Health Centers

What did we do with this consortium? What were the activities? In the health centers we made use of the waiting rooms. That is nothing new, nothing novel. The difficulty of most health centers is that they do not have enough resources to assign a staff member to the waiting room to take advantage of the patients' unoccupied time. By conducting small group sessions focusing on health prevention and promotion, we now have contact with about 390 persons per quarter year in the health centers, where even the environment encourages the discussions.

In School

The schools were another tough situation to approach, but an interested person in the school system said, "Yes, that is an important activity. Let's try to work together on something." When we organized an essay contest for junior high and high schools, students from seven schools contributed essays on what cancer is and how it is related to the Black community. One of the network organizations offered $100 as first prize and $50 as second prize. The students had to read material and produce pamphlets, and they submitted some really interesting papers. The key, of course, was to heighten their awareness and stimulate their thinking, in the hope that this would arouse some discussion at home. The project also involved the teachers who helped the students with their research. We gave awards to the winners and certificates to every student who participated. Some of them were presented by one of the Cincinnati Bengals, and the University of Cincinnati basketball coach came and shook hands. Parents, teachers, and some of the school officials were there; the ceremony turned into a media event through which we promoted the notion of cancer awareness and the possibilities of lowering risks in the Black community.

In Churches

The Black church provided additional challenges. In Gaines United Methodist Church, the pastor's wife had died of cancer, and the pastor was interested in organizing an education program with other Black ministers. In letters signed by the pastor and me, we asked all Black congregations in Cincinnati to recruit one volunteer who could coordinate cancer education activities for that church. The plan was to train the coordinators to organize and lead seminars. The first year 20 church representatives held small workshops with our help, put up posters, and distributed other educational materials in the church, always making sure that the announcements made every Sunday included one about these materials. The church coordinators organized groups on smoking cessation with help from the local American Heart Association and American Lung Association.

In Beauty and Barber Shops

The beauty and barber shops, whose 150 owners we wrote letters, were and still are an interesting experience. Fortunately, because the Health Department formerly licensed and inspected these shops, the proprietors never ignored a communication from us. The 150 requests mailed the first year brought responses from 50 beauty and barber shop operators who said they would come to a training session to learn about cancer concepts, cancer prevention, and the seven warning signs and symptoms and display reading materials and posters in their shops.

Our goal for the second year is to recruit 50 more volunteers from the beauty and barber shops, places nearly everyone visits from time to time. The conversation is usually casual and touches many topics. We train our volunteers occasionally to mention the poster displayed on the wall, not to engage in intellectual dialogue to transmit information but to heighten sensitivity and spark some curiosity. This might lead the other person to pick up a pamphlet or an announcement of a seminar.

Evaluating the Program

Of the three facets of the program — planning, implementation, and evaluation — the last has been more difficult with only $9000 in state funds. Because our project depends on in-kind services from the other organizational participants, we cannot carry out the kind of reliable evaluation we like to do, especially of the project's effectiveness. Health outcome and health status are always difficult to measure and gauge, and so we could only evaluate the program's process.

We documented the number of presentations, displays, participants in the various activities, number and type of pamphlets and posters distributed and type preferred, number of volunteers trained, and number of schools participating in the essay contest.

One of our network agencies conducted a one-day seminar for teachers so they could respond to students' questions related to the essay and any other curiosities aroused by the contest; we measured those ingredients.

We allocated part of the $9000 state grant to the church to help pay some of their costs in producing video announcements. We did wonders with that $9000. I almost felt like I could walk on water after that experience.

The last thing we tried to do was surveys before and after our presentations, but many of those were difficult to conduct because our meetings were informal and unstructured in waiting rooms, barber, and beauty shops.

My principal message is that it is not how much money you have, but what you can do with the resources already in the neighborhood. Key ingredients are creativity, coordination, and consolidation of efforts to address such a serious issue.

11. Cancer Prevention (Smoking) in the Black Population: A Community Research/Intervention Model

William A. Darity, George B. Cernada, Ted T.L. Chen, Harris Pastides, Edward G. Stanek III, Robert W. Tuthill, and Alvin Winder

Introduction

There is evidence of a strong relationship between certain cancers and cigarette smoking. The incidence rates for important smoking-related cancers of the lung, esophagus, larynx, and pancreas are higher in Blacks than in Whites in the United States, and a greater proportion of Blacks smoke cigarettes.

We have developed a community intervention model to test a series of hypotheses about the effectiveness of active community participation and education in promoting smoking cessation at the neighborhood community level.

Background

The cancer mortality rate in the Black population of the United States has been increasing over the last 30 years. In calculating this from a differential deficit ratio (DDR)[1] perspective, there is the increasing gap between the White and the Black population. When 1950 rates are compared with the 1980 rates, the gap becomes wider between the races for both sexes (Darity and Pitt 1979; Darity 1986–1987). In 1950 the number of deaths per 100,000 population from cancer for Black males was 125.4 and for White males, 126.1, for a DDR of −0.0037.[2] In 1980 the rate for Black males was 229.9 and for White males 160.5, for a DDR of 0.432. In other words, the death rate difference between Black and White males changed from a −0.37% lower death rate in Black males compared with White males to a 42.7% higher death rate. In 1950 the death rate per 100,000

---

[1]The differential deficit ratio (DDR) is the percentage deficit observed between the Black population and the white population, even when there are decreases in existing rates of mortality for both groups. The DDR is calculated according to the following formula: $[(B_R - W_R)/W_R = DDR]$ when B_R = rate for Blacks, W_R = rate for whites, and DDR = differential deficit ratio.

[2]The minus symbol indicates the rates are higher in the white population.

from cancer was 131.9 for Black women and 119.4 for White women, the DDR being 0.095. In 1980, when the cancer death rate per 100,000 Black women decreased slightly to 129.7 and a more substantial decrease to 107.4 occurred per 100,000 among White women, the DDR was 0.204, an increase over the 30-year period from a deficit of 9.5% to a deficit of 20.4% (Darity 1982, unpublished).

Cancer Rates and Sites

In comparing smoking-related cancer incidence rates in 1980 among Blacks and Whites by sites, the incidence rate per 100,000 population for esophageal cancer was 12 for Blacks and 3 for Whites, for a rate four times higher in the Black population.

The incidence rate per 100,000 for cancer of the larynx was 4.75 for Whites and approximately 7 for Blacks, yielding a DDR of 47.4%. For lung cancer the rate was 70 for Blacks and 50 for Whites, for a DDR of 40%. And for pancreatic cancer the rate was 14 for Blacks and 9 for Whites, for a DDR of 56% (Baquet et al. 1986).

When racial/ethnic/gender incidence-rate comparisons were made for esophageal carcinoma (McBride and Richter 1985), the incidence for Black males was 28.6/100,000 population and for White males 6/100,000, almost five times higher in the Black population. As McBride and Richter pointed out, the frequency of esophageal carcinoma is increasing among Black Americans; cigarette smoking is a risk factor in the development of esophageal carcinoma and may work concomitantly with alcohol to increase the risk of development of this disease. Prevention of this cancer might be enhanced by health education programs against alcohol and smoking (Pattern et al. 1981).

Age-specific mortality rates of bladder cancer in the U.S. show that the rates for non-White males exceed those for White males at younger ages but that rates are higher for White men after the 35- to 44-year age span. Mortality rates for non-White women are higher than those for White women at all ages up to the 75- to 84-year-old group (Centers for Disease Control 1987; Devesa and Diamond 1983).

In 1984 the annual age-adjusted incidence rates of bladder cancer per 100,000 persons in the U.S. were 31 for White men, 15 for Black men, 7 for White women, and 4.5 for Black women. Bladder cancer incidence and mortality data collected in the Third National Cancer Survey showed a stable mortality rate but a rising incidence in White males. In non-White males, incidence and mortality rates are rising, but incidence is increasing at a faster rate. Both rates are declining in White females, whereas incidence is declining and mortality is remaining stable in non-White females (Baquet et al. 1986).

Evidence from epidemiologic studies consistently shows that cigarette smokers have two to three times the risk of bladder cancer of nonsmokers and that the risk of bladder cancer increases with increasing frequency of cigarette consumption.

In reviewing the relationship of socioeconomic status and lung cancer incidence rates in a metropolitan area in which 2354 cases of lung cancer were diagnosed from 1969 to 1971, Devesa and Diamond (1983) found the age-adjusted rate for the lowest-income White groups was 20% higher than that of the highest-income White group. The patterns in this study were similar among Black and White males, but the difference in range between the lowest-income and highest-income Blacks was much smaller than the difference in range between lowest-income and highest-income Whites (Young et al. 1981).

Cancer Prevention

In discussing cancer prevention, White and his colleagues (1981) wrote:

It appears that the major underlying factor contributing to the poor health status of U.S. Blacks (relative to U.S. Whites) is their relatively low socioeconomic status (SES). The low SES . . . not only makes it difficult for them to obtain the goods and services necessary for a high-quality lifestyle, but makes it difficult to concentrate on more future oriented goals such as regular medical checkups, preventative health practices, and entering the medical system at early stages of disease.

They continued:

The high mortality rates found among U.S. Blacks are, in reality, the end result of many factors. Not only are they the end results of high cancer incidence rates among Blacks and poor survival once cancer is detected, but they are also the results of many indirect contributing factors such as high risk lifestyles, environmental and occupational exposure to carcinogenics, and poor overall health resulting from relatively low SES.

The authors, among their recommendations, emphasized primary prevention as an essential aspect of any cancer program. Stating that "the goal of primary prevention should be to effect the removal of all cancer causing and promoting factors from the environment, thus reducing the occurrence of cancer," they specifically recommended that future cancer research and control programs for Blacks include a greater concentration on primary and secondary cancer prevention among the high-risk Black population; funding of epidemiologic studies in three high-risk Black populations, those of Washington, D.C., Baltimore, and New Orleans; and funding of studies to determine effective methods for reaching Blacks with appropriate health information.

Smoking Incidence

A major contributing factor to the high incidence of cancer is smoking practices among Blacks. For example, the Centers for Disease Control, in a report on cigarette smoking released in September 1987, observed that in 1986 32.5% of Black males in the United States smoked compared with 29.3% of White males. For those between the ages of 25 and 34 years, however, 45.9% of Black men smoked compared with 32.4% of male Whites. When Black and White women were compared, 25.1% of Black compared with 23.7% of White women smoked. At ages 25 to 34, however, the percentage of Black women who smoked was

30.9% compared with 29.1% for White women; for the 35- to 44-year-old group, the rate was 36.4% for Black compared with 27.6% of White women.

Survival Rates

Data from four cancer registries—California, Connecticut, the University of Iowa, and Charity Hospital, New Orleans—showed that for 1964 to 1973, the five-year survival rates for esophageal cancer were 4% for Whites and 2% for Blacks; for cancer of the lung and bronchus, the five-year survival rates were 64% for Whites and 45% for Blacks.

Among women, the five-year survival rates for esophageal cancer were 5% for Whites and 1% for Blacks; for lung and bronchus, 13% for Whites and 9% for Blacks. For cancer of the larynx, the five-year survival rates were 56% for White and 49% for Black women (Myers 1981).

These studies and data indicate a need for research on prevention and for effective methods of intervention.

A Long-Term Smoking Cessation Program

Rationale

Cancer is a leading cause of death in the United States. Through concerted efforts of the National Cancer Institute, voluntary health agencies, and related health institutions, the cancer mortality and morbidity rates of Americans have shown some improvement in the past decade. One exception, however, is that no clear reduction of cancer mortality and morbidity rates have been found among Black Americans, whose rates remain the highest of all racial groups in the United States. When one considers the fact that cigarette smoking has long been recognized as the most preventable risk factor of cancer, the need to reduce the rate of smoking among Black populations to control related rates of cancer morbidity and mortality is apparent, because all data point to highly unfavorable cigarette smoking patterns among Blacks as promoting high rates of some cancers.

The major purpose of our research study, therefore, was to develop a smoking intervention program with the aim of motivating smokers in Black communities to stop smoking cigarettes.

The smoking intervention program consists of two parts, a passive aspect (control) and an active aspect (experimental). The passive intervention consists basically of the use of communication through the mass media. The active intervention consists, in addition to use of mass media, of applying principles of community organization and community education to the problem, establishing community-wide advisory committees and recruiting neighborhood opinion leaders to organize a neighborhood task force for antismoking, identified as smoking and health committees. Health resource agencies, churches, and social action organizations are also being contacted to provide both the programs and a supportive network in the community for the antismoking campaign.

The principles of the health belief model (Rosenstock 1974) are being applied to develop education messages to help smokers recognize that smoking is hazardous to their health, that it is a serious problem, that it is beneficial for them to change the smoking habit, and that an opportunity to quit is available. Moreover, barriers that make it difficult for smokers to change their habits are identified in order to be removed. Self-help kits and mass media messages are being designed to reach Black smokers in their households to provide motivation and guidance for changing smoking behaviors.

The concept of the adoption/diffusion theory (Rogers and Shoemaker 1971) is being applied using early adopters of smoking-behavior change as the models to lead other smokers in the community to change their smoking behavior. Smokers desiring to quit smoking through cessation programs will be invited to enroll in such a program.

The smoking intervention program initiated for this study is a long-term, community-oriented project that emphasizes the application of education principles and involvement of community residents. The variable of community organization will enhance these efforts by providing a supportive atmosphere in the active intervention areas for smokers to quit and to maintain this nonsmoking behavior.

Objectives

The major objective of this five-year study is to develop community-oriented smoking intervention strategies to motivate smokers in Black communities to stop smoking cigarettes.

The subobjectives proposed to achieve the main objectives are to:

1. Investigate the relative efforts of passive and active intervention strategies on changing smoking behaviors in middle- and lower-income Black communities over a three-year period.
2. Determine how smoking-behavior change differs in middle- and lower-income communities, by southern and northern location, by gender, and other characteristics.
3. Assess the cognitive and attitudinal characteristics of Black smokers related to successful smoking-cessation behaviors.
4. Evaluate the effectiveness of the passive and active intervention strategies in increasing knowledge of the health effects of smoking.
5. Compare and document the relative change in community attitudes and behaviors affected by the active and passive intervention program components over a three-year period.

Hypotheses

This is a community-based intervention study in which four communities in three geographic areas (one northern and two southern) form the basis of comparison. The northern site is Hartford, Connecticut, and Springfield, Massachusetts combined; the southern sites are Columbia, South Carolina, and Durham, North Carolina. The intervention control settings designated in the above areas are low-income Black neighborhoods and middle-income Black neighborhoods in which one each will serve as active (experimental) and one each as passive (control) intervention sites. The numerous behavioral objectives targeted for change are phrased in terms of the study hypotheses.

Intervention Strategies

Passive Intervention Goals

The passive intervention campaign beginning in year 2 has as its overall goal, as is also the case of active intervention, the reduction of smoking behavior among the target population. The methods used, however, will be restricted to mass media, particularly radio, newspapers, TV, and indigenous printed news vehicles such as community newsletters and Black newspapers.

Since much of the mass media intervention will, by its nature, reach the active intervention targets, it will be designed to support the active intervention as well. The power of combining mass media and community organization efforts has been well documented—for example, in the North Keralia project's successful efforts to reduce chronic disease rates in Finland (Puska and Koskela 1983).

Both passive and active campaigns will be based on the findings of the year 2 survey, which should provide guidelines for our audience's media habits, including program preferences and trust in specific media and their awareness, knowledge, attitudes, and behavior regarding health and smoking. Newspaper and broadcast authorities will be consulted.

The educational objectives of the mass media campaign can be summarized as twofold: dissemination of information about the negative aspects of smoking and positive health outcomes of stopping cigarette smoking; and dissemination of information about the opportunities for smokers to take action to stop the habit. The former will create awareness as well as provide specific information about health outcomes; the latter will be directed more to smokers who may be ready to quit. The former will receive the heavier emphasis during the early part of the campaign, with mass media messages directed to creating awareness and providing information.

Both public service announcements (PSAs) as well as limited commercial spots will be used on radio and TV. In general, the emphasis will be on brief spot announcements with novel approaches that gear into the cognitive framework of the study audience. To some extent, counteradvertising will be used, particularly in the printed medium.

All materials developed have been pretested in the Springfield area, under the guidance of the University of Massachusetts, for readability, comprehension, believability, personal relevance, recall, and other target-audience reactions. A small number of tests were done for each message and medium used, generally with such cost-effective methods as self-administered questionnaires and intercept interviews at central locations. The sharper targeting of focus group sessions will, however, be emphasized. In addition, printed materials have been pretested for readability. A modified version of the standard set of core questions developed by the Health Message Testing Service (HMTS) of the National Cancer Institute's Office of Cancer Communications will be used as relevant for radio and television PSAs.

The overall goal is to have a fairly standardized media campaign across the three project sites that is targeted to low- and middle-income Black communities. Continual monitoring of the media inputs will be done to assure as much standardization as possible. The general media strategy is to seek high-frequency, high-quality saturation and novel approaches over a reasonable duration of time. Other materials are being developed locally.

Summary of Passive Intervention Activities

Radio. Existing public service announcements will be supplemented by paid commercial spot announcements developed by the project. Primary use will be of local radio stations listened to heavily and trusted by the Black community. Content will focus on positive health and social advantages of not smoking. Local role models who have stopped smoking will be used when possible.

Television. PSAs will be used as available, supplemented by occasional commercial spot announcements developed by the project.

Newspapers. Two media channels will be emphasized: local newspapers (dailies) read frequently and trusted by the Black community and indigenous newspapers directed to the Black community (usually weekly). News releases, letters to the editor, guest columns, and special feature articles will be produced or adapted.

Magazines. Where possible, feature articles will be developed for local magazines (e.g., Sunday newspaper supplements, special geographic interest publications).

Logo. A logo to help the community associate smoking with positive health and social values will be developed and integrated into the overall media campaign.

Active Intervention: Theory

The active intervention program is based on several theories of behavioral science. The first is community organization theory, namely, that effective social planning makes it possible to solve substantive social problems (Abrams et al. 1986; Milroy 1982). The basic strategy of this approach is gathering facts about the problem, in this case, smoking behavior, and deciding how to influence the community and individual members through an effective course of action.

The client role in this model of community organization is that of recipients or consumer participants in the intervention strategies. Specifically, active intervention aims to induce in the consumer an awareness of the need to cease smoking as well as a readiness to participate in community activities that have been organized as opportunities to quit. Participation by community members is further enhanced by local members of the health and smoking committees.

A second, related theory, that of the health belief model (Janz and Becker 1984) is that persons define health and make health judgments according to a framework of beliefs. Although a belief system does not cause action, it stimulates and orients action. According to the health belief model, the likelihood of undertaking health action is a function of a person's beliefs along four subjective dimensions: perceived level of personal susceptibility to a particular condition, perceived degree of severity of consequences that might result from a condition occurring, estimation of the recommended health action's potential benefits or efficacy in preventing or reducing susceptibility, and severity and views of possible psychological and other cost barriers related to the proposed action. In addition, the health belief model stipulates that a stimulus or cue to action is necessary to trigger the appropriate health behavior by making people conscious of their thoughts and feelings about the condition. This final aspect of the health belief model is provided by passive intervention (the media) as well as a newsletter and other active educational efforts. The literature on smoking offers strong support for the idea that beliefs about smoking can be influenced by knowledge about the consequences of smoking (Flay 1987). This support for the influence of the media as a cue to action leads us to contend that a media campaign, with the addition of mobilized community resources and community activities, should have significant change effects.

The community-organization structure of this study is based on systems theory, in which a system is defined as a set of two or more interrelated elements or subsystems that together serve a function. The system used here has a structure of three interacting subsystems—the provider subsystem designed to facilitate the study, the household subsystem in the area of active intervention, and the community subsystem of relevant organizations—and serves to organize the community to work toward smoking reduction.

Active Intervention: Practice

To reach the first objective, awareness and readiness to respond to the campaign, a variety of activities will be directed to the active intervention households. These activities will include brief biofeedback education with use of a carbon monoxide digital breath analyzer, distribution of education materials that include a smoker's self-help kit during the year 2 smoking behavior survey, and a mass media campaign. Newsletters and a telephone hot line will be provided to help smokers develop a positive attitude toward smoking cessation and reduction.

The second objective, to create opportunities to stop smoking, will be met by the activities of the health educator, the neighborhood representatives, and other community leaders working with community groups. These activities may include organized quit nights, national smoke-out week events, neighborhood referral and information services, and smoking cessation workshops.

For the third objective, to maintain a nonsmoking environment, community organization principles will be applied to promoting a policy of nonsmoking in all public places. The health advisory council and health and smoking committee will be encouraged to lead this community movement. Ex-smokers will be organized to provide mutual support for maintenance of nonsmoking behavior and creation of a smoke-free environment.

Summary of Active Intervention Activities

Smoking behavior survey. At the beginning of year 2 trained interviewers will conduct a household survey, during which a carbon monoxide breath analyzer will be used for validation purposes as well as a means of biofeedback education. Educational materials and self-help kits will be distributed to assist smokers in the surveyed households to stop smoking.

Biofeedback education. The interviewer will use the CO breath analyzer as a means of briefly explaining the physiological effects of cigarette smoking and suggesting a change in smoking behavior (Young et al. 1981–1982).

Education materials. A package of education materials will be selected or developed for distribution at baseline survey. The package will include a fact sheet, a self-help kit, and resource list. Additional education materials will be developed later in the study for distribution by neighborhood representatives.

Newsletters. A Health Line type of newsletter will be mailed four times a year, edited by the health educator to contain information supplied mainly by residents in communities being studied.

Telephone hot line. The health educator will operate a telephone hot line to answer residents' questions about cigarette smoking and health and make referrals for further assistance. The phone will be answered by machine when the person is not on duty.

Neighborhood representatives. Neighborhood representatives will be recruited and trained to respond to residents' requests for information and to make referrals.

Quit-nights. A community center such as a church or YMCA will be used to sponsor quit-nights for community residents. These will be scheduled in the spring of year 2 through year 4.

National Smoke-out Week events. During the National Smoke-out Week in the fall of year 2 through year 4, the health educator and health and smoking advisory committee will sponsor antismoking events.

Smoking cessation workshops. Health educators will use the American Lung Association approach to conduct smoking cessation workshops for community residents in years 2 through 4½ once every three months. If possible, participants will be grouped in categories of expectant parents, parents of school-age children, family members of cancer and respiratory disease patients, and the general public.

Ex-smokers clubs. Those who quit smoking through smoking cessation workshops will be encouraged to form ex-smokers clubs, with activities decided and scheduled with help of health educators.

Smoking behavior change survey. During the fourth year, trained interviewers will conduct the second household survey. CO analyzers will again be used for validation purposes as well as a means of biofeedback education. This survey will be the last reminder for hard-core smokers to change their smoking behavior.

Smoke-free community campaign. This campaign will be accomplished through community organization efforts. In conjunction with National Smoke-out Week activities, we will try to persuade the community to adopt a no-smoking policy. Public health professionals in Massachusetts and American Cancer Society staff members have been consulted about the development of related campaign strategies.

Community Organization

The advisory council will be composed of members of community agencies that are relevant to and interested in participating in the study. The council functions to advise the site coordinator (see below), to help with recruitment of community agencies and organizations, and to recruit community leaders from the active intervention areas. These community leaders then become members of the health and smoking committee.

The health and smoking committee is composed of selected community leaders. Its members work with the community subsystem to initiate and develop smoking reduction activities in community agencies and organizations—churches, fraternal organizations, and neighborhood associations. These activities include sending antismoking literature to households in the active intervention areas and sponsoring quit-nights and other antismoking community events. Committee members also work directly with the household subsystem through their contact with the households to insure the awareness of household members of and encourage attendance at community antismoking activities.

The site coordinator, with assistance of the health educators, provides training and oversight to community leaders in their implementation of the program, while the health educators also help area residents with use of antismoking kits.

Methods and Procedures

Initial Survey

An initial survey conducted during year 2 of the study will serve as the baseline for the study. The study design is a quasiexperimental controlled before/after design, with smokers identified in the initial survey serving as the panel to evaluate change in smoking behavior between years 2 and 5. Since a list of smokers is not available in any of the study communities, a simple random sample of smokers in each community is not possible. A sample of smokers will be identified by selecting a simple random sample of households in each community, screening each household sampled for the presence of a smoker aged 18 or older, and listing all such adult smokers in the household.

The list will be ordered alphabetically by first name, and a simple random sample of one subject from the household list will be selected for a detailed interview, which will take place at the time of the initial visit if possible, or at a follow-up time. The interview will deal with the person's smoking history, knowledge of effects of smoking, and media use. In addition, each respondent will receive the breath analyzer test. Smoking histories will also be collected on other smoking adults in the households.

Process Evaluation

Throughout the study active and passive intervention programs will undergo continual internal evaluation. Every six months participation rates of smoking cessation programs will be reviewed, and the results used to modify, augment, and improve the intervention programs. The process will include the extent of activity—number of media spots aired, mailings sent out, and media intervention programs offered—and the extent of participation—number of people calling on hot lines and of participants at each intervention program.

The quality of the event will be assessed by having a random sample of up to 20 people attending an event fill out a brief questionnaire on gain in knowledge, willingness to change their behavior, and other factors.

These measures of process will be collected routinely and formally reviewed at year 2.5, 3, 3.5, 4, and 5. With these data, the plan for interventions can be compared with what was realized, as part of management control.

Special emphasis will be placed on quality control of educational materials and mass media communication. These will include an evaluation of existing educational materials to be adapted or used in their original form; pretesting of media and educational materials for attractiveness, comprehensibility, readability, acceptability, believability, personal relevance, and recall; regular reviews of inventories of educational materials being disseminated by other health providers in the community; routine queries of persons requesting program information and services to find out their sources of information; focus group sessions for targeted audiences on media and educational materials to determine whether these meet their objectives; feedback mechanisms integrated intermittently in the mass media to determine the extent of audience outreach and reactions, for example, letters to the editor/special columnists in local newspapers, quizzes on the radio with small prizes to encourage responses.

Telephone Survey

In each community a telephone survey of the whole original sample participating in detailed interviews during the first survey will be carried out during years 3 to 5. This survey will consist of five- to eight-minute interviews concerning the respondent's continued residency at the address, number of cigarettes smoked last week, attitude to two or three smoking questions, knowledge of two or three smoking issues, and awareness of smoking programs and mass media messages in the community.

Final Survey

After three years of community-based intervention, during year 5 a second home-interview survey will be conducted in each of the study communities. This will include a resurvey of all household members sampled during year 2 who still reside in the study community and an additional random sample of households with smokers who were not included in the initial year 2 sample. Smokers interviewed the first time will be reinterviewed and asked for smoking history and knowledge of and participation in intervention activities as principal response variables. In addition, smoking histories of other smokers in the household will be recorded at the time of the interview, if possible, or by follow-up phone interview. Household members who have moved out of the target community will not be resurveyed.

An additional sample of household members not included in the initial survey will also be interviewed during year 5, details of the sample depending on the estimated number of households with smokers not included in the initial survey, as well as an estimate of mobility. Data on these variables will come from the initial survey and the survey done during the middle of the fourth year. The objective of the additional sample of households will be to assess diffusion of the intervention programs to the community. Retrospective smoking histories will be collected during the year 5 survey, in addition to knowledge of smoking programs in the community.

Sample Size

The sample size required for the surveys conducted in the community is based on the need to detect a differential change in smoking behavior between the active and passive groups. Since smoking behavior will be recorded before and after the intervention programs on the same panel of respondents, change in an individual's smoking behavior will be the key variable under study. The sample size is calculated based on enrolling a single smoker from each household included in the sample. For the purpose of sample-size calculations, it is assumed that similar differential effects between active and passive groups will be observed in each city and each socioeconomic level. The assumption is also that the panel of subjects reinterviewed at year 5 is a simple random sample of smokers; the sample size is based on a change at year 5 in the proportion of subjects who still smoke.

The principal hypotheses of the study concern the rate of cigarette-smoking cessation between active and passive intervention communities in each area. The study is designed to detect a 3% difference in smoking prevalence between the two intervention communities in each area, a difference in prevalence that corresponds to a 10% difference between the active and passive groups in the number of cigarette smokers still smoking at year 5.

The sample size calculation is based on a two-sided test, with alpha set at 0.05 and a power of 0.80. Using these criteria, a total of 200 smokers (identified at baseline) per intervention per area need to remain in the panel and complete smoking histories at year 5 of the study. Because there are two southern areas and only one northern area, sample sizes in the northern areas are twice this number, 400 smokers per intervention. Since there are two interventions per area, and three areas in the study, a total of 1600 smokers (previously identified at baseline and completing both the baseline and year 5 surveys) need to participate in the study.

The study is designed so that 1632 smokers will complete the year 5 survey. A larger number of households must be visited initially for the baseline survey, however, because of nonresponse at the year 5 survey, possible loss of contact with the smoker in the period between the baseline survey and the year 5 survey, nonresponse at the baseline survey, presence of nonsmoking households at the baseline survey, presence of non–Black households in the community, and presence of vacant households in the community.

In calculating the number of households to be selected for visits at the baseline survey, we assumed a 90% response rate at the year 3 survey, a loss-of-contact rate between baseline and year 3 equal to three-fifths of the five-year mobility rate reported by the 1980 census, a 90% response rate to the initial contact at baseline, a 95% response rate to the household roster at baseline, an 80% response rate for the smoking history, and a 90% response rate for the key interview. Finally, we assumed a 30% adult smoking rate for Black households and a percentage of Black household rates and vacancy rates based on 1980 census data. Each of these factors serves to enlarge the number of households that initially have to be contacted at the baseline survey.

As a result of these factors, although only 1600 complete interviews are required for the year 3 survey, we plan to visit 19,360 households for the baseline survey. In these visits, we anticipate contacting 13,007 Black households, resulting in contact with 3336 Black smoking households (based on the percentages mentioned above). As a result of these contacts, we expect to complete 2402 key interviews for the baseline survey. We project that these 2402 respondents at baseline will yield 1600 complete responses at the year 3 survey, after accounting for mobility and nonresponse at that time.

Power Calculations

Power has been calculated for each of the principal hypotheses to be tested in this study, each power calculation is based on an alpha level of 0.05 and assuming a 0.10% smoking cessation rate in the passive communities. The power calculations are summarized in Table 1. The study is designed to have high power (0.80) in detecting differences of 10 percentage points in the quit rates between active and passive groups in each area. Note that a 10% difference in the quit rates between active and passive groups is equivalent to a 3% difference in smoking prevalence between the groups, and a 5% difference in the quit rates of smokers is equivalent to a 1.5% difference in the smoking prevalence between the inter-

TABLE 1. Power calculations for principal hypotheses based on two-sided tests[a]

Hypothesis	Size of Difference	Power
Within Income Level		
Active–Passive		
Separate southern areas	0.05	0.19
Combined southern areas	0.05	0.33
Northern area	0.05	0.33
Separate southern areas	0.10	0.51
Combined southern areas	0.10	0.80
Northern area	0.10	0.80
Within Area		
Active–Passive		
Separate southern areas	0.05	0.33
Combined southern areas	0.05	0.57
Northern area	0.05	0.57
Separate southern areas	0.10	0.80
Combined southern areas	0.10	0.98
Northern area	0.10	0.98
North/South Comparison		
Active–Passive		
Passive–Passive		
Income-level specific	0.05	0.33
Overall income levels	0.05	0.57
Income-level specific	0.10	0.80
Overall income levels	0.10	0.98

[a] Size of difference is the difference between the two groups in proportion of persons who still smoke at year 3.

vention groups. The power for particular hypotheses varies depending on the hypothesis but is generally greater than 0.70.

Pilot Data Collection Sites

To determine the best approach to data collection, pilot study areas were selected at each city site for the pilot studies in year 2. These sites are distant from the intervention sites. About 30 households with smokers will be included from each city site, for a total of 120 households. This will provide an opportunity for fine-tuning procedures and be an opportunity for interviewers to test their skills and be evaluated. These data will be analyzed to give the researchers a better understanding of the various aspects of data management.

Data Management

Because this highly complicated project will produce a large amount of data, a data management team and system were developed to handle this aspect of the study. Staff members who have data management skills, data entry skills, and data analysis skills were hired. They are organizing the system by developing procedures and forms for both process and impact evaluation as well as computer programming for storage and retrieval.

The basic components of the system include (1) constructing a list of households in each geographic area for selection of the baseline sample, (2) developing a household and interview tracking system to monitor and assure quality control of baseline survey interviews (using DBASE-III Plus), (3) establishing procedures for data entry, verification, and documentation of data at the University of Massachusetts coordinating center (using KEYENTRY III software), and (4) developing programs to establish basic files for analysis (using SAS software).

Lists of households are constructed from available city directories, voter registries, property listings, and actual on-site field listings. A composite list is formed for each area that includes all households identified. The interview tracking and monitoring system includes a telecommunication link with the University of Massachusetts coordinating center to assure simultaneous and comparable monitoring of data gathering in different areas. Three quality-control reports focused on interview progress, response rates, and expense will be produced per week. All data entries will be made at the University of Massachusetts coordinating center, with detailed procedures specified for logical checks and follow-back clarification of errors to the area coordinating centers. Final data management and analysis will make use of SAS software.

All components of the system are programmed on microcomputers, with mainframe computers being used as a backup and for storage of large files. Uniform variable names and protocols are being developed to assure consistency between area sites.

Summary

This research study of smoking in the Black population is designed to decrease the incidence of smoking-related cancers. Four cities, each with four neighborhood sites, two low-income and two middle-income each, serving as experimental (active intervention) and control (passive intervention) population sites will form the basis of this intervention study. A series of null hypotheses will be tested.

Both pretesting and pilot testing of the questionnaire and data collection instruments have been done. Intervention will consist of community organization and education media information, neighborhood smoking and health committees, and use of already organized community and church groups starting in year 2. A follow-up in year 5 will assess the impact of the overall program.

Acknowledgment. This research is supported by contract number 6502811 from the National Cancer Institute.

References

Abrams DB et al: Social learning principles for organizational health promotion: An integrated approach. In Cataldo M, Coates T (eds): *Health and Industry: A Behavioral Medical Perspective*. New York: John Wiley & Sons, 1986.

Baquet CR, Ringen K, Pollack ES, et al: *Cancer Among Blacks and Other Minorities: Statistical Profiles*. Bethesda, MD: National Cancer Institute, NIH Publication 86-2785, 1986, pp 75–80.

Centers for Disease Control: Cigarette smoking in the United States. *MMWR* 1987; 36:581–585.

Darity WA: Socio-economic factors influencing the health status of black Americans. *International Quarterly of Community Health Education* 1986-1987;7:91–108.

Darity WA, Pitt ES: Health status of black Americans. In Williams JD (ed): *The State of Black America, 1979*. New York: National Urban League, 1979; pp 125–156, 235–250.

Devesa SS, Diamond EL: Socioeconomic and racial differences in lung cancer incidence. *Am J Epidemiol* 1983;118:818–831.

Flay BR: Mass media and smoking cessation: A critical review. *Am J Public Health* 1987;77:153–161.

Janz NK, Becker MH: The health belief model: A decade later. *Health Educ Q* 1984; 11:1–47.

McBride W, Richter GC: Gastrointestinal malignancies in black Americans. *NY State J Med* 1985;85:157–159.

Milroy L: Social network and linguistic focusing. In Romaine S, Arnold E (eds): *Sociolinguistic Variation in Speech Communities*. London: Edward Arnold, Publishers, 1982, pp 141–152.

Myers MH: Survival from cancer by blacks and whites. In Mettlin C, Murphy GP (eds): *Cancer Among Black Populations*. New York: Alan R Liss, 1981, pp 151–165.

Pattern LM, Morris LE, Blat WJ, et al: Esophageal cancer among black men. *JNCI* 1981;67:777–783.

Puska P, Koskela K: Community based strategies to fight smoking: Experiences from the North Karelia project in Finland. *NY State J Med* 1983;83:1335–1338.

Rogers EM, Shoemaker SF: The innovation decision process. In Rogers EM, Shoemaker SF (eds): *Communication of Innovation: A Cross-Cultural Approach*. San Francisco: Free Press, 1971, pp 98–133.

Rosenstock IM: Historical origins of the health belief model. *Health Education Monograph* 1974;2:328–356.

US Department of Health and Human Services: *Health and Prevention Profile*. Washington, DC, 1983; pp 182–184.

US Department of Health and Human Services: *Health United States*. Washington, DC, 1982; p 9.

White JE, Enterline JP, Zahure A, et al: Cancer among blacks in the United States: Recognizing the problem. In Mettlin C, Murphy GP (eds): *Cancer Among Black Populations*. New York: Alan R Liss, 1981, 35–53.

Young JL, Percy CL, Asire AJ, et al (eds): Surveillance, Epidemiology and End Results Program: Incidence and mortality data, 1973–1977. *NCI Monogr* 1981;57:1–187.

Young S, Chen TL, Cernada GP: An evaluation of a biofeedback smoking education program. *International Quarterly of Community Health Education* 1981–1982;2:330–337.

12. Smoking and Smoking-Related Cancers Among Asian and Pacific Islander Americans

Betty Lee Hawks

The smoking behavior of the group referred to in this paper as Asian and Pacific Islander Americans (APAs) has gone nearly unreported in the literature on smoking and health. This may be so partly because few research possibilities are offered by the existing limited data base on APAs, and because of the relatively small size of this population.

The excess mortality of lung cancer and other smoking-related diseases of American Blacks has focused increasing public health attention on this population, among whom both men and women have some of the highest rates of smoking of all racial groups in the United States.[1] Although smoking-related disease incidence and mortality rates have been lower for Hispanics to date, there is a trend toward higher smoking rates among Hispanic men in particular. This should prompt further research on and the application of culturally appropriate prevention measures now to avert for the Hispanic population the health consequences experienced by the White and Black populations. Given the following review of available data on APAs, one may make similar observations for this group.

Demographics

Asian Americans are defined in this paper as persons who came as immigrants or refugees to the U.S. from Asia, including Pakistan and the countries that lie east of it in South Asia, Southeast Asia, and East Asia (Gardner et al. 1985). Pacific Islanders are persons from the Pacific Basin islands who settled in any part of the U.S., and they include Hawaiians, Samoans, Guamanians, Fijians, and others.

---

[1]According to the National Health Interview Survey 1985, the smoking prevalence rates of American Blacks are the highest for all racial groups sampled, regardless of gender. The Current Population Survey 1985 indicates that American Indians, both men and women, have the highest smoking rates of all groups surveyed.

Although I use the term Asian and Pacific Islander Americans or APAs throughout this paper, I do so for convenience rather than as a reflection of reality. "Asian" encompasses more than 26 different ethnic groups, most of whom come from individual sovereign countries. Pacific Islander Americans probably number at least eight to 10 different groups as well, and they include the Pacific Island tribes and nations who relate to the U.S. as trust territories and Native Hawaiians who are the only Pacific Island people indigenous to a state in the U.S. and whose history most closely resembles that of Native Americans on the U.S. mainland.

Most of the APA groups are differentiated by their own language, culture, religion, art, relations of home country to the U.S., and history in the U.S. as either immigrants, refugees, or even citizens. According to the U.S. census of 1980, the population of APAs was 3,725,987, or 1.6% of the total U.S. population. Asian Americans comprised 3,466,421, that is, more than 90% of the APA category, while Pacific Islanders numbered 259,566, or about 7% (Gardner et al. 1985).

Asian and Pacific Islander Americans are the fastest growing segment of the U.S. population today, having increased by 120% in the past decade compared with a 6.4% increase among Whites, 17.4% increase among Blacks, and 60.8% increase among Hispanics (Gardner et al. 1985). This growth of the APA population has been attributed to immigration, fertility, and to the redefinition of this category to include Asian Indians.

The Population Reference Bureau in Washington, D.C., estimated that the population of Asian Americans would reach more than 5.1 million, an almost 50% increase, by September 30, 1985, based on data on immigration and refugee flows as well as calculations of natural increase since the last census (Gardner et al. 1985). Table 1, reprinted from Gardner et al. (1985), illustrates this point for the total Asian American population as well as for the largest ethnic groups. This anticipated growth would have increased the proportion of Asian Americans in the total U.S. population from 1.5% to 2.1% (Gardner et al. 1985). Furthermore, this population is estimated to grow to 4% of the total population by the year 2000 (Gardner et al. 1985). No estimates are available for the Pacific Islander American population.

Asian Americans

Because related information on Pacific Islanders is unavailable, the following descriptive information focuses on Asian Americans only.

Composition

The most populous groups of Asian Americans are Chinese (23.4%), Filipino (22.6%), Japanese (20.7%), Asian Indian (11.2%), Korean (10.3%), and Vietnamese (7.1%) according to the 1980 census (Gardner et al. 1985). Although there have been important immigration flows to the U.S. from China, Japan, and

TABLE 1. Asian American population: 1980 census and estimates for September 30, 1985.

		April 1, 1980 Census				Estimates for September 30, 1985		
Rank	Ethnic group	Number	Percentage	Percentage foreign-born of group	Ethnic group	Number	Percentage	Percentage increase in number Apr. 1, 1980–Sept. 30, 1985
	Total	3,466,421	100.0	—	Total	5,147,900	100.0	48.5
1	Chinese	812,178	23.4	63.3	Chinese	1,079,400	21.0	32.9
2	Filipino	781,894	22.6	66.3	Filipino	1,051,600	20.4	34.5
3	Japanese	716,331	20.7	28.4	Japanese	766,300	14.9	7.0
4	Asian Indian	387,223	11.2	70.4	Vietnamese	634,200	12.3	158.8
5	Korean	357,393	10.3	81.8	Korean	542,400	10.5	51.8
6	Vietnamese	245,025	7.1	90.5	Asian Indian	525,600	10.2	35.7
	Other Asian	166,377	4.8	—	Laotian	218,400	4.2	358.0
	Laotian	47,683	1.4	—	Kampuchean	160,800	3.1	902.2
	Thai	45,279	1.3	—	All other	169,200	3.3	64.8
	Kampuchean	16,044	0.5	—				
	Pakistani	15,792	0.5	—				
	Indonesian	9,618	0.3	—				
	Hmong	5,204	0.2	—				
	All other[a]	26,757	0.8	—				
	Percentage of total U.S. population (226,545,805) = 1.5%				Percentage of total U.S. population (239,447,000) = 2.1%			

Sources: 1980: Bureau of the Census, 1980 Census of Population, PC80-S1-12, Asian and Pacific Islander Population by State, December 1983, Table B. 1985: Estimates by Bulletin authors. Reprinted from Robert W. Gardner, Bryant Robey, and Peter C. Smith, Asian Americans: Growth, Change, and Diversity, Population Bulletin, Vol. 40, No. 4. Population Reference Bureau, Inc.: Washington, DC, 1985.
[a] Includes Bangladeshi, Bhutanese, Bornean, Burmese, Celebesian, Cernan, Indochinese, Iwo-Jiman, Javanese, Malayan, Maldivian, Nepali, Okinawan, Sikkimese, Singaporean, Sri Lankan, and Asian not specified (e.g., "Asian").

the Philippines beginning in the nineteenth century, these were mere trickles compared to the upsurge in numbers of Asian immigrants following passage of Public Law 89236 in 1965. This law greatly liberalized immigration policy and raised heretofore low ceilings on numbers of immigrants from Asian countries.

Subsequent refugee acts allowed entrance into the U.S. of groups from various parts of the world who suffered political, religious, and other persecution. Many refugees from Southeast Asia, starting in 1975 and particularly those from the second wave beginning in 1979, had lost all their material possessions and often members of their families. According to Gordon, 823,000 Southeast Asian refugees had resettled in the U.S. by April 1987, with an additional 40,000 expected to enter in 1987 (Gordon, personal communication 1987). They started new lives in the U.S. with virtually nothing, oftentimes lacking the education, training, language, and other skills to be immediately employable and the support of established family ties in the U.S.

This contrasted with the situation of contemporary immigrants in general who, upon application for U.S. entrance, have to meet educational or training requirements for occupations with a shortage of workers, or meet the requirements for family reunification that, in brief, allow immediate relatives of citizens to enter the U.S.

Nativity

A result of the increased immigration and migration patterns over the past couple of decades has been that Asian Americans are dominated by a higher proportion of foreign-born, non-Western Hemisphere-born members than any other large minority group in the U.S., with an overall foreign-born percentage of 62%. In individual groups the foreign-born rates are 63% for Chinese, 82% for Korean, and more than 90% for Vietnamese and other Indochinese groups (Gardner et al. 1985). The only Asian group for which this is not true are the Japanese, who have not increased substantially from immigration and whose foreign-born proportion was only 28% in 1980 (Gardner et al. 1985).

Distribution

Asian and Pacific Islander Americans are mostly concentrated in the Western states (56%), with three of four living in seven states, including California, Hawaii, New York, Illinois, Texas, Washington, and New Jersey. These people are overwhelmingly urban dwellers as well (Gardner et al. 1985).

Median Age

The median age of the U.S. population as a whole was 30 years in 1980. Except for Japanese Americans, whose median age was 33.5 years, the remainder of the APA groups had median ages that were lower than the U.S. median. Among the largest ethnic groups, the median ages of the Chinese (29.8 years) and Indians (29.6 years) most closely approached the national median age, followed by

Filipinos (28.4 years) and Koreans (25.9 years). The Vietnamese had a median age of 21.5 years, and other Southeast Asian groups had even younger median ages (U.S. Bureau of the Census 1980).

Bimodal Patterns

The image of Asian Americans as the "successful minority model"[2] has some basis in truth perhaps, but is not generalizable. In most cases, we can describe Asian Americans as following a bimodal or bipolar pattern with respect to many socioeconomic indices (Lin-Fu 1987). Some examples include:

Education

According to the 1980 census, 33% of Asian Americans have completed college compared with 18% of the nonminority group. Asian women are two to three times as likely as nonminority women to have completed college, while Asian men are almost twice as likely as nonminority men to have done so. A contrast is the lack of formal education and literacy in even their own languages, especially among the Southeast Asians (Vietnamese and ethnic Chinese or "boat people," Khmer, Laotians, and Hmong) who arrived during the second wave.

Occupation

For both sexes, more Chinese (19%), Japanese (15%), and Filipinos (14%) than nonminorities (13%) are in professional positions (Asian American Health Forum 1986). If one examines service occupations, however, one also finds higher percentages of Chinese (19%), Japanese (13%) and Filipinos (17%) than nonminorities (11%) (Asian American Health Forum 1986). Given the high educational attainments of Asians in the U.S., their percentage representation in service jobs appears disproportionate. One might expect an even higher percentage of Southeast Asians, particularly the most recent refugees, in service-related work.

Socioeconomic Status

The median Asian American family income in 1979 was $22,075 compared with $20,840 for nonminority families. On the average, however, Asian American

---

[2]Social scientists, educators, and even the media have focused numerous articles on the success stories of members of the Asian American population, citing individual achievements of children of immigrant and refugee parents in math and the natural sciences, art, business, and other fields (see *Time* cover story, Vol. 130, No. 9, 1987). The message seems to be that, given the example of the Chinese, Japanese, or other Asian group, one should be able to improve one's social and economic status in American life through effort, perseverance, and sacrifice. Only recently is there growing awareness that such successes characterize only part of the population and tend to obscure if not distort the public perception of Asian Americans.

households had a higher number of individuals who contributed to the household income (Gardner et al. 1985).

Poverty Level

A higher percentage of Asian Americans (13.9%) lived below the poverty level in 1979 compared with nonminorities (9.4%) (Asian American Health Forum 1986).

Barriers to Health Care

Besides the frequently cited indicators of education, location, transportation, communication, and others, being poor has a direct correlation with ill health and the inability to gain access to services (True 1985). People who are eligible for Medicaid may be able to obtain health services, but with substantial effort, forbearance, paperwork, and patience. Some 35 million Americans, frequently referred to as the working poor, are without the financial resources or private or public insurance to cover the costs of necessary health care.

Another problem encountered by foreign-born Americans is the frequently higher mortality rates they experience compared to the native born (i.e., U.S. born) population. Age-adjusted nativity-mortality ratios, for example, are typically higher for foreign-born than for native-born Chinese Americans (Yu et al. 1985).

Cancer Incidence, Mortality, and Relative Survival Among Asian and Pacific Americans

The following is a brief overview about smoking-related cancer statistics among APAs, as provided in a personal Communication (1987) by J. Horn of the National Cancer Institute (NCI) from data collected by the Hawaii and Oakland-San Francisco registries for the Surveillance, Epidemiology, and End Results (SEER) Program. These are the only two SEER registries in the U.S. that collect cancer data on APAs because large numbers of APAs live in these areas. The specific sites for which statistics are presented include bladder, buccal cavity and pharynx, esophagus, larynx, and lung for which tobacco smoking is the major cancer risk factor. Stomach cancer, a tobacco-related cancer, is not included in the following tables because of the associated risk factor of diet.

Smoking-Related Cancer Incidence Rates

For all sites shown in Table 2, native Hawaiians had the highest incidence rate per 100,000 compared with Whites and the other APA groups. Of all APAs, only Chinese men experienced a higher incidence rate of cancers of the buccal cavity and pharynx than White men. Native Hawaiian men had the highest incidence of

TABLE 2. Average annual age-adjusted incidence rates per 100,000 by racial/ethnic group: selected cancer sites, 1980–1984.

Cancer site	Whites	Japanese	Chinese	Filipinos	Native Hawaiians
All sites	350.4	254.0	269.0	234.3	359.7
Bladder	17.3	8.8	9.6	4.8	7.7
Buccal cavity and pharynx					
Male	17.1	8.0	22.1	10.9	8.9
Female	6.5	2.6	10.1	7.6	6.9
Esophagus	3.0	2.7	3.2	3.6	7.3
Larynx	4.6	2.3	1.8	1.8	3.8
Lung					
Male	83.1	50.2	60.6	41.3	102.6
Female	32.4	11.9	29.4	16.7	49.6

Source: Oakland-San Francisco and Hawaii, SEER Program, National Cancer Institute.

lung cancer, followed by White men. Native Hawaiian men also had the highest incidence of esophageal cancer, Chinese and Filipino men having slightly higher rates than White men. Whites had the highest incidence of cancer of the bladder and larynx of the groups shown.

Compared to the incidence among White women, the buccal cavity and pharyngeal cancer rates were higher among Chinese and Filipino women, and only slightly higher for native Hawaiian women. Native Hawaiian women also had a higher incidence of lung cancer than White women.

Smoking-Related Cancer Mortality Rates

Overall, as the data in Table 3 show, native Hawaiians had the highest mortality rate per 100,000 for all sites shown. Chinese men had the highest mortality rate compared with those of White men and other selected APA groups for cancer of

TABLE 3. Average annual age-adjusted mortality rates per 100,000—Whites and selected Asian groups: selected cancer sites, 1980–1984.

Cancer site	Whites	Japanese	Chinese	Filipinos	Native Hawaiians
All sites	165.6	107.0	132.6	80.6	206.4
Bladder	3.7	1.4	1.9	1.1	3.0
Buccal cavity and pharynx					
Male	4.9	3.1	8.6	3.2	4.8
Female	1.8	0.8	3.5	1.5	2.2
Esophagus	2.7	2.1	2.7	1.8	6.8
Larynx	1.3	0.4	0.6	0.4	1.8
Lung					
Male	70.9	35.7	47.3	21.5	75.4
Female	23.2	8.5	19.4	8.0	38.0

Source: Oakland-San Francisco and Hawaii, SEER Program, National Cancer Institute.

TABLE 4. Five-year relative survival rates—Whites and selected Asian groups: selected cancer sites, 1977–1984.

Cancer site	Whites	Japanese	Chinese	Filipinos	Native Hawaiians
All sites	50.3	51.5	45.8	44.8	42.2
Bladder	76.1	83.8	76.2	65.6	52.9
Buccal cavity and pharynx					
male	52.4	42.5	56.9	37.6	56.4
female	55.4	57.3	51.2	58.4	37.5
Esophagus	6.6	7.4	13.9	3.5	0.0
Larynx	67.1	79.2	65.9	57.6	80.2
Lung					
male	11.7	13.8	13.9	13.3	10.8
female	15.9	15.8	16.1	11.2	15.8

Source: Oakland-San Francisco and Hawaii, SEER Program, National Cancer Institute.

the buccal cavity and pharynx. Native Hawaiians had the highest rate of deaths from cancer of the esophagus, followed by Whites and Chinese. The mortality rate for lung cancer was highest for native Hawaiian men and women.

Smoking-Related Cancer Survival Rates

Of all groups represented in the data shown in Table 4, native Hawaiians experienced the worst five-year relative survival rates for all cancer sites combined, and specifically for cancers of the bladder, esophagus, buccal cavity and pharynx in women and lung in men.[3] Filipinos had the second worst relative survival rates for all sites combined and for cancers of the bladder and esophagus but the worst rates for cancer of the buccal cavity, and pharynx in men, and lung in women. Japanese had the highest relative survival rates overall and for cancer of the bladder. Chinese had the highest survival rates for cancer of the buccal cavity and pharnyx in men, and esophagus and lung, but fared worse than Whites for all sites combined, for cancers of the buccal cavity, and pharynx in women, and larynx.

Smoking Prevalence Among Asian and Pacific Islander Americans

The best national survey data available may be from the National Health Interview Surveys (NHIS) prepared by the National Center for Health Statistics. The inclusion of smoking questions varies from survey to survey, but the surveys have some comparability with regard to smoking rates (G. Hendershot 1987, National

---

[3]Because of the low numbers of Native Hawaiians in the SEER data, rates cannot be generalized beyond this locale and should be used only to point out possible areas of excess mortality and morbidity for this group.

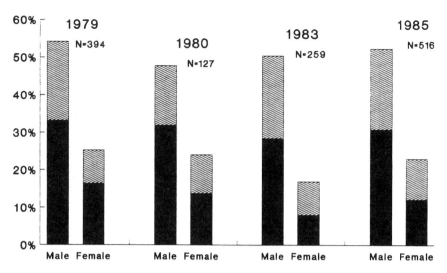

FIGURE 1. ■: Current smokers; □: Former smokers. Prevalence of cigarette smoking among Asian and Pacific Islander Americans by gender and years 1979, 1980, 1983, and 1985. *Source*: National Center for Health Statistics, National Health Interview Survey data tapes for the years indicated.

Center for Health Statistics, personal communication). The smoking rates by gender for APAs obtained from analyses for the NHIS for 1979, 1980, 1983, and 1985 are shown in Figure 1.

As this chart shows, APA males tended to have higher rates of smoking, both as present and former smokers, than APA females.

The data currently available on smoking rates among APAs are limited. National surveys that include a smoking component, for example the National Health Interview Survey, typically have not included a large enough sample of APAs to support any general statements about their smoking behavior. Also, given the large number of different ethnic groups that comprise APAs, it might be more accurate to describe the smoking rates of particular APA groups who have been the subjects of studies, however small a sample.

In the data shown in Table 5, an attempt is made to compare smoking prevalence rates among racial/ethnic groups and men and women, using 1985 NHIS and Current Populations Survey data. Whereas Aleuts/Alaska Natives/Native American and Black men had substantially higher current smoking rates than did APA men, the rate for APA men was only slightly lower than that for White and Hispanic men. Looking only at women's rates, APAs had the lowest prevalence rate for all the racial/ethnic groups.

If one were to combine two or more years of the NHIS data to increase the APA sample size, and look at the age ranges by decade, one would observe higher percentages of smokers in the younger, that is, under 45, age category of APA males. For the age decades from 25 to 44, the percentage of APA male smokers

TABLE 5. Smoking prevalence rates by racial/ethnic groups and gender, 1985.

Racial/ethnic group	Current smokers (%)		Former smokers (%)	
	Men	Women	Men	Women
Blacks	39.6	31.0	21.1	12.7
Whites	31.6	28.1	33.5	19.9
Hispanics	31.3	20.8	23.1	12.8
Asian/Pacific Islanders	30.8	12.2	21.5	10.8
Aleuts/Alaska Natives Native Americans	40.0	35.7	23.6	17.0

Source: Baquet C: The Association of Tobacco to Cancer and Other Health Conditions in Minority Populations. Proceedings from Interagency Committee on Smoking and Health . . . The Impact of Cigarette Smoking on Minority Populations. Publication No. HHS/PHS/CDC-87-8403, pp. 21–45, Mar 1987.

seems to range from 32% to 39%. For the decade from 15 through 24, the smoking prevalence rate for APA males seems to be in the upper twenties. It is not possible to make observations based on a similar analysis of the data on APA females.

The observation on APA male smoking is similar to one made in the *Report on Hypertension and Related Health Problems in California: Results from the 1979 California Hypertension Survey* (California Department of Health 1982). In this study, the higher percentage of smokers was again found among the younger (ages 18 to 49) APA men whose smoking rate was 29.7%. Further studies seem warranted to shed more light on smoking patterns among APA males.

Other local or regional surveys by which smoking behavior information on APAs was collected may give us some idea of smoking rates among the less known of this population, the Southeast Asians sometimes known as the Indochinese. R. G. Rumbaut of San Diego State University conducted a study from 1982 to 1985, the Indochinese Health and Adaptation Research Project, in San Diego County which has about 40,000 Indochinese residents. His preliminary analysis of data from a random sample of 500 Indochinese differentiated by gender and ethnicity (including Hmong, Chinese, Vietnamese, and Cambodians) indicated that the highest smoking rates occurred among males, Cambodian men exhibiting the highest frequency at 70.7%, followed by Vietnamese men at 64.7%, Chinese men at 54.5%, and Hmong at 26.0%. Cambodian women had the highest smoking prevalence at 12.9%, with prevalence among Hmong and Chinese women each at 1.7%, and at 0.0% among Vietnamese women (Rumbaut 1988; personal communication).

Rumbaut found the heavier smokers (who smoked one or more packs a day) among Cambodian, followed by Vietnamese, men. He found a positive correlation between alcohol use and smoking in this population, with greater alcohol consumption among those who also smoked tobacco.

B. Levin, who directs the refugee program of the Department of Health, Cook County, Illinois, reported that a survey she conducted of 250 randomly selected Laotian men indicated about 72% to be current smokers, more than 25% of those smoking one or more packs a day (Levin 1987, personal communication).

Although these are small studies with relatively small sample sizes of APAs, their results point to the need for further surveys and research on APAs and their ethnic groups, such as the Indochinese in the U.S., to better understand their smoking behavior and gather data on their health status.

Smoking-Related Statistics in Asia

Almost three quarters of Asian Americans are foreign-born and it is likely that immigration and migration will continue this trend into the twenty-first century. Some smoking-related statistics from their countries or areas of origin may therefore be informative.

National anti-tobacco campaigns that might emerge in Asian countries will in most cases have a difficult time because of historically state-controlled and state-promoted tobacco industries. More recently, the American tobacco companies have been vying for the Third World markets as political and public sentiments in the U.S. turn increasingly against tobacco use.

Table 6 shows age-adjusted mortality rates per 100,000 population for oral and lung cancer in the U.S. and four areas of Asia. In the period of 1980 to 1981, the highest mortality rates from oral cancer occurred in Hong Kong and Singapore, the lowest in Japan and Thailand. The highest mortality rates from lung cancer occurred in Singapore and Hong Kong, followed by the U.S.

Table 7 shows smoking prevalence rates, gathered from a variety of sources, by gender in selected countries and areas. One will note from the data in Tables 6 and 7 that, despite a high smoking prevalence among Japanese males, the lung cancer mortality rate is comparatively low. I cannot report the lung cancer incidence rate nor do I have information on when smoking tobacco was introduced

TABLE 6. Cancer in the U.S. and Asian areas 1980–1981: age-adjusted death rates per 100,000 population for selected sites.

Country	All sites		Oral		Lung	
	Men	Women	Men	Women	Men	Women
U.S.	215.9	135.5	5.6	1.9	71.6	21.4
Hong Kong	227.4	120.5	19.9	6.6	71.9	29.7
Japan	193.9	108.1	2.5	0.9	33.7	9.5
Singapore	237.3	143.3	17.5	5.9	72.5	23.4
Thailand	57.2	36.7	2.8	1.3	8.0	2.4

Source: Adapted from Silverberg and Lubera 1986, with permission of the American Cancer Society.

TABLE 7. Percentage of smokers in selected Asian areas.

Country	Men	Women
India (Various cities, 1983)	59	3
Japan (National, 1984)	66	14
China (Hunan, 1981)	59	1
China (Shanghai, 1982)	43	3
Hong Kong (National, 1984)	33	4
U.S.A.[a] (National, 1983)	353	32

[a] For comparison purposes.

Source: Glynn 1987, personal communication. Adapted from table, Percentage of Smokers in Selected Countries, presented to Pan American Health Organization, Washington, DC.

and became widely used by Japanese men. This information would help to explain the contrasting observation above. Immigration from Japan to the U.S. is nominal, in sharp contrast to the recent and continued immigration and migration from the other Asian countries and areas, such as China, India, and Southeast Asia where male smoking rates and lung cancer mortality rates are high.

Conclusions

From the information presented here, it is difficult to draw any firm connection between cancer statistics and the smoking behavior of Asian and Pacific Islander Americans. The incidence and mortality rates of certain smoking-related cancers—such as cancer of the lung and esophagus among Native Hawaiians, cancer of the buccal cavity and pharynx among Chinese—are higher for the ethnic APA groups than for nonminorities. The SEER data are limited, however, by the number of U.S. sites at which cancer statistics are collected and by the few subcategories of ethnic groups included in the data gathering. The national surveys, from which the smoking prevalence data given above were derived, are limited by small sample sizes for APAs and, like those of the SEER program, by too few subcategories of ethnic groups.

These data have been useful in at least identifying apparent high rates of smoking-related cancers in particular APA groups and of tobacco use by APA men. More data collection and analysis are obviously needed for the APA population, both in the aggregate and for individual subgroups.

Implications for Future Research

The population of APAs in the United States will continue to increase steadily, as will its proportion of the total U.S. population. At the moment, no one can state conclusively whether this minority group warrants special smoking prevention, let alone cessation, efforts. The available data suggests that gender and ethnicity are predictors of smoking behaviors for this population and that education and nativity (i.e., foreign compared with U.S. birth) are factors to consider. More studies are needed, however, to establish better baseline information on APAs or, more realistically, on the more populous APA ethnic groups or those that appear at this time to be at high risk. Generalizations may be made about APAs at some future time but they should be attempted only after proper groundwork has been done for the major APA ethnic groups.

Some steps that could be taken include:

- National surveys that include questions on smoking behavior, attitudes, and knowledge need to have an improved sampling frame and to oversample APAs. This is the only way to obtain representative statistics on APAs.
- More accurate ethnic classifications of APAs when data are collected with possibly an increase in the number of Surveillance, Epidemiology, and End Results (SEER) sites in SMSAs or states where significant numbers of APAs, and particularly Southeast Asians, live. Los Angeles, San Diego, and New York are possible additional sites. Currently, data on APAs are collected only at Hawaii and San Francisco-Oakland SEER sites.
- Greater care and accuracy at the local level by the professionals (physicians, resident physicians, funeral home directors) who complete death certificates. Their recording of accurate and specific minority/ethnicity identifiers for clients/patients, especially APAs and Hispanics, directly influences the validity of morbidity and mortality data.
- Funding by federal research agencies of interdisciplinary research to gather data on knowledge, attitudes, and practices of different APA groups with respect to smoking-related cancer and tobacco use.

Can We Go Beyond Research Now?

Yes, some public health actions that affect APAs are possible now. For example: Health education materials about the hazards of smoking should be disseminated in various APA languages. Such materials should cover especially the short-range, more immediate health effects, such as shortness of breath, chronic obstructive pulmonary disease, bronchitis, and the effects of second-hand smoke on family members—infants, children, and the elderly—and on pregnancy outcome. Messages should focus on not smoking or quitting smoking for the welfare of the family, and the fact that the health consequences of smoking can prevent one from being able to work and provide for one's family.

Existing, culturally appropriate health education materials should be made more widely available through centers that serve as focal points in communities (E. Carillo 1987, unpublished paper on Hispanics and smoking). For APAs, for example, these would be community health centers and clinics, hospitals, social service centers, and refugee resettlement centers that serve a significant portion of this population. Temples and churches are important social support networks for APAs. Because learning English is a key to the acculturation process, the schools that offer English as a second language, found in every major city, must be included.

Some of these linguistically and culturally appropriate materials on smoking already are available in a few Asian languages such as Chinese and Vietnamese. Community health centers that serve primarily APAs in Boston, New York, San Francisco, Oakland, and Seattle have been sharing their information materials in different languages, and they might be able to work on similar projects with other groups. It is also critical to use other than print media to convey smoking prevention/cessation and other health promotion messages. Although the literacy rate has been relatively high among various Asian ethnic groups in the U.S., illiteracy in their native languages characterizes many of the more recent refugees from Southeast Asia. Use of radio or cable television networks for spot announcements or special health-oriented programs in the native languages may therefore have more impact.

The specific content and context of smoking control messages warrants careful study. These messages must contradict and indict the old image of the Marlboro man as Mr. West, Mr. America. They must convey clearly to our increasingly large foreign-born American population that smoking, and indeed any tobacco use, is neither American nor "fashionable" any longer. It would be a sad commentary if those who came to the U.S. to seek new lives succumbed instead to pressures to begin smoking or to continue smoking, a path that can only hasten their death in the West.

Acknowledgments. I express my appreciation and thanks to the following individuals for the advice, comments, counsel, and information that allowed me to write this paper.

For supporting my interest in the area of smoking and cancer among the Asian and Pacific Islander American population: Thomas Glynn, Ph.D., Program Director for Smoking Research, National Cancer Institute; Joseph Cullen, Ph.D., Deputy Director, Division of Cancer Prevention and Control, and Smoking, Tobacco and Cancer Program Coordinator, National Cancer Institute.

For providing data analyses, statistics, or access to data tapes and personal research data: John Horm, Special Population Studies Branch (formerly with Demographic Analysis Section, Surveillance and Operations Research Branch, National Cancer Institute); Darlene Naughton, formerly with the Operations Research Branch, National Cancer Institute; Lori Crane and Alfred Marcus, Ph.D., Jonsson Comprehensive Cancer Center, University of California, Los Angeles; Linda W. Gordon, Ph.D., Office of Refugee Resettlement, Family Support Administration; William Lynn (formerly with the Office on Smoking and Health), Smoking, Tobacco, and Cancer Program, National Cancer Institute; Ruben G. Rumbaut, Ph.D., Indochinese Health and Adaptation Research Project, San Diego State University; and Barbara Levin, M.A., M.P.H., Director of Refugee Program, Cook County Department of Public Health.

For advice and comments on draft paper and graphics: Claudia Baquet, M.D., M.P.H., Chief, Special Populations Studies Branch; Gayle Boyd, Ph.D., Thomas Glynn, Ph.D., and Margaret E. Mattson, Ph.D., Smoking, Tobacco, and Cancer Program, National Cancer Institute; Richard L. Hawks, Ph.D., Chief, Research Technology Branch, National Institute on Drug Abuse; William J. Mayer, M.D., M.P.H., Health Promotion Sciences Branch; and Thomas Marciniak, M.D., Chief, Computer Systems Section, Surveillance and Operations Research Branch, National Cancer Institute.

For typing assistance and general support: Shirley Wimberly, Smoking, Tobacco, and Cancer Program, National Cancer Institute.

References

Asian American Health Forum: *Facts and Figures About Asian Americans.* Fact sheet provided at First National Conference of the Asian American Health Forum, New York, 1986.

Brand D, Hull J, Park J, et al: The new whiz kids: Why Asian Americans are doing so well, and what it costs them. *Time* 1987;130(9):42–51.

California Department of Health: *Report on Hypertension and Related Health Problems in California: Results from the 1979 California Hypertension Survey,* 1982.

Gardner RW, Robey B, Smith PC: Asian Americans: Growth, change, and diversity. *Population Bulletin* 40(4). Washington, DC: Population Reference Bureau, Inc., 1985.

Lin-Fu JS: Population characteristics and health care needs of Asian Pacific Americans. *Public Health Reports* 1988;103:18–21.

National Center for Health Statistics. National Health Interview Surveys; data tapes on smoking prevalence among Asian and Pacific Americans, 1979, 1980, 1983, and 1985. Washington, DC.

Rumbaut RG: Portraits, patterns and predictors of the refugee adaptation process. In Haines DW (ed): *Refugees as Immigrants: Cambodians, Laotians, and Vietnamese in America.* Totowa, NJ: Roman & Littlefield, 1988.

Silverberg E, Lubera J: Cancer statistics, 1986. *CA* 1986;36:20–21.

True R: Access to health care. Commissioned paper for Department of Health and Human Services Task Force Report on Black and Minority Health. Washington, DC, 1985.

US Bureau of the Census. Census of the Population, 1980. Asian and Pacific Islander population by states, 1980. Supplementary Report PC 80-S1-12. General social and economic characteristics, US summary. Publication No. PC 80-1-C1. Washington, DC: US Government Printing Office, 1983.

Yu ESH, Chang CF, Liu WT, et al: Asian-white mortality differentials: Are there excess deaths? Commissioned paper for Department of Health and Human Services Task Force Report on Black and Minority Health. Washington, DC, 1985.

13. The Targeting of Minority Groups by the Tobacco Industry

Alan Blum

For health professionals, especially those who work in governmental, academic, or voluntary health agency settings, this discussion may be hazardous to their preconceptions about the smoking pandemic and how to end it. Although there is hardly anyone over the age of two who hasn't heard that smoking is hazardous to health, the facts remain that a significant decline in smoking among minority groups has not occurred and that consumption may actually be rising among such immigrant groups as the Vietnamese, Haitians, and Hispanics.

I will focus on Black and Hispanic tobacco users and will propose guidelines for counteracting the influence of the purveyors of tobacco products. The objective of this discussion is to challenge health care professionals to reexamine their preconceptions and their very vocabulary in order to begin looking at the tobacco problem as much in terms of marketing the message of not buying cigarettes as in terms of the health behavior of not smoking. Such a view may lead to a better understanding of why tobacco advertising has been so much more successful than has health education and why, in most instances, the tobacco companies could be considered our leading health educators.

Antismoking Literature Lacking

In 1983 and 1984, during my preparation of the two issues of the *New York State Journal of Medicine* (1983, 1985) devoted to the world cigarette smoking pandemic, there was little in the medical literature on minorities and smoking. One of the few available documents was a brochure from the American Cancer Society (ACS) (1981) entitled *Smoking and Genocide*. Considering the disproportionate toll that smoking-related diseases take in minority communities, it was encouraging to find one group that felt it necessary to challenge conventional health vocabulary. Unfortunately, the issue did not take hold among black leaders or civic organizations, some of which receive financial support from the tobacco industry. Moreover, although the ACS assigned an employee to work full time on cancer prevention in Blacks, the word genocide was removed from subsequent editions of the ACS brochure out of fear of offending potential contributors (personal communication, Dan Hoskins 1987).

Similarly, while perhaps 50,000 physicians may have seen the two smoking pandemic issues of the *New York State Journal of Medicine*, which included an incisive review article by Cooper and Simmons (1985) on smoking among Black Americans, it is unlikely that more than a small part of the contents reached the general public. Although *The New York Times* wrote about Cooper and Simmons' conclusions in its main news section, no newspaper or magazine directed to Blacks mentioned their article. Perhaps the most influential sources of health information in minority communities are such publications as *The National Enquirer*. In almost every issue of *The Enquirer* articles describe the prevention of cancer, often based on reports from the ACS, the National Cancer Institute, and medical research centers. The catch is that smoking is seldom singled out as the predominant cause of cancer in the United States, and cigarette advertising is often juxtaposed with articles on cancer. Virtually the only advertising in this 10 million circulation publication, apart from the prostate rejuvenators, horoscopes, and bust developers, is for cigarettes. Such an influence is felt not just in the tabloid press but also in such credible publications as *Time*, *Newsweek*, *US News & World Report*, *Sports Illustrated*, *Ms.*, *Ladies' Home Journal*, and *Family Circle*, all of which not only underplay the subject of tobacco-caused disease but also actively solicit cigarette advertising. Perhaps the greatest concentration of tobacco company advertising is in Black publications such as *Jet*, *Essence*, and *Ebony*, where as many as one in three color advertisements in some issues is for cigarettes. *Ebony*, which reaches more than a third of the adult Black population, has had an enormous influence on the Black community. Yet in its more than 40-year history, it has never published a major article on the leading cause of death among Black Americans: tobacco. Nor did *Ebony* editors express any interest in covering the historic conference on the Realities of Cancer in Minority Communities, the source of this book. One complaint concerned the conference's alleged emphasis on smoking, notwithstanding the fact that only a handful of presentations addressed this subject.

The Health Status of Minorities

The fact that cigarette smoking has become less fashionable among upper- and middle-income groups over the last decade may have lulled the public into believing that the United States is well on its way to reducing the enormous toll taken by smoking. Although overall cigarette consumption has declined slightly, by an average of 1% per year since 1980, the United States still has one of the highest smoking rates in the world—approximately 3,500 cigarettes per adult per year. An increasing percentage of these cigarettes is smoked by those with the lowest levels of income and education. And as the Task Force on Black and Minority Health of the Department of Health and Human Services pointed out in its report in 1985, there are substantial inequities in the health status of ethnic and minority groups in the United States as compared with that of the White majority. The report noted that there are 58,000 excess deaths each year among Black Americans compared with the death rate for the White population. Although the task force called for more research on the disparity in health status between the White and non-White population, there is little doubt that the improvement in health among the educated and privileged has not been shared by those in minority and low-income groups.

Principal among the rising, preventable causes of death are cardiovascular disease and lung cancer (US Department of Health and Human Services 1985) — the two major consequences of smoking. Blacks and Hispanics have the highest rates of these diseases in our population, a fact that Cooper and Simmons (1985) allege is obscured by a tendency in medicine to focus attention on the rare but highly publicized diseases that are more common in Blacks than in others, such as sickle cell anemia. Yet fewer than 300 of the 58,000 excess deaths among Blacks each year are due to sickle cell anemia and related blood conditions — only a small fraction compared with the number of deaths attributable to smoking.

The results of a survey published in 1986 in the *American Journal of Preventive Medicine*, for which nearly 1,000 Chicago adults were interviewed, suggested that insofar as cardiovascular risk factors are concerned, the public has *not* heard it all before. Few respondents could identify all three of the major risk factors — high blood pressure, cigarette smoking, and high cholesterol. Given a list of nine risk factors and asked to choose three, only 11% of the Black respondents and 18% of the Hispanic respondents included cigarette smoking (Dolecek TA et al. 1986). Ethnographic research by Carol Hall of Georgia State University indicated that although most Blacks surveyed answered affirmatively when asked directly "Is smoking hazardous to your health?" only 2% of Black women identified smoking with low birth weight (personal communication, Loudell Snow, Michigan State University, 1987).

Advertising Downplays Risk

Smoking thus continues to go unrecognized by the public as far and away our leading health problem, largely because cigarettes are the most heavily advertised product in America. This advertising not only recruits new users but also buys the complacency of those who do not smoke. Although an enormous amount of behavioral and consumer research has been done on the Black population, very little of it is publicly available because much of it was sponsored by the tobacco and alcohol industries. And there is substantial evidence to suggest that these industries are aiming their advertising at very young consumers.

To approach smoking in a way that is commensurate with its worldwide importance as a cause of death and disease, one would do well to consider smoking as a parasitic disease. In this disease model one must study the life cycle of the parasite in order to understand how to interfere with its activities and to eradicate it. Smoking does not exist in a vacuum. Unlike AIDS or hypertension, it is the only major risk factor that is both entirely preventable and actively promoted. In contrast to health officials who are charged with eradicating infectious diseases (or to tobacco company employees who are charged with selling more cigarettes), few if any health professionals have jobs that depend on there being a decline in tobacco consumption.

A crucial phase in American public health will be reached when the seven major tobacco companies in the U.S. are recognized as seven of its leading parasites: Philip Morris (makers of Marlboro, Virginia Slims, and Benson & Hedges); RJR-Nabisco (R. J. Reynolds Tobacco Company: Winston, Salem, More, and Camel); Loews (Newport and Kent); Brown and Williamson division of British-American Tobacco (Kool and Barclay); American Brands (also known as American Tobacco: Carlton, Lucky Strike, and Pall Mall); Liggett and Meyers (generics); and UST (United States Tobacco Company: Skoal Bandits spitting tobacco).

Phony Debates

Over the years, tobacco companies have created catch-phrases and artificial debates through their public relations arm, the Tobacco Institute, in an attempt to suggest that there is disagreement among scientists about the adverse health effects of smoking. As the evidence against smoking is well accepted, it stands to reason that the industry would direct a major part of its propaganda to the least educated and least sophisticated consumers. Without question, the news media's acceptance of the tobacco industry-coined phrase "smoking and health controversy" delayed public understanding of the fact that there are not two sides to this issue. In the late 1960s the campaign for another tobacco industry pipe dream, the low-tar or "safer" cigarette, led the National Cancer Institute to invest almost its entire budget on smoking — in excess of $40 million — in finding a "safe" way to smoke. One claim of safer smoking was ridiculed in a British Health Education Council campaign, which suggested that smoking a so-called safer cigarette was like jumping from the 36th floor of a skyscraper instead of the 39th.

Yet even today the American Cancer Society and other health organizations have not sufficiently ridiculed the notion that low-tar filtered cigarettes offer the slightest protection from disease. And the National Cancer Institute continues to conduct chemoprevention experiments in which beta carotene and other substances are given to so-called committed smokers as a potential means of preventing lung cancer.

By the mid-1970s, the tobacco industry had created the illusion of another great debate — between the smoking public and the "antismokers." In this most successful of tobacco industry efforts, those who oppose smoking are portrayed as misanthropic. The tobacco industry, by seeming to defend the very consumers that it is helping to kill, has avoided the sobriquet of "anti-health."

By the end of 1985, when even the conservative and antiregulatory American Medical Association had joined other health groups in calling for a total ban on tobacco advertising and promotion, the tobacco industry had succeeded in creating the image of a debate between "neo-prohibitionists" and "First Amendment protectionists." In November 1985, Philip Morris hosted 93 publishers of Black newspapers at its corporate headquarters in New York for a forum on preserving freedoms in American life. (The company has never gathered White editors as a group for a similar meeting.) Early in 1986, these Black publishers voted to condemn the call for a ban on tobacco advertising.

The tobacco industry's advertising credo could well be "Ubiquity, Propinquity, Iniquity." If a lie is glorified day and night on billboards on every street corner, as is found in totalitarian societies, people begin to believe it. In many ethnic neighborhoods, virtually 80% to 90% of all advertising is for brands of tobacco and alcohol products (personal surveys and personal communication, Ed McMahon, Coalition for Scenic Beauty, Washington, DC, 1988). In Black communities especially, cigarette advertising is the single, common theme in a variety of retail outlets from food stores and supermarkets to beauty parlors and barber shops (as well as dry cleaners, laundromats, gas stations, and bars and grills). Mass transit systems, relied on more by lower-income commuters than by others, are an increasing showcase for such cigarette brands as True Gold and Richland.

As for propinquity, cigarette brand names are associated with popular events such as fashion shows, automobile races, and tennis tournaments. They are on the scoreboards of basketball, baseball, and football stadiums (22 of the 24 American major league baseball teams have either a Marlboro or Winston logo on their scoreboards (Blum 1985). Because of its low literacy rate, the Black community depends on television as its prime medium of communication and information (Marketing to Blacks May 18, 1981). Taking advantage of this, tobacco companies make an end run around the Public Health Cigarette Smoking Act of 1971 by getting their names on sporting event broadcasts through an extensive purchase of space at key camera angles. And although professional athletes had stopped appearing in cigarette advertisements, the United States Tobacco Company could still attract popular Black football players such as Earl Campbell and Lawrence Taylor well into the 1980s to promote the use of its Skoal Bandits spitting tobacco.

As for iniquity, the image of tobacco use must appear to be somewhat sinful. Otherwise, a person who smokes wouldn't have to shrug off warnings from family, preachers, health professionals, and others about the dangers of the "evil weed." Advertising of tobacco products, thus, perpetuates an anti-authoritarian mentality.

Advertisers' Goals

The purpose of tobacco advertising goes beyond just selling the product. Of course, such advertising maintains existing users. This is what the industry says it is doing—aiming its advertising at those who already smoke. But the industry's argument that the advertising is aimed only at getting people who already smoke to switch brands is, of course, absurd. Only 10% of people who smoke switch brands in a given year (personal communication, Kenneth Warner, University of Michigan, 1987). That is fewer than five million people a year, yet $3 billion a year is spent on cigarette advertising—more than double the amount spent on the next leading advertised products in our society—pharmaceutical products and alcohol. The tobacco industry's most important goal in advertising, then, is to create social acceptability for smoking. Tobacco companies aim to buy the complacency of those of us—even health care professionals who turn past the cigarette advertising in our magazines and newspapers without a second thought—who may not quite believe the Surgeon General's claim that smoking is our No. 1 killer.

Because 1.5 million people quite smoking each year—one way or another—tobacco companies must recruit replacement smokers, and these 1.25 million new users come almost entirely from the 8- to 18-year-old age group (personal communication, John Pierce, Office of Smoking and Health. More than 90% of people who start to smoke do so before the age of 21, and more than half do so before the age of 16. Although the tobacco industry is quick to cite peer pressure and parental modeling as "proven" causes of childhood smoking, the industry does not acknowledge the influence of its advertising. Indeed, in congressional testimony, industry spokesmen have testified that if the advertisements were banned, people would no longer see the warnings on cigarette packages. However, the relative size and frequency of the brand name versus that of the warnings in advertisements suggest that cigarette advertising is an attempt to negate the health information. Thus many who would like to stop smoking are discouraged through advertising, and those who have stopped are likely to be tempted to start again.

The most insidious effect of tobacco company advertising—now including enormous television and radio buying power through subsidiary corporations in high-visibility consumer products such as food and beverages—has been the immunity from journalistic scrutiny it buys. Thus while newspapers and other media corporations may have begun to editorialize against smoking, no major American newspaper has supported a ban on cigarette advertising. This is in stark contrast to the situation in Canada, where between 1985 and 1987 (well before the passage of bill C-51 by Parliament, which prohibits cigarette advertising entirely), no fewer than 10 of the country's largest newspapers stopped accepting tobacco advertising, stating that they could no longer put profit above public health.

Ironically, money-saving offers are perhaps the major appeal that the tobacco industry is making to the people with the lowest disposable income. There has been a dramatic increase in the number of rebate coupons in magazines and newspapers, good for up to a 40% discount on cartons of cigarettes. The free distribution of sample packs also is especially common in inner-city communities. The fact that a pack-a-day smoker spends more than $7,000 in 10 years on cigarettes is not highlighted in the advertising.

Fighting Back

Efforts to counteract the industry's propaganda have been largely unsuccessful. Unfortunately, the warning labels and brochures that health care authorities have relied on to communicate smoking risks refer to seemingly abstract things such as lung cancer that smokers may experience 10, 20, or 30 years down the line. Instead, the antismoking focus should be on looks, sex, and money—things that may matter more to people. And rather than continuing to rely on pamphlets, posters, preaching, and 3 a.m. public service announcements, health care professionals must figure out ways to compete with the cigarette pushers. To look more closely at the targeting of ethnic markets, one must turn to advertising and marketing publications such as *Advertising Age* and *Ad Week* as well as, of course, to Black-directed publications, including local newspapers. One must walk through Black neighborhoods and repeatedly visit retail establishments. After bemoaning their lack of financial resources to compete with the tobacco industry, public health professionals, and government and voluntary health care agencies simply have not done their homework and remain mired in an unimaginative vocabulary describing health behaviors. These health care forces have not even made use of the simplest of marketing tools, such as a calendar, a map, and lists of popular events and places.

In contrast, the tobacco industry has been especially adept at exploiting racial identity in defining a profitable market among ethnic minorities. R. J. Reynolds sponsors Hispanic street fairs in Los Angeles, and Brown and Williamson foots the bill for numerous Spanish and jazz musicals in Miami and in Hispanic communities elsewhere. Brown and Williamson presents annual "Kool Achiever" awards (named for Kool cigarettes) to people who want to improve the "quality of life in inner-city communities." The tobacco company has even enlisted the National Urban League, the National Newspaper Publishers Association, and the NAACP in the nominating process. During "Black History Month" (February), R. J. Reynolds has featured discount coupons in Black magazines for various brands of cigarettes, complete with pictures of famous Black scientists such as George Washington Carver.

By creating awards for almost any occasion, the tobacco industry maintains a presence in the Black press that extends into the news and sports columns and even the nutrition pages. Although such tactics may follow the pattern of strategies used in the white press, about the best that can be said for such an argument is that it is equal-opportunity exploitation. Black magazines are an especially powerful focus of attention for tobacco companies, and even relatively small-circulation weekly Black newspapers contain cigarette advertising. (Upper, income suburban newspapers seldom receive tobacco advertising money.) The leading advertiser in *Ebony, Jet*, and *Essence*—which reach 47% of the Black women and 38% of the Black men in America—is the tobacco industry (Marketing to Blacks, May 18, 1981). *Essence*, which positions itself as a Black lifestyles magazine and frequently highlights health topics on the front cover, regularly runs cigarette advertisements on the back cover. Not a single article on smoking, much less on cigarette advertising, has ever appeared in *Essence*.

Publishers who accept tobacco advertising are not reluctant, disinterested, or passive recipients of revenue from advertising that is intended to promote the use of a harmful but legal product in a free society. To the contrary, like their White counterparts at *Time* and *Newsweek*, Black publishers aggressively court tobacco advertisers by emphasizing their credibility and their reach in the community they purport to serve. Johnson Publications, publisher of *Ebony* and *Jet*, adds another insidious twist by permitting itself to be the apparent sponsor of a national traveling fashion fair that is in large part paid for by R. J. Reynolds to promote its More brand of cigarettes. Similarly, Philip Morris, without identify-ing itself as a cigarette manufacturer, has sponsored cultural events such as the Alvin Ailey American Dance Theatre, jazz concerts, and a photographic display of the late Dr. Martin Luther King. At the same time that Philip Morris is spon-soring an upscale exhibition of Black artists at the Whitney Museum, it is plaster-ing Black neighborhoods with hundreds of larger-than-life billboards for Virginia Slims, Benson & Hedges, and Marlboro Lights Menthol cigarettes.

Even a single paid counteradvertising billboard in each minority neighborhood could begin to turn the picture around by galvanizing attention to the pervasive-ness of tobacco industry propaganda. According to the Eight-Sheet Outdoor Advertising Association (the trade organization for $5' \times 11'$ billboards), fully 50% of all eight-sheet advertising in the United States is for cigarettes (Eight-Sheet Outdoor Advertising Association 1986). In many Black and Hispanic areas, this figure may reach as high as 90%. "Outdoor advertising reaches ethnic groups better than any other medium aimed at ethnic groups" reads the headline from a promotion by the Gannett Corporation (publisher of *USA Today* and 83 other newspapers) in *Advertising Age*. Until these eyesores are banned outright, this simple, cost-effective advertising medium must be a fixture of every health promotion campaign.

Tackling just four of the top 10 Hispanic markets — Los Angeles, New York, Miami, and San Antonio — could reach nearly 70% of the Hispanic population in this country. The Hispanic population is a very important growth segment for the tobacco companies. It encompasses in excess of 15 million people and is the fastest growing minority group in the country. Hispanics' buying power is an extraordinary $45 billion a year, and Hispanics are a young population. In New York and Los Angeles, 40% of the Hispanic population is under 18, and 70% is under 35. Puerto Ricans, Mexican Americans, and Cuban Americans largely compose the Hispanic market. Tobacco advertisers have learned to appeal to each segment well. In Puerto Rico, R. J. Reynolds' Winston brand sponsors numerous cultural activities using local ethnic themes. Philip Morris' Marlboro is the sole national advertiser in a number of Hispanic publications in the United States, such as *La Informacion* in Houston. Marlboro, R. J. Reynolds' Winston and Salem, and Loews' Newport brands are perhaps the most prevalent brand-name products advertised on billboards in Spanish communities and in mom-and-pop grocery stores.

Recommendations

What, then, are the measures that might be taken in planning strategies for preventing and ending the use of tobacco in minority communities? First and foremost, there must be additional research, only a small part of which should be directed toward studying health habits, smoking-related disease incidence, and attitudes toward smoking. Health advocates must take the lead from tobacco companies and other purveyors of unhealthful products who have sought to overcome the burden of scientific research concerning smoking and other harmful habits. Health professionals need to conduct far more *consumer* research, including face-to-face surveys and in-store observations of buying behavior in lieu of telephone surveys of health behaviors. Even before this step, health professionals must learn more about the basic history and customs of minority communities and must be sensitive both to ethnic characteristics and to the aspirations of minority groups. It is imperative to recognize that minority communities are no more homogenous than is the rest of American society. In this light, one can learn a great deal by studying the techniques of the tobacco industry, which are in sharp contrast to those of health agencies.

The steps toward ending the cigarette smoking pandemic are not unidimensional; rather they are multifocal and require concomitant strategies. Paid counteradvertising ridiculing specific tobacco brand names and advertising images is the single most important force that will result in a declining consumption. An excise tax dedicated solely to the purpose of counteradvertising space would be ideal, but the investment must be made even without such tax support. A ban on tobacco advertising is another ideal, but without paid counteradvertising it might be an illusive initial step.

The passage of clean indoor legislation has been the single major advance in this country in terms of reducing cigarette consumption, thanks to the efforts of activist nonsmokers' rights groups. Unfortunately, Black and Hispanic membership in these organizations is small, and the success of tobacco companies in winning over minority group lawmakers has been a major disgrace. As incredible as it may seem, Black and Hispanic legislators have fallen for the tobacco industry line that efforts to restrict smoking in public places are designed to bring back racial segregation.

There is a great need for a no-holds-barred revocabularization, that is, a new set of terms, images, and other symbols with which to communicate to the public about tobacco products and the manufacturers—child molesters, if you will—who promote them. Such counteradvertising has the potential to discourage the next generation from ever buying a pack cigarettes or a tin of tobacco.

To this end, school-based programs must be made more engaging—and enraging—based on an equal emphasis on the "three Ps": peer pressure, parental modeling, and propaganda. Curriculum designers might well employ a simple formula of fear, humor, and anger. Too few educational programs in or out of the classroom go beyond scare tactics and cognitive objectives about the dangers of smoking. By analyzing and satirizing the promotional techniques of tobacco companies and their media allies, students can delight in turning the tables on Madison Avenue. In studying the long arm of the tobacco industry around the world and making the connection between tobacco advertising and the deaths of family members and friends from tobacco-related diseases, students may learn to redirect their anger away from teachers, parents, and health professionals onto the authority figures in our society who attempt to promote unhealthful products to children.

Because the onus for ridding society of tobacco and its promotion should not rest solely on parents, teachers, and health care officials, reinforcement strategies must be created in health care settings, religious and civic organizations, cultural and sports arenas, and the mass media. Health care authorities and legal scholars have an ideal opportunity to combine forces in litigation by suing those who make and promote irredeemably harmful tobacco products. This includes seeking redress on behalf of those killed or injured in fires caused by cigarettes, which are designed to keep burning even when unattended.

Regrettably, existing regional, national, and international coalitions to carry out a multilevel strategy to end the tobacco pandemic are few. However, as the consumption of cigarettes very slowly declines in the United States, American companies are dramatically expanding their markets in Asia, Africa, and Central and South America. Thus, although much emphasis has been placed on complaining about the absurdity of government price supports for tobacco, little clamor has been raised to end foreign trade in tobacco products. Similarly, a disproportionate allocation of resources and personnel for smoking cessation programs for adults may have come at the expense of a concerted mass media primary prevention effort designed for young people.

The age-old problems caused by tobacco in American society are dramatically worse in minority communities. All responsible citizens, health organizations, and corporations must put their money where their mouths are to end the tobacco pandemic and laugh the pushers out of town.

References

American Cancer Society: *Smoking and Genocide.* New York, 1981.

Blum A: Deadly pushers: How sports sells tobacco. *Miami Herald*, Aug 25, 1985, p 1E.

Blum A (ed): The world cigarette pandemic. Part I. *NY State J Med* 1983;83:1242–1377.

Blum A (ed): The world cigarette pandemic. Part II. *NY State J Med* 1985;85:278–477.

Cooper R, Simmons BE: Cigarette smoking and ill health among black Americans. *NY State J Med* 1985;85:344–349.

Dolecek TA, Schoenberger JA, Omam JK, et al: Cardiovascular risk factor knowledge and belief in prevention among adults in Chicago. *Am J Prev Med* 1986;2:262–267.

Eight-Sheet Outdoor Advertising Association: *National Advertising Report and 1985 Summary.* Independence, MO, 1986.

Marketing to Blacks: *Advertising Age* (Suppl), May 18, 1981.

US Department of Health and Human Services: *Report of the Task Force on Black and Minority Health.* Washington, DC, 1985.

Section 4

Cancer Research

Introduction to Section 4

Edith P. Mitchell

Patterns of cancer incidence, mortality, and survival vary among population groups according to racial and ethnic background. Blacks have the highest overall age-adjusted rates of cancer incidence and experience poorer survival than any other United States population. Data analyzed from the Surveillance, Epidemiology, and End Results (SEER) Program of the National Cancer Institute from 1973–1981 showed, in general, survival rates for most minorities were lower than for nonminorities. However, of the 25 primary sites for which survival data were available, Blacks had lower survival rates than any other population group for all except three cancers—brain, multiple myeloma, and ovarian (Young et al. 1984; Cancer Patient Survival, 1977).

It is well recognized that for a specific cancer site, survival time following diagnosis depends on several factors, including the stage or extent of disease, tumor biologic characteristics, host performance status, and effectiveness of treatment. However, little is known regarding the factors that account for the poorer survival observed among minority populations. Lower socioeconomic status has been implicated as a primary factor (Bergdow et al. 1977) and may correlate with the increased incidence of certain cancers.

Lung cancer is a major health problem in the United States, with age-adjusted cancer death rates for both males and females doubling every 15 years (Rosenow and Carr 1979; Jett et al. 1983). Lung cancer is the leading cause of cancer death in men aged 35 years or older, and the leading cause of cancer deaths in women 35 to 74 years old (Silverberg 1986).

Using data from the Third National Cancer Survey, Devesa and Diamond (1983) evaluated the association of lung cancer incidence with income and education and the effect of adjustment for socioeconomic distribution on Black-White differences in lung cancer rates. Strong significant inverse trends between lung cancer incidence and both income and education were apparent among White and Black males, and the effect of income exceeds that of education. Lung cancer rates among Black males compared with those for White males were significantly higher before socioeconomic adjustments, rose significantly higher after adjustment for education, and were nonsignificantly lower after adjustment for income. Strong trends in risk with income or education were not observed for lung cancer among females of either race.

Approximately 40,000 new cases of head and neck cancers occur annually, with no major change in the incidence over the past three decades. Tobacco and alcohol have been implicated as the primary causative factors, and the effects seem to be additive (Hardingham et al. 1977).

Cancers of the esophagus account for approximately 8,000 deaths per year and constitute 7% of all gastrointestinal cancers. Gastric cancer remains a major cause of cancer deaths in the United States: approximately 25,000 new cases are diagnosed annually. Although the overall incidence has decreased in the United States over the past three decades, the incidence in Black populations has increased slightly (Weisburger and Rainiri 1978).

Environmental factors have been implicated as having a major role in the development of gastric cancers. It is widely hypothesized that nitrates and secondary amines in the diet influence the in vivo synthesis of mutagenic and carcinogenic nitrosocompounds and that these may be involved in mutations to epithelial cells.

Cancers of the colon and rectum account for approximately 94,000 new cases annually and 50,000 deaths. It is likely that environmental factors are important in the etiology of colorectal cancer. It has been suggested that there is an association between high dietary fat and beef intake and the lack of dietary fiber and the high incidence of colon cancer in some populations. Diet influences intestinal mucosal microsomal mixed-function oxidases, thereby possibly causing carcinogenesis (Weisburger et al. 1977).

Cancer of the breast is the second leading cause of cancer death in American women. Each year more than 100,000 women will develop the disease and approximately 35,000 will die of the disease. The major risk factors for development of breast cancer include early menarche and late menopause, nulliparity or bearing the first child after age 30, a family history of breast cancer, and exposure to ionizing radiation (Ries et al. 1983; McMahon et al. 1973).

The recurrence of breast cancer following surgery or other methods of local control is primarily dependent on the stage of disease at diagnosis. However, other factors correlate with survival, including the presence of estrogen receptors and high nuclear and low histologic grade. For breast cancer, in each stage, Whites had higher survival rates than Blacks.

Further studies are needed to investigate the role of additional factors in the survival differentials of racial/ethnic groups and whether intervention ultimately will affect survival.

In a multi-institutional, prospective clinical trial, differences in age at diagnosis, tumor diameter, and estrogen receptor (ER) level were found between White and Black women with breast cancer. Black women tended to be younger, have larger tumors, and have lower ER levels. Disease-free survival was higher for Whites than Blacks (Gordon and Pearson 1987). Similar results were found by other investigators (Mohla et al. 1982).

Much has been accomplished in pediatric oncology in recent years. The effectiveness of therapy in increasing the duration of disease-free survival and the rate of cure has improved. Most studies show no major differences in the disease incidence or survival of Blacks and Whites (Van Eys 1988).

References

Bergdow, Ross R, Latourette HB: Economic status and survival of cancer patients. *Cancer* 1977;39:467–477.

Cancer Patient Survival, Report Number 5. DHEW Publication No (NIH) 77-992, 1977.

Devesa SS, Diamond ES: Socioeconomic and racial differences in lung cancer incidence. *Am J Epidemiol* 1983;118:818–831.

Gordon N, Pearson O: Race and prognosis in breast cancer. *Reviews on Endocrine Related Cancer* 1987;27:17–20.

Hardingham M, Dalley VM, Shaw HJ: Cancers of the floor of the mouth: Clinical features and results of treatment. *Clin Oncol* 1977;3:227–246.

Jett JR, Cortese DA, Fontana RS: Lung cancer. Current concepts and prospects. *CA* 1983;33:74–86.

McMahon, B, Cole P, Brown J: Etiology of human breast cancer: A review. *JNCI* 1973;50:21–42.

Mohla S, Sampson CC, et al: Estrogen and progesterone receptors in breast cancer in black Americans: Correlation of receptor data with tumor differentiation. *Cancer* 1982;50:552–559.

Ries LG, Pollack ES, Young JL Jr: Surveillance, Epidemiology, and End Results Program 1973–79. *JNCI* 1983;70:693–707.

Rosenow EC III, Carr DT: Bronchogenic carcinoma. *CA* 1979;29:233–246.

Silverberg E: Cancer statistics 1986. *CA* 1986;36:7–25.

Van Eys J: Pediatric cancers. *Cancer Bulletin* 1988;40:88.

Weisburger J, Rainiri R: Dietary factors and etiology of gastric cancer. *Cancer Res* 1978;35:3469–3474.

Weisburger J, et al: Colon cancer: Its epidemiology and experimental production. *Cancer* 1977;40:2114–2420.

Young JL, Ries LG, Pollack ES: Cancer patient survival among ethnic groups in the United States. *JNCI* 1984;73:341–352.

14. Hormone Receptors, Tumor Differentiation, and Breast Cancer in Black Americans

Suresh Mohla, Walter M. Griffin, Calvin C. Sampson,
Jerome Wilson, Vandana Narang, and LaSalle D. Leffall, Jr.

One of 11 women will develop breast cancer during her lifetime (Cancer Facts and Figures 1986). Although the disease occurs more frequently in White than in Black women, mortality rates in the two groups are comparable (Cutler and Young 1975; White and Enterline 1980) because Blacks have a poorer survival rate from breast cancer than Whites. Not only is breast cancer in Blacks detected at a relatively more advanced stage than in Whites, but it also shows a consistently lower rate of survival when calculated by disease stages (Myers and Hankey 1980; Nemoto et al. 1980). Thus, a question arises to whether biological differences (independent of socioeconomic status) may account for the survival differential within stages between Blacks and Whites.

Estrogen receptors (ER) and progesterone receptors (PR) in breast cancer have been shown to play an important role in predicting a patient's response to endocrine therapy, as predictors of disease-free interval and overall survival for patients with primary disease (Clark et al. 1984; Fisher et al. 1981, 1983; Howat et al. 1985; McGuire and Clark 1985; Vollenweider-Zerargui et al. 1986; Walt et al. 1976; Witliff 1984).

Earlier reports showed a significant association between the growth fraction of a breast cancer (as measured by the thymidine labeling index, TLI) and ER. A low TLI was associated with ER positivity and a high TLI with ER negativity (Meyer et al. 1977; Rao and Meyer 1977; Silvestrini 1984). A significant association between tumor grade and ER had been documented with the observation that well- and moderately well-differentiated tumors usually contain ER, whereas most poorly differentiated tumors are devoid of these receptors (Fisher et al. 1981; Lesser et al. 1981; Maynard et al. 1978; Mohla et al. 1980, 1982a and b, 1984; Parl and Wagner 1980; Rich et al. 1978). Recent observations also indicated a relationship between disease-free interval, ER, and tumor differentiation (Knight et al. 1977; Rich et al. 1978). Although the disease-free interval is independent of ER in both well- and moderately well-differentiated tumors, a shorter disease-free interval was observed for patients with poorly differentiated ER-negative tumors and a longer disease-free interval for those with poorly differentiated ER-positive tumors (Maynard et al. 1978).

Earlier studies from Japan (Matsumoto and Sugano 1978; Ochi et al. 1978) on the distribution of ER and PR had revealed significant ethnic differences in the incidence of ER-positive tumors in postmenopausal Japanese women, the incidence in Japanese patients being similar for premenopausal and postmenopausal patients. In Western patients the incidence is higher in postmenopausal patients.

Earlier data from one of our laboratories (Mohla et al. 1980, 1982a and b, 1984) indicated a predominance of ER-negative and poorly differentiated breast cancers in a predominantly Black American patient population, and our results on the predominance of poorly differentiated tumors in Black Americans were confirmed (Ownby et al. 1985). In addition, several studies from South Africa demonstrated significant differences in the distribution of ER among White, Black, and Asian patients (Collings et al. 1980; Pegoraro et al. 1986; Savage et al. 1981).

This report summarizes data on estrogen and progesterone receptors, histologic characteristics, and tumor differentiation in 413 patients with primary breast cancer from the Howard University Hospital, Washington, D.C.

Materials and Methods

Patients. All tissue samples discussed here were derived from 413 women patients, ages 28 to 97 years, treated at Howard University Hospital between June 1977 and December 1986.

Tissue collection, pathology, and preparation. Fresh tumor specimens were received in an ice bath from the laboratory of surgical pathology immediately after excision. All histologic preparations were examined and graded (Bloom and Richardson 1957). Based on the criteria, each case was placed into one of three categories: (1) well-differentiated (WD), (2) moderately well-differentiated (MWD), or (3) poorly differentiated (PD).

Tissue homogenization, cytosol preparation, and incubation of cytosols for ER and PR assays, which were done using the sucrose density-gradient method, have

TABLE 1. Distribution of estrogen receptors in primary breast cancer.

Patient's menopausal status	Estrogen receptors[a]			Significance	Estrogen receptors	Significance
	> 10	3–10	< 3		Pooled < 10	
Premenopausal	44	15	65	χ^2 7.21 df 1	80	χ^2 6.63[b] df 1
Postmenopausal	144	28	117	$P < 0.03$	145	$P < 0.01$

[a] fmoles/mg protein
[b] Compared with > 10 fmoles/mg protein group

TABLE 2. Relationship between estrogen and progesterone receptors.

Estrogen[a] receptors	All patients		Premenopausal patients		Postmenopausal patients	
	Progesterone[a] receptors		Progesterone receptors		Progesterone receptors	
	> 10	< 10	> 10	< 10	> 10	< 10
> 10	70	84	17	22	53	62
< 10	11	188	5	66	6	122
Significance	$P < 0.0001$[b]		$P < 0.0001$		$P < 0.0001$	

[a] fmoles/mg protein
[b] Fisher's exact test

been described (Mohla et al. 1981a, 1982b). The results were expressed as femtomoles of receptor per milligram of cytosol protein. For ER, a value of more than 10 fmoles/mg protein was classified as ER-positive (+), a value of 3 to 10 fmoles/mg was classified as borderline (±), and a value of less than 3 fmoles/mg was classified as ER-negative (−). Tumor specimens with more than 10 fmoles/mg of 8S (Suedberg units) + 4S PR or more than 3 fmoles/mg of 8S-complex were classified as PR+. Tritiated estradiol (estradiol [2,4,6,7-^{3}H(N)]) and ^{3}H-R5020 (promegestone [17α-methyl-^{3}H]) were used as ligands for ER and PR, respectively. Each sample was assayed in the absence or presence of a 200-fold excess nonradioactive hormone.

Results

The distribution of ER and PR in 413 specimens from patients with primary breast cancer revealed 46% (188/413) ER+, 10% (43/413) ER±, and 44% ER− (182/413) tumors in these patients. There was a higher incidence of ER+ samples in postmenopausal than in premenopausal patients; this trend was maintained whether the small number of ER± patients were grouped separately or pooled with ER− patients (Table 1). Progesterone receptors were detected in 45% of ER+ and 6% of ER− patients; this trend was independent of menopausal status (Table 2). The majority of patients exhibited tumor histopathologic characteristics of infiltrating ductal carcinoma (IDCA). Forty-six percent of all IDCA were ER+; 10% and 44% of the IDCA were ER± and ER−, respectively. Only 3% (14/413) of the tumors were WD, 21% (87/413) were MWD, and 76% (312/413) were PD. A significant correlation was found between tumor grade and ER+ samples whether the small number of WD tumors were pooled with MWD or analyzed separately (Table 3). Thus more than 87% of all ER− tumors (159/182) were poorly differentiated. In contrast, tumor grade was not correlated with menopausal status; the percentages of poorly differentiated tumors in pre- and postmenopausal patients were 77.4% and 74.7, respectively. Tumor

TABLE 3. Relationship between estrogen receptors and tumor differentiation.

Tumor grade	Estrogen receptors			Significance	Estrogen receptors	Significance
	$> 10^a$	3–10	< 3		Pooled < 10	
WD	10	2	2		4	
				χ^2 25.60		$\chi^2 14.23^b$
MWD	52	14	21	df 4	35	df 2
				$P < 0.0001$		$P < 0.001$
PD	126	27	159		186	

Abbreviations: WD, well-differentiated; MWD, moderately well-differentiated; PD, poorly differentiated.
[a] fmoles/mg protein
[b] Compared with > 10 fmoles/mg protein group

TABLE 4. Relationship between estrogen receptors (ER) and tumor grade, adjusted for menopausal status.

Patient's menopausal status	ER^a	Tumor grade		Significance[b]
		WD + MWD	PD	
Premenopausal	> 10	15	29	
	< 10	13	67	χ^2 12.35
				df 1
				$P < 0.005$
Postmenopausal	> 10	47	97	
	< 10	26	119	

Abbreviations: WD, well-differentiated; MWD, moderately well-differentiated; PD, poorly differentiated.
[a] fmoles/mg protein
[b] Mantel-Haenszel analysis

TABLE 5. Relationship between progesterone receptors and tumor grade.

Progesterone receptors[a]	Tumor grade			Significance	Tumor grade	Significance
	WD	MWD	PD		WD + MWD	
> 10	5	23	59	χ^2 6.21	28	χ^2 4.74[b]
				df 2		df 1
< 10	6	47	211	$P < 0.05$	53	$P < 0.05$

Abbreviations: WD, well-differentiated; MWD, moderately well-differentiated; PD, poorly differentiated.
[a] fmoles/mg protein
[b] Compared with PD group

TABLE 6. Relationship between progesterone receptors (PR) and tumor grade, adjusted for menopausal status.

Patient's menopausal status	PR^a	Tumor grade		Significance[b]
		WD + MWD	PD	
Premenopausal	> 10	9	16	
	< 10	16	67	χ^2 47.22 df 1 $P < 0.03$
Postmenopausal	> 10	19	43	
	< 10	37	144	

Abbreviations: WD, well-differentiated; MWD, moderately well-differentiated; PD, poorly differentiated.
[a] fmoles/mg protein
[b] Mantel-Haenszel analysis

differentiation was correlated with estrogen receptors even when adjusted for menopausal status (Table 4); 54% of WD and MWD tumors in premenopausal and 64% in postmenopausal patients were ER+. In contrast, 30% and 44% of PD tumors were ER+ in premenopausal and postmenopausal patients, respectively. PR positivity was also correlated with low tumor differentiation (Table 5), a trend independent of menopausal status (Table 6). The relationship between tumor grade and histology is shown in Table 7. Intraductal tumors showed a higher percentage of WD and MWD characteristics whereas all lobular carcinomas were PD. However, fewer than 4% of all patients had lobular and intraductal carcinomas.

TABLE 7. Relationship between tumor grade and histopathology in patients with primary breast cancer.

Tumor histology	Number of patients (%)		Tumor grade	
			WD + MWD	PD
1. Intraductal	7	(1.7)	4	3
2. Infiltrating ductal	356	(86.2)	83	273
Adenoid-cystic	1	(0.24)	1	
Medullary	15	(3.6)	3	12
Mucoid	19	(4.6)	7	12
Papillary	7	(1.7)	2	5
Squamous	1	(0.24)		1
Tubular	1	(0.24)	1	
3. Lobular	6	(1.5)		6
Total	413	(100)	101 (24.4%)	312 (75.6%)

Abbreviations: WD, well-differentiated; MWD, moderately well-differentiated; PD, poorly differentiated.

Discussion

Our data on predominantly Black patients indicated a lower incidence of ER+ and a higher incidence of ER− breast cancers compared with published data on predominantly White patients; data from several laboratories have now confirmed these results (Hulka et al. 1984; Natarajan et al. 1985). Our results were also consistent with recent reports from South Africa on the significant differences in the distribution of ER between Black and White patients with breast cancer (Collings et al. 1980; Pegoraro et al. 1986; Savage et al. 1981). The present results confirmed our earlier ones (Mohla et al. 1980, 1982a and b, 1984).

The findings also showed several similarities in ER distribution: a higher incidence of ER+ samples in postmenopausal than premenopausal patients and a higher incidence of PR+ samples in ER+ than ER− patients. Earlier data from our institution also showed a higher incidence of ER positivity in tumor specimens taken from the primary than those from the metastatic tumor site (Mohla et al. 1982a and b). These data are in agreement with earlier findings from several laboratories.

Another observation that was significantly different from previous reports was a higher incidence of PD tumors in our patient population (Table 8). These results on the predominance of poorly differentiated tumors in Black Americans compared with their White counterparts have been confirmed (Ownby et al. 1985). The incidence of ER positivity in WD, MWD, and PD tumors was similar, however, to what has been reported (Fisher et al. 1981; Lesser et al. 1981; Maynard et al. 1978; Parl and Wagner 1980; Rich et al. 1978); ER positivity was lower in PD tumors compared with WD or MWD tumors. Further, this relationship between ER and tumor grade was independent of the patients' menopausal status.

Several factors have been suggested to influence the ER status of a tumor specimen, including menopausal status and seasonal variation (Hughes et al. 1976; McGuire 1978), rate of cell replication, local lymphocytic reaction, tissue cellularity (Meyer et al. 1977; Rao and Meyer 1977; Silvestrini 1984), and tumor grade (Fisher et al. 1981; Lesser et al. 1981; Maynard et al. 1978; Mohla et al. 1980, 1982a and b, 1984; Parl and Wagner 1980; Rich et al. 1978). Although the rate of cell proliferation, tissue cellularity, and local lymphocytic reaction were not studied in this investigation, our data clearly indicated that the high frequency of ER− and low frequency of ER+ tumors may, among other reasons, have resulted from the higher incidence of PD tumors in our patient population.

As mentioned, even though breast cancer occurs more frequently in White than in Black women (Cutler and Young 1975), the breast cancer mortality rates for the two groups are comparable (White and Enterline 1980) because Black women with breast cancer have a notably poorer survival rate than their White counterparts (Myers and Hankey 1980). Although certain risk factors (family history, benign breast disease, early onset of menarche, late menopause, delayed

TABLE 8. Breast cancer and tumor differentiation: data comparison of present findings with those of other researchers

	Present study 413[a]	Maynard et al. 1978 200	Rich et al. 1978 140	Parl & Wagner 1980 116	Heuson et al. 1975 85	Matsumoto & Sugano 1978 102	Boyd et al. 1981 698
Tumor Grade							
WD	14(3%)	41(19%)	26(19%)	20(19%)	18(21%)	10(10%)	111(16%)
MWD	87(21%)	82(37%)	86(61%)	57(49%)	38(45%)	57(56%)	377(54%)
PD	312(76%)	97(44%)	28(20%)	39(34%)	29(34%)	35(34%)	210(30%)
χ_2		74.50	140.23	77.24	68.07	63.32	217.66
df		2	2	2	2	2	2
P		< 0.001	< 0.001	< 0.001	< 0.001	< 0.001	< 0.001

Abbreviations: WD, well-differentiated; MWD, moderately well-differentiated; PD, poorly differentiated.
[a] Number of patients.

age at first pregnancy, nulliparity, failure of ovulation, obesity, high intake of fats in diet, socioeconomic status, and body weight) have been implicated in the incidence of breast cancer (Blot et al. 1977; Cole and Cramer 1977; Lesser et al. 1981; Mohla and Criss 1981b; Vorherr 1980), relatively little is known about the role of such risk factors in relation to survival. One reason for this survival difference is that breast cancer in Blacks is detected at a more advanced stage than in Whites (Mohla et al. 1982a and b; Myers and Hankey 1980; Natarajan et al. 1985; Nemoto et al. 1980). However, Black women also have poorer survival rates at each stage of the disease compared with those of Whites (Nemoto et al. 1980). Thus, the biologic differences observed in our study, that is, a high incidence of PD and ER− tumors, may provide at least a partial explanation for within-stage survival differences between Blacks and Whites.

Loss of differentiation has been shown to result in loss of ER, which in turn has been associated with an increase in tumor growth fraction (Meyer et al. 1977; Rao and Meyer 1977). Furthermore, data from other studies suggested both a longer disease-free interval in ER+ patients than ER− patients (Clark et al. 1984; Howat et al. 1985; Ownby et al. 1985; Rich et al. 1978; Vollenweider-Zerargui et al. 1986). A longer disease-free interval in patients with ER+ PD tumors compared with those with ER− PD tumors has been reported (Maynard et al. 1978). A determination of whether these findings help to explain poor within-stage survival among Blacks will require further study.

Earlier studies (Walt et al. 1976) showed, however, that "estrogen receptor negative patients have a shorter life span after discovery of the tumors and are more likely to develop dominant visceral metastases" known to be associated with very poor prognoses. In contrast, the dominant metastatic sites in ER+ patients were soft tissues and bone; this distribution of metastatic sites between

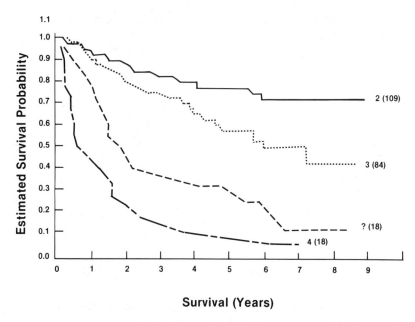

FIGURE 1. Kaplan-Meier survival estimates for 230 breast cancer patients by stage diagnosed during the period of 1977 to 1981. Patients were classified as stage 1 (cancer in situ), stage 2 (local), stage 3 (regional) and stage 4 (distant). There were 18 patients with stage unknown (?). Numbers in parentheses indicate the number of patients. There was only one patient with stage 1 disease, and this patient is still alive.

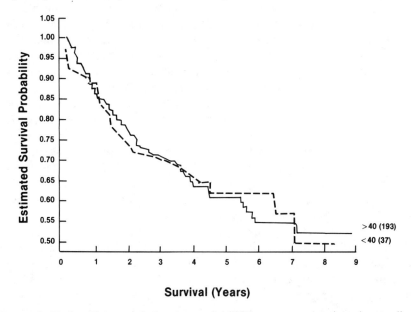

FIGURE 2. Kaplan-Meier survival estimates for 230 breast cancer patients by age diagnosed during the period of 1977 to 1981. Number of patients older and younger than 40 years are shown in parentheses.

ER+ and ER− was highly significant ($P < 0.0005$; Walt et al. 1976). Further, as Walt et al. reported, "life expectancy from the time breast lump was noted until death demonstrated increased longevity in the estrogen receptor positive groups," and this was independent of stage or delay in seeking medical treatment (Walt et al. 1976). "It is possible that ER positive patients are likely to live longer due at least in part to their greater responsiveness to hormonal therapy but also possibly to the less immediately lethal distribution of their metastases," Walt et al. (1976) wrote.

Current efforts are to determine the overall survival in ER+ and ER− patients, with data controlled for tumor grade. However, our data on survival of all patients diagnosed between 1977 and 1981 indicated a correlation between survival and stage at diagnosis (Figure 1) and no significant difference in survival between patients younger or older than 40 years (Figure 2).

The clinical significance of our results lies in the observations that ER− and PD tumors indicated both histopathologic and biochemical evidence of dedifferentiation and hence may also indicate aggressive disease. These results may be a partial explanation of the overall poorer survival of Black breast cancer patients compared with that of Whites. Whether these differences are caused by ethnic or environmental factors, or both, remains to be elucidated. The recent work of Slamon et al. (1987) demonstrated a correlation between the amplification of HER-2/neu oncogenes and survival and time to relapse in patients with breast cancers. HER-2/neu was amplified two- to 20-fold in 30% of the tumors. Compared with currently used prognostic factors, including ER and PR, the amplification of this specific oncogene in breast cancer patients had greater prognostic value in node-positive patients. The Slamon group's 1987 data suggested that HER-2/neu oncogene amplification in breast cancers may play an important role in determining the biologic behavior or pathogenesis of human breast cancer. Research in the area of oncogenes may prove beneficial in delineating causes for the overall poorer survival of Black Americans with breast cancer compared with that of their White counterparts.

Acknowledgments. This investigation was supported by grant NCI-5P30-CA-14718 awarded by the National Cancer Institute. We gratefully acknowledge the secretarial assistance of Joyce Dempsey.

References

Bloom HJG, Richardson WW: Histologic grading and prognosis in breast cancer. *Br J Cancer* 1957;11:359–369.

Blot WJ, Fraumeni JF, Stone BJ: Geographic patterns of breast cancer in the United States. *JNCI* 1977;59:1407–1411.

Boyd NF, Meakin JW, Hayward JL, et al: Clinical estimation of the growth rate of breast cancer. *Cancer* 1981;48:1037–1042.

Cancer Facts and Figures: American Cancer Society, New York, 1986.

Clark GM, Osborne CK, McGuire WL: Correlations between estrogen receptor, progesterone receptor, and patient characteristics in human breast cancer. *J Clin Oncol* 1984;2:1102–1109.

Cole P, Cramer D: Diet and cancer of endocrine target organs. *Cancer* 1977;40:434–437.

Collings JR, Levin RJ, Savage N: Racial differences in oestrogen receptor and peroxide status of human breast cancer tissue. *S Afr Med J* 1980;57:444–446.

Cutler JJ, Young JL: Third national cancer survey: Incidence data. *US Department of Health, Education and Welfare* Publication No. (NIH) 75-787, pp. 122, 1975.

Fisher B, Redmond C, Brown A, et al: Treatment of primary breast cancer with chemotherapy and tamoxifen. *N Engl J Med* 1981;305:1–6.

Fisher B, Redmond C, Brown A, et al: Influence of tumor estrogen and progesterone levels on the response to tamoxifen and chemotherapy in primary breast cancer. *J Clin Oncol* 1983;1:227–241.

Heuson JC, Leclercq G, Longeval E, et al: Estrogen receptor: Prognostic significance in breast cancer. In McGuire WL, Carbone PP, Vollmer EP (eds): *Estrogen Receptor in Human Breast Cancer.* New York: Raven Press, 1975, pp. 57–72.

Howat JMT, Harris M, Swindell R, et al: The effect of oestrogen and progesterone receptors on recurrence and survival in patients with carcinoma of the breast. *Br J Cancer* 1985;51:262–270.

Hughes A, Jacobsen NI, Wagner RK, et al: Ovarian independent fluctuations of estradiol receptor levels in mammalian tissues. *Mol Cell Endocrinol* 1976;5:379–388.

Hulka BS, Chambless LE, Wilkinson WE, et al: Hormonal and personal effects on estrogen receptors in breast cancer. *Am J Epidemiol* 1984;119:692–704.

Knight WA, Livingston RB, Gregory EJ, et al: Estrogen receptor as an independent prognostic factors for early recurrence in breast cancer. *Cancer Res* 1977;37:4669–4671.

Lesser ML, Rosen PP, Senie RT, et al: Estrogen and progesterone receptors in breast carcinoma: Correlations with epidemiology and pathology. *Cancer* 1981;48:299–309.

Matsumoto K, Sugano H: Human breast cancer and hormone receptors. In Sharma RK, Criss WE (eds): *Endocrine Control in Neoplasia.* New York: Raven Press, 1978, pp. 191–208.

Maynard PVR, Blamey RW, Elston CW, et al: Estrogen receptor assay in primary breast cancer and early recurrence of disease. *Cancer Res* 1978;38:4292–4295.

McGuire WL: Hormone receptors: Their role in predicting prognosis and response to endocrine therapy. *Semin Oncol* 1978;5:428–433.

McGuire WL, Clark GM: Role of progesterone receptors in breast cancer. *Semin Oncol* 1985;12:12–16.

Meyer JS, Rao BR, Stevens SC, et al: Low incidence of estrogen in breast carcinomas with rapid rates of cellular replication. *Cancer Res* 1977;40:2290–2298.

Mohla S, Clem-Jackson N, Hunter JB: Estrogen receptor and estrogen-induced gene expression in the rat mammary glands and uteri during pregnancy and lactation: Changes in progesterone receptors and RNA polymerase activity. *J Steroid Biochem* 1981a;248:6366–6374.

Mohla S, Criss WE: The relationship of diet to cancer and hormones. In Newell GR, Ellison NM (eds): *Nutrition and Cancer: Etiology and Treatment.* New York: Raven Press, 1981b, pp. 93–110.

Mohla S, Enterline JP, Sampson CC, et al: A predominance of poorly differentiated tumors among black breast cancer patients: Management and screening implications. *Prog Clin Biol Res* 1982a;83:249–258.

Mohla S, Sampson CC, Khan T, et al: Estrogen and progesterone receptors in human breast cancer in black patients. *Med Pediatr Oncol* 1980;9:95.

Mohla S, Sampson CC, Khan T, et al: Estrogen and progesterone receptors in breast cancer in black Americans: Correlations of receptor data with tumor differentiation. *Cancer* 1982b;52:552–559.

Mohla S, Sampson CC, Enterline JP, et al: Predominance of estrophilin-negative and poorly differentiated breast cancer in black patients. In Ames FC, Blumenschein GR, Montague ED (eds): *Current Controversies In Breast Cancer.* Austin: University of Texas Press, 1984, pp. 603–616.

Myers MH, Hankey BF: Cancer patient survival experiences. *US Department of Health, Education and Welfare* Publication No. (NIH) 80-2148:1–15, 1980.

Natarajan N, Nemoto TJ, Mettlin C, et al: Race related differences in breast cancer patients: Results of the 1982 national survey of breast cancer by the American College of Surgeons. *Cancer* 1985;56:1704–1709.

Nemoto TJ, Vana RN, Bedwani HW, et al: Management and survival of female breast cancer: Results of the national survey by the American College of Surgeons. *Cancer* 1980;45:2917–2924.

Ochi HT, Hayashi K, Nakao E, et al: Estrogen, progesterone and androgen receptors in breast cancer in the Japanese: Brief communication. *JNCI* 1976;60:291–293.

Ownby HE, Frederick J, Russo J, et al: Racial differences in breast cancer patients. *JNCI* 1985;75:55–60.

Parl FF, Wagner RK: The histopathological evaluation of human breast cancers in correlation with estrogen receptor values. *Cancer* 1980;47:362–367.

Pegoraro RJ, Karnan V, Nirmul D, et al: Estrogen and progesterone receptors in breast cancer among women of different racial groups. *Cancer Res* 1986;46:2117–2120.

Rao BR, Meyers JS: Estrogen and progestin receptors in normal and cancer tissues. In McGuire WL, Raynaud JP, Baulieu EE (eds): *Progesterone Receptors in Normal and Neoplastic Tissues.* New York: Raven Press, 1977, pp. 155–169.

Rich MA, Furmanski P, Brooks SC, et al: Prognostic value of estrogen receptor determinations in patients with breast cancer. *Cancer Res* 1978;38:4296–4298.

Savage N, Levin J, DeMoor G, et al: Cytosolic oestrogen receptor content of breast cancer tissue in blacks and whites. *S Afr Med J* 1981;58:623–624.

Silvestrini R: Cell kinetic and ER assays in breast cancer. *Reviews on Endocrine Related Cancers* 1984;18:15–19.

Slamon DJ, Clark GM, Wong SG, et al: Human breast cancer: Correlation of relapse and survival with amplification of HER-2/neu oncogene. *Science* 1987;235:177–182.

Vollenweider-Zerargui L, Barrelet L, Wong Y, et al: The predictive value of estrogen and progesterone receptors' concentration on the clinical behavior of breast cancer in women. *Cancer* 1986;57:1171–1180.

Vorherr H (ed): *Breast Cancer; Epidemiology, Endocrinology, Biochemistry and Pathology.* Baltimore: Urban and Schwarzenberg, 1980.

Walt JA, Singhakovinta A, Brooks SC, et al: The surgical implications of estrophile protein estimations in carcinoma of the breast. *Surgery* 1976;80:506–512.

White JE, Enterline JP: Cancer in non-white Americans. *Curr Probl Cancer* 1980;4:1–34.

Witliff JL: Steroid hormone receptors in breast cancer. *Cancer* 1984;53:630–643.

15. Cancer of the Corpus Uteri in Black Women

John G. Boyce and Rachel G. Fruchter

The differences between racial/ethnic groups in cancer incidence and survival are greater for cancer of the uterine corpus than for any other major cancer site. According to 1978–1981 data from the Surveillance, Epidemiology, and End Results (SEER) Program (Baquet et al. 1986), the incidence of corpus cancer ranged from 2.6 per 100,000 Native Americans to 27.1 per 100,000 Native Hawaiians with a White:Black ratio of 1.9 (Table 1). The five-year survival ranged from a high of 88% in Whites to 57% in Blacks, a difference of 31%. For breast cancer, in comparison, the White:Black incidence ratio was only 1.2 and the difference in five-year survival was only 12%. Since corpus cancer is the fourth most frequent cancer in U.S. women, with 35,000 new cases estimated for 1987, its diagnosis and treatment involves much expensive medical care, and its prevention is clearly of great significance. The existence of differences between populations often suggests that some aspects of a disease are indeed preventable and thus justifies a detailed analysis of ethnic differences in all factors that contribute to the incidence and mortality of corpus cancer.

The marked disparity between the incidence of corpus cancer in Black and White women is a relatively recent phenomenon. Haenszel and Hillhouse (1959) reported that the White:Black ratio of the age-adjusted incidences was about 1.1.

Differences in Incidence

Histologic Differences

Adenocarcinomas of the endometrium comprise more than 90% of corpus cancers, but whereas they constitute about 95% of cancers in Whites, they account for only 85% of the cancers in Black women (Baquet et al. 1986). In contrast, sarcomas comprise only 5% of corpus cancers in White women but more than 13% in Black women. The disproportion in incidence results not only from a much higher incidence of carcinomas in Whites than in Blacks but a higher incidence of sarcomas in Blacks than in Whites. In Brooklyn, New York in 1978–

TABLE 1. Differences between racial/ethnic groups in incidence, survival, and mortality from cancer of the uterine corpus

Population group	Incidence[a] per 100,000 females	Five-year survival (%)	Mortality per 100,000 females
Whites	25.1	88	3.9
Blacks	13.4	57	6.6
Hispanics	11.1	86	n/a
Japanese	18.6	86	3.9
Chinese	17.6	87	4.3
Filipinos	11.7	78	2.0
Native Hawaiians	27.1	80	3.0
Native Americans	2.6	66	1.8
Ratio White:Black	1.9	1.5	0.6

[a] Age-adjusted to the 1970 U.S. population.
Adapted from Baquet et al. 1986.

1982, for example, the Black:White ratio of the age-adjusted incidence of carcinomas was 0.7, whereas for sarcomas it was 2.0. In the SEER areas, the Black:White incidence ratio for sarcomas is also 2:1 (Harlow et al. 1986).

Most sarcomas of the uterus are either leiomyosarcomas (LMS) of the myometrium or malignant mixed mesodermal (Mullerian) tumors (MMMT) of the endometrium. A very small proportion are endometrial stromal sarcomas (ESS). In the Harlow group's (1986) SEER study and in Brooklyn, the relatively high incidence in Blacks held for both LMS and MMMT. Occult LMS are sometimes identified in a uterus removed at hysterectomy for benign leiomyoma. Since Black women in the U.S. have higher rates of hysterectomy than White women do (Easterday et al. 1983), more surgery might account for some of their higher incidence of LMS. Differential rates of surgery would not explain the higher incidence of MMMT in Black women, however, because MMMT is usually diagnosed in postmenopausal women presenting with vaginal bleeding.

A higher incidence in Blacks of extrauterine as well as uterine sarcomas was demonstrated in the SEER population (Harlow et al. 1986) and in New York state (Polednak 1986). One suggestion was that the relatively high incidence in Blacks of certain benign mesenchymal neoplasms, such as leiomyomas of the uterus, and dermatofibromas or "keloids" of the skin may be related to the higher incidence of sarcomas and that both may have an underlying genetic determinant (Polednak 1986).

Differences in Risk Factors for Carcinoma of the Corpus

Many factors have been demonstrated to be associated with the incidence of carcinomas of the uterine corpus, and we will attempt to discuss each insofar as it may help explain these ethnic differentials.

TABLE 2. Incidence of corpus cancer by country.

| Country | Incidence/100,000 females[a] | |
	White	Black
United States		
SEER 1973–77	26.1	11.4
SEER 1978–81	20.9	11.0
Brooklyn 1978–82	16.9	11.2
Jamaica (Kingston, St. Andrews) 1973–77		7.8
The Netherlands Antilles 1973–78		6.1
Senegal (Dakar) 1970–71		1.5
England 1973–77	5.4–10.7	
Poland (Warsaw) 1973–77	9.7	
Italy 1976–77	14.2	
New Zealand 1972–76	11.2	
Australia 1977	15.0	

[a] Age-adjusted to the standard world population.
Adapted from Waterhouse et al. 1982, with permission of the International Agency for Research against Cancer, and from Horm et al. 1985.

Country of Residence

In addition to ethnic differences among women in the U.S., large differences in incidence are found among women in different countries (Table 2) (Waterhouse et al. 1982). The incidence of corpus cancer in the U.S. is much higher than in any industrialized or developing country in the world. In Eastern and Western Europe and in Australia and New Zealand, the incidence of corpus cancer ranged from 5 to 16 per 100,000, in contrast to the United States, where the incidence was more than 25 per 100,000 during the same period (1973–1977). The incidence of corpus cancer in Black women in the U.S. (11 per 100,000) was similar to the incidence in all women in many other industrialized countries, but it was higher than the incidence in the Black populations of Jamaica, The Netherlands Antilles, and Africa.

The large gap between the incidence of corpus cancer in White women in the U.S. and in other industrialized countries does not exist in the case of breast or colon cancer. The incidence of corpus cancer in White women in Alameda County, California, for example, was more than three times that of New Zealand Whites, whereas the incidence of breast, colon, and ovarian cancers were 1.1, 0.9, and 1.2 times the New Zealand rates (McTiernan et al. 1985).

Age

The incidence of carcinoma of the endometrium increases rapidly after menopause at approximately 50 years of age. In White women the increase in age-specific incidence starts younger, rises higher, and peaks at a younger age (60 to 64 years) than in Black women (75+ years) (Horm et al. 1985) (Figure 1). In

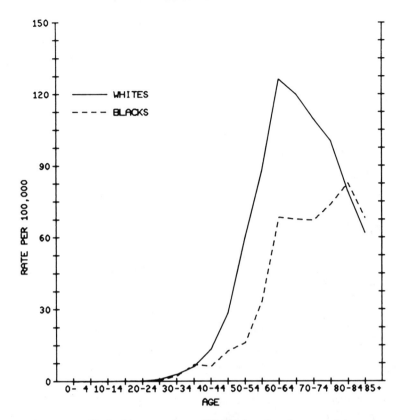

FIGURE 1. Age-specific incidence rates per 100,000 females of cancer of the corpus uteri for Black and White women: 1978–1981 U.S. (Baquet et al. 1986). Reprinted by permission of the National Cancer Institute.

other countries with relatively low incidences of corpus cancer, the peak age-specific incidence also occurs later than in the White U.S. women (Waterhouse et al. 1982).

The rate of increase with age is much steeper for corpus cancer than for cancers of the ovary and breast in both low-incidence and high-incidence populations.

Socioeconomic Status

The incidence of corpus cancer is associated with socioeconomic status (SES), the highest incidence occurring in the most affluent groups (Elwood et al. 1977; Austin and Roe 1979). Standardization for socioeconomic status would undoubtedly reduce the differential between Blacks and Whites because the incidence in the highest socioeconomic quartile is 1.4 to 2.0 times the rate in the lowest quartile (Austin and Roe 1979). Some of the factors that may contribute to this socioeconomic differential are obesity, diet, and use of medical care.

Reproductive Endocrine Disorders

Anecdotal reports by gynecologists that carcinomas of the endometrium are often associated with primary infertility and disorders of the reproductive endocrine system have been confirmed by case-control studies (De Waard 1982; Elwood et al. 1977). A high risk of endometrial cancer is associated with early menarche, late menopause, primary infertility, and anovulation. In premenopausal women in particular, more than half of endometrial carcinomas are associated with disorders of estrogen metabolism. The specific endocrine abnormality that is more frequent in women with endometrial carcinoma or its precursors is the preferential conversion of dehydroepiandrosterone to estrone rather than estradiol. There is, however, no evidence of major differences between Black and White women in the frequency of primary infertility or reproductive endocrine disorders, so this risk factor throws little light on the differential incidence of concern here.

Obesity and Diet

Gynecologists have long been aware that a triad of medical conditions — diabetes, hypertension and obesity — is often associated with carcinomas of the endometrium, and these observations have been confirmed by case-control studies. Obesity probably is the critical variable in this triad, with hypertension and diabetes reflecting the obesity. The association between obesity and endometrial cancer is believed to be linked to excessive estrogen production in the adipose tissue where Δ^4-androstenedione produced by the adrenal cortex is metabolized to estrone.

Although obesity may explain the high incidence of corpus cancer in some population groups, specifically Native Hawaiians and New Zealand Maoris, it does not explain the difference in incidence among Black and White women. In the U.S., obesity is inversely associated with SES, and Black women have a higher frequency of obesity than White women do (National Center for Health Statistics 1981). This suggests that if obesity is a significant risk factor in determining the incidence of endometrial carcinoma, it is overridden by some more powerful factor associated with race and SES.

Studies of cancer incidence in different countries have led to theories that the high incidence of breast, colon, and ovarian cancers observed in many industrialized countries may result from the high-fat, low-fiber diets characteristic of affluence. In the U.S., both breast and colon cancers, as well as corpus cancer, are associated with high SES. Carcinomas of the endometrium have some risk factors in common with breast, colon, and ovarian cancer, and all these cancers are sometimes associated as multiple primary lesions in the same individual. If diet is involved, it is not through the simple intermediate of obesity. One dietary factor that deserves evaluation, in view of the powerful effects of exogenous estrogen described below, is the role of estrogens fed to livestock to promote growth. This practice is more common in the U.S. than elsewhere, and meat consumption, like endometrial cancer, is associated with affluence.

Iatrogenic Factors

Estrogen Replacement Therapy

Although estrogens have been prescribed in increasing quantities for post-menopausal symptoms from the 1950s on, and although a steadily increasing incidence of corpus cancer was noted, not until the mid-1970s did case-control studies show a significant association between the two trends. Then, within a few years, a series of studies (Smith et al. 1975; Ziel and Finkle 1975; Mack et al. 1976; McDonald et al. 1977; Gray et al. 1977; Antunes et al. 1979; Hulka et al. 1980) with various methods of selecting cases and controls and analyzing data were published that constituted clear evidence that exogenous estrogen was associated with an increased incidence of endometrial carcinoma. The risk of developing the cancer increased with dosage and duration of use of the hormone. The publication of these studies was followed in the United States by a rapid decline in the incidence of endometrial cancer from 29.4 per 100,000 in 1973–1977 to 24.2 per 100,000 in 1978–1981 (Horm et al. 1985), and there was a concomitant decline in the number of prescriptions of estrogens and in the dosage prescribed (Kennedy et al. 1985). However, whereas the incidence of corpus cancer in White women declined 18% in this period (from 30.5 per 100,000 to 25.1 per 100,000), the incidence in Black women declined only 4% (from 14.0 per 100,000 to 13.4 per 100,000). This suggested that a considerable proportion of the difference between Black and White women in incidence was the result of higher use of exogenous estrogens by White women. That this excessive use of estrogens by White women primarily reflected their higher socioeconomic status was demonstrated in studies from British Columbia (Elwood and Boyes 1980) and California (Austin and Roe 1979), where among 50- to 74-year-old White women in the highest socioeconomic quartile the incidence of corpus cancer increased by almost 60% between 1969 and 1973, whereas among women in the lowest socioeconomic quartile the incidence increased by only 10%.

Carcinomas of the endometrium associated with estrogen use are usually diagnosed at younger ages and at an earlier stage than carcinomas not associated with estrogen use (Collins et al. 1980; Elwood and Boyes 1980). The decline in incidence in White women from 1973–1977 to 1978–1981 has been associated with a shift to diagnosis at older ages, the greatest drop in incidence occurring between ages 50 and 59. Thus the pattern in White women is now closer to that in Black women and also in White women in low-incidence countries such as England or Italy. The decreased incidence at ages 50 to 59 probably reflects the fact that estrogens are most likely to be prescribed in these perimenopausal years. Since estrogen prescription requires surveillance by a physician, this surveillance may account for the fact that exogenous estrogen-associated carcinomas are likely to be diagnosed at a localized stage and at a more differentiated grade. Alternatively, there may be a biological reason for the association between early-stage, well-differentiated tumors, and estrogen replacement therapy.

The epidemiologic studies of the 1970s demonstrating the cancer-estrogen link were critical not only in decreasing the incidence of endometrial cancer but in stimulating more careful, although still incomplete, epidemiologic studies that have demonstrated a significant role for exogenous estrogen in preventing osteoporosis (Kelsey 1984). More detailed studies of the association between estrogen and endometrial cancer now suggest that estrogen functions as a promoter of tumor growth rather than an initiator. Preliminary studies suggest that if estrogen is given in minimal doses cyclically in conjunction with a progestin so that the endometrial lining is sloughed off regularly, the positive effects of estrogen in remitting menopausal symptoms and preventing osteoporosis may be achieved without increasing the incidence of endometrial cancer (Gambrell et al. 1983).

The data described above suggest that low-income women and minorities in the United States may have been protected from a high incidence of endometrial cancer by their limited use of preventive medical and gynecologic care.

Oral Contraceptives

In 1975 an unusual increase in endometrial carcinomas in young women was noted to be associated with the use of sequential oral contraceptives that consisted of estrogen alone, followed by estrogen and progestin, in a sequence designed to mimic the hormonal output of the ovaries. The use of such contraceptives was discontinued in 1976 (Silverberg et al. 1977).

More recently, in a large case-control study, the Centers for Disease Control (1983) established that the use of combined (estrogen plus progestin) oral contraceptives decreases the risk of developing endometrial carcinoma in later years. The protective effect seems to be related to duration of use and presumably acts by affecting the normal estrogen function.

How much combined oral contraceptive use will affect the difference in incidence between Blacks and Whites is hard to tell, given the changing patterns of contraceptive use. In 1976–1980, 20.3% of Black women and 18.4% of White women were estimated to use oral contraceptives (Russell-Briefel et al. 1985). Although there is a trend among both White and Black women to rely on surgical sterilization in their later years, the side effects and limited availability of intrauterine devices mean that young women of all ethnic groups will undoubtedly rely heavily on oral contraceptives.

The number of women in the U.S. who will be taking estrogen and progestin at all ages is clearly very large, and it is essential that evaluation of the complex effects of exogenous hormones on cancers and other diseases continue. Physicians can contribute to this effort by ensuring that accurate and thorough histories are taken for women of all ages.

Hysterectomy

The incidence of endometrial cancer in a population is calculated as cases per 100,000 women, which is an underestimate of the true risk because the denominator includes women who have had hysterectomies. Most hysterectomies (65%) in the United States are performed before the age of 45 (Easterday et al. 1983) and before the rapid increase in the incidence of endometrial carcinoma. Howe (1984) estimated that if the hysterectomy rate were taken into account, the true incidence of corpus cancer in New York state would be increased by 21%. Easterday et al. (1983) reported that in 1978 the hysterectomy rate in Black women aged 15 to 44 (972 per 100,000) was 25% higher than the rate in White women (777 per 100,000). Moreover, White women were 1.5 times more likely than Black women to have a vaginal rather than an abdominal hysterectomy according to the study. This difference probably reflects the relatively high frequency of uterine leiomyoma in Black women compared with that in White women and the higher incidence of pelvic infection associated with low socioeconomic status. Whatever the cause, it is apparent that the higher hysterectomy rate in Black women could account for a significant portion of their lower incidence of uterine corpus cancer.

The hysterectomy rate in the United States is considerably higher than in many other industrialized countries. Probably, therefore, the gap between the U.S. and other countries in the incidence of corpus cancer in both Black and White women is actually wider than reported.

Summary

In summary, the differential use of medical care may explain a part of the difference in the incidence of corpus cancer in Black and White women. First, greater use of preventive medical/gynecologic care has led to more frequent use of exogenous estrogen, which has contributed to a higher incidence of corpus cancer in affluent White women. Second, the medical and social conditions that lead to a higher hysterectomy rate have contributed to a lower incidence of corpus cancer in Black women.

Clearly, the iatrogenic factors involved in endometrial carcinoma are consistent with the observed pattern of incidence – the notable increase in incidence in the last 30 years and the increasing differential between Whites and Blacks. Despite evidence of the estrogen-cancer link, the incidence has not declined to the rates of 30 years ago or to the rates in other countries. Since there is considerable pressure to continue estrogen-containing drugs, studies must be done to establish whether there is indeed a clear benefit to exogenous estrogen in preventing osteoporosis and to clarify the precautions necessary to prevent endometrial carcinoma.

In contrast to the case with iatrogenic factors, much more study is needed to clarify the interactions between race, socioeconomic status, obesity, body build, endogenous estrogens, and diet when iatrogenic factors are not involved. These complexities are well illustrated by the fact that Black women, although more obese than White women, are at lower risk for both osteoporosis and endometrial cancer.

Differences in Survival

The major determinant of survival in most cancers is how far the disease has spread at diagnosis, and this is as true for corpus cancers as any other malignant lesion. If a cancer is treatable, then other factors including general health and access to appropriate medical care may also contribute to survival.

In our experience in Brooklyn, more than 50% of sarcomas in both Black and White women were diagnosed after the tumor has spread beyond the uterus, and there was no difference in survival between Black and White women. Since there is little effective therapy for advanced sarcomas, ethnic or socioeconomic differences in access to or quality of medical care have no effect on survival. For the uterine sarcomas, the major determinant of survival is histologic characteristics. The five-year relative survival for patients with MMMT is only 15%, but for LMS it is about 70% and for ESS about 93%. Steinhorn et al. (1986), in a study of the SEER population, also found no difference in survival between Black and White women with sarcomas.

In contrast to the data for sarcomas, in the case of carcinomas Black and White women show a major difference in stage at diagnosis. In a study of women in the SEER Program, Steinhorn and colleagues (1986) noted that 84% of White women but only 69% of Black women had localized (stage I) adenocarcinoma of the corpus. In Brooklyn in 1978–1982, the proportions were 71% localized adeno–carcinoma in White women (including Hispanics) and 61% in Black women.

One problem in comparing survival by stage is the different definitions of stage used in different studies. The International Federation of Gynecologists and Obstetricians (FIGO) classifies gynecologic cancers by strict clinical criteria. The five-year survival for endometrial carcinomas in the international FIGO data ranges from 75% at stage I, through 58% at stage II and 30% at stage III, to 11% for stage IV (Petterson 1985). Using such clinical criteria, we observed – stage for stage – a lower survival in Blacks than in Whites in Brooklyn.

Most U.S. tumor registries, including SEER, use a staging definition that may include surgical-pathologic data. The survival rates at stage I are higher than in the FIGO series (more than 80% five-year survival), but Black women consistently have poorer survival for both stage I and stage II cancer of the corpus (Baquet et al. 1986).

The many surgical-pathologic features within each stage that affect prognosis in endometrial cancer are well defined. Depth of invasion of the myometrium, extension to the pelvic lymph nodes, and degree of differentiation of the carcinoma all predict outcome. It would be valuable to know the comparative frequency of occurrence of these prognostic factors in the endometrial carcinomas of White women compared with those of Black women. Estrogen-associated endometrial carcinomas are of lower stage than non-estrogen-associated carcinomas (Collins et al. 1980; Elwood and Boyes 1980; see also Mohla et al. in this volume). Furthermore, in the case of stage I endometrial tumors, estrogen-associated carcinomas are better differentiated and invade the myometrium less deeply. Therefore, stage for stage, the survival of women with estrogen-associated tumors is superior. If Black women have fewer estrogen-associated carcinomas, at least part of the difference in survival is explained.

Differences in survival are anticipated among different socioeconomic groups for reasons that range from overall health status of the populations to differences in access and quality of medical care. These factors would be expected to play a role in the difference between Black and White women in survival from corpus cancer. A study of women in the SEER population with corpus carcinoma (Steinhorn et al. 1986) showed that for both Black and White women, those who had graduated from high school survived longer than those who had not, and more affluent women survived longer than poor women. However, even when the survival rate was adjusted for differences in stage, age, and socioeconomic variables, Steinhorn and colleagues found a residual superior survival for White women, implying that one or more additional factors were involved. One possibility is that the White women had more estrogen-associated carcinomas with better prognosis.

If stage were the major determinant of survival, prevention of death would imply a reduction in the stage of disease. We have seen, however, that the advantage of Whites over Blacks in survival is partly spurious because their excess incidence of low-stage carcinomas is no real advantage. If primary prevention of endometrial cancer were achieved by a reduction in the use of unopposed estrogens, the probable effect would be a decrease in localized cancer and a decrease in the five-year survival rate of White women. The most recent survival data from SEER (American Cancer Society 1987) do indicate a decrease in the relative five-year survival rate of White women with corpus cancer from 89% in 1974–1976 to 85% in 1977–1983. For Black women, however, there was a corresponding decrease from 62% to 54%, actually increasing the gap from 27% to 31%. This is not consistent with a relative decline in estrogen-associated carcinomas with good prognosis in White women. Clearly, further investigation of the continuing disparity in survival is needed.

The potential for *secondary* prevention (early diagnosis and treatment) of corpus cancer is difficult to assess because no screening tests equivalent to the Pap smear are available for cervical cancer. Several precursors, including polyps and cystic and adenomatous hyperplasia of the endometrium, may precede the frank endometrial carcinoma by many years. Endometrial sampling in asymptomatic postmenopausal women reveals about 6 cases of endometrial cancer or its precursors per 1000 women (Koss et al. 1984). However, such sampling has not been accepted as a routine screening method. Mass cytologic screening programs, aimed primarily at detecting cervical cancer, consistently reveal some cases of endometrial cancer through occult bleeding or unreported symptoms. In a Brooklyn study, we found that duration of symptoms (usually vaginal bleeding) was correlated with the surgical-pathologic stage of endometrial cancer (Fruchter and Boyce 1981). We believe that delay in reporting symptoms and seeking medical care by elderly women who are unfamiliar with or fearful of gynecologic examinations may contribute to advanced cancer stage and mortality. Since women with low incomes and belonging to minority groups are less likely to obtain preventive gynecologic care, there may be significant scope among these women for reducing the stage at diagnosis of corpus cancer by more extensive care, and thus reducing the difference in mortality rate between Black and White women.

Socioeconomic status is a critical variable in ensuring prompt diagnosis and compliance with optimal treatment and providing the material and social supports necessary to the cancer patient. The quality of the surgical technique and of the staff and hospital, the availability of state-of-the-art radiotherapy equipment and of transportation and other support services may be critical in improving the survival of minority cancer patients.

In summary, although a genetic component may underlie the difference in incidence of uterine sarcomas, for endometrial carcinomas most of the factors affecting the large disparity in incidence and survival between Black and White women can probably be related directly or indirectly to differences in socioeconomic status. A small component of ethnic differences may be related to culturally specific factors such as diet. Given the major effect of medical practices on this cancer, however, it is extremely important to scrutinize closely the trends in incidence and survival.

References

American Cancer Society: *Cancer Facts and Figures – 1987*, p 17. New York: American Cancer Society, 1987.

Antunes CMF, Stolley PD, Rosenshein NB, et al: Endometrial cancer and estrogen use: Report of a large case-control study. *N Engl J Med* 1979; 300:9–13.

Austin DF, Roe KM: Increase in cancer of the corpus uteri in the San Francisco-Oakland Standard Metropolitan Statistical Area, 1965–75. *JNCI* 1979; 62:13–16.

Baquet CR, Ringen K, Pollack ES, et al: *Cancer Among Blacks and Other Minorities: Statistical Profiles*. National Cancer Institute. Bethesda, MD: NIH Publication No 86–2785, 1986.

Centers for Disease Control Cancer and Steroid Hormone Study: Oral contraceptive use and the risk of endometrial cancer. *JAMA* 1983; 249:1600–1604.

Collins J, Donner A, Allen LH, Adams O: Oestrogen use and survival in endometrial cancer. *Lancet* 1980; 2:961–964.

De Waard F. Uterine corpus. In Schottenfeld D, Fraumeni JF (eds): *Cancer Epidemiology and Prevention*, 2nd ed, Philadelphia: Saunders, 1982, pp 901–908.

Easterday CL, Grimes DA, Riggs JA: Hysterectomy in the United States. *Obstet Gynecol* 1983; 62:203–212.

Elwood JM, Boyes DA: Clinical and pathological features and survival of endometrial cancer patients in relation to prior use of estrogens. *Gynecol Oncol* 1980; 10:173–187.

Elwood JM, Cole P, Rothman K, Kaplan SD: Epidemiology of endometrial cancer. *JNCI* 1977; 59:1055–1060.

Fruchter RG, Boyce JG: Delays in diagnosis and stage of disease in gynecologic cancer. *Cancer Detect Prev* 1981; 4:481–486.

Gambrell RD, Bagnell CA, Greenblatt RB: Role of estrogens and progesterone in the etiology and prevention of endometrial cancer: Review. *Am J Obstet Gynecol* 1983; 146:696–707.

Gray LA, Christopherson WM, Hoover RN: Estrogens and endometrial carcinoma. *Obstet Gynecol* 1977; 49:385–389.

Haenszel W, Hillhouse M: Uterine-cancer morbidity in New York City and its relation to the pattern of regional variation within the United States. *JNCI* 1959; 22:1157–1181.

Harlow BL, Weiss NS, Lofton S: The epidemiology of sarcomas of the uterus. *JNCI* 1986; 76:399–402.

Horm JW, Asire AJ, Young AJ, et al: *Cancer Incidence and Mortality in the United States, SEER, 1973–81.* US Department of Health and Human Services. Bethesda, MD: NIH Publication No 85-1837, 1985.

Howe HL: Age-specific hysterectomy and oophorectomy prevalence rates and the risks for cancer of the reproductive system. *Am J Public Health* 1984; 74:560–563.

Hulka BS, Fowler WC, Kaufman DG, et al: Estrogen and endometrial cancer: Cases and two control groups from North Carolina. *Am J Obstet Gynecol* 1980; 137:92–101.

Kelsey J: Epidemiology of osteoporosis. In Gold EB (ed): *The Changing Risk of Disease in Women.* Lexington, MA: Collamore Press, 1984, pp 287–298.

Kennedy D, Baum C, Forbes MB: Noncontraceptive estrogens and progestins: Use patterns over time. *Obstet Gynecol* 1985; 65:441–446.

Koss LG, Schreiber K, Oberlander SG, et al: Detection of endometrial carcinoma and hyperplasia in asymptomatic women. *Obstet Gynecol* 1984; 64:1–11.

Mack TM, Pike MC, Henderson BE, et al: Estrogens and endometrial cancer in a retirement community. *N Engl J Med* 1976; 294:1262–1267.

McDonald TW, Annegers JF, O'Fallon WM, et al: Exogenous estrogen and endometrial carcinoma: Case-control and incidence study. *Am J Obstet Gynecol* 1977; 127:572–580.

McTiernan A, Chu J, Thomas DB: Cancer incidence in Caucasians living in the Pacific Basin. *NCI Monogr* 1985; 69:65–72.

National Center for Health Statistics: *Height and Weight of Adults Ages 18–74 Years by Socioeconomic and Geographic Variables: United States 1971–74.* US Vital and Health Statistics Series 11, No 224. Washington DC: US Government Printing Office, 1985.

Petterson F. *Annual Report on the Results of Treatment in Gynecological Cancer*, Vol 19. Stockholm, Sweden: Radiumhemmet, 1985, pp 123–136.

Polednak AP: Incidence of soft-tissue cancers in Blacks and Whites in New York State. *Int J Cancer* 1986; 38:21–26.

Russell-Briefel R, Ezzati T, Perlman J: Prevalence and trends in oral contraceptive use in premenopausal females aged 12–54 years, United States, 1971–80. *Am J Public Health* 1985; 75:1173–1176.

Silverberg SG, Makowski EL, Roche WD: Endometrial carcinoma in women under 40 years of age. *Cancer* 1977; 39:592–598.

Smith DC, Prentice R, Thompson DJ, et al: Association of exogenous estrogen and endometrial cancer. *N Engl J Med* 1975; 293:1164–1167.

Steinhorn SC, Meyers MH, Hankey BF, Pelham VF: Factors associated with survival differences between Black and White women with cancer of the uterine corpus. *Am J Epidemiol* 1986; 124:85–93.

Waterhouse J, Muir C, Shanmugaratnam K, et al: *Cancer Incidence in Five Continents.* IARC Scientific Publications No 42. Lyon, France: International Agency for Research against Cancer, 1982.

Ziel HK, Finkle WD: Increased risk of endometrial carcinoma among users of conjugated estrogens. *N Engl J Med* 1975; 293:1167–1170.

16. Cancer of the Cervix in the Rio Grande Valley of South Texas

Mario O. Gonzalez

My purpose here is threefold. I shall try to present an overall description of the patient population in the South Texas Valley region with cancer of the cervix. (The population of this geographic region is predominantly Hispanic.) Second, I shall assess the place of this group in the overall state population, and third, I shall review a series of patients with cancer of the cervix treated at the Rio Grande Cancer Treatment Center in McAllen, Texas. Detailed descriptions and statistics of disease characteristics such as survival and death rates, tumor grade, and stage of disease are not included because I believe them to be not fundamental to this section of the book. Suffice it to say that survival rates for patients with cervical cancer in the valley region of South Texas parallel standard survival curves reported in the United States and Puerto Rico for persons of similar ethnic background, disease stage, grade, and type of treatment. Our patients do as well as those treated in other parts of the country, although, as will be shown later, they come to treatment with more advanced stages of disease.

I shall also describe the Dysplasia Clinic in Harlingen (35 miles east of McAllen), a detection and screening service provided since 1977 by The University of Texas Medical Branch at Galveston in conjunction with the health departments of the state of Texas and Cameron County. This information is important and relevant to this discussion because since the first description of the Papanicolaou test in the late 1940s and its subsequent general use and application, this test has greatly improved survival from cancer of the cervix through early detection of malignant transformation. Unfortunately, in the Rio Grande Valley region, not many health care facilities are able to offer this type of screening test to the indigent and the less socioeconomically fortunate.

Some gains, however, have been made in the last 10 years. We now have excellent facilities for radiation therapy and chemotherapy. We also have excellent hospitals and outpatient clinics as well as the Dysplasia Clinic, but there is still a great deal to be done.

The Valley Population

Most of the health problems in the South Texas Valley area stem from the socioeconomic depression of this region. Our Valley is a stricken land, with an unemployment rate of over 20%, the highest in the state and in the country. This area also has the highest percentage of people living below the poverty level in the state and the highest in the country as a whole. The tax base of our county and city government has been greatly depressed in the last five years because of hardships created by two consecutive winter freezes and also because of the devaluation of the Mexican peso. The business and industry of McAllen, a city only seven miles from the Mexican border, is highly dependent on trade from Mexico. Since the peso was devaluated five years ago, the Mexican economy has gone steadily downhill and has brought the economy of the South Texas Valley down with it. Thus, an area never wealthy or even affluent is now becoming even poorer. We are now in dire need of additional state and federal financial help to provide better education and health care for this distressed and deprived Valley population.

In Texas, a large proportion of the increase in population is the result of immigration. Immigration, as I use the word here, refers to people who move from other countries or states to Texas. In the Valley region we have a problem with immigration in that most of it is illegal or "underground." This influx of people is a steady stream through the many crossings along the Rio Grande River from neighboring villages and cities of northern Mexico into the United States and is made up largely of poor individuals and migrant laborers. McAllen and other cities close to the border are their first stop in the United States; many stay in the Valley area, and although they have no legal papers, they get sick and require attention and medical treatment. At the Rio Grande Cancer Treatment Center and at other health facilities in McAllen, we provide treatment for any sick person regardless of nationality, creed, or ability to pay.

According to a study by researchers of the department of sociology of Pan American University at Edinburg, Texas, the increase in population has been mainly among the aged—what they call the "graying of the Valley." Between 1960 and 1980, the population of people over 60 increased by more than 144%, a huge increase compared with the 21% rise in persons 14 years old and younger. This research, still going on and not yet published, is funded by the National Institute on Aging and by the United States Department of Health and Human Services. It is a study of the Hispanic elderly's health status, needs, and use of health services. Because cancer of the cervix is a disease predominant among adult and elderly women, the study's finding of an increasing aged population in the Valley area can be used to project a similar increase in cases of cancer of the uterine cervix among women in the area. The study also shows that the elderly in Cameron County do not receive adequate health care. There is a higher percentage of poverty in the Valley area, and use of health care facilities is much lower among Hispanics than among non-Hispanic residents of the Valley or the general U.S.

population. Further epidemiologic public health and gerontologic health care studies are thus warranted to assess the financing needed for adequate medical services to treat or prevent cervical cancer in the population.

According to the latest published data, the Texas county of Hidalgo has almost 370,000 people, 87% of whom are of Hispanic origin or have Hispanic surnames. Also, the average level of education among the adult population of this area is very low compared with that of the rest of Texas and the United States. Other reports in this volume stress that poverty, low educational level, and low socioeconomic status go hand-in-hand with high cancer mortality. According to 1980 census data, more than 67% of the population in the South Texas Valley area came from a family group with an income of less than $10,000. Forty-seven percent had fewer than eight years of formal education, and only 18% had any education at the high school level.

Mortality from cancer of the uterine cervix for this group is slightly higher than that for the whole Texas population, and Spanish-surnamed patients in this Valley region account for 48% of all deaths from cancer in Texas. The peak incidence of cancer of the cervix among Valley residents occurs at a earlier age than that reported in other studies. Most of our patients are in the 45-, 50-, and over-60-year-old age groups.

The Valley region has been blessed by nature with beautiful scenery and landscapes and agriculturally rich terrain. In fact, our economy depends mainly on agriculture—the growth of citrus fruits, vegetables, and other produce crops. Thus, the area has a large number of migrant farm workers, many of whom are illegal aliens. The winter freezes of 1982 and 1983 almost completely decimated the citrus crop industry, however, which by some estimates lost more than $150,000,000 after the freeze of 1983. Recovery from that disaster has been slow.

Our Medical Facilities

The McAllen area has two hospitals that provide some care for indigent patients. These facilities are partly subsidized by the county government, which allocates 10% of its annual budget for health care of indigent patients, thus allowing the hospitalization of those who need radium insertion, surgery, or biopsy. Unfortunately, the subsidy is not enough to accommodate large numbers of patients or an expensive hospital stay. Both McAllen hospitals are part of national proprietary chains and are for-profit institutions.

The Rio Grande Cancer Treatment Center

Another facility for treating patients who have cancer of the cervix is the Rio Grande Cancer Treatment Center, built in 1976 and sponsored, designed, and staffed in its early years by The University of Texas M. D. Anderson Cancer Center. M. D. Anderson Cancer Center was very much involved in the Rio

Grande Center's design and staffing until 1983, when the foundation that owns and funds the center, the Rio Grande Radiation Treatment and Cancer Research Foundation, decided to separate its business, finance, and internal structure from M. D. Anderson. The Rio Grande Cancer Treatment Center still maintains a clinical and teaching affiliation with M. D. Anderson Cancer Center. The Rio Grande Radiation Treatment and Cancer Research Foundation is a nonprofit, purely volunteer, autonomous organization created on the initiative of R. Lee Clark when he was president of M. D. Anderson. Clark assembled a group of prominent professionals, businessmen, and other concerned individuals from the Valley and South Texas from Laredo to Brownsville and organized, chartered, and authorized the foundation to raise funds to build a facility and equip it with state-of-the-art equipment for radiation therapy and chemotherapy. The Rio Grande Cancer Treatment Center is the only facility of its kind in the geographic region between Monterrey in northern Mexico and Corpus Christi and San Antonio in South Texas.

The purpose of the center, which was also partially financed by Hill-Burton funds, is to provide the best quality of care for cancer patients in the area. It is nondiscriminatory and treats all referred patients regardless of ethnic origin or financial situation. During the winter season, it has a unique patient load as the area has now become a haven for retired elderly citizens from cold northwestern and midwest states who flock to the Valley to escape the cold winters; these are the so-called Winter Texans or Snowbirds. Naturally, this population has many of the diseases peculiar to the aged. The elderly can also get adequate medical treatment at the facility in McAllen.

In 1986, the Rio Grande Cancer Treatment Center administered radiation therapy to 700 new patients and gave chemotherapy to more than 1000 new patients. The center's staff includes three physicians, all board-certified oncologists, as well as paramedical and clinical laboratory personnel. It provides radiation and chemotherapy in accordance with the protocols used at M. D. Anderson Cancer Center. Additionally, it serves as a "liaison center" for the neutron program of M. D. Anderson in recruiting patients who may require this type of high-energy-level radiation therapy. The Rio Grande Center is equipped with a high-energy linear accelerator and a cobalt unit that still has many clinical uses in radiation oncology. It also has modern equipment for treatment simulation, treatment planing, and computerized dosimetry, as well as all of the complementary radioactive sources and applicators for the intracavitary treatment of cancer of the uterus and uterine cervix.

In addition, the center has a clinical laboratory and a department of social work that is involved in public information and outreach education and that has recently received a $300,000 grant from the Texas Cancer Council to research cancer among Hispanics in the South Texas Valley and then design educational programs and diagnostic and awareness clinics directed to serve this minority group. The center also has a dedicated group of volunteers and auxiliary members, and chaplaincy staff members who minister to the patients, spiritual needs.

Cervical Cancer Patients

Based on information obtained from a review of the treatment charts, I will report on a series of 294 patients with cancer of the uterine cervix treated at the Rio Grande Cancer Treatment Center in McAllen, Texas, from April 1976 through December 1986. The patients received a combination of external radiotherapy plus intracavitary radiation by radium insertion as well as other treatments with either radiation plus surgery, radiation plus chemotherapy, or surgery alone.

The majority of these patients were residents of Hidalgo and Cameron counties in the southernmost tip of Texas along the Rio Grande border of northern Mexico. Eighty-seven percent had Hispanic surnames. The great majority spoke only Spanish, and few had an education above the eighth-grade level. The percentage of Hispanic patients treated was slightly higher than the percentage of Hispanics in the Texas population, probably because of the many Mexican nationals in the area who are not officially counted among the Hispanic residents of Texas. More than two thirds of the patients were older than 40 years of age, 21% were 40 to 49 years old, 28% were in their 50s, and 20% in their 60s and 70s. There were only two young patients, aged 22 and 23 years.

As evidenced in this patient population, not only does cancer of the cervix have a higher incidence among Hispanic women than that noted among similar groups in other studies, but it also appears at an earlier age, mainly because of the cultural and socioeconomic factors such as early marriage and intercourse, multiparity, and related factors that characterize the Hispanic population and account for the higher incidence of carcinoma of the cervix among them.

The histopathologic types of tumors seen in the 294 patients was similar to those seen elsewhere in the country or for that matter in the world. Most were squamous cell carcinoma, with only a few of the glandular or adenocarcinoma type. Most of the patients had advanced stages of disease, which of course carried a poor prognosis and survival rate. Furthermore, most of these patients were elderly and could not tolerate some kinds of treatment as well as younger patients do. Since survival from cancer of the cervix is a function of the patient's physical status, performance status, general health, and age, these factors make the problem of cervical cancer among Hispanic females worse than in the rest of the population.

Dysplasia Clinic

Early detection of and screening for carcinoma of the cervix are fundamental to controlling and treating cancer of the uterine cervix. In our area at present, such facilities are available only in the Dysplasia Clinic located in Harlingen. Before this clinic was established, indigent women had no place to be screened for carcinoma of the cervix or to obtain the required follow-up with colposcopy or biopsy when indicated after examinations at health department clinics.

The Dysplasia Clinic is located in the Harlingen branch office of the Cameron County Health Department. Initially it was staffed on alternate months by staff gynecologists and gynecology residents from The University of Texas Medical Branch at Galveston, who flew to Harlingen for that purpose. At first, the clinic was open only one day every other month, but because of the explosive increase in requests for appointments and the need for its services, it is now open all day three times a month. Patients were initially referred from the Hidalgo and Cameron county health departments, but at present many other health providers also make use of the service for their indigent patients. Other referral sources include the community health centers in the Brownsville Community Health Clinic, the clinics of Su Clinica Familiar, the Hidalgo County Health Care Corporation, the region and field offices of Willacy and Starr counties, the five Planned Parenthood Associations of Hidalgo County, the three Planned Parenthood Associations of Cameron County, the Planned Parenthood Association of Willacy County, and some private gynecologists who have patients who cannot afford the cost of colposcopy and biopsy in private facilities.

At present, more than 250 new patients are examined in the clinic every month; in the first three months of 1987, 120 new patients were seen. There is constant juggling of appointments to allow sicker patients to be seen ahead of those diagnosed with mild dysplasia. Currently, some of the patients have to be kept on waiting lists for at least six weeks because of limitations of space and equipment.

The criteria for referral are according to the protocol designed by the Department of Gynecology and Obstetrics of the University of Texas Medical Branch at Galveston. Any patient with severe dysplasia is seen at the earliest possible date.

Since the initiation of the program, 1229 patients have made a total of 1689 visits to the Dysplasia Clinic. Of the 1229, 157 (12%) required hospitalization for cone biopsy; vaginal, abdominal, or radical hysterectomy; or radiation, laser ablation, or chemotherapy. Cryotherapy was used to treat 16.5% of the women, and 79 patients underwent conizations. A total of 891 patients were treated in the three years, from 1983 through 1986. In that period 72 patients underwent hysterectomy and 203 had cryotherapy. The patients' ages ranged from 19 to 62 years. The majority were in their late 20s and early 30s.

It is well known that successful treatment of cancer of all sites, and more so of cancer of the cervix, is a function of its early diagnosis. The availability of the Dysplasia Clinic, which identifies cancer at its earliest noninvasive or early invasive stages, thus plays a very important role in cancer control. However, there are still large numbers of women not being reached by these screening programs because of the lack of information and education about them and because of the lack of appropriate screening and treatment facilities.

Acknowledgments. My thanks for help in collecting data for this paper to Julian Castillo, Ph.D., director, Division of Health Related Sciences, and Rumaldo Z. Juarez, Ph.D., chair, Department of Sociology and Social Work, Pan American University, Edinburg; Sister Mary Nicholas Vincelli, R.N., program manager, Family Health Services Program, Texas Department of Health, Public Health Region 8, Harlingen; and Rosalie R. Turner, A.R.T., director, Medical Records Department, Rio Grande Cancer Treatment Center, McAllen, Texas.

17. The Heterogeneity of Prostate Cancer: Implications for Research

Andrew C. von Eschenbach

Cancer does not treat all its victims equally. Some progress rapidly from diagnosis to death; in others the disease advances almost imperceptibly. This variation in malignant expression is certainly apparent from one type of cancer to another. In the case of melanoma and basal cell carcinomas of the skin, for example, even the same tumor type may act differently in two patients. As a model of heterogeneity, prostate cancer is of particular importance because of its variable behavior in patients belonging to various minorities (Young et al. 1984).

The growth and progression of a malignant tumor is a result of a complex interaction between the tumor and its host. The tumor begins when genetic or epigenetic events transform a cell and initiate uncontrolled proliferation and inappropriate growth that violates all of the body's homeostatic mechanisms. It seems logical that the major determinant of tumor behavior is the magnitude of disorder imparted to the cell by the etiologic factor or factors that initiated and promoted the malignant transformation. It is equally logical to assume, however, that the tumor's milieu also plays a significant role in modulating its activity. These host factors may be immunologic, endocrinologic, or biologic. The process of malignant expression is a dynamic one, the result of the everchanging interaction between tumor cell and host environment. This is why cancer can take on many characteristics and why the same type of cancer may seem to change its behavior capriciously. Among patients or groups of patients, such as members of minority groups, dramatic differences may occur in incidence and mortality rates because of these different host-tumor relationships.

The study of a malignant tumor type among minorities is one perspective on the heterogeneity of cancer, and as such it is an important aspect of our understanding the biology of cancer as a disease. Adenocarcinoma of the prostate represents one of the most common malignant transformations that occur in men, yet its clinical incidence and mortality rates vary widely with genetic or racial factors as well as ethnic and geographic ones (Figure 1). Although rare before age 50, malignant growth of the prostate increases in such a nearly linear fashion thereafter with increasing age that one might say if men lived long enough, all would eventually develop prostate cancer.

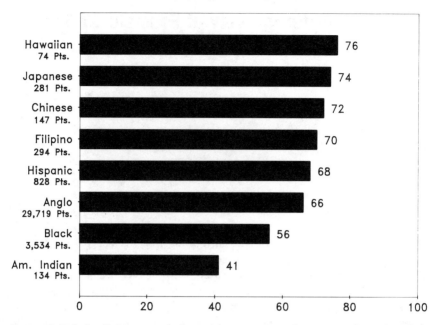

FIGURE 1. Relative five-year survival rates, in percentages, for prostate cancer by ethnic group. Standard error for Hawaiian and American Indian figures is 10% to 20% of the rate. Adapted from Young et al. 1984 with permission.

Cancer of the prostate is a cancer of aging but it may originate quite early in life. Its expression may be variable, some cancers seeming biologically inert and never posing a threat to the patient's health, and other tumors undergoing long and slow local growth before demonstrating a transition to metastasis. Unfortunately, many tumors appear to be able to disseminate and proliferate as widespread lethal metastasis while the primary tumor in the prostate is still small and perhaps clinically unrecognized. In 1987 about 25,000 patients died as a result of prostate cancer, accounting for 10% of all cancer deaths; 96,000 cases were diagnosed clinically during that year. If we can extrapolate from autopsy data that reflect the frequency of clinically unsuspected disease, however, then the American male population includes about 750,000 to one million men who have unrecognized malignant prostate tumors. Why does prostate cancer kill some men and not affect others?

Environmental and Genetic Differences

The problem of the heterogeneity of prostate cancer begins with this variable clinical expression and is reflected in the expression of prostate cancer among minority groups. Although the etiology of prostate cancer is not known, its clinical behavior is apparently influenced by many epidemiologic factors; most important among these are race and diet. Racial differences suggest that there is a variance in genetic susceptibility to both the occurrence of prostate cancer and its subsequent virulence. Clinical incidence studies indicate that, among Oriental persons, mortality rates from prostate cancer are quite low, whereas among Caucasians the mortality rates are significantly higher and vary with ethnic background. Occidental people from Western European countries have unusually high death rates from prostate cancer, but the highest mortality rates in the world occur among Blacks of American nationality.

Whether these observed differences in mortality rates reflect genetic differences in race or are environmental is a question to be investigated; both factors seem to be important. Analyses of the effect of migration suggest that a change in cultural environment may modulate racial genetic expression but not completely efface underlying genetic differences. In the study of Nisei, first-generation Japanese living in Hawaii (Haenszel and Kurihara 1968), the mortality rate of prostate cancer increased notably from that of native Japanese but did not approach that of Caucasians living in Hawaii.

Most significant of all environmental factors that influence mortality from prostate cancer appears to be diet (Rose 1986). The lower mortality rates observed among Orientals are associated with a diet low in saturated animal fats and high in green and yellow vegetables, whereas the diet of Western Europeans and Americans is high in saturated animal fats. Hispanics, whose mortality rates from prostate cancer are lower than those of Caucasians, have diets that are higher in carbohydrates and lower in fat compared with those of Blacks and Whites. When we compared the diets of Black, White, and Hispanic patients seen at UT M. D. Anderson Cancer Center because they had prostate cancer, we found the diet of Blacks highest in fat content, that of Whites highest in protein, and that of Hispanics highest in carbohydrates (G.R. Newell, personal communication). That environment and diet may modulate racial factors in disease is also supported by comparative studies of African and American Blacks, which demonstrated lower mortality rates among Africans (Thind et al. 1982).

One major issue concerning prostate cancer in minority persons is the influence of socioeconomic factors on diagnosis and detection of disease at a time when therapy may affect clinical outcome. Since poorer people are likely to have less access to medical facilities, they would be expected to have more advanced disease at the time of diagnosis and therefore a poorer outcome (Dayal and Chiu 1982). However, tumors among Blacks are also of a higher grade and more malignant, and perhaps this reflects a true difference in tumor biology (Mettlin and Natarajan 1983).

Numerous studies of prostate cancer have failed to determine the mechanisms by which these epidemiologic factors influence the clinical expression of prostate cancer. We need to know whether the biologic difference in tumor behavior reflects differences in the tumor imparted by these etiologic factors, or whether it is an expression of differences in the host, the result of endocrine or immune system mechanisms that are favorable to tumor growth. Does a diet high in animal fat, for instance, contain a carcinogen that affects the tumor cell's genome, or does the high-fat diet influence the patient's metabolism of steroid hormones? More than interesting speculations, these issues demand scrutiny because they may influence future strategies for reducing mortality from prostate cancer and possibly even its frequency of occurrence.

Differences in Tumor Progression

The problem of the diversity of prostate cancer behavior extends to tumors at various sites and even to different cells in the same tumor. This heterogeneity suggests that tumor cells take on a variety of phenotypes as they proliferate. In specific patients, these differences in tumor behavior must be understood so that appropriate and effective therapy may be chosen. At present, therapy is usually selected based on the extent of disease or its stage at the time of the evaluation. Stage is a static parameter, however, and does not predict a tumor's behavior. In his discussion of the natural history of prostate cancer, Whitmore (1973) pointed out the failure of this disease to progress in an orderly fashion through stages of intracapsular microscopic disease (stage A) to macroscopic intracapsular tumors (stage B) to extracapsular growth (stage C) and then finally to systemic dissemination (stage D). There is a wide variation in behavior among tumors of the same stage, and a variety of staging system modifications and subdivisions have been introduced to subcategorize tumors into relatively homogeneous groups for purposes of selecting therapy and comparing results (Figure 2).

It is now apparent that the histologic grade of the primary tumor is an important parameter in assessing a tumor's behavior. The most popular grading system is one proposed by Gleason et al. (1974), which categorizes tumors according to their pattern of gland formation. Because a tumor may have a mixture of patterns, and because the biologic behavior of prostate cancer seems to depend on the average of the histologic pattern rather than the most dedifferentiated portion, Gleason proposed grouping tumors according to the grade of their primary and secondary patterns. This results in Gleason scores ranging from 2 through 10. The clinical behavior of the tumor and the survival rates of patients are directly proportional to the primary tumor's Gleason score.

At M. D. Anderson Cancer Center, a grading system has been proposed that simply defines the number of quartiles of the tumor that are made up of glands. Thus, a grade 1 tumor is one that, according to the pathologist's estimate, consists of 75% glands. In a grade 4 tumor, in contrast, only 25% or less is made up of glandular structures, the remaining 75% being a solid pattern made up of single cells (Brawn et al. 1982).

The effect of categorizing tumors according to this grading method was apparent in our assessment of the survival of a group of 182 patients who were diagnosed as having clinical stage C (extracapsular extension) tumors without radiographic evidence of metastasis, and who underwent external beam megavoltage radiation therapy. These patients' overall five-year survival rate was 62%.

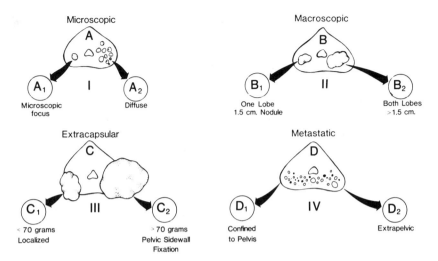

FIGURE 2. Various staging classifications of prostatic carcinoma that have been devised in an effort to define homogeneous groups for selection of therapy and analysis of results. (Reproduced from Johnson et al. 1988, Appleton & Lange.)

When survival was analyzed according to tumor grade, however, there was a statistically significant difference in outcome. Among patients with grade 1 tumors, Kaplan-Meier projected survival was 91% at five years, similar to that of age-matched controls without cancer. For patients with grade 4 tumors, however, the five-year survival rate was only 15%. The histologic appearance of the tumor is therefore a useful way of determining tumors that have a more malignant phenotype.

One important aspect of the study of the impact of prostate cancer on minorities is to determine whether a difference in etiology imparts a difference in histologic subtypes among these patients. Dayal and Chiu (1982) reported that 42% of Blacks in their series had poorly differentiated tumors, compared to 30% of Whites. If histologic grade and racial origin are related, the factors responsible must be identified.

Variations in Response to Therapy

Another important issue in tumor heterogeneity and differences in survival among population groups is whether tumors in persons of various ethnic groups will respond similarly to therapy. The standard method of treating patients for metastatic prostate disease is androgen deprivation. But not all tumors respond equally to androgen withdrawal (Grayhack et al. 1987). Lymph node metastasis may respond more dramatically than osseous metastasis, and the rate at which tumor regression occurs may be quite variable. Even when tumors become endocrine-unresponsive, they retain heterogeneity in response to cytotoxic chemotherapy. Logothetis et al. (1983), after treating 62 such patients at M. D. Anderson with combination chemotherapy consisting of doxorubicin, mitomycin C, and 5-fluorouracil, reported a 48% objective response rate, although the magnitude of response and duration of survival varied with the site and extent of metastasis. For patients with visceral metastasis to the lung, response rates were 88%, compared with 33% for patients with osseous metastasis to the axial skeleton and diaphyseal and distal extremities. In spite of dramatic response rates, median survival among the responding patients was only 47.5 weeks, compared with 23.8 weeks for the nonresponding patients. This study pointed out that, even in the case of end-stage disease, the malignant expression of prostate cancer varies. At some sites the response is more dramatic than at others or for a longer period. The factors that determine these expressions are unknown, but its seems appropriate to speculate that both tumor and host factors are involved in a dynamic interplay. Do prostate cancers that occur in American Blacks have a phenotype that is inherently more unresponsive to therapy? What factors are responsible for resistance to therapy, and can they be modulated?

Research proposals for evaluating these factors in the impact of prostate cancer are both crucial and frustrating. They are crucial because the problem of prostate cancer will increase in magnitude. By the year 2000, with an increased number of men older than 50 and with an absolute rise in the incidence rates of prostate cancer, the estimate is that the disease will be diagnosed in more than 125,000 Americans yearly. Thus, there is great concern that the number of deaths caused by prostate cancer may far exceed current rates of about 25,000 a year. If certain minority groups such as American Blacks are uniquely susceptible to a lethal form of prostate cancer, then the death rates among this group may reach considerable proportions. Research into methods to prevent this are needed now. Proposals for such research are indeed frustrating to develop because of the lack of suitable experimental models and the difficulty of evaluating all of the many possible variables that may influence the expression of malignant transformation, regulate tumor growth rate, and determine the tumor's potential for metastasis.

Perhaps by focusing research on prostate cancer in minority communities, some of the factors that determine its heterogeneity will be defined, and then therapeutic strategies could be developed to modulate malignant expression in all patients. The challenge is to find strategies to alter the biologic behavior of prostate cancer. The answers might be found by studying the tumor patterns that exist in minority populations.

References

Brawn PN, Ayala AG, von Eschenbach AC, et al: Histologic grading study of prostate adenocarcinoma. *Cancer* 1982; 49:525–532.

Dayal HH, Chiu C: Factors associated with racial differences in survival for prostatic carcinoma. *J Clin Res* 1982; 35:553–560.

Gleason DF, Mellinger GT, and The Veterans Administration Cooperative Urological Research Group: Prediction of prognosis for prostatic adenocarcinoma by combined histological grading and clinical staging. *J Urol* 1974; 3:58–64.

Grayhack JT, Keeler TC, Kozlowski JM: Carcinoma of the prostate: Hormonal therapy. *Cancer* 1987; 60:589–601.

Haenszel W, Kurihara M: Studies of Japanese migrants I. Mortality from cancer and other diseases among Japanese in the United States. *JNCI* 1960; 40:43–68.

Johnson DE, Swanson DA, von Eschenbach AC. Tumors of the genitourinary tract. In Tanagho EA, McAninch JW, eds, *General Urology*, 12th Ed. Norwalk: Appleton & Lange, 1988.

Logothetis CJ, Samuels ML, von Eschenbach AC, et al: Doxorubicin, mitomycin-C and 5-fluorouracil (DMF) in the treatment of metastatic hormonal refractory adenocarcinoma of the prostate with a note on the staging metastatic prostate cancer. *J Clin Onocol* 1983; 1:368–379.

Mettlin C, Natarajan N: Epidemiologic observation from the American College of Surgeons survey on prostate cancer. *Prostate* 1983; 4:323–331.

Rose DP: The biochemical epidemiology of prostatic carcinoma. In: *Dietary Fat and Cancer*, New York: Alan R Liss, 1986, pp 43–68.

Thind, IS, Najem R, Paradise J, et al: Cancer among blacks in Newark, New Jersey 1970–1976. *Cancer* 1982; 50:180–186.

Young JL Jr, Ries GL, Pollack ES: Cancer patient survival among ethnic groups in the United States. *JNCI* 1984; 73:341–352.

Whitmore WF Jr: The natural history of prostate cancer. *Cancer* 1973; 31:1104–1112.

18. Head and Neck Cancer
in Minority Populations

Isaiah W. Dimery, Waun Ki Hong, and Robert M. Byers

Although they account for only 5% of cancers, cancers of the head and neck are among the most devastating in terms of their effects on the patient and his family. Because most of these tumors are readily evident at some point as an abnormal swelling in the face or neck and are accompanied by hoarseness, pain, difficulty in swallowing, or weight loss, one would assume early diagnosis to be the rule. In fact, however, because of a combination of factors (denial, inaccessibility of prompt medical care, initial misdiagnosis, the aggressive growth characteristics of the tumor, or even sometimes the initial absence of symptoms), most patients have advanced disease at diagnosis, and only about a third of these patients are successfully treated with the standard approaches of surgery, radiation therapy, and a combination of these modalities.

In the United States, the impact of head and neck cancers on racial minorities seems to be disproportionately great, especially among Blacks. Incidence and mortality are increasing among both men and women of minority groups. In this chapter, we review current knowledge about differences in trends of incidence and survival in the United States between majority and minority racial populations as these trends relate to head and neck cancer. We also discuss etiology and review preventive strategies.

Incidence and Survival

The incidence and survival figures for head and neck cancers in the American population are well known (Figures 1–4). The estimate based on Surveillance, Epidemiology, and End Results (SEER) data was that more than 41,000 new cases resulting in more than 13,000 deaths (32.5%) would be diagnosed in 1987 (American Cancer Society 1986). Some 5000 of these cases were expected to occur in Blacks, with 2000 resulting deaths (40%). The site of origin was predicted to be the oral cavity and pharynx in 29,800 of the patients and the larynx in 12,100 patients (American Cancer Society 1986, 1987). In general, of treated patients who present with locally advanced squamous cell carcinoma of

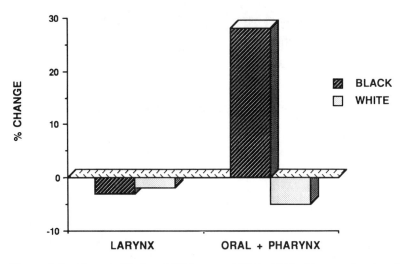

FIGURE 1. Incidence in Black and White men, 1975 to 1984, of laryngeal and oral cavity plus pharyngeal cancer, shown as percentage change. Adapted from SEER data base.

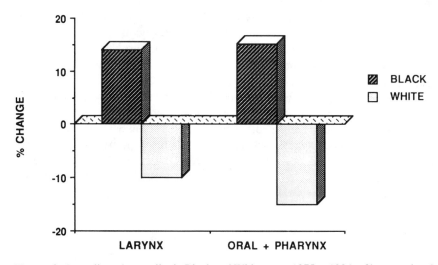

FIGURE 2. Age-adjusted mortality in Black and White men, 1975 to 1984, of laryngeal and oral cavity plus pharyngeal cancer, shown as percentage change. Adapted from SEER data base.

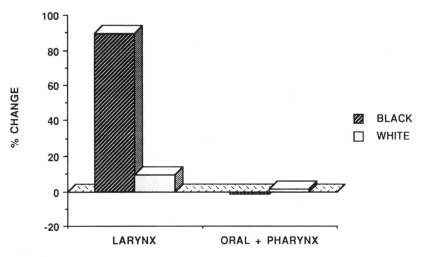

FIGURE 3. Incidence in Black and White women, 1975 to 1984, of laryngeal and oral plus pharyngeal cancer, shown as percentage change. Adapted from SEER data base.

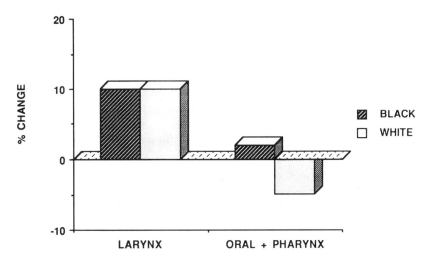

FIGURE 4. Age-adjusted mortality in Black and White women, 1975 to 1984, of laryngeal and oral cavity plus pharyngeal cancer, shown as percentage change. Adapted from SEER data base.

the head and neck, 50% to 60% develop local recurrences, 20% to 30% develop distant metastasis (80% within two years of diagnosis), and 10% to 40% develop a second primary malignancy, usually in the upper aerodigestive tract, lungs, or bladder (Hong and Bromer 1983).

Few published studies however, have been dedicated to the occurrence of head and neck cancers and related survival among racial minorities; fewer still specifically describe the outcome in these groups by tumor location in the larynx, pharynx, or oral cavity (Fontaine et al. 1972; Henschke et al. 1973; Seidman et al. 1976; Garfinkel et al. 1980). Other than SEER assessments (which underrepresent minorities and may not yield an entirely accurate picture of cancer incidence in the United States for all sites), the only surveillance programs of head and neck cancer have been on a small scale (Preston-Martin et al. 1982). Nonetheless, taking head and neck cancers as a whole, oral and pharyngeal cancers have been shown to predominate in Blacks. Head and neck cancers, with one exception, occur less frequently in Hispanics; that exception is paranasal sinus carcinoma, which is seen twice as often in Hispanics (at an incidence per 100,000 of 0.80 in Hispanic men and 0.47 in Hispanic women, compared with 0.41 and 0.24 per 100,000, respectively, in non–Hispanic Whites) as among the general population and is strongly related to occupational exposure to metal and organic dusts or fumes (Preston-Martin et al. 1982). Americans of Chinese ancestry are at a greatly increased risk of nasopharyngeal carcinoma.

The overall risk of developing and dying from head and neck cancers also seems to be greater for Blacks than Whites. Since 1950, the age-adjusted mortality rate per 100,000 population for buccal cavity and pharyngeal cancers has decreased from 6.6 to 4.7 for White males while increasing from 4.9 to 10.2 for Black males (McKay et al. 1982). Although the incidence of these tumors in men is generally higher than in women in all groups (probably as a direct relationship to etiologic factors), the incidence in Black women seems to be catching up with that of Black men. Between 1975 and 1984, oral cancer incidence increased 28% in Black males, accompanied by a 15% increase in mortality, while oral cancer mortality decreased by 10% to 15% for White males (Figures 1 and 2). During that period, the incidence of laryngeal cancer increased 90% among Black but less than 10% among White women (Figure 3), although the mortality rates of the two groups were comparable (Figure 4) (Sondik et al. 1987).

Survival for patients with laryngeal cancer is typically longer than for those with cancers at other sites because symptoms develop early, allowing early diagnosis and treatment. Recently, Wasfie and Newman (1988) reviewed their experience with laryngeal cancer in Black patients treated at Harlem Hospital in New York. Laryngeal carcinoma, described in 113 patients, occurred in patients younger than those reported in other studies, had a higher incidence in females, was diagnosed at a more advanced stage, and therefore had lower one-, three-, and five-year survivals, than in comparable studies. Even patients with stage I or II disease had a one-year survival rate of 50% to 70%, which fell to 30% and 16%, respectively, at five years. These figures are in drastic contrast to those of previous studies. That these persons delayed seeking medical attention because of socioeconomic reasons as well as the presence of dietary and environmental factors can only be implied to have resulted in such a poor outcome.

Earlier, a 15-year study exclusively of head and neck cancer in Blacks was reported by Leffall and White (1965) from Freedman's Hospital in Washington, D.C. Although the population was comparatively small, trends in primary site incidence were illustrated, as was the generally poor outcome in these patients: oral cavity carcinomas predominated, and overall three-year disease-free survival was 24%. Slotman et al. (1983) of the Rhode Island Hospital found that Black patients at their institution who had head and neck cancers were younger (45 years old or younger) ($P < 0.001$) than their White counterparts and had a much poorer prognosis both at two years (28% compared with 40% survival) and five years (5% compared with 13% survival). In general, these younger patients did less well than older patients from the same institution. These results were felt to reflect an earlier initiation of tobacco and alcohol use among Blacks (Slotman et al. 1983).

Etiology and Risk Factors

Alcohol and tobacco usage, socioeconomic, dietary, environmental, and possibly genetic factors both directly and indirectly affect the development of head and neck cancers (Schottenfeld and Bergard 1985) and may correlate directly with racial incidence patterns of these cancers.

First and foremost, the intake of alcoholic beverages, particularly undiluted liquors or large quantities of other beverages that contain lesser percentages of ethanol, is clearly associated with an increased risk of oral cancer. When heavy consumption of alcohol is combined with heavy cigarette smoking, the risk of oral cancers increases to six- to sevenfold of that seen among light drinkers and smokers (Graham 1977). This figure is derived from the evaluation of a White population; the exact relative risk patterns among minorities are not well known. However, the increased tumor incidence in Black women is probably related to changing patterns of alcohol consumption and smoking.

Alcohol consumption is strongly associated with age (the incidence increases among 20- to 34-year-olds), education (incidence increases along with educational attainment), and income. People in lower-income groups have been found to be less likely to drink than those with higher incomes yet more likely to have more drinks at one sitting. Blacks and Hispanics (48% and 56%, respectively), compared with Whites (31%), were more apt to abstain (defined as taking fewer than 12 drinks per year) or less apt to have had more than five drinks on at least one day in the past year (30% for Blacks compared with 38% for Whites) (Schoenborn and Cohen 1986).

The prevalence and patterns of smoking seem to differ among Blacks and Whites. In a recent survey, 41% of Black men reported that they smoked, compared with 32% of White men; 32% of Black women surveyed smoked, compared with 28% of White women surveyed (Centers for Disease Control 1987). In the same survey, Hispanic men reported approximately the same smoking prevalence (31%) as did White men, whereas Hispanic women had a much lower smoking rate (21%) than did either White or Black women. Despite the higher percentages of Black smokers, analysis of similar data obtained from household interviews of the National Health Interview Survey indicated that the higher per capita usage was offset because more than half (55%) of Black smokers smoked fewer than 15 cigarettes per day, compared with 24% of the whites (Schoenborn and Cohen 1986). Whether filtered or nonfiltered brands were consumed and how completely the cigarettes were smoked was not described in these studies. An aggressive promotional campaign aimed at the minority communities supports the higher usage of tobacco products, which is generally felt to be directly linked to increasing cancer incidence (Davis 1987; Blum 1986). A case-control, multi-institutional study of 1114 patients with oral and pharyngeal cancer and 1268 population-based controls demonstrated the effects of smoking and alcohol on cancer incidence (Blot et al. 1988). This study demonstrated that the relative risk patterns were similar among Whites and Blacks but that the prevalence of drinking and smoking was higher among the Black general population. Evaluation of the Hispanic population revealed smoking and drinking to be less prevalent. The cessation of alcohol and tobacco usage after 10 years reduced the risk of cancer development to that of the general population (Blot et al. 1988).

From these differing data, it appears that Blacks may have a universal, overwhelmingly increased exposure to carcinogens that accounts for the discrepancies in cancer incidence. Blacks may not, however, have an increased age-associated risk of head and neck cancers compared with Whites (Satariano et al. 1982). The higher rate of laryngeal cancer seen among Black females in most age groups may, however, reflect a different rate of susceptibility or exposure to risk factors.

Nonetheless, a lower socioeconomic status is associated with higher risk among both Blacks and Whites, and whether this heightened risk is strongly related solely to the amounts and types of alcohol and cigarettes used remains in question (Graham et al. 1977). The diets of heavy smokers and drinkers are usually deficient in certain vitamins, such as vitamins A and C, and in certain trace elements. Animals experimentally deprived of vitamin A or its derivatives (retinoids) were more likely to develop certain epithelial tumors when exposed to carcinogens, and development of the tumors was reversible or preventable upon reconstitution of the diet (Goodman 1984; Moon et al. 1983). The vitamin A analogue 13-*cis*-retinoic acid has been shown to reverse precancerous oral lesions (leukoplakia) in human trials (Hong et al. 1986) strengthening the argument for the role of diet in carcinogenesis and cancer prevention.

The incidence of sinus carcinomas is related to occupational exposure to smoke, dust, and fumes. Those at greatest risk seem to be Mexican-born Hispanic men and women, who may have had a history of an increased environmental exposure to carcinogen-laden inhalants (i.e., from cooking fires) than did their American-born counterparts (Preston-Martin et al. 1982). Careful case-control studies need to be done to test this theory, not only in cities with large Hispanic populations such as Los Angeles but in other large metropolitan cities as well.

Differences in cancer incidence may be the result of some differential alteration induced in the immune system upon exposure to potential carcinogens.
Alfred et al. (1982) examined lymphotoxin release from peripheral blood lym-
phocytes co-cultured with 3-methylcholanthrene in Black patients with head and
neck and lung cancers and in Black controls. The concentration of lymphotoxin
released was lower in the cancer patients overall as compared with controls,
possibly reflecting impairment of cell-mediated immunity. Among patients with
cancer, those with lung cancer produced less lymphotoxin than those with head
and neck cancer. Both intra- and interracial studies along these lines should
prove useful.

Access to Treatment

Obviously, oral cancers and precancerous lesions can be identified at much
earlier stages in those who have regular dental examinations, heightening the
chance for cure or elimination of the abnormal area before malignant transformation occurs. Unavailability of such care, for whatever reason, is reflected in the
more advanced stage of most tumors at initial diagnosis.

Our hope is that new treatment approaches—for example, incorporating neo-
adjuvant chemotherapy into the standard surgery, radiotherapy, and combined
surgery-radiation regimens—will improve long-term survival rates for patients
with head and neck cancers. The required additional hospitalization and pro-
longation of treatment will make the cost of such treatment even greater,
however, and will thus make treatment potentially even less accessible.
Moreover, patients often need speech, swallowing, and physical therapy as well
before they can resume their pretreatment functional status. Significant
resources are required to deliver full medical support and rehabilitation services,
and few hospitals and medical centers are so equipped. Notably, however,
although survival of cancer patients has been found to be affected by racial and
socioeconomic status (Berg et al. 1977; Axtell et al. 1975; Axtell and Myers
1978), these factors became negligible when health care was uniform (Page and
Kuntz 1980).

We evaluated by race (White compared with Black or Hispanic) patients seen
for head and neck cancer at M. D. Anderson Cancer Center between 1974 and
1983 for primary diagnosis and definitive therapy, excluding those who had had
prior therapy elsewhere. Patients are described in Table 1. Our hospital is the
comprehensive cancer referral center for the southwestern United States, a state-
supported facility where the ability to pay for treatment is not a limiting factor
for state residents. Seventy-five percent of Black and Hispanic patients seen
during the study period were financially disadvantaged (as determined by health
insurance status and income level) compared with 42% of Whites. These statistics may reflect the patterns of patient referral. The anatomic site of the primary
disease was quite similar among these groups, whereas the disease stage at diagnosis tended to be more extensive in non–Whites at most sites (Table 2). Analysis
of survival data for patients with oral cavity/oropharyngeal primary tumors

TABLE 1. Patients with head and neck cancer seen 1974–1983 at M. D. Anderson Cancer Center.[a]

	White		Black		Hispanic	
Number	1987		151		113	
Male/female percentage	70/30		74/26		77/23	
Site						
Oral cavity	29%		26%		20%	
Oropharynx	27%		20%		23%	
Hypopharynx	9%		8%		10%	
Larynx	27%		37%		35%	
Other	8%		9%		10%	
Stage						
Local	30		15		25	
Extensive	32		33		34	
Nodes	9	70%	7	85%	7	75%
Extensive + nodes	23		34		25	
Distant	6		11		9	

[a] For primary diagnosis and definitive treatment, excluding patients treated previously here or elsewhere.

(stages T3-4 and N+) did not demonstrate any greater disadvantage for the non-White population in a stage-for-stage comparison. For this group, the prognosis was poor with a median survival of 18 months, whether surgery was used alone or was followed by radiotherapy. Detailed evaluation of patients with earlier-stage disease at other sites, who routinely have a longer survival (i.e., patients with cancer of the larynx) might prove to be more meaningful and important.

Nasopharyngeal Carcinoma

In the United States, race is a particularly important factor in the occurrence of nasopharyngeal carcinoma, which accounts for 0.3% of all malignant conditions and 2% of head and neck cancers in this country. It is unique among upper aero-digestive tumors in that its etiology is strongly associated with the Epstein-Barr virus (EBV) and the ingestion of salted fish (Levine 1985; Yu 1986). The incidence is 4 per one million of North Americans in general but is 25 times higher in Chinese Americans. The incidence decreases in second-generation relatives, but even third-generation Chinese Americans have a 10 times greater risk of developing this cancer than do members of the general population. Nonrandom chromosomal abnormalities indicate that an acquired genetic predisposition is induced by the EBV genome into the normal host tissues (Fedder and Gonzales 1985); Moloy et al. 1985). Measurement of EBV antibodies in serum may identify a high-risk population, but because of the ubiquitous nature of subclinical EBV infections, evaluation for the antibody may not be an effective screening tool in prevention trials.

TABLE 2. Racial comparison by disease stage of patients with head and neck cancers at M. D. Anderson Cancer Center 1974–1983.

Site	Local		Extensive		Distant Metastases	
	White N(%)	Black and Hispanic N(%)	White N(%)	Black and Hispanic N(%)	White N(%)	Black and Hispanic N(%)
Oral	224/581 (38%)	17/62 (27%)	329/581 (56%)	41/62 (65%)	28/581 (5%)	4/62 (6%)
Oropharynx	97/528 (18%)	5/58 (9%)	403/528 (76%)	43/58 (74%)	28/528 (5%)	10/58 (17%)
Hypopharynx	17/185 (9%)	1/23 (4%)	142/185 (77%)	19/23 (82%)	26/185 (14%)	3/23 (13%)
Glottis	222/526 (42%)	23/96 (24%)	284/526 (54%)	68/96 (70%)	20/526 (4%)	5/96 (5%)
Sinuses	31/123 (25%)	5/22 (22%)	78/123 (63%)	12/22 (54%)	14/123 (11%)	5/22 (22%)

Discussion

So little is known at this point about the behavior of head and neck cancer in minority populations that any sound clinical studies would be a significant contribution to existing knowledge.

The critical analysis of differences in the incidence of and treatment outcome for head and neck cancers in minority populations may allow identification of significant but subtle causative environmental and of inherent–genetic or immunologic–factors that account for the observed trends. Preventive programs could then be designed to address this issue (Wynder and Kabar 1981). Such an analysis would require the concerted effort of surgeons, radiotherapists, medical oncologists, and epidemiologists interested in head and neck cancers. Currently, there is no reported breakdown to show which patients do well and which do poorly. Prospective comparative analyses of treatment results of White and non-White populations would be interesting, not only from the aspect of survival outcome but also in terms of the histologic differentiation of the tumor, patterns of distant metastases, responses to surgery/radiotherapy and chemotherapy, and disease-free survival. Expansion of preliminary results (Alfred et al. 1982) to include full immunologic evaluation should be pursued, along with evaluations of possible differential responses of lymphoid tissues in culture to carcinogens.

Finally, minority patients should avail themselves of programs designed to evaluate new (possibly experimental) treatment approaches, either as the primary treatment for or to prevent head and neck cancers. Only through continued innovative approaches to the prevention and treatment of this disease can progress be accomplished.

Acknowledgments. Thanks to Dr. Margaret Spitz for her contribution and review, to Suzanne Simpson for editing, and to Pamela Ansley and Cynthia Argo for preparation of the manuscript. We thank Vincent Guinee, M.D. and Mr. Rick Shallenberger of the Department of Epidemiology and Patient Studies for their assistance and advice in the preparation of this manuscript.

References

Alfred LJ, Venkatesan N, Mandal AK, et al: Release of lymphotoxin by control and chemical carcinogen-treated lymphocyte cultures derived from black healthy subjects and cancer patients. *J Natl Med Assoc* 1982;74:775–781.

American Cancer Society: *Cancer Facts & Figures for Minority Americans – 1986.* New York: American Cancer Society, 1986.

American Cancer Society: *Cancer Facts & Figures – 1987.* New York: American Cancer Society, 1987.

Axtell LM, Myers MH, Shambaugh EM: *Treatment Survival Patterns for Black and White Cancer Patients Diagnosed 1955 through 1964.* Bethesda, MD: US Department of Health, Education and Welfare, DHEW publication No. (NIH) 75-712, 1975.

Axtell LM, Myers MH: Contrasts in survival of black and white cancer patients, 1960–73. *JNCI* 1978;60:1209–1215.

Berg JW, Ross R, Latourette HP: Economic status and survival of patients. *Cancer* 1977;39:467–477.

Blot WJ, McLaughlin JK, Winn DM, et al: Smoking and drinking in relation to oral and pharyngeal cancer. *Cancer Res* 1988;48:3282–3287.

Blum A: Selling cigarettes: The blue-collar, black target. *Washington Post*, May 18, 1986.

Centers for Disease Control: Topics in minority health: Cigarette smoking among blacks and other minority populations. *MMWR* 1987;36:404–407.

Davis RM: Current trends in cigarette advertising and marketing. *N Engl J Med* 1987; 316:725–732.

Fedder M, Gonzalez MF: Nasopharyngeal carcinoma: Brief review. *Am J Med* 1985; 79:365–369.

Fontaine SA, Henschke UK, Leffall LD, et al: Comparison of the cancer deaths in the black and white populations from 1949 to 1967. *Annals of the District of Columbia* 1972;41:293–298.

Garfinkel L, Poindexter CE, Silverberg E: Cancer in black Americans. *CA* 1980;30: 39–44.

Goodman DS: Vitamin A and retinoids in health and disease. *N Engl J Med* 1984;310: 1023–1031.

Graham S, Dayal H, Rohrer T, et al: Dentition, diet, tobacco, and alcohol in the epidemiology of oral cancer. *JNCI* 1977;59:1611–1618.

Henschke UK, Leffall LD, Mason CH, et al: Alarming increase of the cancer mortality in the U.S. black population (1950–1967). *Cancer* 1973;31:763–768.

Hong WK, Bromer R: Chemotherapy in head and neck cancer. *N Engl J Med* 1983;308: 75–79.

Hong WK, Endicott J, Itri LM, et al: 13-*cis*-retinoic acid in the treatment of oral leukoplakia. *N Engl J Med* 1986;315:1501–1505.

Leffall LD, White JE: Cancer of the oral cavity in Negroes. *Surg Gynecol Obstet* 1965; 120:70–72.

Levine PH, Connelly RR: Epidemiology of nasopharyngeal cancer. In Wittes R (ed): *Head and Neck Cancer.* Cancer Investigation and Management Series. New York: John Wiley & Sons, 1985, pp 13–34.

McKay FW, Hanson MR, Miller RW: *Cancer Mortality in the United States: 1950–1977. NCI Monogr* No. 59 NIH publication 82-2435. Bethesda, MD: National Cancer Institute, 1982.

Moloy PJ, Chung YT, Krivitsky PB, et al: Squamous carcinoma of the nasopharynx: Medical Progress. *West J Med* 1985;143:66–69.

Moon RC, McCormick DL, Mehta RG: Inhibition of carcinogenesis by retinoids. *Cancer Res* 1983;43(Suppl):2469–2475.

Page WF, Kuntz AJ: Racial and socioeconomic factors in cancer survival. A comparison of Veterans Administration results with selected studies. *Cancer* 1980;45:1029–1040.

Preston-Martin S, Henderson BE, Pike FMC: Descriptive epidemiology of cancers of the upper respiratory tract in Los Angeles. *Cancer* 1982;49:2201–2207.

Satariano WA, Albert S, Belle SH: Race, age, and cancer incidence: A test of double jeopardy. *J Gerontol* 1982;37:642–647.

Schoenborn CA, Cohen BH: *Trends in Smoking, Alcohol Consumption, and Other Health Statistics: No. 118.* DHHS Pub. No. (PHS) 86-1250 Public Health, pp 1–16. Hyattsville, MD: US Public Health Service, 1986.

Schottenfeld DS, Bergard BM: Epidemiology of cancers of the oral cavity, pharynx, and larynx. In Wittes R (ed): *Head and Neck Cancer.* Cancer Investigation and Management Series. New York: John Wiley & Sons, 1985, pp 3–12.

Seidman H, Silverberg E, Holleb AL: Cancer statistics, 1976: A comparison of white and black populations. *CA* 1976;26:2–30.

Slotman GJ, Swaminathan AP, Rush BF Jr: Head and neck cancer in a young age group: High incidence in black patients. *Head Neck Surg* 1983;5:293–298.

Sondik EJ, Young JL, Horm JW, et al: *1986 Annual Cancer Statistics Review.* Bethesda, MD: National Cancer Institute. NIH publication 87-2789.

Wasfie T, Newman R. 1987. Laryngeal carcinoma in black patients. *Cancer* 1988;61:167–172.

Wynder EL, Kabat GC: Opportunities for prevention of cancer in blacks. In Mettlin C, Murphy GP (eds): *Cancer Among Black Populations: Proceedings of the International Conference on Cancer Among Black Populations.* New York: Alan R. Liss, Inc, 1981, pp 237–252.

Yu MC, Ho JHC, Lai S-H, Henderson BE: Cantonese-style salted fish as a cause of nasopharyngeal carcinoma: Report of a case-controlled study in Hong Kong. *Cancer Res* 1986;46:956–961.

19. Lung Cancer in Black Populations of the United States: Overview and Update

Kenneth Olden, Ki-Moon Bang, Sandra L. White,
and Barry Gause

Epidemiologic Trends

Incidence

In 1986 in the United States, 100,000 men and 49,000 women were expected to develop lung cancer according to an American Cancer Society (ACS) (1986) estimate. This represents about 15% of all cancer cases (22% in men and 11% in women); the incidence of lung cancer has been increasing at up to 10% per year since the 1930s (Cutler and Devesa 1973; Devesa and Silverman 1978). Among the major ethnic groups, Blacks have the highest overall incidence of lung cancer and American Indians the lowest. A recent report (Horm and Kessler 1986) indicated that the incidence of lung cancer in White men had dropped for the first time, from 82.7 per 100,000 in 1982 to 79.3 in 1983. For Black men, the incidence appeared to have increased slightly in this same period (Table 1). In 1983 the incidence for Black men was 125.3, 58% higher than that for White men. The incidence of lung cancer in both White and Black women had not shown any change during the previous decade, and Blacks had higher age-specific rates than Whites (National Cancer Institute [NCI] 1985).

The age-specific trends of lung cancer incidence have been continuously falling since 1973 for White men aged 35 to 44 years but have increased for those 50 years old and older. For Black men aged 35 to 54 years, the age-specific incidence rates were about double those for White men (Horm and Kessler 1986).

Mortality

Lung cancer is the leading cause of cancer death in the U.S. In 1986, about 150,000 Americans died from this disease. It now accounts for 25% of all cancer deaths, 35% of all deaths from cancer in men, and 19% of all deaths from cancer in women (ACS 1986). Age-adjusted cancer death rates for both males and females are doubling approximately every 15 years (Minna et al. 1985). In Blacks, the age-specific mortality rate for lung cancer is higher than in Whites

TABLE 1. Incidence and mortality rates (per 100,000 population) of male lung cancer by race, 1973–1983.

	Incidence		Mortality	
Year	White	Black	White	Black
1973	72.3	103.9	61.6	74.6
1977	79.5	107.7	66.8	87.4
1981	82.8	123.8	70.1	95.0
1982	82.7	122.8	71.3	97.5
1983	79.3	125.3	71.2	97.3

Source: Surveillance, Epidemiology, and End Results Program, National Cancer Institute.

until ages 70 to 74. At this age the rate begins to decrease, according to data from the NCI's Surveillance, Epidemiology, and End Results (SEER) Program during the period of 1978–1981 (NCI 1985) (Figure 1).

In Whites mortality from lung cancer rose by 2.1% per year from 1973 to 1977 and 1.1% per year from 1978 to 1982. The slight decrease from 1982 to 1983 was the first decrease in age-adjusted mortality for lung cancer since 1950 (Horm and Kessler 1986). The mortality rate for Black men increased continuously until 1982 and then decreased slightly but not significantly between 1982 and 1983 (Table 1). Mortality from lung cancer among women has continuously increased at about 6% per year (Horm and Kessler 1986) such that in the last 30 years, women's lung cancer death rates have increased by more than 300%. In 1986, lung cancer was expected to surpass breast cancer as the No. 1 cancer killer among women (ACS 1985).

Until the early 1950s, cancer mortality rates for Blacks were lower than those for Whites (White and Enterline 1980). Over the past decades, however, cancer deaths among Black men have risen even faster than those for White men. From 1955 to the present, they have been higher for Blacks.

Recent decreasing trends in incidence of and mortality from lung cancer in White men may signal the beginning of a downturn in lung cancer from 1982 on. The trend may be related to the lower percentage of smokers (50% in 1965 and 38% in 1980) since the Surgeon General's first report on smoking and health (US Department of Health, Education, and Welfare 1964). If there is a 20- to 25-year latency period of lung cancer after smoking, one would expect the incidence of lung cancer to decrease over the next 20 to 25 years.

Survival

The five-year survival rate of lung cancer patients after diagnosis was 11% for Blacks compared with 13% for Whites during the period of 1977–1981 (NCI 1985). Only 13% of all lung cancer patients live five years after diagnosis (ACS 1986), a rate that has improved only slightly over the last decade. The five-year survival rate for Blacks with localized stage I lung cancer was 36% compared

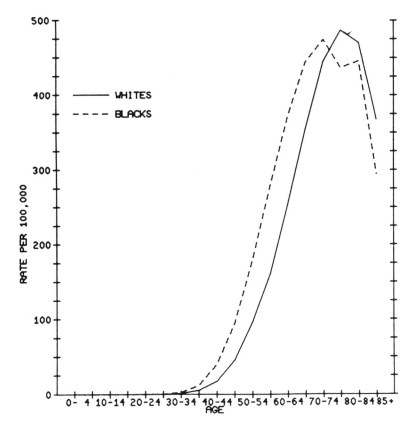

FIGURE 1. Age-specific mortality rates for lung cancer per 100,000 men in the United States, 1973–1981. Source: *Cancer Statistics Review*, National Cancer Institute (1985).

with 41% for Whites, but at advanced stage III, the rate was only 1% for Blacks and 5% for Whites. Patients with epidermoid cancers have the best survival, followed by those with adenocarcinoma and large cell carcinoma. Rarely will a patient with small cell carcinoma survive for five years (Minna et al. 1985). At the time of diagnosis, the disease has spread to regional lymph nodes or distant sites in 70% of patients with small cell lung cancer (National Institutes of Health [NIH] 1977), which may account for the poor survival rate of patients with this disease.

In general women have a better five-year survival than men for as yet unknown reasons. This is not explained by the patient's age or by tumor resectability or location (Watson and Schottenfeld 1968). The difference is particularly marked for women with localized disease who undergo surgical resection (Minna et al. 1985). In a recent study, Weiss and Daniels (1978) reported an interesting association of increased one-year survival in non-small cell lung cancer with the presence of human leukocyte antigens of the AW19 and B5 complexes.

TABLE 2. Environmental and occupational causes of lung cancer.

Agent	Type of exposure	Attributable percentage
Tobacco smoke	Cigarette smoking	80–85%
Asbestos	Manufacturing and application	
Arsenic (inorganic)	Mining and smelting of certain ores	
Bischloromethylether	Manufacture of ion exchange resins	
Chromium compounds	Manufacturing	5–10%
Mustard gas	Manufacturing	
Nickel dust	Refining	
Polycyclic hydrocarbons	Coal carbonization products	
Radon	Uranium mining	

Risk Factors

Although cigarette smoking is the principal cause of lung cancer, epidemiologic researchers have discovered other environmental and occupational risk factors that may be involved in the development of lung cancer. The occupational causes of cancer, which may account for 5% to 10% of lung cancer cases, are listed in Table 2.

Smoking, however, contributes directly to from 80% to 85% of deaths from lung cancer in the United States (US Department of Health and Human Services 1983), and the risk of developing lung cancer is 10 times greater for smokers than nonsmokers (ACS 1985). Many cohort studies in various parts of the world have consistently demonstrated the association between smoking and lung cancer, among them the American Cancer Society follow-up of one million persons for more than six years (Hammond 1972), the 20-year evaluation of mortality of 34,000 male British physicians (Doll and Peto 1976), and the 8.5-year follow-up of 290,000 United States veterans (Kahn 1966). All showed that excess risk of lung cancer was directly proportional to the number of cigarettes smoked per day and the duration of smoking, the risk for male smokers of two or more packs per day being nearly 20 times that of nonsmokers. For ex-smokers, lung cancer mortality is related to the number of years since they stopped smoking. In their landmark study of British physicians, Doll and Peto (1976) showed that an ex-smoker who had not smoked for five years had a lung cancer mortality about 40% that of a current smoker.

Smoking seems to induce lung cancers of all major histologic types (Vincent et al. 1977; Wynder and Stellman 1977); the strongest associations have been found with squamous cell and small cell carcinomas, but dose-response relationships for adenocarcinomas and other cell types have also been reported.

Changes in the number of lung cancer cases paralleled smoking patterns over the past 20 years. The 1965 figure, 52% of adult males smoking cigarettes, fell to 30% in 1980 and to 35% in 1983. There were differences by race, however, as nearly 45% of Black men smoked in 1980 compared with 37% of White men (National Center for Health Statistics 1984). Fewer women stopped smoking, and the lung cancer rate of women smokers dropped less than that of men smokers. Although the lung cancer rate among women is still one-third that of men, women are catching up: over the past decade both new case and death rates for lung cancer among women increased about 6% annually.

Since the first such report by Hirayama in 1981, several others (ACS 1986) have found an increased risk of lung cancer among nonsmoking wives of cigarette smokers.

Asbestos-induced lung cancer is characterized by a latency period of 20 years or longer between the start of exposure and onset of the disease. Its synergistic relationship to cigarette smoking (Saracci 1977) was also demonstrated by a review of 276 lung cancer deaths among insulation workers by Hammond et al. (1979). This study revealed a relative risk of about 5 deaths from asbestos exposure alone, 10 deaths from cigarette smoking alone, and 50 from combined exposure. Among the other environmental risk factors, radon is responsible for the elevated risk of lung cancer among uranium miners in Canada and Czechoslovakia (Sevc et al. 1976), and an excess of lung cancer cases was reported among workers who had manufactured mustard gas in Japan and Germany (Wada et al. 1968; Weiss and Weiss 1975). For polycyclic hydrocarbons, which have been reported to induce lung cancer in gas workers, coal workers, coke oven workers, and steelworkers, the associated excess mortality from lung cancer occurred among men who worked at the coke ovens and rose 10-fold among those who had worked five years or longer at the top of the ovens (Lloyd 1971).

Industrial exposures to beryllium, acrylonitrile, and vinyl chloride are also suspected to cause lung cancer (Wagoner et al. 1980; O'Berg 1980; Buffler et al. 1979).

Histopathologic Characteristics

There are many histopathologic classifications for bronchogenic carcinoma, which divide these tumors into 4 to 12 categories. The most reasonable ones, those that correlate with differences in therapeutic options, clinical presentation, and survival, are based on the World Health Organization classification, which divides lung cancer into four major categories (Table 3). Twenty years ago squamous cell carcinoma accounted for 35% to 50% of cases of bronchogenic carcinoma. Recently, however, the percentage of cases of adenocarcinoma has risen such that data collected over the past five years indicate that adenocarcinomas and epidermoid carcinomas each make up 30% to 35% of lung cancers whereas the percentages of small cell (20% to 25%) and large cell cases (10% to 15%) have remained constant. In some patient series, adenocarcinomas have been the most frequently occurring form (Martin 1982). The reasons for this are not clear although the increasing number of women with lung cancer has been postulated as one possible cause (women as a group have a higher incidence of adenocarcinoma than men). In Blacks overall, epidermoid cancer remains the most frequent type seen. This has some survival implications in that patients with epidermoid

TABLE 3. Histologic classification of bronchogenic carcinoma.

Squamous cell (epidermoid carcinoma)
Adenocarcinoma
   Bronchial-derived (acinar, papillary, solid)
   Bronchioloalveolar
Small cell carcinoma
   Oat cell (lymphocyte-like)
   Intermediate cell (polygonal)
   Combined (usually with squamous)
Large cell carcinoma (undifferentiated, giant cell, clear cell)
Combined squamous cell carcinoma and adenocarcinoma

Source: World Health Organization.

carcinoma, because of the cancer's tendency to grow locally and therefore its increased resectability, have a higher five-year survival rate than do patients with adenocarcinoma (Katlic and Carter 1979; NCI 1985, NIH 1977). This rise in adenocarcinoma cases could negate improvements one might see in survival as a result of more effective treatment.

Bronchogenic carcinomas usually arise from the first-, second-, or third-order bronchi. Some, predominantly adenocarcinomas of the bronchoalveolar type, arise from the alveolar septa and terminal bronchioles. Pathogenetically, bronchogenic carcinoma is believed to arise as a response to repeated irritation, with subsequent injury and repair. The initial response of the bronchioloalveolar surface epithelial cells to injury is proliferation, followed by replacement of normal columnar epithelia with metaplastic stratified squamous epithelia. The epithelia then become disorganized and form atypical nuclei in a dysplastic change. This is followed by carcinoma in situ and then invasive cancer as the basement membrane is breached.

This process usually develops for one to two decades before a patient shows evidence of malignancy, a prolonged period that has obvious implications for early detection or prevention.

Signs and Symptoms

The clinical presentation of patients with lung cancer depends on the location of the primary tumor, the presence or absence of local extension or metastatic disease, and the presence of remote tumor effects not related to metastasis, that is, paraneoplastic syndromes. These characteristics are to a great degree related to the histologic type of the tumor. Small cell and epidermoid carcinomas, for instance, tend to present as central lesions with hilar and mediastinal adenopathy. This location leads to large-airway obstruction with subsequent atelectasis and pneumonia. Adenocarcinomas tend to occur as peripheral lesions, which lead to early pleural involvement and effusions. As the disease progresses, airway obstruction and atelectasis may also become a problem. Large cell carcinomas also tend to occur in a peripheral location but they are usually much larger at diagnosis than adenocarcinomas. Patients with large cell carcinoma may, therefore, show evidence of pleural involvement and central large-airway obstruction when they are first seen.

Because of the tumors' relatively central location, then, patients with epidermoid or small cell lung cancer will have symptoms of airway irritation and obstruction such as dyspnea, coughing, wheezing, hemoptysis, pain in the midchest area, and postobstructive pneumonia. Tumor extension into the mediastinum may lead to recurrent laryngeal nerve paralysis with subsequent hoarseness or dysphagia or both and superior vena cava syndrome; dysphagia and hoarseness are more common with disease on the left and superior vena cava syndrome with disease on the right side of the chest. Esophageal compression may also lead to dysphagia.

Adenocarcinomas, in contrast, with their peripheral locale, cause symptoms of pleural irritation, such as pain on inspiration, and pleural effusion. The inspiratory pain may lead to the feeling of dyspnea that is different from the dyspneic sensation observed in patients with central obstructive lesions, because this type of dyspnea is related to a voluntary decrease in pulmonary expansion secondary to pain. Patients with large cell tumors usually do not have any characteristic symptoms on presentation other than the tendency to form pulmonary cavitations.

Patients dying of lung cancer commonly have metastatic disease. Other than small cell cancer, however, which may present with metastasis in as many as 10% of cases, most types of lung cancer develop only as intrathoracic disease.

Some patients may show remote effects of the tumor, unrelated to metastasis. These so-called paraneoplastic syndromes occur in up to 50% of lung cancer cases and tend to manifest themselves up to two years before the symptoms of intrathoracic disease occur. Some of these syndromes tend to be specific to certain tumors: the Eaton-Lambert syndrome, inappropriate antidiuretic hormone and inappropriate ACTH secretion to small cell carcinoma, hypercalcemia to epidermoid carcinoma, and hypertrophic pulmonary osteoarthropathy to adenocarcinoma.

Blacks tend to present with more extensive disease and complications that may be immediately life threatening, such as severe hemoptysis, pneumonitis and sepsis, and large pleural effusions (White and Enterline 1980). In Black patients with lung cancer, the immune system also tends to be more severely depressed than in Whites. This has implications for disease complications, for the ability of the patients' immune systems to control the disease, and for their ability to respond to chemotherapy.

A perplexing syndrome of weight loss and anorexia is seen in about 30% of patients with lung cancer and in a higher percentage of Blacks who have this disease. Related to the extent of disease at diagnosis, this syndrome is a major determinant of response to therapy and survival.

Managing the Problem

As mentioned previously, research in the area of lung cancer etiology consistently defines smoking as the causative factor in 80–85% of the cases. The obvious conclusion from this data therefore is that lung cancer is basically a preventable disease if individuals never start smoking (ACS 1985). It is also well established that smoking cessation is followed by a reduced risk of cancer; e.g., 10 to 15 years after quitting, the risk of developing carcinoma of the lung and larnyx approaches that of nonsmokers (Holbrook 1983). There is also increasing evidence from basic and epidemiologic research that certain micronutrients, specifically vitamin A and its analogues, may prevent cells from progressing from metaplasia to carcinoma. This relationship between vitamin A and cancer was first documented in 1926, when Fujimaki noted the development of stomach carcinoma in rats maintained on a vitamin A-deficient diet. Also, a vitamin A-deficient diet led to metaplastic changes in the respiratory, gastrointestinal, and urogenital tracts of experimental animals (Rowe and Gorlin 1959; Saffiotti et al. 1967). These findings led researchers to postulate that vitamin A might have a role in cancer prevention by inhibiting the earliest changes in the malignant process. In a study using the Syrian hamster, Rowe and Gorlin (1959) showed that vitamin A deficiency and exposure to a carcinogen markedly increased the incidence of oral cancer above that of the control animals. Saffiotti et al. (1967) reproduced these results with the same animal model when they instilled benzpyrene into the animals' tracheas and found that high doses of vitamin A could prevent metaplasia and delay or prevent the subsequent development of cancer. Other investigators (Wald et al. 1980; Wolback and Howe 1985) showed that methylcholanthrene could induce pulmonary carcinogenesis in rats when vitamin A was eliminated from the diet.

Secondary Prevention (Screening)

Patients with lung cancer, like those with most solid tumors, have the best chance of being cured if the disease is detected at an early stage, when surgery and radiation can be used with curative intent. Survival data have shown that 24% to 42% of patients with stage I disease (small tumor, no nodes, no metastasis) survive at least five years, whereas only 10% of patients with disease at stages II and III (tumors of larger size, one or two positive nodes, no metastasis) will survive that long. The idea of screening individuals who are asymptomatic but at high risk of developing lung cancer therefore seems the prudent thing to do.

Chest X ray and sputum cytology are the most effective screening procedures for detection of stages I, II, and III lung cancer in asymptomatic individuals. However, intensive screening of high-risk populations has not significantly improved detection of stage I disease, hence routine screening of the general population is not highly recommended. The use of conventional markers, such as carcinoembryonic antigen, calcitonin, and ACTH have been shown to have no value in screening tests because of their low sensitivity and specificity. If more sensitive screening procedures were available, the lung cancer mortality could be dramatically reduced. For example, survival is about 80% for patients with stage I disease, 50% for those with stage II, and 10% for stage III.

The results of screening studies were not stratified by race, and thus far no similar studies examining the prevalence of lung cancer in high-risk Black populations have been published. All data concerning Blacks have dealt with survival rate and disease stage at diagnosis in patients with symptomatic cases of lung cancer. This information is not pertinent for evaluating the usefulness of screening programs. We cannot, therefore, be certain whether the results of screening reported in the literature would hold true for Black populations.

Treatment

Two important issues must be considered before appropriate therapy for lung cancer can be instituted: (1) the histologic type of the tumor and (2) the stage or extent of the disease at the time of diagnosis. For example, the optimal therapy for stage I or II lung cancer is definitive surgery with curative intent. In selected patients with stage III disease, such as some with superior sulcus (pancoast) tumors, the combination of surgery and radiotherapy has resulted in statistically significant increases in long-term survival and should be considered. In general, after routine examination and work-up including chest X–ray, laboratory studies, radionuclide scans, and mediastinoscopy, about 40% of patients will be candidates for surgery. At the time of surgery, another 5% will be found to have regional spread and will be considered inoperable. Only 35% of patients with non-small cell lung cancer (NSCLC) will have resectable lesions. In Black populations in the U.S., the percentage of patients whose tumors are resectable is about 20% to 25%, and their operative mortality rate is 5% to 10%, compared with 3% in most studies involving Whites. The percentage of Blacks who are considered to be without evidence of disease after surgery generally is about 25% to 30%.

Chemotherapy and radiation are the mainstays of therapy for patients with advanced (Stages IIIB and IV) NSCLC. The response rate to chemotherapy is 39%, with some evidence of longer survival among responders. For patients with small cell lung cancer (SCLC), the primary method of treatment has shifted over the past 30 years from surgery to radiotherapy and now to chemotherapy. The use of surgery and radiation alone yielded five-year survival rates of less than 1%; but now, with the advent of aggressive combination chemotherapy, we are seeing 5% to 15% of patients surviving free of disease for 18 to 30 months.

Because of the improvements achieved with chemotherapy and radiation therapy for patients with SCLC, researchers began to reevaluate the role of surgery for patients with limited-stage disease (stages I and II), and adjuvant surgery for patients who have a complete response to chemotherapy. Results of a prospective trial by the Veterans Administration Surgical Oncology Group (VASOG) showed that resection was indicated in patients with one small tumor, no nodal involvement, and no metastasis and may be indicated in patients with a larger primary tumor or those with one involved node.

Future Investigations

The prevention of lung cancer is a formidable task. This disease is caused primarily by the self-imposed behavior of tobacco use. Since this information was first published widely during the 1960s, the percentage of Americans who smoke has decreased, but the total number of smokers has continued to increase as the population has grown. This is reflected in the continual increase in the number of lung cancer cases diagnosed. Obviously, decreasing or eliminating tobacco use will be of major importance in the control of this disease.

Since we also know from therapy of other chronic diseases, such as hypertension and diabetes, that it is easier to get people to take a pill than to eliminate a habit that is detrimental to their health, future investigations into the use of possible cancer preventive agents, such as vitamin A analogues, will be useful.

Research needs to be done on appropriate mechanisms for early detection of lung cancer. Studies on the use of chest X–ray, and sputum cytologic assay, need to be done with Black participants, and other screening tests, such as the evaluation in high-risk individuals of sputum cells to look for oncogene amplification or chromosomal abnormalities, are needed.

Investigations in the use of chemotherapy must be continued. This is particularly true for SCLC because the high response rates we have seen may indicate that we are only one drug away from developing curative therapy, similar to that for Hodgkin's disease 25 years ago and testicular carcinoma 15 years ago. For NSCLC, we are approaching response rates for patients with metastatic disease similar to those achieved 15 years ago for patients with advanced-stage breast cancer. If additional drugs could be developed that would give an overall response rate of more than 50%, we could begin to evaluate the use of chemotherapy as adjuvant treatment with increased hope for longer survival. Clinical trials have already begun to evaluate this situation.

References

American Cancer Society: *1986 Cancer Facts and Figures*. New York, 1986.

American Cancer Society: *General Facts on Smoking and Health*. New York, 1985.

Buffler PA, Wood S, Eifler C, et al: Mortality experience of workers in a vinyl chloride monomer production plant. *J Occup Med* 1979;21:195–203.

Cutler SJ, Devesa SS: Trend in cancer incidence and mortality in the U.S.A. In Doll R, Vodopija J (eds): *Host Environment Interactions in the Etiology of Cancer in Man*. Lyon, France, 1973. JARC, pp 15–43.

Devesa SS, Silverman DT: Cancer incidence and mortality trends in the United States: 1935–1974. *JNCI* 1978;60:545–571.

Doll R, Peto R: Mortality in relation to smoking: 20 years' observations on male British doctors. *Br Med J* 1976;2:1525–1536.

Fujimaki Y: Formation of gastric carcinoma in albino rats fed on deficient diets. *J Cancer Res* 1926;10:469–477.

Hammond EC: Smoking habits and air pollution in relation to lung cancer. In Lee DHK (ed): *Environmental Factors in Respiratory Disease*. New York: Academic Press, 1972, pp 177–198.

Hammond EC, Selikoff IJ, Seidman H: Asbestos exposure, cigarette smoking and death rates. *Ann NY Acad Sci* 1979;330:473–490.

Hirayama T: Non-smoking wives of heavy smokers have a higher risk of lung cancer: A study from Japan. *Br Med J* 1981;282:183–185.

Horm JW, Kessler LG: Falling rates of lung cancer in men in the United States. *Lancet* 1986;1:425–426.

Kahn HA: The Dorn study of smoking and mortality among U.S. veterans: Report on 8½ years of observation. *NCI Monogr* 1966;19:1–125.

Katlic M, Carter D: Prognostic implications of histology, size and location of primary tumors. *Progress in Cancer Research and Therapy* 1979;11:143–150.

Lloyd IW: Long-term mortality study of steelworkers. V. Respiratory cancer in coke plant workers. *J Occup Med* 1971;13:53–68.

Martin N: Results of the Memorial Sloan-Kettering lung project. *Recent Results Cancer Res* 1982;82:174–178.

Minna JD, Higgins GA, Glatstein EJ: Cancer of the lung. In Devita V Jr, Hellman S, Rosenberg SA (eds): *Cancer: Principles and Practice of Oncology*, Vol. 1. Philadelphia: JB Lippincott, 1985, pp 507–597.

National Cancer Institute: *Cancer Statistics Review: Black, White, and Other Groups Comparisons.* Bethesda, MD, 1985.

National Center for Health Statistics, Division of Health Interview Statistics: *Data from the National Health Interview Survey.* Washington, DC, 1984.

National Institutes of Health: *Cancer Patient Survival.* Report No. 5. Washington, DC: Department of Health, Education, and Welfare. Publication No. (NIH) 77-992, 1977.

O'Berg MT: Epidemiologic study of workers exposed to acrylonitrile. *J Occup Med* 1980;22:245–252.

Rowe NA, Gorlin RJ: The effect of vitamin A deficiency on experimental oral carcinogens. *J Dent Res* 1959;38:72–83.

Saffiotti U, Montesano R, Sellakumar AR, et al: Experimental cancer of the lung: Inhibition by vitamin A of the induction of tracheobronchial squamous metaplasia and squamous cell tumors. *Cancer* 1967;20:857–864.

Saracci R: Asbestos and lung cancer: An analysis of the epidemiological evidence on the asbestos-smoking interaction. *Int J Cancer* 1977;20:323–331.

Sevc J, Kunz E, Placek V: Lung cancer in uranium miners and long-term exposure to radon daughter products. *Health Phys* 1976;30:433–437.

US Department of Health, Education and Welfare: *Smoking and Health: Report of the Advisory Committee to the Surgeon General of the Public Health Service.* Washington, DC: Public Health Service Publication No. 1103, 1964; pp 1–387.

Vincent RG, Pickren IW, Lane WW, et al: The changing histopathology of lung cancer. A review of 1682 cases. *Cancer* 1977;39:1647–1655.

Wada S, Mivanish M, Nishimoto Y, et al: Mustard gas as a cause of respiratory neoplasia in man. *Lancet* 1968;1:1161–1163.

Wagoner JK, Infante PF, Bayliss DL: Beryllium: An etiologic agent in the induction of lung cancer, nonneoplastic respiratory disease, and heart disease among industrially exposed workers. *Environ Res* 1980;21:15–34.

Wald N, Idle M, Boreham J, et al: Low serum-vitamin-A and subsequent risk of cancer: Preliminary results of a prospective study. *Lancet* 1980;2:813–815.

Watson WL, Schottenfeld D: Survival in cancer of the bronchus and lung, 1949–1962: Comparison of men and women patients. *Dis Chest* 1968;53:65–72.

Weiss GB, Daniels JC: A re-evaluation of the association between prolonged survival in lung cancer and HLA antigens AW19 and B5. *Clin Res* 1978;26:687A.

Weiss A, Weiss B: Carcinogenesis due to mustard gas exposure in man: Important sign for therapy with alkylating agents [in German]. *Dtsch Med Wochenschr* 1975;100:919–923.

White JE, Enterline JP: Cancer in nonwhite Americans. *Curr Probl Cancer* 1980;4:3–34.

Wolback SB, Howe PR: Tissue changes following deprivation of fat soluble A vitamin. *J Exp Med* 1985;42:753–777.

Wynder EL, Stellman SD: Comparative epidemiology of tobacco related cancers. *Cancer Res* 1977;37:4608–4622.

20. Childhood Cancer in Minorities

Jan van Eys

Childhood cancer is curable more often than not. This claim can be made with confidence. It is not an extrapolation from limited research experience when the claim is made that if all children were treated similarly, the cure rate would be greater than 50%. Rather, the curability of childhood cancer is now reflected in the vital statistics of the United States (Miller and McKay 1984). This excellent result is also seen in Western European countries, but it is not shared worldwide. The treatment of childhood cancers is arduous, prolonged, and expensive. Only a rich nation can afford pediatric cancer care as it is currently delivered in the United States.

It is reasonable, therefore, to ask whether, even in nations that can deliver such care, all children partake equally of this medical miracle of childhood cancer cure, and if not, why not? One explanation could be inherent differences in cancer rates and in the distribution of diagnoses among population sets grouped on racial and ethnic bases. Further, one could postulate that racial and ethnic groupings are not independent variables from economic groupings. One could postulate that there is etiologic diversity among groups. Precisely because there is such a high cure rate in childhood cancer, one can approach some of these questions.

Cancer in children is often curable. However, certain variables determine the probability of a good outcome: disease burden, patient characteristics, and specific disease etiology. Recently, refinements in nosology have made it clear that apparent differences in outcome often are in reality attributable to differences in subtypes of otherwise similar diseases. However, outcome is also a function of social variables. Even in a given type of host for a specific disease, there are non-disease-related factors that are beyond the control of the patient and family and factors that are the direct consequence of actions by the patient and family.

My hypothesis is that the outcome of pediatric cancer therapy is, in the United States, determined about equally by forces over which the family has no control and by those that are self-determined. To put this in perspective, it is important to dissect the components of cancer care from the beginning to the end (Table 1).

TABLE 1. Childhood malignancies.

	Outside forces	Self-determination
Incidence	+ + + +	+/−
Diagnosis	+ + +	+
Therapy	+ +	+ +
Compliance	+/−	+ + + +
Outcome	9.5	7.5

Major factors are the incidence of the disease, diagnosis, therapy, and compliance with the recommendations. Each of those factors can be modified by actions under personal control and by forces neither child nor family can modify. I shall discuss this issue and contrast the overall outcome of cancer care for children in the United States with the outcome for patients with other diseases.

Incidence

Black children are less likely than White children to have cancer and, specifically, less likely to have certain tumors (Table 2) (Haddy 1982). The data from the Third National Cancer Survey show that for almost all cancers the incidence is

TABLE 2. Incidence of 13 types of malignant tumor in Black and White children in the United States, in order of decreasing frequency, from the Third National Cancer Survey, 1969–1971.

	Rate (per million and per year)	
Diagnosis	Black children	White children
1. Leukemia	24.3	42.1
2. Central nervous system	23.9	23.9
3. Lymphoma	13.9	13.2
4. Sympathetic nervous system including neuroblastoma	7.0	9.6
5. Soft tissue	3.9	8.4
6. Kidney, including Wilms' tumor	7.8	7.8
7. Bone	4.8	5.6
8. Retinoblastoma	3.0	3.4
9. Gonadal and germ cell	2.6	2.2
10. Liver	0.4	1.9
11. Melanoma	0.0	0.7
12. Teratoma	0.4	0.3
13. Miscellaneous	5.7	5.4

Modified from Young JL et al. (1986), with permission.

either the same or lower for Black children than it is for White children. The lower rate of leukemia among Black children translates into a lower overall rate of cancer among Black children because of the dominance of that disease. Certain tumors are very rare in the Black child. Ewing's sarcoma for example, is effectively not seen in Black children (Polednak 1985).

The differences in cancer incidence between Black and White children that are seen in the United States are accentuated in countries where the discrepancies in the environments of children in different racial or ethnic groups are more pronounced. For instance, the differences among ethnic groups in incidence, cell type, and survival for children with acute leukemia in South Africa are quite distinct from the patterns seen in the United States (MacDougall et al. 1986).

The incidence data from the National Cancer Institute's Surveillance, Epidemiology, and End Results (SEER) Program for the 10-year period 1973–1982 show that incidence rates have changed very little since the late 1960s (Young et al. 1986). This stability indicates it is unlikely that life-styles have a major effect on the incidence of childhood cancer in the United States. The differences among geographic population groups do suggest environmental effects on cancer incidence (Kramer et al. 1983). It is assumed that Blacks and other non–Whites have higher exposure to noxious environmental stimuli. In the United States, however, exposure to such environmental factors probably does not constitute a selection toward cancer. In fact, from the lower overall cancer incidence among Blacks, the opposite seems to be true. Cancer in children is often an acute disease. Therefore, parents can do little to modify the incidence.

There are also hints of genetic influences on cancer incidence. For instance, the experience of the Pediatric Oncology Group showed an association of a particular allele whose gene lies within the major histocompatibility complex with acute lymphocytic leukemia in both Black and White children (Budowle et al. 1985).

Diagnosis

It is clear that diagnostic categories as they are now used in the various surveys are grossly inadequate to prognosticate outcome and indicate treatment. This is best illustrated by the description of leukemia nosology.

Initially, no distinction was made between types of leukemia. It soon became apparent, however, that morphologic characteristics showed different outcomes among patients given the same therapy. Separate treatments were developed for what are now known as acute lymphocytic leukemia (ALL) and acute myelogenous leukemia. However, even in ALL, the treatment effectiveness plateaued. Close examination showed that within ALL, many subtypes corresponded to the differentiation of the lymphoid system in normal individuals. The distribution between what are now called early pre-B, pre-B, T, and B cell leukemia is shown in Table 3 (Crist et al. 1986).

TABLE 3. Frequency of the four major phenotypes of childhood acute lymphocytic leukemia.

	Number of patients	%
Early pre-B cell	209	67.2
Pre-B cell	56	18.0
B cell	2	0.6
T cell	44	14.2
Total	311	100.0

Adapted from Crist et al. 1986.

More important, the subtypes of leukemia responded differently to a given
therapy and therefore came to be viewed as prognostically significant. For
instance, pre-B cell leukemia, which cannot be distinguished easily by laboratory
and clinical clues from early pre-B or common leukemia, has a much poorer outcome than does the common variety. There seemed to be some indication that the
relative incidence of the pre-B cell ALL phenotype was higher in Black children
than in non–Black children (Crist et al. 1984). Later data derived from a large
group of patients did not bear this out, although there seemed to be a slight
preponderance of T-cell disease among that group of Black children (unpublished
data, Pediatric Oncology Group). Even when these data were collapsed to compare Black with non–Black patients in terms of best outcome, no dominance of
unfavorable leukemia types was evident.

We do not know what factors influence the relative distribution of the various
subtypes of leukemia. Therefore, it remains uncertain whether this distribution
shows a significant distinction between Black and White children on a popula-
tionwide basis. Given the same treatment for the same disease, however, Black
and White children do not seem to fare differently. The results of the Pediatric
Oncology Group study on acute myelogenous leukemia show clearly, for example, that there is no distinction in outcome between Black and White children,
although Hispanic children fared worse than did the others.

Furthermore, prognostic factors are artifacts of the therapy used. If the therapy
is tailored to the specific subset of leukemia, variations disappear. Other prognostic factors may be more important than subsets of leukemia. For instance,
data from prospective studies showed clearly that the degree to which the chromosomes are disordered has a great bearing on outcome. This overshadows any
prognostic indication that subtypes of leukemia are believed to signify. The
abnormalities in the chromosomes do not differ among ethnic groups (unpublished data, Pediatric Oncology Group).

It is therefore primarily important that diagnosis be made promptly and that
the diagnostic approach used measure up to modern standards. Different institutions have different capabilities. To the extent that patient and family control the
selection of the initial diagnostic center, there is an element of self-determination
in the diagnosis. However, it is important to consider to what degree the diag-

nosis of cancer must be taken on trust. Especially in leukemia, there are very few signs that will make the patient capable of self-diagnosis. This is in vast contrast with self-detection of a breast lump in breast cancer, an enlarged testicle in testicular cancer, or intestinal obstruction in colorectal cancer.

Therapy

Therapy for childhood cancer is done almost exclusively under the aegis of one of two national cooperative groups, the Children's Cancer Study Group and the Pediatric Oncology Group. Smaller institutions have affiliated with larger ones, so that up-to-date therapy has reached far into the community. Furthermore, most diagnostic centers and individual pediatricians are quick to refer children with cancer, when it is diagnosed, to larger treatment centers. Modern therapy is available to every child in the United States if the patient and family are willing to participate. Much of this therapy is linked to prospective and randomized or other types of therapeutic trials. Almost every child with cancer is touched by experimental therapy. However, there is no evidence of racial bias in this participation. Furthermore, there is ample evidence that the participation in research trials is, on the whole, beneficial to the child (Hammond et al. 1980).

Nevertheless, the treatment must be accepted by the child and family. At this point, the family begins to exercise more control. The treatment is arduous and long. A standard ALL protocol lasts for three years, and multiple drugs are administered on a complex schedule. Adherence to the schedule is believed to be important to the outcome of treatment.

It is not true, however, that all centers are alike even when they use the same treatment. A recent experience of the Pediatric Oncology Group brought this home strongly. In a test of a specific chemotherapy regimen, a number of centers began to administer the antibiotic trimethoprim-sulfamethoxazole (TMP-SMX) to their patients to avoid infectious complications. When the data were analyzed, it seemed that the administration of TMP-SMX was a beneficial influence on the outcome of leukemia. When this association was tested in a prospective randomized trial, however, no such beneficial effect was seen. What was observed in the nonrandomized trial was a comparison between institutions rather than the effect of a drug. Once the variation among institutions was removed by use of randomization, the drug showed no further effect (van Eys 1987).

This issue is difficult for health consumers to grasp. Many institutions are proud of their affiliation with the cooperative groups. A great deal of pressure is put on parents by saying, "We can do everything the big center can." But, in general, the outcome of any procedure is better when the person who supervises the procedure is more experienced. Chemotherapy for childhood leukemia or solid tumors is no different.

TABLE 4. Mean annual cost by year since diagnosis by diagnostic and prognostic groups.

Diagnostic group	Cost per year ($)				
	1	2	3	4	5+
Acute lymphocytic leukemia	29,572	25,865	20,194	20,443	25,980
Other acute leukemias	62,577	22,348	16,678	–	17,443
Chronic myelogenous leukemia	33,432	21,367	6,614	–	–
Non-Hodgkin's lymphoma	48,937	41,470	11,130	5,845	2,403
Hodgkin's lymphoma	42,902	28,665	35,471	22,537	7,869
Bone	63,498	40,366	30,724	1,433	7,167
Soft tissue sarcoma	37,366	31,845	2,395	4,826	26,784
Brain	29,455	25,032	12,446	4,623	13,435
Wilms' tumor	23,644	53,719	4,383	6,462	12,705
Neuroblastoma	26,422	11,285	17,497	35,164	19,939
Germ cell	23,103	55,671	17,634	–	3,436
Retinoblastoma	32,239	8,620	17,271	–	3,029
All other	22,255	12,261	11,064	–	11,866

Adapted from Bloom et al. (1985) in JAMA 253(16):2393–2397; Copyright 1985, American Medical Association.

Compliance

The most difficult aspect of treatment outcome is the degree to which patients comply with recommendations. Multiple studies show that compliance is poor, even with simple prescriptions, such as a 10-day antibiotic course for a streptococcal pharyngitis. It is, therefore, not surprising that the compliance rate with complex therapies, such as those indicated for leukemia, varies widely.

Some of the factors responsible for poor compliance are inherent in human nature. In general, when the drug is to be administered intravenously at the treatment center, compliance is better than it is when oral administration is required. However, intravenous administration means a trip to a center. It is not often realized how expensive childhood cancer treatment is.

Bloom et al. (1985) gave us the epidemiology of disease expense for children with cancer. Table 4 shows an illustrative example of the cost of disease by year beginning with diagnosis. The patients who did poorly had the highest expense. Although the total out-of-pocket cost was lower for families with low incomes, this was entirely the result of lower amounts of wages lost (Table 5). The out-of-pocket costs other than lost wages did not vary greatly from family to family regardless of income.

Economic pressures do bear on compliance. McWhirter et al. (1983) showed that, in Australia, social class is a prognostic variable for patients with ALL. However, in the United States there is a great deal of secondary gain for the institutions to continue contact with the patients under their care. As a result, enormous pressure is placed on families to continue compliance. Furthermore, children are considered the concern of society at large. Denial of potential curative therapy for children with cancer is considered a form of child neglect in many

TABLE 5. Distribution of annual family income and annual out-of-pocket costs by quartile.

Quartile	Annual family income ($)	Total out-of-pocket costs	Wages lost ($)	All other out-of-pocket costs ($)
1	≤ 15,000	4,853	1,283	3,570
2	15,001–20,000	10,240	4,663	5,577
3	20,001–30,000	8,967	4,229	4,738
4	> 30,000	16,054	9,540	6,514
P value		0.004	0.01	0.3

Adapted from Bloom et al. (1985) in JAMA 253(16):2393–2397; Copyright 1985, American Medical Association.

instances. For this reason, societal pressure for patient compliance is higher for ill children than for ill adults. Finally, cancer is a disease whose treatment frequently is reimbursable under the Crippled Children's Service program. Therefore, hospital care often is available for children of low-income families in the United States.

The quality of care for childhood cancer is proportional to the experience of health care personnel and not proportional to hospital resources. Therefore, access barriers to childhood cancer therapy are not nearly as great as they are for adults with cancer. It is at diagnosis that the problem of access can be great, not during treatment.

Outcome

Childhood mortality is higher among Blacks than it is among Whites. Table 6 shows overall mortality figures for the United States population, as derived from the annual summary of vital statistics for 1985 (Wegman 1986). This must be contrasted, however, with the outcome as deduced by the SEER program for children with cancer. There is no significant effect on the relative survival at five years of Black and White children (Table 7) (Young et al. 1986).

The overall statistics are dampened by the lower incidence of cancer in Blacks and the rarity of some of the diseases. However, if one were to take a specific example of patients treated in modern fashion at a given hospital for a specific diagnosis, the same data emerge. For instance, the generally presumed poorer prognosis of cancer in Black children does not apply to osteogenic sarcoma patients (Huvos et al. 1983).

This similarity in outcomes for Black and non–Black children with cancer contrasts with experiences elsewhere. The treatment of acute leukemia in Johannesburg, South Africa, shows a marked distinction in outcome between Black children and White children (MacDougall et al. 1986). The difference was largely attributed to different prognostic factors. Yet many of the differences in prognostic factors refer to extent of disease rather than to the specific type of

TABLE 6. Death rates, crude and age-adjusted, with gender and race ratios for leading causes of death in the United States, 1985 and 1984.[a]

| | 1985[b] | | | 1984 | | |
	% of All deaths	Crude death rate	Age-adjusted death rate	Age-adjusted death rate	Ratio M/F	Ratio B/W
All causes	100.0	874.8	545.9	545.9	1.75	1.4
Major cardiovascular diseases	47.4	410.7	225.0	228.4	1.80	1.3
Malignant neoplasms	22.1	191.7	132.5	133.5	1.48	1.3
Respiratory diseases	.0	0.2	31.8	30.0	2.13	1.0
Accidents	4.5	38.6	34.3	35.0	2.80	1.1
Diabetes mellitus	1.9	16.2	10.1	9.5	1.07	2.2
Perinatal conditions and congenital anomalies	1.5	13.1	[c]	[c]	[c]	[c]
Suicide	1.4	12.0	11.2	11.6	3.60	0.5
Chronic liver disease and cirrhosis	1.3	11.2	9.6	10.0	2.20	1.7
Homicide and legal intervention	0.9	8.1	8.1	8.4	3.33	5.3

Source: Adapted from Wegman 1986, with permission of *Pediatrics*, Vol. 78, p. 983, Copyright 1985.
[a] Data from National Center for Health Statistics. Percentages shown total 81% of all causes. Rates are per 100,000 population.
[b] Provisional data.
[c] Because almost all deaths occur in infancy, no age-adjusted rates are shown for these causes.

TABLE 7. Survival rates for all forms of cancer in children younger than 15 years by race and gender, 1973–1981.[a]

Race and sex	No. of cases	Relative survival (%) 1 Year	3 Years	5 Years
All races				
Both sexes	5296	80	63	57
Males	2853	79	61	54
Females	2443	81	66	60
Whites				
Both sexes	4539	80	64	57
Males	2464	79	61	54
Females	2075	82	66	61
Blacks				
Both sexes	519	78	62	57
Males	259	78	60	56
Females	260	79	64	58

Adapted from Young et al 1986, with permission.
[a] Data from Surveillance, Epidemiology, and End Results (SEER) program.

disease. Cancer diagnosed early is easier to manage than is late-diagnosed cancer. These data suggest again that the outcome differential for children in a given locality is more likely to stem from problems at the diagnostic than at the treatment level.

Children fear cancer greatly. Michielutte and Diseker (1982) reviewed the perceptions of a sample of seventh-grade students of cancer in comparison with their perceptions of heart disease, diabetes, and mental illness. The results indicated that children generally view cancer as more severe than the other diseases (except for heart disease) and see themselves as more susceptible to and less likely to be cured of cancer than of other illnesses. These perceptions did not differ by sex, socioeconomic background, or knowledge of cancer. However, it was extremely interesting that Black children believed that they were personally more susceptible than White children. Actually, the contrary is true.

Future Problems

The data do not bear out that minority children with cancer fare poorer in cancer care than do nonminority children when results are adjusted for type of disease and treatment. Furthermore, Black children in general have a lower incidence of cancer than do White children. It has been suggested that improvements could be made largely through the actions of the family and the child rather than that the system must markedly improve. However, there are many threats to the current situation that now seem reasonably good.

First of all, cancer is a catastrophic illness. For children, catastrophic illness is often covered by third-party payment if it happens after the immediate neonatal period. This may not be true much longer, as budgets of Crippled Children's Service programs are being curtailed. Second, a great deal of benefit has been derived from the use of therapeutic research as a mode of treatment for children with cancer. Investigators reaped great secondary gain from pursuing the therapy for each child. Consumers of health care received a moderate but real secondary gain in that part of the treatment was either free or supported, and society pressured the social service agencies to assist families to continue compliance with treatment. The current curtailment of research budgets at the National Cancer Institute threatens this safeguard for children with cancer.

Finally, children have been the primary beneficiaries of entitlement programs. Children have been a privileged subclass in society, and to a large degree being a child has dominated being White or Black. The entitlement structure is extraordinarily complex, however, and therefore susceptible to reform. The privileged status of children in society is quite new, and it is not impossible that a significant retrenchment in the privileged status of children will occur.

Nevertheless, the greatest obstacle now is at the level of diagnosis. Utilization of proper diagnostic centers, therefore, is the primary determinant of overall outcome.

References

Bloom BS, Knorr RS, Evans AE: The epidemiology of disease expenses. The costs of caring for children with cancer. *JAMA* 1985;253:2393-2397.

Budowle B, Dearth J, Bowman P, et al: Genetic predisposition to acute lymphocytic leukemia in American blacks. A Pediatric Oncology Group study. *Cancer* 1985;55:2880-2882.

Crist W, Boyett J, Pullen J, et al: Clinical and biologic features predict poor prognosis in acute lymphoid leukemias in children and adolescents: A Pediatric Oncology Group review. *Med Pediatr Oncol* 1986;4:135-139.

Crist W, Boyett J, Roper M, et al: Pre-B cell leukemia responds poorly to treatment: A Pediatric Oncology Group study. *Blood* 1984;63:407-414.

Haddy TB: Cancer in black children. *Am J Pediatr Hematol Oncol* 1982:4:285-292.

Hammond D, Chard R, D'Angio GJ, et al: Pediatric malignancies. In Hoogstraten B (ed): *Cancer Research: Impact of the Cooperative Groups.* New York: Masson Publishing, 1980, pp 1-23.

Huvos AG, Butler A, Bretsky SS: Osteogenic sarcoma in the American black. *Cancer* 1983;52:1959-1965.

Kramer S, Meadows AT, Jarrett P, et al: Incidence of childhood cancer: Experience of a decade in a population-based registry. *JNCI* 1983;70:49-55.

MacDougall LG, Jankowitz P, Cohn R, et al: Acute childhood leukemia in Johannesburg. Ethnic differences in incidence, cell type, and survival. *Am J Pediatr Hematol Oncol* 1986;8:43-51.

McWhirter WR, Smith H, McWhirter KM: Social class as a prognostic variable in acute lymphoblastic leukaemia. *Med J Aust* 1983;2:319-321.

Michielutte R, Diseker A: Children's perceptions of cancer in comparison to other chronic illnesses. *J Chronic Dis* 1982;35:843-852.

Miller RW, McKay FW: Decline in US childhood cancer mortality, 1950 through 1980. *JAMA* 1984;251:1567-1570.

Polednak AP: Primary bone cancer incidence in black and white residents of New York State. *Cancer* 1985;55:2883-2888.

van Eys J, Berry D, Crist W, et al: Effect of trimethoprim-sulfamethoxazole (TS) prophylaxis on outcome of childhood lymphocytic leukemia. *Cancer* 1987;59:19-23.

Wegman ME: Annual summary of vital statistics — 1985. *Pediatrics* 1986;78:983-994.

Young JL Jr, Ries LG, Silverberg E, et al: Cancer incidence, survival, and mortality for children younger than age 15 years. *Cancer* 1986;58:598-602.

Section 5

Treatment

Introduction to Section 5

Eddie Reed

It has long been recognized that some malignancies appear to be more aggressive in some minority populations than in Caucasian groups. Such tumors include breast cancer, prostate cancer, and invasive cancer of the uterine cervix (National Cancer Institute 1986). In addition, when one compares relative five-year survival figures of Blacks and Whites for the 18 most common tumors in the United States, Blacks have a poorer survival with 13 of those tumors (American Cancer Society 1986). A question of concern to all those who are involved in the care of cancer patients is, Can this difference in survival between ethnic groups be explained by differences in the biology of the diseases based on the genetic milieu of the hosts, or is this difference in survival simply a reflection of the relative ability to deliver optimal health care to different ethnic populations? In this context, four minority clinical research scientists individually discussed the delivery of the four major cancer treatment modalities and discussed the impact of AIDS on minority communities.

Dr. Neil J. Clendeninn discussed the delivery of chemotherapy. Although local modalities of treatment (surgery and radiation therapy) are ideal approaches for localized tumors, a very large number of individuals diagnosed with cancer have widespread disease at the time of diagnosis. For that reason, treatment with systemic chemotherapy has become an important tool in cancer treatment. Dr. Clendeninn feels that there are 13 cancers that are curable with chemotherapy and that there are many others that may benefit from this treatment approach. Herein he discusses the developmental process for new anticancer agents, including drug discovery, drug screening, animal testing, and clinical testing. Although there may be some ethnic differences in response rates to treatment, Dr. Clendeninn feels that if minority patients and Caucasian patients with the same stage of disease were compared, both groups would probably respond comparably well. He feels that this question could be definitely answered by entering more minority patients onto randomized, controlled clinical trials.

Dr. Jerrold Saxton discussed the delivery of radiation therapy to minority populations. Dr. Saxton reported that the majority of the problems seen by the radiotherapist involve cancers of the lung, colon, breast, prostate, and gynecologic organs. Upon reviewing data on cancer incidence in White versus minority populations, and with focus on the stage of the disease at the time of diagnosis, Dr. Saxton concludes that "the issue is not simply one of genetics but more of socioeconomic status," noting that the incidences of lung cancer and prostate cancer are greater in Black populations than in White populations. Implicit in such a view is the assumption that socioeconomic status results in environmental exposures that may lead to an increased incidence of certain types of cancer. According to Dr. Saxton, this difference in cancer incidence may account for most of the differences in five-year survival seen between Blacks and Whites in these two diseases. Another example of this is colorectal cancer, for which cure rates are high when the disease is detected in its early stages. In his experience, early detection on internal malignancies is less likely to occur in the lower socioeconomic strata of our society. He indicates that all patients, regardless of race, are treated by methods that are based on the disease type and the extent of disease present at the time of treatment and that meaningful increases in the cure rates of cancer can be best achieved when cancer is detected early. In respect to minority populations, he feels strongly that the actual management of patients who have malignant disease will not improve "until this country can provide every citizen with equal access to jobs, housing, and medical care."

Dr. Robert DeWitty discussed the roles of surgery in the management of malignant disease. These roles may be diagnostic as well as therapeutic. He emphasized that the treatment approach must always be multimodal, with consideration of the possible utility of radiation therapy, chemotherapy, and immunotherapy in every case. Each individual must be assessed for the possibility of cure—the removal of every cancer cell from the body. Also to be considered are issues related to pain management and, in the case of breast cancer, possible breast reconstruction. In many cases, the ability to treat the patient in an optimal fashion may depend upon a third-party carrier, who may sometimes disagree with physicians as to what diagnostic studies are needed for patient management and as to what care is optimal for a given patient.

Surgery is the oldest member of the anticancer armamentarium, and only relatively recently was it realized that more often than not, surgery does not remove all cancer cells from the body. Consequently, surgery is often combined with other modalities in the treatment of diseases such as cancers of the breast, colon, and head and neck. In treating these diseases, surgery has a diagnostic role, can be curative in early-stage disease, but can be disfiguring. In those cases where disfigurement may be considerable, support groups become important parts of the therapy team.

Dr. DeWitty discussed several patients from his own practice experience whom he felt represented a somewhat common situation in the Black community. In two separate cases, a Black woman presented with far-advanced breast cancer. One case was notable for an extremely large breast mass; the other was notable for disease that eroded the chest wall. These lesions were painless, and in both cases, the patient had been aware of her breast lesion for months. But these individuals sought medical care only after these lesions interfered with their private interpersonal relationships. In situations such as these, surgery may or may not be used in combination with other modalities depending upon whether the goal is cure, palliation, or simple tumor debulking.

Dr. Adan Rios (whose paper was not submitted for this book) discussed AIDS as it affects Black and Hispanic communities in the United States, based on data collected by the Centers of Disease Control (CDC) in Atlanta. Since cancer develops in approximately 40% of persons with AIDS, this topic was felt to be quite appropriate for this symposium. AIDS in Black and Hispanic communities tends to be associated more with intravenous (IV) drug use and heterosexual transmission than in White communities, where homosexuality appears to be the main association. When comparing the incidence of AIDS in different ethnic groups, it becomes apparent that the epidemic has affected Black and Hispanic groups disproportionately, although in absolute numbers Whites comprise most known cases of the disease. In American men, the incidence of AIDS in Hispanics is 560 cases per one million population; in Blacks, 593 per one million; and in Whites, 224 per one million population. In Hispanic women, the incidence is 58 cases of AIDS per one million population; in Black women the incidence is 79 per one million; and in White women the incidence is 6 per one million. Most experts agree that these differences in the incidence of AIDS in different ethnic groups in the United States can be attributed for the most part to IV drug use, usually in inner cities.

Dr. Rios pointed out that at this time, therapeutic options against AIDS are limited. Drugs that appear to be effective are expensive and are not widely available, and the development of an effective vaccine may be years away. Therefore, prevention is the only realistic option available to most Americans. Prevention at this time means curbing IV drug abuse, prostitution, and sexual promiscuity. Only in these ways can we begin to blunt the growth of the most serious contagious disease epidemic of our time.

The discussion that followed the four presentations outlined above was spirited. A consensus developed on several points. First, it appears that differences in cancer survival rates between Black and White Americans are probably related to socioeconomic factors. Socioeconomic differences between ethnic groups appear to result in minority patients seeking care at later stages of their disease and in a relative inability to afford state-of-the-art medical care. However, it should be emphasized that this has not been scientifically proven. Second, AIDS is a major public health problem with particularly frightening implications for minority communities. A third point is that improvements in cancer survival in minority populations may be intimately linked to other social aspects of our society, including ethnic trends in employment, housing, and education.

References

American Cancer Society: *1986 Cancer Facts & Figures*. New York, 1986.

Baquet C, Ringen K, Pollack ES, et al: *Cancer Among Blacks and Other Minorities: A Statistical Profile*. Washington, DC: National Institutes of Health, 1986.

21. Chemotherapy for Minorities and the Drug Development Process

Neil J. Clendeninn

Black and other minority cancer patients may respond differently to chemotherapy than do Whites. However, few studies have addressed this issue at all, and the results of those studies that have considered it have been flawed by a small sample size of minority cancer patients. Increasing the participation of minorities in clinical trials could produce statistically sound numbers that would allow researchers to determine whether Whites and minorities respond differently to the same chemotherapeutic agents and combinations. One explanation that could be examined is whether cancers in people in lower socioeconomic groups generally are diagnosed at a later stage than are those in people with better access to medical care. In addition, if perceived differences are not related to socioeconomic status, researchers can begin to explore whether genetic or environmental factors promote the differences in response. Findings from these studies could change the way minorities are treated for cancer and might improve their prognosis as well.

Nevertheless, treatment for cancer in Whites and minorities will involve chemotherapeutic drugs. In understanding cancer and its treatment, it is important to consider how new chemotherapy drugs are developed and what improvements can be made in that process. The four major methods of new drug discovery are targeted synthesis, random synthesis, testing of natural products, and computer modeling. In targeted synthesis, we attempt to make active drugs more active. We examine a certain molecule or the portion of the molecule that seems to convey the most specific activity in destroying tumor cells and try to develop new drugs by modifying the chemical groups on the molecule. Random synthesis, in contrast, involves creating and developing a molecule and then testing it in a model system, such as cells in tissue culture, to determine whether it kills some of them.

New chemotherapeutic agents can also be discovered through the isolation of natural products, that is, compounds from certain plants used in traditional medicines claimed to have cured people of cancer. We try to distill from those natural products the component that seems to be active.

The fourth method is computer modeling. Using computer models of DNA or enzyme structures we can design compounds to fit into these structures and ultimately prevent cell growth. In designing these compounds, we search for cellular structures that are more common to cancer cells than to normal cells.

Once we have selected a drug, we must determine whether it is active. The systems that we have available for this are in vitro and in vivo models. With in vitro antiproliferative tests of cells in tissue culture, we attempt to determine whether tumor cells are killed when the drug is present. These cells may be animal tumor cells or human tumor cells that are derived from patients. Human or animal cells placed into mice form the basis of our in vivo system. Normally, human cells placed in mice or cells from one species that are placed into an animal of another species will be killed because the host immune system perceives them as foreign. If one immunocompromises mice, that is, diminishes their immune function, one can then put human tumor cells into these mice to test a drug's effect on these human tumor cells. On the other hand, we can inject cells from mouse or rodent tumors into normal mice or rodents, respectively, and use the resulting tumors as models to screen for drugs.

Using animal models, the National Cancer Institute (NCI), which probably is the major screening house for anticancer agents, tests more than 15,000 compounds a year; from these, a few are deemed suitable to be tested in man. However, we suspect that the common screening systems used today are able to detect only a small portion of all possibly active compounds. When we add a new screen, sometimes we may include the present area, and often we can discover a few more active drugs. If we add a different type of screen, we may be able to pick up different drugs that are active. However, we may still miss a segment of compounds because our tests are neither broad enough nor foolproof. Researchers are exploring ways of improving drug screening methods to find more active compounds. Because we cannot take compounds that are found by targeted synthesis or from natural products and simply give them to man, we need to find a way of differentiating or screening drugs that is both effective and minimally toxic.

The traditional drug screening process that the NCI has used, which has recently changed, was a series of stages. Stage I involves a murine tumor, the P388 screening model, and tries to identify dose-response delineation in animals. This is the first screen, to determine whether the drug is active. In the second stage, the drug is tested against a panel of cell lines. Results with these cells may also give researchers an indication of the types of tumors that may be sensitive to the drug. We also want to determine whether the drug will actually reach the tumor. This is accomplished, for example, by placing the tumor in the footpad of mice, giving the drug intravenously or intraperitoneally, and determining whether it gets into the footpad to kill the tumors cells. Preliminary identification of major pharmacologic actions are also observed at this stage.

An important next step is to try to optimize the dose and schedule, that is, to determine whether we should give the drug once a day, twice a day, every hour, or continuously. We then look at a broader panel of tumor lines that represent such diseases as lung and colon cancer, at human cells in the stem cell assay, and at mouse models again. We test cells that we know are resistant to certain existing agents. We also look at different types and methods of dosing the drug and begin our pharmacological screen. This is generally the type of analysis we go through in trying to find an active drug.

There are pitfalls. For example, in the mouse model, the standard tumors that are placed into mice involve short-term experiments, 30 days or 60 days at the most for an experiment that allows you to test the drug and either decide to do something further with it or not. The tumor is a mouse tumor, and it is growing in a mouse, its normal host, but not in quite its normal setting. But the mouse tumor, as mice are not men, is not a precise model for human tumors. Not only are their tumors different from human tumors but mice also metabolize drugs differently than man. In addition, the cells in this model are fast-growing, rather than the more typical, slow-growing tumors seen in medical practice. If we use human tumors in the immunocompromised mice, although the target is human, the organism that we are testing it in is a mouse, and again, the tumor, because its is in a different organism that is immunocompromised and not quite normal, could behave differently than it would in man. So again, it is not a perfect system.

Another tumor model system is naturally occurring animal tumors. These tumors spontaneously develop in animals such as dogs, mice, or rats. The problem is that they are spontaneous tumors, and we cannot guarantee that all our test animals will develop tumors. This requires experiments with large populations of animals in hopes that the tumor, which you believe has a fairly high rate of occurrence, will spontaneously occur in nearly equal numbers in both your control and your treatment groups.

With all our testing methods, the total number of drugs has been increasing but not dramatically so. Each year, we are producing new drugs, but the drug development process has not been rapid.

Once we have completed our screenings and have decided that we have selected, based on the degree of activity in our diverse model systems, an active drug, what happens next? We now want to test these drugs in man. One of the first problems is whether the compound is easy to synthesize in large quantities. This can be a difficult and/or expensive problem. Some compounds that look active are virtually impossible to make in large quantities, especially some natural products. The next problem is to find a convenient formulation in which to administer the drug. A number of anticancer compounds are large, with bulky structural groups, and are insoluble in almost everything but very toxic material. You cannot give a drug that cannot be solubilized and expect it to get into biological spaces.

We must also perform toxicology testing. We need to look at the effect of giving the drug to an animal. Some of the compounds that tested as active in vitro could, for example, produce instant seizures when given to a dog. Certainly, one would not want that to happen in man. (Sometimes, however, these observed effects are peculiar to the animal being tested.) Drugs need to be tested in animals to see what their toxic effects might be. Finding out how they work in animals allows researchers to predict likely side effects. Is the drug going to cause seizures? Is the drug going to cause cardiac effects? Is it going to affect the muscles? This is information that will be needed to determine what end points may be observed in man. At this stage, we also examine the tissue distribution, plasma levels, and metabolism of the drug in vivo.

After all of these tests have been completed, the drug is ready for human trials. Clinical trials in cancer are done sequentially as phase I, phase II, phase III, and phase IV trials. In phase I trials, one tries to identify the maximum tolerated dose and the qualitative toxicity profile. These studies are usually done with patients who have no other treatment options. This trial starts at a prescribed dose equivalent to that found safe for a majority of a species in toxicology tests. Pharmacokinetics and dosing schedules are examined. For example, you may try continuous infusion, an everyday dosing for five days, or a weekly schedule to see which schedule offers an advantage, at least in reducing toxicity. In the phase II trial, we attempt to identify various tumors, such as lung cancer, colon cancer, or melanoma, that we suspect the drug may be active against. A trial on each is done using the maximum tolerated dose and the schedule from our phase I trial. The phase II trial is usually done with patients who have failed all known effective therapies, if there are known effective therapies for that particular type of cancer. These trials are initially done in about 14 patients in an attempt to determine the statistical response rate to expect when the agent is given to many patients.

Next is phase III. Once we have established that the drug does have some activity, based on results with those 14 patients and additional patients in phase II, we begin to test the drug in a large number of patients with the particular type of cancer that responded to the drug in phase II. We test the drug either as a single agent or in combinations to compare whether it is better than the therapies we have. At this point, if the drug does prove to be efficacious, it may be granted a license by the FDA. Once licensed, although the drug is available on the market, we try to further integrate it into our total cancer treatment of patients by doing additional, phase IV clinical trials.

At present, about 13 cancers are curable with chemotherapy: ovarian, testiculae, and small-cell lung cancer; diffuse histiocytic, nodular mixed, and Burkitt's lymphomas; Hodgkin's disease; acute lymphocytic and acute myelogenous leukemias; choriocarcinoma, Wilms' tumor, embryonal Rhabdomyosarcoma, and Ewing's sarcoma. Although the 5-year survivals may not be extremely high, most people would probably say that most of these cancers are curable. A lot of these tumors are pediatric, but there are occasional adult tumors. These cancers account for about 10% of all cancers per year and 10% of all cancer deaths per year. We also have a group of cancers that are probably responsive to chemotherapy but probably are not cured. We do see definite regressions in tumors—and occasional patients probably are cured—but certainly we would consider chemotherapy to be only a portion of the treatment in these patients. A lot of major cancers fit into this category: breast cancer, small cell lung cancer, gastric cancers, prostatic cancer, soft tissue sarcoma, multiple myeloma, and head and neck cancer. Chemotherapy does work for these patients, but it is not curative.

Cancers in this group account for about 40% of all new cancers per year and about 30% of all cancer deaths. Cancers for which we show no demonstrated improvement in survival include some of our major cancers: lung cancer, colorectal cancer, bladder cancer, carcinoma of the cervix, kidney cancer, and melanoma. These cancers, which account for about 35% of all cancers and 30% of all cancer-related deaths do not respond well to chemotherapy. For example, in colon cancer, our standard therapy is 5-fluorouracil. In various studies, the response rate to this drug varies from 5% to 30% and probably averages only about 10%.

An example of a tumor that is responsive to chemotherapy and in the short-term probably curable is small cell lung cancer, which is not the most common type of lung cancer. Adenocarcinoma, large cell, and squamous cell lung cancer are much more common than small cell. Small cell lung cancer has generated a lot of interest in chemotherapy trials because it is so responsive. We have found agents that seem to have definite activity against this disease, even as single agents. Drugs that produce at least a 20% response rate as single agents are usually combined with other agents to improve response rates. In some studies that have looked at combination chemotherapy, complete response rates tended to be better than with single drugs. Generally, patients respond better when more drugs are used. If, we also combine modalities of treatment, such as radiation therapy and chemotherapy, that trend continues. The more drugs that are used along with the radiation, the better. Therefore, we now use multiple agents and what has been called non-cross-resistant drug combinations. This concept involves the initial use of a number of chemotherapeutic agents that work differently, followed by a secondary group of agents, also with different mechanisms of action. This is to prevent resistant cancer cells from developing.

Chemotherapy results in another major problem, drug resistance. A large number of tumors start out to be responsive to a chemotherapeutic agent but eventually no longer respond, resulting in regrowth of tumors. For some curable tumors, response or remission rates are very high and 5-year disease-free survival tends to be maintained. For diseases that respond to chemotherapy, an initial high response rate often is followed by the rapid development of drug resistance. There are a large number of reasons and causes of drug resistance. More research to increase our understanding of the resistance mechanism in tumor cells is needed.

I hope this paper has given you some idea of how chemotherapy agents are developed and tested. There is still a great need to scientifically study these agents. It is important that minority patients participate in clinical trials that offer the latest therapy for the treatment of cancer. Increasing minority participation in clinical trials could, in addition to improving therapy for minorities, further our overall understanding and treatment of cancer.

22. Use of Radiation Therapy in Treatment of Malignant Tumors

Jerrold P. Saxton

In 1986, the American Cancer Society estimated that 930,000 people would be diagnosed as having cancer, among whom 10% would be Black. For the 93,000 projected new cases, the approximate anatomic distribution of cancer would be as listed in Table 1.

Survival rates by cancer site and race are shown in Figure 1, and Figure 2 shows a comparison of incidence and mortality among Black men and women.

In the case of cancers of the lung, pancreas, and ovaries, in which the incidence percentage is exceeded by the percentage of deaths, the cancer curability rate is obviously limited. An evaluation of the mortality rate among the Black population shows an increase in deaths from lung, prostate, and, to a lesser degree, breast and colorectal carcinoma (American Cancer Society 1986).

A comparison of five-year survival rates of Blacks and Whites is distressing. When one looks at the percentage of patients surviving local compared with metastatic disease in each group, the White population has an approximate 10% advantage. The difference may be explained in part by the fact that there are different stages of localized disease with a range of survival rates. Survival rates have been increasing for cancer at most disease sites as treatment has improved, but again with an advantage for White patients (American Cancer Society 1986).

The estimate is that 145 Black persons die each day as a result of cancer, averaging one every 10 minutes. Overall, cancer incidence rates for Blacks increased by 27% compared with 12% among Whites (American Cancer Society 1986).

Although the development of cancer is closely associated with socioeconomic status, as is the availability of medical treatment, the fact that Blacks of different cultures do not show the same predilection for developing cancer as American Blacks do demonstrates that the issue is not simply one of genetics but more of socioeconomic status.

Radiation Therapy

Many advances have been made in the treatment of malignant lesions, with more effective chemotherapeutic agents, immunologic agents, and more intricate

TABLE 1. Projected anatomic distribution of cancer in Black patients.

Site	Number of patients
Digestive organs	23,000
Colorectal	12,000
Respiratory	18,425
Lung	16,600
Genital	19,000
Prostate	12,250
Uterus	6,750
Breast	11,000

Source: Cancer Facts & Figures for Minority Americans 1986, American Cancer Society.

surgical procedures, while radiation therapy has remained an essential as well as improving part of multimodality treatment.

Radiation therapy is essentially the use of ionizing radiation to treat malignant lesions. The basic principles of radiation therapy are coordination of treatment, careful treatment planning with attention to minute detail, optimal equipment, and trained personnel. There have been major advancements in the equipment available to the radiation therapist, both in delivery of radiation therapy and in treatment planning with the help of sophisticated computer planning techniques, even in three-dimensional form. Units have advanced from orthovoltage through cobalt-60 therapy units to high-energy linear accelerators that use electricity rather than radioactive materials to produce radiation.

Advances in modern equipment have increased the need to broaden the radiation therapy team to include the medical physicist, dosimetrist, nutritionist, radiation oncological nurses, and specifically, well-trained radiation therapy technicians. High linear energy transfer equipment employing neutrons, protons, alpha particles, and pi-mesons is commonly used. The radiation therapy team members are responsible for selecting, planning, and combining the various sources available to develop the best treatment program for each patient: to deliver the most effective tumoricidal dose with the least side effects and the least acute and chronic complications.

Radiation therapy has proved effective in nearly every aspect of cancer treatment, and especially for cancer types that have high incidence rates in economically disadvantaged patients (Fletcher 1980; Perez and Brady 1987). For patients with prostate and colorectal tumors, a combination of good technique, of pinpoint localization, and good equipment, has rendered radiation a valuable tool in cancer management, both in definitive and adjuvant form. Radiation is used as either pre- or postoperative treatment as well as in a sandwich technique combining both (Fletcher 1980; Perez and Brady 1987). Exposures of bowel and bladder to radiation are minimized by precise treatment planning, special bowel localization technique, and accurate dose delivery. The precise localization is demonstrated in Figures 3 and 4.

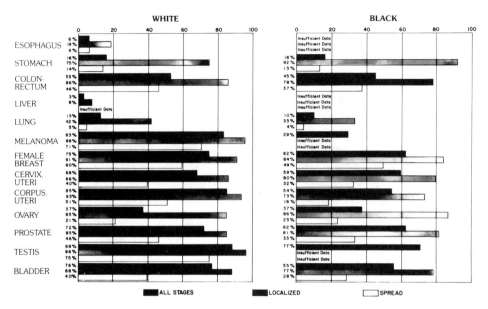

FIGURE 1. Five-year cancer survival rates (adjusted for normal life expectancy) for selected sites by race. Chart is based on cases diagnosed from 1977 to 1982. Source: American Cancer Society 1986.

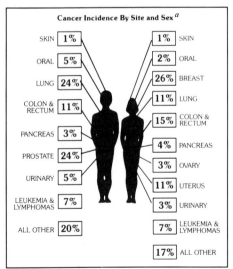
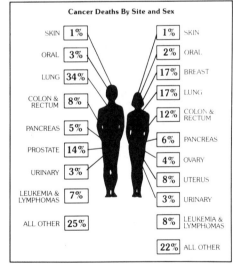

FIGURE 2. Cancer incidence and mortality among black women and men, 1986.
[a] Excludes nonmelanoma skin cancer and carcinoma in situ.

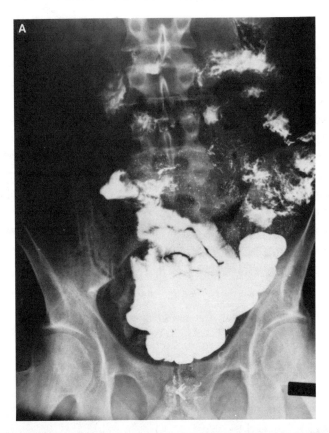

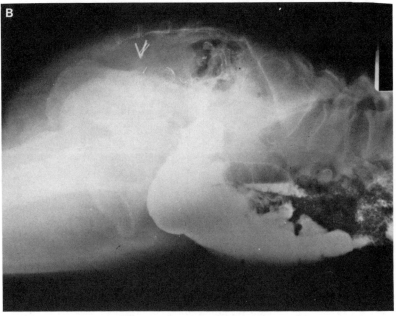

These methods enable the radiation therapist to minimize acute and chronic complications as a result of treatment and to produce high cure rates in patients at early stages of disease. Local control rates for stage B and stage C lesions of the prostate have been reported to be as high as 90% and 80%, respectively, although some patients die of distant metastases (Fletcher 1980; Leibel et al. 1984; Perez and Brady 1987).

In patients who have cancer of the cervix, different modalities of treatment have produced excellent and stable results. High-energy external radiation therapy is combined with localized cesium or radium systems to produce high cure rates with minimal complications, substantiating the fact that most tumors are curable when diagnosed early (Fletcher 1980; Perez and Brady 1987). Newly designed equipment is making hospitalization for brachytherapy unnecessary and minimizing the radiation exposure of radiation therapy and hospital personnel. In addition, this drastically reduces the cost of this portion of the patient's medical care.

For breast cancer, the ideal management remains controversial. Some physicians believe that breast cancer is a systemic disease, but if this were true, no patients would be cured by solely local treatment, which has been successful in many cases (Arriagada et al. 1985; Botnick et al. 1985; Fisher et al. 1985; Veronesi et al. 1986). That most early diagnosed disease is readily curable with local management has been repeatedly documented. This is a cancer type and anatomic area for which good radiation therapy technique is of utmost importance. Good radiotherapeutic management of early breast cancer has substantially reduced the need for extensive, mutilating surgery, as was demonstrated by the results of the National Surgical Adjuvant Project for Breast and Bowel Cancer and those of several European trials (Arriagada et al. 1985; Botnick et al. 1985; Fisher et al. 1985; Peirquin et al. 1986; Veronesi et al. 1986). The five- and 10-year cure rates are the same as for radical surgery but with excellent cosmetic results as well. Recently, despite excellent results obtained with conservative resection and irradiation, the use of modified radical mastectomies and immediate reconstruction has increased, reportedly because of the difficulty of reconstructing the breast after radiation therapy. The results of the studies mentioned show that, with good technique in both surgery and radiation, reconstruction is often unnecessary. The initial surgical procedure is the most important factor in whether the patient will need breast reconstruction at any time. Irradiation is a

◄ FIGURE 3. X-rays taken two to three hours after patient drinks barium. Figure 3A, showing barium limited to the small bowel, was taken in an anterior projection that reveals a significant amount of small bowel in the pelvis. Figure 3B shows the patient in prone position with a cross-table exposure, again revealing the small bowel in the pelvis but primarily in the anterior part. Using a posterior and two lateral fields makes it possible to irradiate a lesion in the posterior portion of the pelvis. This spares most of the small bowel, which improves the patient's tolerance of radiation and avoids long-term complications.

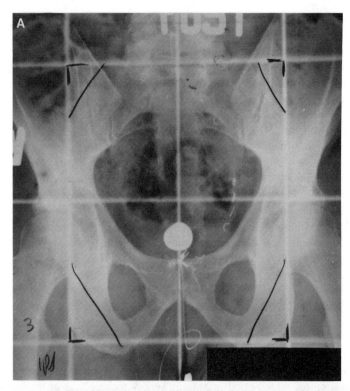

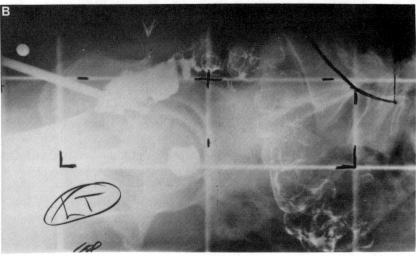

FIGURE 4. Simulation films outlining the intended area of treatment. Figure 4A is a posterior view with the patient in prone position. Figure 4B, a cross-table lateral view with the patient in prone position, outlines the treatment volume and enables the physician to spare a significant portion of small bowel that was identified with the modified small bowel meal as shown in Figure 3. The treatment portals will subsequently be reduced at specified tumor irradiation doses, again increasing the patient's acute tolerance and decreasing the risk of long-term complications.

useful means of palliating patients who have incurable disease and who may need help with pain management or other difficult problems.

It is important to identify, to the best of our ability, sites and types of cancer for which the incidence is rising among minority group patients and to make everyone aware of early warning signs and effective treatment methods. It is painfully clear, in my view, however, that cancer is partly but significantly related to lifestyle as are most other disease entities, but that poverty continues to dictate that disadvantaged minorities will continue to show the highest incidence of cancer and the lowest survival rates. When a patient has to decide between an elective visit to the doctor and paying for a meal, the decision is fairly predictable. Until this country can provide every citizen with equal access to jobs, housing, and medical care, disadvantaged minorities will not benefit to the same extent from medical breakthroughs and advances in medical care that otherwise might prolong health and improve their quality of life.

References

American Cancer Society: *Cancer Facts and Figures for Minority Americans 1986*. New York, 1986.

Arriagada R., Mouriesse H, Sarrazin D, et al: Radiotherapy alone in breast cancer. I. Analysis of tumor parameters, tumor dose and local control: The experience of the Gustave-Roussy Institute and The Princess Margaret Hospital. *Int J Radiat Oncol Biol Phys* 1978; 11:1751–1757.

Botnick LE, Harris JR, Hellman S: Experience with breast conserving approaches at the Joint Center for Radiation Therapy, Boston. In Tobias JS, Peckham MJ (eds): *Primary Management of Breast Cancer: Alternatives to Mastectomy*. London: Edward Arnold, 1985, p 103.

Fisher B, Bauer M, Margolose R, et al: Five-year results of a randomized clinical trial comparing total mastectomy and segmental mastectomy with or without radiation in the treatment of breast cancer. *N Engl J Med* 1985; 312:665–673.

Fletcher G (ed): *Textbook of Radiotherapy*, 3rd Ed. Philadelphia: Lea & Febiger, 1980.

Leibel S, Hanks G, Kramer S: Pattern of case outcome studies: Results of the national practice in adenocarcinoma of the prostate. *Int J Radiat Oncol Biol Phys* 1984; 10:401–409.

Peirquin B, Mazeron Jean-Jacques, Glaubiger D: Conservative treatment of breast cancer in Europe: Report of the Groupe Européen de Curietherapie. *Radiother Oncol* 1986; 6:187–189.

Perez C, Brady L (eds): *Principles and Practice of Radiation Oncology*. Philadelphia: Lippincott, 1982.

Veronesi U, Zucali R, Luini A: Local control and survival in early breast cancer: The Milan trial. *Int J Radiat Oncol Biol Phys* 1986; 12:717–720.

23. Surgery and Patient Support Services

Robert L. DeWitty, Jr.

Introduction

Surgery plays a major role in the management of most cancers. This role is divided into two broad categories: diagnosis and treatment. Treatment can be further divided into two main areas: cure and palliation. Each of these will be discussed in the text that follows.

Surgical Diagnosis

Before treatment for cancer can be instituted, a diagnosis must be made and its extent determined. Treatment, except in a few situations, should never be started until a pathologic diagnosis is made because there are a number of benign conditions that are grossly similar to cancer.

Diagnosis involves some form of biopsy. The more common biopsy techniques used are excisional biopsy, incisional biopsy, and aspiration biopsy.

Aspiration biopsy is performed by using a fine needle in a forward-backward motion once the mass has been entered. This motion is designed to dislodge cells within the mass, allowing them to be aspirated into the needle's hub and syringe. The specimen obtained is then stained and can be read almost immediately. This cytologic specimen requires a skilled pathologist for accurate interpretation (Smith et al. 1985). A negative report may result if that portion of the mass containing cancer cells was missed during the sampling process. Therefore, fine-needle aspiration biopsy is only valid if a positive diagnosis is obtained. There are two advantages of fine-needle aspiration; ease of execution and low incidence of morbidity. Depending on the location of the tumor, fluoroscopy, computed tomography (CT) scan, and ultrasound are used for more accurate tumor localization and higher yield during the aspiration biopsy procedure.

Incisional and excisional biopsy are techniques used in sampling tumors where a portion of the tumor or all of the gross tumor is removed, respectively. These techniques provide tissue for histologic diagnosis. Pathological diagnosis is more precise from tissue as compared to the cytological diagnosis made from the fine needle aspiration. In some instances, excisional biopsy can serve not only to diagnose cancer but also as the definitive surgical treatment of the disease.

Treatment

Once a definitive diagnosis of cancer has been established, treatment can then be instituted. The treatment of cancer involves an interdisciplinary approach that includes the medical, radiation, and surgical oncologists. This paper will focus on the surgical management of cancer.

Surgical treatment can either be curative or palliative. The ideal surgical management objective is to cure the patient by complete surgical removal of all the disease. This is possible when the disease is localized to its site of origin, small in size, and can be removed with a margin of normal tissue without jeopardizing vital structures. After the primary site of cancer has been treated, the surgeon attempts to remove the regional lymph node drainage areas. Removal of these lymphatic nodal areas not only removes potential sites for cancer growth but also allows staging of the disease. In certain instances, when there is removal of gross disease, but there still remains a possibility of microscopic disease, or in partial resection of disease, radiation therapy can be employed to further sterilize the area and effect a cure. Examples of this would be radiation given after a lumpectomy for breast cancer and radiation used in conjunction with surgery for head and neck cancer (Fletcher 1976; Jesse 1977).

In many circumstances, cure of the cancer patient is not possible. The goal of management under these circumstances is to provide an improved quality of life. Surgery is performed to relieve obstruction, stop hemorrhage, clear infection, relieve pain, and address anticipated cancer complications prophylactically.

For example, tumors occurring primarily in the gastrointestinal tract (GI) or one of its derivatives (i.e., pancreas) can cause obstruction by invading a portion of the GI tract. Lesions that develop primarily in the GI tract should be removed if possible. This is to prevent obstruction, bleeding, and perforation. For lesions outside the GI tract proper but causing obstructions, i.e., pancreatic cancer, bypassing that portion of the GI involved will allow continued oral alimentation, which provides worthwhile palliation.

Tumors invade blood vessels or erode into blood vessels, resulting in hemorrhage. Surgical intervention is indicated to arrest this condition. These same tumors outgrow their blood supply, resulting in tumor necrosis with abscess formation. Surgical intervention (either percutaneous or by direct exposure of the abscess cavity) is needed to treat this development adequately.

Pain Management

Pain management is of paramount importance for the cancer patient. Pain serves as a constant reminder to the patient of his illness, which (in many instances) cannot be cured. Therefore, pain relief eliminates one of the primary indicators to the patient of his disease state. Usually, when pain becomes a significant problem for the cancer patient, cure is no longer possible (DeVita et al. 1985). When pain is a problem and the tumor can be resected successfully and/or irradiated, the pain disappears. The following discussion of pain management is directed to those patients with pain from incurable cancer.

The management of pain can be through systemic, local, or regional methods. Systemic medications cause a reduction in pain by attacking the centrally located pain center. This causes an overall reduction in pain sensation regardless of the site of origin. The usual routes of medication administration are orally, intramuscularly, intravenously, or by rectal suppository. Nonnarcotic and/or narcotic medications are used either alone or in combination. Usually a nonnarcotic preparation is used initially, moving to a narcotic substance as symptoms warrant. Long-term narcotics used systemically result in the need to increase the dose of medication given to effect the same level of relief previously enjoyed. This ever-increasing dose of narcotic may lead to drug addiction. This addiction is not a concern in the cancer patient with incurable disease, for whom the main problem is providing the patient with enough medication to obtain the same relief without causing excessive mental and respiratory depression.

Local and regional pain control may be achieved through surgery, irradiation, or regionally administered medications. Surgery is used to remove a tumor resting on or invading a nerve. This approach is practical when the tumor is external to a body cavity. For tumors in the abdominal cavity, i.e., in the pancreas, chemical splanchnicectomy has been used to interrupt the nerve fibers emanating from the celiac plexus. This procedure is performed by using the technique of percutaneous injection of neurolytic agents into the celiac plexus. Pain relief produced by this technique has been variable, with some studies reporting pain relief lasting several months (Howard and Jordan 1977; Brooks 1983).

Radiation can be quite successful in treating pain due to metastatic cancer. Notable examples are pain associated with metastatic bone disease. The relief obtained can be complete. However, if the pain returns, in most instances, radiation cannot be used again because of its deleterious effects on surrounding tissue.

An example of regionally administered medication would be epidural or intraspinal agents. Regionally administered narcotic (morphine) is the newest modality used at Howard University Hospital to control pain secondary to incurable cancer. The morphine is delivered to the intraspinal space by an intraspinal catheter connected to a subcutaneously implanted continuous infusion morphine pump. Since we began using this method of managing pain three years ago, 36 patients have been treated. The primary tumor sites in patients treated by this method have been breast (5), colon and rectum (7), pancreas (5), head and neck (6), and other sites (13). All catheters were inserted into the spinal canal from a lumbar approach except in three patients with head and neck cancer. Here, the catheters were inserted into the intra-cranial ventricular system.

Prior to pump and catheter insertion, each patient was given a test dose of morphine. This was done for two reasons: (1) to determine if this method of administration would be effective, and (2) to determine the daily dose needed and the therapeutic duration of the medication. Patients were able to resume previous activities after pump insertion. Follow-up visits were scheduled every 14 to 21 days for refilling of their pumps. Pain relief in these patients has been good to excellent. Some patients require nonnarcotic oral medications to supplement their intrathecal doses of morphine. Complications have been few, consisting mainly of pump-pocket seroma. It is our opinion that this form of therapy represents the treatment of choice in selected patients with pain resulting from incurable cancer (Bryant et al. 1987).

Support Services

After a diagnosis of cancer has been made and treatment given, many patients as well as their families need supportive services. This needed support is either financial or psychological in nature. Organizations are available to provide cancer patients and their families with these necessary services. Some organizations are locally based, whereas others have a nationwide and even world-wide network.

Initial support begins in the institution where surgery is performed. These services may come from the hospital social services department, which can assist in qualifying the patients for needed financial assistance and making necessary contacts with local cancer rehabilitation. Physical medicine and rehabilitation services can provide required physical reconditioning exercises or the artificial appliances for rehabilitation.

Some of the more common local and national support groups are described below.

Reach to Recovery

This support program was started in 1952 in New York City by a woman who had undergone a mastectomy. She felt that there was a need for a program to provide emotional support for postmastectomy patients. In 1969, the program was brought under the auspices of the American Cancer Society (ACS).

Reach to Recovery is made up of women volunteers who have had mastectomies. These women are trained by the ACS and not only provide emotional and psychological support but also provide women undergoing mastectomies with information on types of permanent prostheses and where they can be obtained locally.

I Can Cope

Any cancer patient can participate in this support program. In consists of four sessions with health care professionals giving pertinent information about cancer or cancer patients sharing their personal experiences with newly diagnosed patients. This support program is available to patients, their family members, or interested persons.

Lost Chord Support Group

This program was formed in 1952 by participants who had had laryngectomies. The patients must have a speech therapist or physician referral to participate. Patients are given laryngectomy kits which contain information about the organization, rehabilitation, hygiene, first-aid, and self-help. Families of patients can also be included in the support group.

United Ostomy Association

The United Ostomy Association is a volunteer support group that assists in the education and rehabilitation of people who have or will have surgery resulting in the creation of a colostomy, ileostomy, or urinary diversion. The association provides patients with information that will assist them in understanding their preoperative and postoperative course. During their period of rehabilitation, volunteers (who are ostomates) are available to share experiences with the new ostomates. Educational programs and counseling are available for the new ostomates and their families. The association also helps the general public understand the problems, concerns, and needs of ostomates.

Summary

Surgery is the principal modality used in diagnosing and treating most cancers. Cure is the desired objective and requires a multitreatment modality plan consisting of surgery, radiation, and sometimes chemotherapy. This approach has been demonstrated to be the most effective.

When cure is not possible, meaningful palliation can be provided. This palliation may include relieving obstruction, stopping hemorrhage, debridement, drainage of abscesses, and controlling pain.

A number of support services exist to assist the cancer patients and their families in coping emotionally and physically with their disease. These services are conducted mainly by volunteers who have had similar experiences.

References

Brooks JR: Cancer of the pancreas. In Brooks JR (ed): *Surgery of the Pancreas*. Philadelphia: WB Saunders, 1983, pp 263-298.

Bryant D, Dennis GC, DeWitty RL: The Infusaid pump in the management of intractable cancer pain. *J Natl Med Assoc* 1987; 79:305-311.

DeVita VT, Hellman S, Rosenberg SA: *Cancer Principles and Practice of Oncology.* Philadelphia: JB Lippincott, 1985, p 669.

Fletcher GH: Reflections on breast cancer. *Int J Radiat Oncol Biol Phys* 1976; 1:769-779.

Howard JM, Jordan GL: Cancer of the pancreas. *Curr Probl Cancer* 1977; 2:1-52.

Jesse RH: The philosophy of treatment of neck nodes. *Ear Nose Throat* 1977; 56(3):125-129.

Smith TJ, et al: Accuracy and cost-effectiveness of fine needle aspiration biopsy. *Am J Surg* 1985; 149:540-545.

Section 6

Support Resources and Provider Roles

Introduction to Section 6

Geraldine V. Padilla

This section includes papers that address a variety of issues concerning culture and health care delivery. For example, Dr. Vallbona emphasizes the importance of including in general screening activities diagnostic tests for cancers known to be prevalent in certain ethnic, sex, and age groups. He encourages primary care physicians to take an active role in promoting primary prevention behavior in their patients. Ms. Esparza discusses the importance of recognizing that the cultural backgrounds of both the patient and health care professional can interfere with effective communication, promote stereotyping, and hamper the delivery of health care services. Education and research should address these cultural issues.

Ms. Villejo recommends that the health care system reach out to minorities and the disadvantaged with a multidisciplinary, bicultural, bilingual approach to developing and translating educational material. Ms. Perez speaks of the need for financial and social service programs targeting the minority and disadvantaged cancer patient. These programs should guide minority patients through complex health care structures, and assist the disadvantaged cancer patient to find the financial resources and support systems necessary to cope with their disease and treatment. Finally, Ms. Guillory discusses an important problem faced by the disadvantaged cancer patient, the lack of a home environment essential to proper and safe home care.

24. The Role of Primary Care Physicians in Primary and Secondary Prevention of Cancer in Minority Persons

Carlos Vallbona

Introduction

One of the problems facing primary care physicians who deliver comprehensive care to low-income, predominantly minority, persons, in the metropolitan area of Houston is the primary and secondary prevention of cancer. This is a major problem because physicians usually give higher priority to the management of acute emergencies or chronic problems than to the systematic screening for hidden illnesses, the assessment of risk factors, and the education of patients, their families and the community-at-large.

The purpose of this chapter is to present specific guidelines for the primary and secondary prevention of cancer in minority persons who receive care in a network of community health centers. Although these guidelines are intended for primary care physicians, they are also used by the physician extenders, nurses, and allied health professionals of the centers because the prevention of cancer requires a multidisciplinary and community-oriented approach. Indeed, oftentimes minority persons fail to recognize the presence of risk factors for cancer or the early clinical manifestations of some types of cancer. Accordingly, by the time they may seek medical care the cancer is too advanced and frequently incurable.

Before discussing the guidelines in detail, it would seem appropriate to describe the health care settings for which these guidelines are intended and some general principles of preventive medicine on which they are based.

Description of the Network of Community Health Centers

Since its creation by referendum in 1965, the Harris County Hospital District has been responsible for the delivery of medical care to the indigent population of Harris County (metropolitan Houston area), providing both inpatient and outpatient facilities at Ben Taub General Hospital and at Jefferson Davis Hospital (the latter for obstetrics, neonatology, pulmonary disease, and rehabilitation).

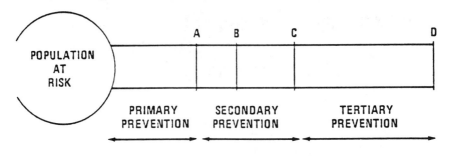

A: Biologic Onset
B: Possible Detection
C: Clinical Onset
D: Endpoint (cure, death)

FIGURE 1. Phases of prevention (adapted with permission from Hutchison, Pergamon Press 1960).

A satellite clinic program was begun in late 1966 when the district assumed responsibility for a clinic that the Baytown Health League had started many years before the low-income residents of Baytown, a city located 22 miles east of Houston. In 1967, at the request of the citizens of the low-income Settegast community, the district established the Settegast satellite clinic, which was staffed by community physicians. There was no formal liaison between this clinic and the central facilities of the Ben Taub General Hospital and the Jefferson Davis Hospital. In 1969, Baylor College of Medicine established a Department of Community Medicine, which was given the task of organizing a Community Medicine Service for the district that would be responsible for the medical staffing of a network of community health centers. At the same time, the district administration established a Community Health Program to coordinate the administrative and allied health program services of the network of centers.

Currently, the network includes eight community health centers and two satellite clinics. Additionally, a centrally located community dental center provides primary dental care.

Each community health center is located in an area populated by low-income, predominantly minority, groups. Although there are no specific geographic boundaries for each center, in general they are targeted to serve a community of approximately 30,000 to 40,000 individuals. At present, an average of 15,000 to 20,000 active patients seek comprehensive care at each center. A total of about 130,000 patients are officially registered as receiving primary care in the network.

The medical staff of the health centers includes board-certified or certification-eligible family physicians, general internists, and pediatricians. All the physicians are members of the faculty of Baylor's Department of Community Medicine and, in addition to their clinical responsibilities, participate in the teaching of medical students and family practice residents. Physician extenders (physician assistants or nurse practitioners) are also part of the medical staff and provide a useful liaison between the physicians and other health professionals of the center. Each center is equipped with a laboratory, electrocardiography and x-ray equipment, and a pharmacy. Simple cytology tests are carried out routinely, although specimens may be sent to the central laboratory facilities at Ben Taub General Hospital.

Patients who require clinical consultation or special tests such as imaging or endoscopy are sent to the appropriate specialists at the outpatient or inpatient services of Ben Taub General Hospital.

The volume of services in the network is very high, and each physician sees from 20 to 25 patients in a typical day. As is usually the case in primary care settings, most of the active patient population includes children, young women in the fertile age group, and elderly persons of both sexes. In general, the male-to-female ratio of physician visits is 1:3.

Phases of Prevention

The Hutchinson model identifies four critical points in the course of a disease that may occur in a population at risk (Hutchison 1960). The first is the point of biologic onset, when physiological changes are occurring but are not yet detectable by diagnostic tests. As changes progress, the disease may be detected by special tests, but the patient has no clinical manifestations. The patient later has the typical signs and symptoms of the disease. From then on, depending on the nature of the disease and efficacy of treatment, the disease progresses to the end point, which is either cure or death (Figure 1).

Primary prevention includes interventions before the onset of disease. An example is the prevention of infectious diseases by vaccination.

Secondary prevention encompasses interventions aimed at early detection of a disease before it is symptomatic. For example, secondary prevention of some forms of cardiac disease (e.g. left ventricular hypertrophy) is possible by screening for hypertension and instituting treatment of such precursor of heart disease.

Tertiary prevention refers to interventions after the onset of symptoms in order to delay, arrest, or reverse the course of a disease. An example is the management of diabetes to prevent its complications (nephropathy, retinopathy, neuropathy, etc.).

The major problem in the primary prevention of cancer lies in the fact that we do not know precisely when the biological onset occurs nor all of the mechanisms that enter into play in the genesis of cancer. Furthermore, for several types of cancer we do not have useful and simple screening tools that will allow us to establish that a person has already gone beyond onset of the disease before overt symptoms and signs appear. Thus, secondary prevention of cancer is also jeopardized for a good many of the cancers that are most prevalent in minority communities.

Epidemiological Considerations

We subscribe to the following set of general principles of epidemiology as the basis for preventive action by primary care physicians working in community health centers.

1. The primary care physician must be aware of the age and sex specific incidence and prevalence of various types of cancer in the general population and in minority populations. Although the incidence and prevalence of cancer in minority populations is not as high as those of hypertension or diabetes, the physiological, psychological and social impacts for the patient, the family and the community are certainly greater than those of the majority of chronic illnesses.
2. The relative risk of having certain types of cancer is greater in the United States minority populations than in the general population. There is abundant literature that clearly shows the increasing death rates from lung, prostate, breast, colon and rectum cancer for Blacks in this country.
3. Specific risk factors for cancer have been clearly identified.
4. Several risk factors for cancer are associated with other diseases. Indeed, smoking is a risk factor for cancer and for heart disease. The same applies to excessive ingestion of fat as a risk factor for heart disease and for cancer of the intestine. Thus, whenever a primary care physician investigates the existence of risk factors in a patient, it should be clear that many of these risk factors apply to cancer and to other illnesses.
5. Screening for cancer in minority populations should be part of the general screening for the most prevalent conditions in a given age and sex group. The idea of having somebody go to a primary care clinic just for the purpose of screening for cancer is not cost-effective. Yet, whenever a patient seeks medical care for any type of complaint, it is important to uncover the existence of risk factors for cancer and for other chronic illnesses.
6. Delayed detection of cancer in minority populations may account for the fact that their five-year survival rates are lower than those of the general population. The literature has consistently shown that the five-year cancer survival rates for almost all sites is lower in Blacks than in Whites. This is true for practically all types of cancer, whether localized or spread.

Risk Factors For Cancer in Minority Populations

Table 1 shows a summary of the risk factors for the types of cancer that are of greatest importance in minority populations. The risk factors in this table apply to persons of both sexes.

Table 2 presents the risk factors for cancers that are particularly common in minority women.

Table 3 shows the risk factors for the specific types of cancer that are common in the male minority population.

TABLE 1. Risk factors for both sexes.

Disease	Risk factor
Lung cancer	Exposure to asbestos
	Exposure to radiation
	Smoking
Colorectal	Family history of colorectal cancer
	Personal or family history of polyps
	Inflammatory bowel disease
	Diet high in fat
	Diet low in fiber
Oral cancer	Cigarette, cigar, and pipe smoking
	Smokeless tobacco use
	Alcohol
	Black population
Esophageal cancer	Black population
	? Alcohol
	? Poor nutrition
Leukemia	Down's syndrome
	Hereditary abnormalities
	Radiation exposure
	Benzene exposure
Stomach cancer	Hispanic population
	from Central America
	Asian population
	? Diet

TABLE 2. Risk factors for females.

Disease	Risk factor
Breast cancer	Age over 50
	Family history of breast cancer
	Nulliparity
	First child after 30
Cancer of cervix	Early age of first intercourse
	Multiple sex partners
	History of genital herpes
Endometrial cancer	History of infertility
	Failure of ovulation
	Prolonged estrogen therapy
	Obesity
Ovarian cancer	Age over 65
	Nulliparity
	History of breast cancer
	History of endometrial cancer
	History of colorectal cancer

TABLE 3. Risk factors for males.

Disease	Risk factor
Prostate cancer	Age over 65
	Black population
	Family history of prostate cancer
	Exposure to cadmium
	Diet
Bladder cancer	Smoking
	Dye, rubber, and leather work
	Urban dwellers
	? Artificial sweeteners
Pancreatic cancer	Age over 30, especially over 70
	Smoking
	Black male population

Primary Prevention of Cancer

Primary prevention refers to steps that should be taken to avoid the following specific factors that might lead to the development of cancer.

Smoking. It is particularly important to emphasize the importance of avoiding or quitting smoking because minority populations have taken up smoking in greater proportion than whites in the last 10 years. The problem is of considerable magnitude in recent immigrants from Hispanic countries.

Sunlight. Although this risk factor is not particularly relevant to Black persons, it nevertheless is definitely a risk factor for cancer of the skin. Therefore inappropriate exposure to ultraviolet rays should be avoided.

Alcohol. This is also an important risk factor, especially when associated with other risk factors for certain types of cancers, such as cancer of the mouth, esophagus, and perhaps stomach. This is not to say that alcohol should be completely forbidden, but it should be taken in moderation, keeping in mind the potential risks that it may have for minority persons.

Smokeless tobacco. Unquestionably, there is a high association between the habit of chewing tobacco and cancer of the oral mucosa, as well as periodontal problems. Perhaps because of its widespread use among professional baseball players, the habit of chewing tobacco is taken up by some high school students, who then become more vulnerable to cancer of the tongue and buccal mucosa, not to speak of gingival or dental problems.

Estrogens. The pharmacological administration of estrogens had been considered to be a risk factor for cancer of the uterus in menopausal women. However, new formulations of estrogens seem to be exempt of risk and should be routinely prescribed along with dietary supplements of calcium for women at the menopause in order to prevent a major problem for women, i.e. osteoporosis. For unknown reasons osteoporosis is not as severe among Black as among White women. However, osteoporosis occurs in women of all races and its progression can be slowed down by administering the combination estrogen-progesterone after the menopause, and by calcium dietary supplements, appropriate protein intake, and physical exercise.

Radiation. Exposure to various types of radiation is known to be a risk factor that should be particularly avoided in all populations, regardless of race or ethnicity.

Occupational hazards. Exposure to nickel, chromate, asbestos, vinyl chloride, cadmium, and other similar substances are occupational hazards that have been associated with various types of cancer as shown in Tables 1–3. Some of these risk factors have a multiplying effect when combined with the risk factor of smoking.

Nutrition. Time and again, it has been demonstrated that a diet rich in fiber and low in saturated fat seems to be preventive against several types of cancer (especially of the gastrointestinal tract). Dietary recommendations that take this into consideration are particularly important also for the prevention of heart disease and other chronic illnesses.

Secondary Prevention of Cancer

In our network of community health centers, we have taken into consideration the recommendations made by various committees regarding screening for cancer in men and women at various ages. Some of the recommendations, especially those of the American Cancer Society as they refer to mammography, have been impractical for us because of the high cost and the inadequacy of our screening facilities.

In Table 4, we list the age-specific recommendations for women, for men, and for persons of both sexes.

TABLE 4. Secondary prevention in primary care.

Age and sex	Screening procedure
Women	
Age 25+	(Earlier in sexually active females)
	Annual pelvic, pap smear,* breast exam
Age 20–50	Baseline mammogram
Age 50+	Mammogram yearly
Men	
Age 20–40	Instruct in testicular self-exam
Both sexes	
Age 20+	Stool hemoccult in high-risk persons
Age 40+	Digital rectal examination yearly
	Stool hemoccult yearly: six smears in three stools
Age 50+	Flexible sigmoidoscopy every three to five years following two negative yearly exams

*Once every three years, after two consecutive negative tests.

A detailed account of each of these recommendations and the description of the screening techniques are beyond the scope of this report.

It should be emphasized at this point that the guidelines in Table 4 represent a set of minimum recommendations. Needless to say, in the presence of specific risk factors, physicians are well advised to carry out an in-depth screening for cancer in all persons regardless of their age. Such screening should be done as frequently as the physician deems pertinent.

Community Education

It is extremely important to increase public awareness about the incidence and prevalence of cancer and of its risk factors in minority communities. For the reasons stated earlier, minority persons should be well educated on the principles of primary and secondary prevention of cancer. It is for this reason that we have encouraged our primary care physicians and physician extenders to participate in a variety of community education programs, as well as in health fairs that are conducted yearly in our community health centers for the purpose of giving an opportunity to the low-income communities of Harris County to undergo at least yearly screening for cancer, as well as for other chronic illnesses.

Conclusions

Cancer is a major problem in minority populations. Although its incidence and prevalence are not as high as those for other chronic conditions, they still have a major physiological, psychological, and social impact on the individual, on the family, and on the community. It is for this reason that physicians who provide primary care to low-income minority persons in community health centers must be familiar with the epidemiology of cancer, of its risk factors, and of the availability of primary and secondary preventive measures for persons of all ages.

Reference

Hutchison GB: Evaluation of preventive services. *J Chron Dis* 1960;11:497–508.

25. The Influence of Ethnic Patient Values on Cancer Nursing

Dolores M. Esparza

Caring for cancer patients who have diverse ethnic backgrounds requires sufficient foresight and understanding to keep differences in language, values, and customs from creating conflicts between health care providers and patients. As the number of minority patients increases, nurses must take steps to understand the effects of ethnic values on patients and on their treatment outcomes.

The issue of minority (ethnic) patient values is not new. Perhaps the first documented nursing conference on minority patients was held in 1972, when delegates of the American Nurses Association created an affirmative action program. As a direct result of this action, two regional conferences entitled Quality Nursing Care for Ethnic Minority Clients in a Multi-Racial Society were sponsored in 1975. These events marked the beginning of the profession's commitment to minority issues in health care delivery.

As health professionals, we see large numbers of Blacks, Hispanics, and Southeast Asians in addition to Haitians, Middle Easterners, East Indians, Samoans, and Native Americans. Each of these ethnic groups has distinct characteristics that can become obstacles if they are not understood by the health care provider.

Numerous social transitions have occurred in communities to accommodate the nation's influx of minority group members. Businesses, schools, and other institutions have organized multilingual programs and hired bilingual personnel. In many health care facilities, support personnel are specially hired to be bilingual translators.

Although eliminating language barriers is the first, obvious step in developing effective communication with diverse patient populations, other steps must be taken to bridge the more subtle cultural barriers that can exist between patients and health care providers. Understanding the ethnic patient requires learning about the customs, beliefs and traditions that the patient and family practice in relation to medication, response to illness and their sense of independence.

Minority Population Characteristics

The Black, Hispanic and American Indian cultural groups will be highlighted to provide examples for comparison. A focus will be on the health practices of these groups.

Values

For members of the Hispanic population, who place great value on respect, authority, and family, the premise of individualism in decision-making is quite foreign. Not that their values are dramatically different from those of Anglo-American society—it is the degree of emphasis on them that makes their ideas unique and thus a potential source of misunderstanding. Hispanics, for instance, consider suffering a part of life and an act of God (Kagawa-Singer 1987). They may be willing to delay treatment, as may Native Americans, to consult with a family member because the family is a source of security and identity for these groups.

The concept of family is so important to Hispanic patients that they may be more concerned about the effects of their disease on their families than they are about the organic characteristics of the disease. Hispanics also have a great fear that a loved one will be alone at the time of death. This explains why working with Hispanic families often entails chasing droves of people out of the room (American Nurses Association 1976).

Different groups also hold different philosophies about disease and treatment. For instance, some Black, Hispanic, and American Indian populations may believe that disease is caused by supernatural forces to punish or test them. Once diagnosed, they may feel their disease is God's will and react somewhat passively, as opposed to the angry reaction commonly seen in patients from Anglo-Saxon cultures.

Often, minority patients will seek out practitioners of folk medicine, whose remedies may provide a sense of hope and security as well as reaffirm self-worth and social integration. Nurses and other health care professionals need to be familiar with different cultural world views, including opinions on folk medicines, and encourage patients to uphold their beliefs. If this issue is not dealt with appropriately, it may create barriers to patient compliance and communication between patients and providers, severely hampering the effectiveness of care.

The belief that the values and practices of one's own culture are the best and, in some cases, the only appropriate ones is known as ethnocentrism. Reducing ethnocentrism can be an effective tool for dealing with patients who have non-Anglo-Saxon values (Theiderman 1986).

Compliance

Low patient compliance may result from cultural barriers. Hispanics are known for poor compliance with their medication instructions. We may believe they are denying the disease or being stubborn or difficult, but their lack of compliance often arises from the cultural belief that they are incapable of changing their destiny as well as from not trusting the efficacy of medication.

For American Indians, who customarily take large quantities of herbs, the idea of taking one pill at four different times during the day could be a peculiar notion. In some cases, they have instead taken all four pills at once (Primeaux 1977; Polacca 1973).

Additionally, if symptoms are not present, some patients will stop taking their medications because they believe they are cured. It is difficult for these patients to understand that they may not be healthy even though they feel much better physically.

Economic Factors

Minority populations have an overall greater incidence of infections and chronic diseases, including cancer. Health care is often not available to minorities, and the quality of the care that is made available is often poor. Early diagnosis of disease, a phenomenon crucial to successful treatment outcomes in cancer, is practically nonexistent for these populations.

The scarcity of high-quality health care for minority populations may be a function of income rather than cultural factors. According to the U.S. Department of Health and Human Services (1986), Black and Hispanic households were more than twice as likely as their non-Hispanic White counterparts to be living below the poverty line. This means in 1984, 33.8% of the Black population and 28.4% of the Hispanic population lived in poverty, as opposed to 11.4% of their non-Hispanic White counterparts.

Lack of financial resources severely limits minorities' access to health care. As a group, they are less likely to have annual checkups and are more likely to have problems with transportation and payment. Therefore, many minority patients may not receive routine treatment.

The Provider

Patient variations in values, etiquette, and religion, as well as variations in response to pain, may affect the ability of nurses to perceive patients accurately and to act efficiently and compassionately. Patient ethnic backgrounds coupled with the nurse's cultural beliefs yield a potential area of conflict.

Conflict arises when a dominant cultural group tries to impose its beliefs, practices, or values on an individual. As health professionals we tend to impose values associated with the Anglo-Saxon biomedical system. In this system, three principles are assumed that may or may not be shared by people from different cultures. These beliefs include the notions that life is sacred and should be preserved at all costs, that patient autonomy in decision-making is essential, and that suffering is not acceptable (Silberfarb 1982). These assumptions are the seeds of many conflicts and misunderstandings that arise between nurses and cancer

patients of different ethnic backgrounds. Results of such conflicts include alienation of patients, low compliance with treatment, and lack of communication
between patients and caregivers. It is realistic to note that not all nurses are able
to interact positively with ethnic populations.

Every health care practitioner approaches cross-cultural interaction differently. Some will be interested in and will want to be involved with people of
different cultures. They attempt to bridge the world of the cultural group and that
of their own. They generally develop trust between a patient and themselves. On
the other hand, some practitioners may not care to be involved. They will remain
emotionally detached and will only accomplish what is required during an eight-
hour work day. These individuals generally do a good job in their roles, but a
cohesive relationship between patients and providers will not be formed
(Leininger 1973). Other nurses stereotype minorities as inferior. If this is a conscious or unconscious thought, they will undoubtedly feel uncomfortable working
with minority patients and will ask not to work with them. Nursing supervisors
and managers should recognize potential problems early and devise a plan that
will work well for employees and patients.

The Minority Provider

Affirmative action has brought increased educational opportunities for minorities, and the number of minority health care professionals is increasing. The
problems minorities experience in the workplace are very similar to those of
patients. The first is language. Some patients may have difficulty understanding
what the caregiver is saying. Some minority employees may upset the normal
staffing schedule as well by insisting on taking cultural holidays.

People from different countries also have different work styles. For example,
Hispanics may be hesitant to discuss problems with supervisors (Poteet 1986).
They frequently seek out a social worker to discuss a problem with before telling
their supervisors, in order to decide how to best approach their employers. They
often wait until the last moment, when a problem has expanded to near-crisis
proportions, before they bring it to the attention of a supervisor or manager.

Achieving true cross-cultural communication requires learning. It requires
patience, curiosity, and a great deal of understanding and acceptance. Providers
must keep an open mind when working with patients from a cultural group they
have not encountered before. This may require a great deal of study: reading
about the history and customs of the culture in addition to working directly with
its people. Providers may have to visit the communities where these people live
to begin to understand their lives and beliefs.

Hospitals also can help break down cultural barriers by establishing programs
and policies such as in-house continuing education programs that offer classes
and resources on bicultural issues (American Nurses Association 1976), recruitment of minority personnel particular to the specific patient populations of an
institution, in-service training to help employees learn the needs of different

cultural groups during the different stages of cancer treatment (including hygiene and nutrition needs), and visitor policies that accommodate patients and their families.

Summary

Ethnic patient values and the nurse's beliefs and values can become barriers in caring for patients with cancer.

Black, Hispanic, and American Indian populations share interesting beliefs about disease and death that affect their degree of compliance with treatment and response to health teachings.

Conflict arises when a dominant cultural group imposes beliefs and values on a minority group. These conflicts appear in the form of alienation of patients, low compliance with treatments, and language barriers.

Breaking down these cultural barriers requires learning about the beliefs and practices of a cultural group. Nurses should study bicultural issues offered through in-house training classes.

Acknowledgments. My sincere gratitude to Lee Montgomery for her assistance in the preparation of this paper.

References

American Nurses Association: *Toward Quality Nursing Care for a Multiracial Society*, 1976, p 28.

Kagawa-Singer M: Ethnic perspectives on cancer nursing: Hispanics and Japanese-Americans. *Oncology Nursing Forum*, 1987;14:59–65.

Leininger M: Becoming aware of type of health practitioners and cultural imposition. American Nurses Association, 1973; pp. 9–15.

Polacca K: Ways of working with the Navajos who have not learned the white man's ways. In Reinhardt AM, Quinn MD (eds): *Family Centered Community Nursing: Sociocultural Framework*. St. Louis: CV Mosby, 1973.

Poteet GW: Ethnic diversity. *J Nurs Adm* 1986;16:6.

Primeaux M: Caring for the American Indian patient. *Am J Nurs* 1977;77:91–94.

Silberfarb, PM: Research in adaptation to illness and psychosocial intervention. *Cancer* 1982;50(suppl):191–195.

Thiederman S: Ethnocentrism: A barrier to effective health care. *Health Care Issues* 1986;11:52–59.

US Department of Health and Human Services: *Health Status of the Disadvantaged*. Washington, DC, 1986.

26. Social Service Programs for Cancer Patients

Blanca A. Perez

The original focus of my chapter was on programs available to minority cancer patients at the leading cancer treatment institutions. In calls to some of my colleagues affiliated with these cancer centers, I learned that not one of these treatment facilities, including The University of Texas M. D. Anderson Cancer Center, has a program specifically designed to assist the center's minority patients. Their services do, however, provide for the special needs of minority patients.

I chose to discuss the needs of indigent and socially disadvantaged minority cancer patients because I see them as having the greatest need for our services, and we do not have ample resources to meet their needs.

Social Services in Medical Settings

Most social service departments in medical settings provide two types of service: concrete services and discharge planning. In a cancer treatment center, however, these departments' functions are extended to include psychosocial assessment, counseling, education concerning living with cancer, and information and referral services for cancer patients. Specifically, these functions include an assessment of the patient's awareness of his or her medical situation and psychological coping strength; an evaluation of the patient's economic situation and ability or inability to pay nonmedical expenses during the hospital stay; help with transportation, housing, and linking with community and government resources; and, in discharge planning, teaching the patient how to get in touch with resources available to cancer patients.

The special needs of most minority patients are evident from their lack of financial resources for dealing with this illness, an economic disadvantage more profound and more common than among nonminority patients. Often their local communities are also at a loss to help them. Only a small percentage of indigent cancer patients are able to receive the medical care they need in their home-towns; usually they must travel to receive state-supported care. Then, although they may not have to pay enormously high medical bills, they must handle the costs involved in being treated – costs of transportation, housing, food, parking, and perhaps child care at home.

At M. D. Anderson Cancer Center, where we are fortunate to have the means of providing for some of these "getting care" costs, funds and other resources are nevertheless limited, and we must find reimbursement for funds used. We are also constantly trying to find new ways of reducing our expenditures without sacrificing our goal of providing good and decent care for our patients.

Everyone facing a diagnosis of cancer feels tremendous stresses and pressures. But when the person has never traveled outside his or her own community, does not speak the medical language at all and speaks the English language uncomfortably, and lacks the skills for dealing with a complex bureaucratic system, these stresses are even more disturbing. The patient benefits from having someone help to secure the concrete things he or she needs and to guide him or her through the system. That is what we do. The new patient referral office notifies the social work department of problems they identify during any patient's preregistration phase. By contacting patients before they enter the clinic or hospital, we can assess their needs and direct them to local resources. We also give them a brief orientation on the clinic and hospital system and the name of a person to call for additional help.

Most patients see their social workers again during their medical work-up or admission. At that time, we interview the patients and family members to find out how much they know about their diagnosis and treatment, how they have coped with the illness and its surrounding problems up to now, and what resources they have and which ones are appropriate and available to them. Throughout the patients' course of treatment and follow-up period, a social worker will be available to them.

Community Resources

Programs available near the patient's local community are few in number and have limited funds. County welfare offices, county courts, and charitable organizations can usually provide only funds for transportation – resources that are small and often exhausted. Because few agencies or programs can help families of patients with lodging and maintenance, we try to discourage family members from accompanying adult patients when they have no community resources.

Yet no one who is already facing so many difficulties should have to be at a cancer center alone. The American Cancer Society has one of the few programs with resources for lodging, although its service is limited. Our institution provides housing for out-of-town indigent patients but has no housing for families. We depend on the generosity of the medical center hotels to offer discount rates and, when possible, courtesy rooms to our patients. For emergency financial assistance, we depend on private donations and other special funds.

Support Programs

A cancer center's supportive programs exist to help patients and families deal with the disease as well as with issues of death and dying. Counseling in our institution is offered by certified social workers to patients and families individually or in groups. Also available within our institution, our cancerWISE Bureau, staffed essentially by volunteers, organizes a weekly Living with Cancer group and other small seminars for patients and families. Bereavement groups are conducted by the American Cancer Society and hospice agencies, and the American Cancer Society sponsors many other education and support activities.

Needs of Minority Cancer Patients

Based on my working experience and my view of the needs of minority cancer patients, I recommend that:

- The medical institution approve and designate funds to be used for minority patients,
- our representatives' budget include special funds for related medical treatment costs, and that fund-raising be done for that purpose also,
- city and county officials and agencies referring indigent patients take more financial responsibility for these patients,
- researchers include medical treatment-related costs for patients in grant proposals for research studies,
- all clinical departments set aside an emergency fund for patient needs,
- patients be encouraged, when appropriate, to receive treatment in their home communities,
- more minority and Spanish-speaking staff members be hired.

We have many resources at our disposal to assist patients at M. D. Anderson Cancer Center. More remains to be done, however, by our government, our Texas institutions, our departments, and ourselves to help minority patients get the treatment they need and deserve.

27. Home Health Care

Joyce A. Guillory

With the advent of hospital charges governed by diagnosis-related group (DRG) rates and overcrowded hospitals, attention has been focused on reducing health care costs and the length of hospitalizations. Patients with cancer are going home sooner and may require more costly home health care than before.

While a patient is hospitalized, various forms of reimbursement are available —private insurance, Medicare, or Medicaid. Once the patient is discharged and cared for at home, however, the financial picture changes. Some private insurance companies do not compensate at all for care given at home, and others pay 60% to 100%. Frequently, patients who do not meet the requirements for Medicare or Medicaid are discharged from the hospital prematurely and confronted by home health care costs they cannot afford.

Under the most recent Medicare laws, a person may receive daily home care for up to 38 days, approximately twice the number of days reimbursable under the old Medicare rule. Medicare recipients are also granted prescription drug coverage. The old law had no prescription drug coverage, which was a constant concern for many older and deprived people.

There are still questions as to whether the physician will be reimbursed if chemotherapy was given on an outpatient basis. Before the new rules, if chemotherapy is administered on an outpatient basis, either the medication was paid for or the doctor's fee was paid for.

Rise in Home Health Care

Over the last few years, we have seen an explosion in home health services, and the number of home health agencies is expected to increase 15% to 20% annually, with a projected revenue of $12 billion to $15 billion per year by 1990. The nature of these agencies has changed as dramatically as their numbers have. In 1980, most home health agencies were not affiliated with any institution, and most were visiting nurses' associations or local public health agencies (Weinstein 1985). As of June 1984, there were actually fewer public agencies and many more for-profit as well as institution-based agencies. The estimate is that nearly 90% of our nation's hospitals will offer home health services in the near future (Weinstein 1985).

Regulations

A licensed home health care agency is an organization or corporation that meets federal and state regulations to provide skilled nursing and other therapeutic services to a patient in the home setting (Studebaker 1985). The primary purpose for licensure, usually a state regulatory function, is to "assure that all home health services provided to a person are performed under circumstances that ensure quality care" (Illinois Department of Public Health 1978).

Skilled nursing is care provided by a licensed professional nurse (RN). If LPN/licensed vocational nurse (LPN) services are used, the LPN must be supervised by a registered nurse (RN), and only the RN is permitted to sign the patient's records for procedures routinely performed by LPNs in hospital are not permitted to be performed in the home setting by anyone other than a registered nurse (Weinstein 1986).

Medicare regulations describe a home health agency as a public agency or private organization, or a subdivision of such an agency or organization, that (1) is primarily engaged in providing skilled nursing services and other therapeutic services, such as physical, speech, or occupational therapy, medical social services, and home health aide services; (2) has policies established by a professional group associated with the agency or organization to govern the services and provides for supervision of such services by a physician or registered professional nurse; (3) maintains clinical records on all patients; (4) is licensed in accordance with state or local law or is approved by the state or local licensing agency as meeting the licensing standard; (5) meets other conditions set by the Secretary of Health and Human Services (U.S. Department of Health and Human Services 1986).

In general, home health care is usually provided by a Medicare-certified, licensed agency. All agencies are divided into two classes of licensure, Medicare A and Medicare B. Class A agencies provide a private-duty nurse or long-term staffing (Studebaker 1985).

A Medicare A home health classification enables an agency to provide home care services on an intermittent basis to a homebound patient who requires skilled nursing care, physical therapy, occupational therapy, speech pathology, medical social work, or care provided by a home health aide.

A Class B licensure is required for an agency to handle equipment and bill for drugs and other items not covered under Class A.

Reimbursement

Compensation for nursing care in the home is customarily transacted by payment from the patient, private insurance, Medicare, or Medicaid.

Medicare itself has been the primary federally funded medical assistance program for the elderly and disabled since 1966. Medicare provides limited benefits for post-hospital care, including home care. As in hospitals, the Medicare population served by specific home care agencies will vary, with some reporting as few as 10% Medicare patients and others as many as 99% of patients served (Weinstein 1985).

Medicaid assistance, jointly funded by state and federal money, is intended to cover the medical costs of the "categorically needy," those who would become indigent if required to pay individual medical expenses (Weinstein 1985).

To be eligible for Medicare home health benefits, the patient must be homebound, that is unable to leave the home, be receiving medical treatment, and have the doctor certify medical needs. There must be a well-written plan of care and the patient must require only intermittent skilled nursing care, which means care delivered daily for two to three weeks.

To be reimbursed by Medicare, a home health agency must meet certain requirements for skilled services: (1) the nurse/therapist must justify all services rendered by documenting them, (2) the patient's homebound status and number of visits made by the nurse must be consistently documented (nurses frequently complain about the amount of paperwork), and (3) the use of all supplies must be documented (Studebaker 1985).

Home enteral and parenteral nutrition is covered exclusively under Medicare's prosthetic device benefit. Products associated with this treatment modality are reimbursed, therefore, if the patient has a permanently impaired body organ or function that prevents ingestion or digestion of food. Medicare will pay for supplies for 30 days on any given claim.

Administration of Intravenous Therapy in the Home

The concept of providing intravenous therapy in a nonhospital setting dates back to 1963. Because this method was a new approach to the delivery of medical care, its initial use was limited to hyperalimentation, hemodialysis, peritoneal dialysis, and chemotherapy in the home, where it was shown to be as effective as hospital-based administration (Kasmer 1987).

Recent improvements in chemotherapy and methods of administering drugs have made it possible to deliver antineoplastic drugs over short as well as long periods of time. The administration method chosen may depend on the drug's stability, its pharmacokinetics, and side effects (Schaffner 1987). The nurse is primarily responsible for the administration of drugs in the hospital as well as in the patient's home environment.

One major difference between chemotherapy in the home and the hospital is that Medicare is not likely to pay for chemotherapy given at home. Another is that the home health nurse works alone and must be knowledgeable about antineoplastic drugs, dosage, reconstitution, storage, handling, administration, and side effects. The nurse must be aware of safety rules for handling these drugs, being as careful in the home as in the hospital (Schaffner 1987). All nurses who administer these drugs must receive special training in managing the drugs and avoiding potential hazards.

Intravenously administered antineoplastic medications like doxorubicin (Adriamycin) are prepared by the pharmacist, reconstituted if necessary, added to an appropriate solution such as normal saline, and labeled (Schaffner 1987). The bag is wrapped or packed to protect the nurse.

Usually, a 24-hour supply of drug is delivered to the patient's home and then stored in the refrigerator. Some home health agencies recommend that such drugs be stored in a refrigerator other than the one used for food. If this is impossible, as it is in many cases, medication is placed on a separate shelf in the refrigerator, and the patient and family members are advised not to tamper with the bags.

When the primary care nurse visits the patient, she evaluates the patient and reinforces what the patient and family have learned about chemotherapy from the hospital nurses (Schaffner 1987). Family members are always encouraged to take part in the patient's care.

Before the nurse actually administers the chemotherapy, she checks the venous access to make sure it is functional. In many cases, the patient and family members are able to perform the task of catheter care, which consist of daily heparin flushes, weekly or biweekly dressing changes, and frequent observations. Patients are often selected for home intravenous therapy because they are capable of managing this aspect of their care.

Nursing Care in an Economically Deprived Environment

Nurses should know and be sensitive to their patients' socioeconomic status, especially at home, be acquainted with the patients' verbal and nonverbal behaviors, and understand the patients' basic beliefs. In giving instructions, the nurse must avoid medical jargon and be sure the patient comprehends them.

Home health care is a necessary component of comprehensive health care today. It is successful when hospitals select their patients carefully for home care and seek agencies that will provide care at a reasonable cost.

References

Curtis F: Reimbursement dilemma regarding home health care products and services. *American Journal of Hospital Pharmacy*, 1984.

Gardner C: Home I.V. therapy: Part I. *National Intravenous Therapy Association* 1986; 9:95–103.

Health Care Financing Administration. *Home Health Agency Manual*. Washington, DC: Superintendent of Documents; HCDAD Publication no. HIM-11, Section 203 and 204. 1986.

Home health care programs and the law. *Intravenous Therapy News* 1984;27–30.

Illinois Department of Public Health. *Rules and Regulations for Home Health Agencies*, August 1978.

Kasmer RJ, Hoisington LM, Yukniewicz S: Home parenteral antibiotic therapy, Part 1: An overview of program design. *Home Health Care Nurse* 1987;5:12–18.

Metzyer KV: Why some patients can't afford to go home. *RN* 1986;72:56–57.

Mizuri E: There is no place like home. *Am J Nurs* 1984;84:646–648.

Schaffner A: Safety precautions in home chemotherapy. *Am J Nurs* 1984;84:346–347.

Sheehan K, Gilder J: Home antibiotic therapy: A less-than-ideal candidate. *Journal of the National Intravenous Therapy Association* 1985;8:157–159.

Smith E: DRGS: Making them work for you. *Nursing 85* 1985;15:34–41.

Studebaker E: Home health agencies: Functions and reimbursement. *Journal of the National Intravenous Therapy Association* 1985;8:43–46.

US Department of Health and Human Services: *Medicare Home Health Agency Manual.* Washington, DC: Social Security Administration, HIM 11, 1986.

Weinstein SM: The how-to's of home care. *Journal of the National Intravenous Therapy Association* 1986;8:227–230.

Weinstein SM: Regulations governing home care programs. *Journal of the National Intravenous Therapy Association* 1985;8:361–362.

28. Patient Education for Hispanic Cancer Patients

Louise A. Villejo

Greater racial and ethnic diversity is a given in contemporary American life. Combined with unequal access to economic resources and political power, that diversity has created sharp differences in the racial and ethnic composition of the social classes in American life. One manifestation of that difference is the wide disparity in the racial and ethnic characteristics of those who provide and those who receive medical and social services. The exchange of professional services between persons who differ in race, ethnicity, and cultural orientation is therefore inevitable.

What do we know about cultural differences and cross-cultural exchange and their influence on access to and compliance with medical treatment generally and cancer treatment in particular? Can health care providers be taught sensitivity to cultural differences without spending years in cross-cultural training? Are there keys to working successfully with different cultural groups? What principles and skills can we extract from existing knowledge to include in programs of professional, public, and patient education?

My goal here is to provide an overview of how best to convey information—specifically cancer patient education—to the Hispanic population and to encourage those who must deal with these issues daily.

As a case study, I will use the efforts of The University of Texas M. D. Anderson Cancer Center's Bilingual Information and Education Advisory Group to meet the needs of Spanish-speaking patients and family members.

The Cross-Cultural Patient and Health Education Project

The American Medical Association's (AMA) Cross-Cultural Patient and Health Education Project focused on problems encountered in treating Hispanic patients (*American Medical News* 1983).

Their recommendations included:

• Encouraging patients to take Spanish-English courses and to achieve at least a high school education,
• improving the ability of physicians to communicate in Spanish,
• producing AMA health materials in good, understandable Spanish — not only translating but also originating materials in Spanish,
• training more Spanish-speaking health educators,
• and developing concisely written patient education materials for Hispanic patients.

The cultural differences of Hispanic and Anglo-Americans and the impact of these differences on access to medical care and compliance with cancer treatment in particular, have been studied repeatedly. Nall and Speilberg (1967) found that use of folk healers did not inhibit compliance with modern medical treatment regimens as much as a person's submersion in the ethnic community. Strong kinship bonds, the family's conception of its obligations to the patient, and the patient's resistance to separation from the family seemed to be paramount among the cultural factors inhibiting the acceptance of modern medical treatment.

The American Cancer Society (ACS) and the National Cancer Institute (NCI) focused attention over the last several years on how to communicate with Hispanic people more effectively. The National Cancer Institute brought together Hispanic health professionals — statisticians, physicians, public health administrators, and patient educators — to initiate a program in the Division of Cancer Prevention and Control to focus on cancer control in Hispanic populations. The American Cancer Society (1985) conducted a national study of

TABLE 1. Profile of the Hispanic population: summary.

	Percentage of Hispanic population	Percentage of 1980 U.S. Census
Age		
Under 35 years	48	39
65 years and older	6	17
Education		
Less than high school education	61	29
Some college/ college education	17	33
Income		
Under $10,000	31	25
Language at home		
Spanish	63	NA
English	37	NA

Adapted from American Cancer Society 1985, with permission.

TABLE 2. Interest in cancer education programs.

About cancer of	Percentage of Hispanic population surveyed	Percentage of Anglo population surveyed
Breast	62	48
Lung (and smoking)	62	51
Skin	56	52
Colon and rectum	46	51
Uterus	45	43
Prostate gland	39	41
Oral cavity	37	39
Testicles	34	36

Adapted from American Cancer Society 1985, with permission.

Hispanics and cancer in 1983. As demographics summarized in Table 1 show, the Hispanic population is young, with an average age of 25 years, and under-educated; nearly a third is in the lowest socioeconomic group, and the majority speaks Spanish.

The ACS study found also that two of three Hispanics prefer to use a doctor who speaks Spanish fluently and that 61% prefer information programs given in Spanish. The topics listed in Table 2 were rated by Hispanics surveyed according to their interest in learning more about these cancers.

Data from the ACS survey also showed that the incidence of cancer among Hispanics is lower than among the general population, although 4 of 10 persons reported that someone in their family has had cancer. When asked what disease Hispanics worry about most, the answer was cancer. Hispanics seemed to be more fearful of developing cancer than people in the general population (59% compared with 54%) and also more fearful of specific types of cancer.

Hispanics are less familiar with the warning signs of cancer than are persons in the general population. Among three Hispanic groups, Cuban Americans were least likely to identify the cancer warning signals, followed by Puerto Ricans in the middle, and Mexican Americans, who were most knowledgeable.

In looking at trends in cancer tests and treatments, the ACS found Hispanics also less aware of available cancer screening tests than were members of other groups. The one cancer test well known among Hispanic women is the Papanicolaou smear.

According to ACS data (1985) although Hispanics were fairly hopeful, they were in fact much less convinced of the effectiveness of cancer treatments than the general public. And, like the general public, Hispanic Americans were worried about the side effects of treatments, especially of irradiation and chemotherapy.

How can we use this information about Hispanics to provide them with more information regarding their diagnosis and treatment?

The Anderson Experience

As the largest of 20 comprehensive cancer centers in the country, the University of Texas M. D. Anderson Cancer Center's primary mission is to serve the people of Texas. The patient education office supports the hospital's commitment to excellent patient care by a compassionate staff. Our task is to support patient care by providing consultation for the planning and development of educational resources for hospital and clinic patients and their families. This activity takes place from the time of a patient's admission through diagnosis, treatment, rehabilitation, and continuing care, and it ends with the assurance that the patient and family caregiver are prepared for home health care.

Our goal is to help the medical staff provide all patients with information regarding their diagnosis, treatment, and prognosis in terms the patients can understand, to insure the patients' participation in decisions involving their health care, and to provide patients with the information they need to give informed consent before starting any procedure or treatment. All cancer patients have special education and information needs, and these include understanding their disease and treatment, overcoming myths, misunderstanding, and misconceptions about cancer, and dealing with the severe emotional stress created by concerns about mutilation, alienation, vulnerability to recurrence, and mortality.

Patients want and need to play a much larger role than has been customary in managing their own care. The skills they need to do this may be the short-term ones of wound care, mixing medication, or administering injections, whereas the long-term ones may be caring for stomas or using prostheses. These skills are initially taught to individual patients and family members by health care staff members, and they are reinforced several times before patients and family members can comfortably perform these tasks alone.

Barriers to effective patient education arise from several problems. For health care professionals, these may include time limitations, uncertainty of what to teach, unfamiliarity with resources, and discomfort with teaching techniques. Other hurdles for health care providers not familiar with the Hispanic culture may be the obvious language problem, a preconceived bias, or the discomfort of using teaching materials in a language other than English.

For cancer patients, stresses of the diagnosis and treatment, weakened physical condition, lack of interest or unwillingness to learn, sensory deficit, anxiety related to other issues, feelings of powerlessness and loss of control, and the need to absorb an overwhelming amount of information about the disease and its treatment may all be learning handicaps — as may the patient's age and educational level, environmental distractions, or discontinuous care.

Language and cultural factors have been major barriers for Hispanic patients. Different beliefs regarding death and a fatalistic perspective on illness must also be taken into account.

At M. D. Anderson, a bilingual information and education advisory group including physicians, social workers, nurses, dietitians, interpreters, volunteer coordinators, and public and patient education specialists has attempted to identify and meet the needs of Spanish-speaking patients and their families. Since 1983, these group members have evaluated and promoted Spanish-language patient education activities and improved communication between health professionals and patients and their families.

Originally, 10 volunteers were recruited to translate materials chosen by head nurses of the inpatient and outpatient services. Advisory group members reviewed the translated material, which was then sent to an editor for review and comment.

Bilingual persons or those who have attempted to learn another language know that translation and interpretation is an art and a science, especially in the case of medical and technical information. The process took 10 times as long as it would have if a professional translator had been hired, but it achieved our primary goal of having materials available in Spanish.

Over the years we abandoned this cumbersome process because we found that, although volunteers were willing, their translating skills were often inadequate.

Now an Anderson staff member with a master's degree in translation voluntarily assists us with translation and editing. We also request funds from department heads whose staff members and patients need translated materials, and we write proposals for grants from other sources in and outside the institution (e.g., community groups and pharmaceutical companies).

The bilingual advisory group provides a forum for Spanish-speaking patients and family members' concerns, and its members act as advisors to the hospital administration. Our achievements include developing and conducting patient education classes in chemotherapy and central venous catheter care in Spanish; publishing more than 175 printed and audiovisual materials in Spanish, making available Spanish-language materials from ACS, NCI, and pharmaceutical companies, and helping select books and other materials for our Health Information Center; establishing a Spanish-language student internship at a local university; constructing Spanish-language bulletin boards in clinics and hospital to promote all Spanish-language resources; writing the *Guia para Pacientes* that promotes institutional resources and educational opportunities; and organizing a Spanish class for the pediatric staff.

After two years of these activities, we surveyed Spanish-speaking patients and family members to find out whether they are being adequately informed about their diagnostic tests, procedures, and treatment and how they learn about available educational programs and resources. Overall, the results were encouraging. About half of the Hispanic patients and their families stated that they had received adequate information and were confident about the self-care they had to do. A majority (79%) stated that they preferred receiving their information on a one-to-one basis. Other educational strategies—videos, print, materials, and group classes—were ranked somewhat lower at 37%, 32%, and 16%, respectively. A majority of the patients surveyed had been exposed to these resources, 32% had received print materials from health care team members,

53% had attended patient education classes, and 68% had viewed a patient education videotape. Several respondents suggested topics for new materials, classes, and videotapes.

We encountered several challenging problems, one arising from the fact that this is a volunteer effort with a constantly changing staff. Another was that most volunteers were native speakers but not necessarily good translators or writers, and the interns who were learning the language were not good translators either.

As a whole, however, this program has given our patients and family members new resources. The bilingual advisory group has been good not only in fostering Spanish-language activities but also in encouraging our hospital administration to meet the unique educational and informational needs of our Spanish-speaking patients.

References

American Cancer Society: *A Study of Hispanics Attitudes Concerning Cancer and Cancer Prevention*. New York: American Cancer Society, May 1985.

American Medical News, October 28, 1983. MDs study better ways to help Hispanic patients.

Nall FC, Speilberg J: Social and cultural factors in the responses of Mexican-Americans to medical treatment. *J Health Soc Behav* 1967;8:299–308.

Section 7

The Role of Historically Black Colleges
and Universities, the Government,
and National Health Agencies

Introduction to Section 7

Lovell A. Jones, Judith Craven, and Mickey Leland

Minority medical schools, the federal government, and the American Cancer Society are trying to reduce the high incidence of and mortality from cancer in Black and other minority communities through a number of strategies.

Dr. Herbert Nickens of the Office of Minority Health (OMH) describes that federal agency's efforts to improve access to health care. His agency was created after the 1985 report of the Secretary of Health and Human Services Task Force on Black and Minority Health, which pointed out significant disparity in the health status of Whites and minorities. The OMH has seven working committees that are trying to encourage more healthful practices and address the inequities in the health care system and the environmental hazards associated with housing and working conditions.

The National Cancer Institute's efforts were outlined by Dr. Barbara Bynum. She notes that as early as 1976, studies indicated the huge disparity in cancer mortality for minorities compared with that for Whites. The NCI sees improving the health status of minorities to close that gap as critical to achieving its national goal of a 50% reduction in cancer incidence by the year 2000, she says. NCI's continuing efforts to disperse up-to-date information into both communities and medical centers and to fund more minority-oriented cancer research will help, she says.

Nationwide programs also are being offered by the American Cancer Society, which has sponsored several recent workshops and forums on Black and Hispanic health, the society's Dan Hoskins reports. The ACS has studied Blacks' attitudes about cancer in hopes of encouraging prevention efforts. The ACS is also funding minority-oriented research, and the society is also trying to tailor services to needs of minority populations.

A number of critical questions are being addressed by coalitions of Black medical schools and other minority professional schools, as Dr. David Satcher of Meharry Medical College reports. Minority medical schools have four major roles—educating a large share of Black health professionals, providing role models for students, encouraging their graduates to work in underserved areas, and responding to the needs for education, health care, and research in Black and other minority communities. The issues these institutions will and must take on include the disparate outcomes of cancer in Black and White communities; the role of socioeconomic status, life-style, genetics, and racial discrimination; and how to encourage behavior changes.

The following chapters will, I hope, provide information from the government, minority medical schools, and the American Cancer Society, brought together for the first time in one book. They provide no easy answers. Finding solutions will hinge on vigorous health education efforts and health care promotion throughout the minority community. However, these chapters do describe how these agencies are attempting to address the problem of cancer among Black and other socioeconomically disadvantaged groups.

29. The Perspective of the Office of Minority Health

Herbert Nickens

In minority populations, more than 60,000 "excess deaths" occur each year, according to a federal report on health and mortality in the Black, Hispanic, Asian/Pacific Islander, and Native American populations. Excess deaths are deaths that would not occur if minorities had the same death rates as the majority White population. The report by the Department of Health and Human Services Task Force on Black and Minority Health identified six causes that accounted for 80% of that excess: cancer, cardiovascular disease and stroke, chemical dependency (measured by deaths due to cirrhosis), diabetes, violence and infant mortality (U.S. Department of Health and Human Services 1985). For example, about 140,000 Blacks die every year before age 70; of these about 42% would not have died if Blacks had the same death rate as the White population.

The task force had trouble quantifying minority health status because of substantial gaps in the data, particularly concerning non–Black minorities. Our data problems were even greater for subgroups of minorities, such as the Chinese within the larger group of Asian/Pacific Islanders. The Hispanic population is just beginning to be counted accurately in national statistics, because Hispanics have sometimes been considered an ethnic group and sometimes a race. Often, Hispanics have been counted as White or Black, depending on their physical appearance. Despite these shortcomings in data collection, we have a general idea of the health status of the four major minority groups: Asian/Pacific Islanders, Blacks, Hispanics, and Native Americans.

The task force made hundreds of recommendations, which can be grouped into six categories: health information and education, access to and financing of health services, health professions development, cooperative efforts with the nonfederal sector, data, and research. The Office of Minority Health (OMH) was created to ensure the implementation of these recommendations.

Since the task force report was written, the OMH has also been involved in the AIDS issue. About 26% of persons with AIDS are Black, about 15% are Hispanic, and about 1% belong to other minorities; overall, then, more than 40% of persons with AIDS are members of minority groups. Among subgroups of persons with AIDS, the statistics are even more alarming. About 75% of women and children who have AIDS are Black or Hispanic (Centers for Disease Control 1988). This excessive minority representation among persons with AIDS needs to be better known if we are to develop adequately targeted education strategies, which are now our only defense against AIDS.

Opportunities to Improve Minority Health Status

To influence health outcomes, we must be concerned with health care system characteristics, the physical environment, and the individual's knowledge, attitudes, and practices regarding health. I will comment on each of these in turn.

Obviously, health care costs are rising out of sight. Health care costs as a percentage of the gross national product have increased from about 5% in 1960 to about 11% today, about $500 billion. This is substantially higher than what other Western nations spend on health care. Therefore, the resulting pressure in this country to contain costs is here to stay. It began under the Carter administration, has been accelerating under the Reagan administration, and will certainly continue.

Revisions in health care financing methods are being discussed in Congress and elsewhere. A dramatic one is relative-value scales. Such efforts are profound when one considers that 20 or 30 years ago physicians were firmly in control of the medical establishment, including pricing. More familiar changes are represented by the alphabet soup that has come into being in the past few years: HMOs (health maintenance organizations), PPOs (preferred provider organizations), and DRGs (diagnosis-related groups), all of which aim to control costs. We now have to think about health care system plans and health care expenditures as if we were dealing with a zero-sum game: any expenditure must be viewed in light of what has to be cut to finance it. Financing issues must be kept in mind as we forge a strategy for dealing with cancer in minorities. That is true of preventive, diagnostic, and treatment services.

At the OMH, we believe that minority people and institutions must play a larger part in this strategy. Health maintenance organizations, for example, can offer participants the opportunity of receiving preventive care and achieving better health status. Our office will hold a financing and HMO conference in mid-1989 on the role that HMOs can play in minority communities both to improve health care and provide opportunities for entrepreneurship and minority business control.

A second sphere important to health status is the physical environment. In general, when we think about this, we include a range of environmental hazards from a lack of window grates—recent news stories have concerned children of poor families falling out of windows in New York—to the problems associated with lead paint. With regard to cancer, perhaps the most important physical-environmental issues are occupational and home exposure to carcinogens. Unfortunately, many of these agents appear to have synergistic effects with more familiar risk factors, such as tobacco. Minority people have disproportionately high carcinogen exposures because often they are employed in blue collar and agricultural occupations and may be exposed to more carcinogens at home, as well because they are clustered in urban locations and substandard housing. They also have other disease risk factors, such as high rates of smoking. Although important progress has been made toward reducing environmental risks in the past few decades, we have far to go. The shift in our economy from a manufacturing and farm-labor base to a service-oriented job base may reduce exposure to some kinds of carcinogens, but we are learning about a whole new set of exposure problems, like those associated with work in the electronics industry.

The third major effect on health status arises from individual behavior, knowledge, attitudes, and practices. I believe it is fair to say that, generally, people in minority communities have been more preoccupied with issues of day-to-day survival and have not been involved in the increasingly intense pursuit of health promotion and disease prevention. This is probably also true for the poor White population. Our challenge is to encourage minority people to think about their health in a long-term sense and to begin organizing around health issues. We have instituted a program that we hope addresses that challenge.

The issue of behavior also raises the issue of blaming the victim. My view of prevention is that it is a no-fault enterprise; there is no room for being judgmental. Changing behavior may be a constant struggle, especially in the case of habits such as drinking alcohol and smoking.

The relationship of poverty to minority health is often brought up. Many times when we talk about the Office of Minority Health or minority health issues, people look us in the eye and ask, "Aren't you really just talking about the effects of poverty?" I don't think it is that simple. It is true that low socioeconomic status has been associated with poor health since the 12th and 13th centuries. Poverty and poor health status are related unquestionably. However, the problem of poverty is not so simple. We need to research what it means to be poor. Is poverty only a matter of education or income level? Why do all groups with similar poverty rates not have similar health status? In general, higher cancer rates are associated with lower socioeconomic status for almost all cancers except melanoma and breast cancer. Yet we also see dramatic differences in cancer rates among populations with equally low socioeconomic status.

Even if we accept the view that poverty is a central factor in minority health status, what shall we do about it? Most societies, including ours, have not done a good job of eliminating poverty. Those of us in the public health community cannot wait for economic parity before we proceed; we must do what we do best—offer public health programs.

At OMH, we have put our money where our mouths are; our first and most substantial project is our Minority Community Health Coalition grant program, which funds coalitions of community-based organizations that aim to reduce risk factors and conduct other kinds of health activities. These organizations include churches, school systems, fraternities, sororities, police departments, and mayors' offices. We awarded six grants in both the first and second years and have reannounced the program in the *Federal Register*, adding AIDS as a seventh disease area to be targeted.

We have also supported a large number of conferences financially and organizationally. Our intent is to get the word out, to disseminate information to get people thinking about and acting constructively on minority health issues.

One activity tied to these efforts was our Conference for States and Locales: Developing Minority Health Strategies, held in September 1987 in Washington, D.C. This conference brought together people involved in a large number of state and local efforts devoted to minority health (several states now have black and minority health task forces); our Coalition grantees; federal, state, and local health officials; and national minority organizations. Part of the rationale for holding this conference was that more and more human service decisions are made at state and local levels.

One of the most difficult challenges the OMH faces is how, as a small office, we can coordinate minority health issues for the entire Department of Health and Human Services. We have organized nine health-issue working groups representing each of the six disease categories mentioned earlier and the crosscutting issue of data collection, health care access and financing, and health professions. Together, these groups include more than 100 people who will try to answer the question: Now that we have the data of the Task Force report and its recommendations, what constructive implementation steps can HHS take within its budgetary and programmatic constraints?

The OMH also has given seed funding to a cancer network that is being organized by Howard, Meharry, Drew, and Morehouse medical schools. The people in this network will do coordinated, collaborative research in what we believe is an important and historic effort.

Finally, we are beginning to think about how to market health to minority populations. We need to emulate the techniques and successes of such enterprises as beer, fast food, and, unfortunately, even the tobacco companies. Anyone who spends time in minority communities or studies the mass media knows that these companies understand the cultures and tastes of various minority groups and know how to create demand. Those of us in the health care business must learn how to do this; health care messages cannot just be negative, telling us what to stop doing. We must be prepared to offer positive messages. I not only believe it is possible to "sell" health, but also that our lives and our children's lives require it.

References

Center for Disease Control: AIDS Weekly Surveillance Report. Atlanta, GA, May 30, 1988.

US Department of Health and Human Services: Report of the Task Force on Black and Minority Health. Washington, DC, 1985.

30. The Role of the National Cancer Institute

Barbara S. Bynum

The National Cancer Institute (NCI), established under the National Cancer Act of 1937, is the federal government's principal agency for cancer research and training. The National Cancer Act of 1971 directed the institute to "plan and develop an expanded, intensified, and coordinated cancer research program, encompassing the programs of NCI, related programs of other research Institutes, and other Federal and non-Federal programs." To speed the translation of research results into widespread application, the Act authorized a cancer control program to demonstrate and communicate to both the medical community and the general public the latest advances in cancer prevention and treatment.

To fulfill this mandate, NCI sponsors a broad range of research and research-related activities, both intramural and extramural, which include basic and applied research and a variety of educational and public demonstration programs. In addition to conducting investigative projects in its own laboratories and clinics, NCI provides grant and contract support for basic and clinical cancer research and training as well as cancer control programs at institutions in the United States and abroad.

Now, because of the rapid advances being made in these areas, as well as in prevention research, the NCI has set a major goal to reduce the nation's cancer mortality rate by 50% by the year 2000.

Several challenges have emerged recently that clearly require reexamination of the role of minority individuals and institutions in this national cancer effort. One is that posed by the 1985 Report of the Secretary's Task Force on Black and Minority Health, which addresses emphatically the continuing disparity in the burden of death and illness experienced by Black and other minority Americans as compared with our nation's population as a whole. Another is that revealed by the National Cancer Institute's own Surveillance, Epidemiology, and End Results (SEER) Program, which acknowledges the gravity of the cancer incidence-mortality disparity between minorities, especially Blacks, and the general population.

Dr. Vincent DeVita, former director of the National Cancer Institute, has on many occasions cited the essentiality of addressing this disparity as a critical element in achieving the national goals of the institute.

The Division of Extramural Activities (DEA) at NCI has historically been the institute's operational focus for cooperative funding of research and research training through its Comprehensive Minority Biomedical Program (CMBP), although the institute has continued to encourage minority involvement through the traditional extramural support mechanisms. Several of its programs have addressed, in a generic fashion, specific aspects of cancer in defined minority populations.

The paucity of information about the nature of the specific, and perhaps singular, problems of cancer in the minority community has raised questions about the efficacy of addressing these issues along traditional lines using traditional methodology. The extensive network of NCI-supported investigators and facilities constitutes a national resource that the National Cancer Institute has now moved to make more accessible to the minority academic and biomedical community. Perhaps more important, minority individuals and institutions are themselves being increasingly recognized as potential resources for both long- and short-term solutions. It hasn't been too long, certainly no more than a decade or so, since it was the rule, rather than the exception, for minorities in this country to deny the reality of cancer as a major health problem in their communities. This book is an acknowledgment not only of the reality of cancer in minority populations but also of the magnitude and seriousness of its incidence, morbidity, and mortality in minority groups.

The National Cancer Institute's current efforts span the spectrum from surveillance and detection through prevention/awareness and intervention to research, clinical treatment, patient management, and provision of support systems. This range of programmatic activities represents a concerted effort to move beyond the research orientation that we share with other components of the National Institutes of Health into a framework wherein we approach cancer as a public health problem, rather than only as a subject for investigation of the molecular and cellular basis of its etiology or of the biochemical and synthetic parameters to be considered in the design of therapeutic drugs.

Against the background of public recognition of the deteriorating health status of the minority population, the role of the National Cancer Institute is posited as a broad-based approach to every aspect of the issue—from training and manpower development to prevention and awareness heightening, from increased funding for research by minority scientists to enrollment of larger numbers of minority physicians and patients in the NCI clinical trials program.

We are totally cognizant of the recommendations of the Minority Health Task Force report and, consistent with those recommendations, are involved in a major campaign aimed at encouraging minority Americans to minimize their risks of cancer. We recently announced a special initiative that will involve the Historically Black Colleges and Universities in programs designed to heighten awareness about cancer in their communities. We are developing concepts for implementing screening and detection programs in Hispanic communities; the Special Populations Branch of the Division of Cancer Prevention and Control supports studies of avoidable mortality, health services access and utilization,

(Dollars in Thousands)

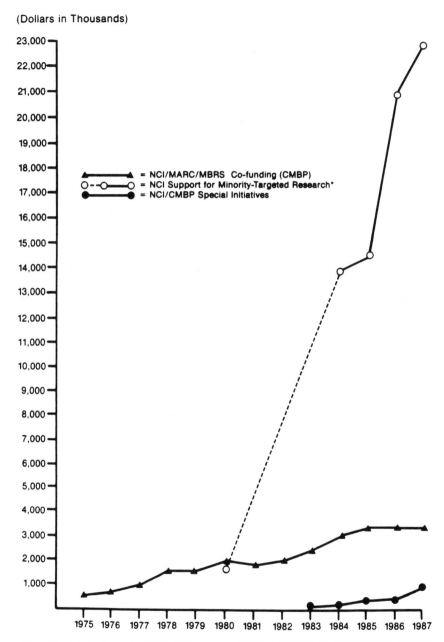

*Complete data for the period 1975–1983 are not available; funding levels given for 1980–1983 are estimates.

FIGURE 1. From "Minority Involvement in Cancer-Related Research and Training Activities," USDHHS Administrative Report, National Cancer Institute, 1987.

and intervention control and prevention strategies that focus on these populations. Our Cancer Treatment Division continues to promote and support participation of minority patients and their physicians in our Clinical Cooperative
Groups and to offer treatment programs at hospitals and institutions that serve
large or predominantly minority populations. In addition, the National Cancer
Institute has been given lead-agency responsibility for the Department of Health
and Human Services Task Force Working Group on Cancer in Minorities.
Finally, we have made it a critical function of the National Cancer Institute to
provide support and assistance in the development of minority manpower and in
strengthening the training and research capabilities of minority institutions in
general and of the minority health professional schools in particular.

In summary, the statement of the NCI Year 2000 goals, following the earlier
publication of the pertinent SEER data on minorities, clearly had major significance in defining the role of the National Cancer Institute in the present context. The subsequent commitment made by the institute to address cancer in
minorities as a critical component of its broader objective and as a viable aspect
of the NCI mission has begun to command a steadily increasing share of its
resources and is one to which we, the National Cancer Advisory Board and each
of the NCI divisions through its programmatic orientation, are unreservedly
dedicated.

31. Cancer and the Disadvantaged —A Crisis

Daniel Hoskins

The American Cancer Society, Inc. (ACS) Study on Cancer in the Disadvantaged (Funch 1985) was summarized in a special report to the ACS Board of Directors (ACS Subcommittee on Cancer in the Economically Disadvantaged, June 1986), along with recommendations on what the ACS might do about the report findings. The special report was approved and disseminated to all ACS committees and departments. These committees were charged with developing short- and long-range plans outlining action it would take toward implementation of each recommendation.

We recognized that a critical element in the planning process to address these recommendations would be to reveal the findings to knowledgeable individuals and institutions in a forum that would provide opportunity for exchange of data and input from others with related concerns. Cosponsoring the symposium on the "Realities of Cancer in Minority Communities" conducted April 22–25 in Houston, Texas, with M. D. Anderson Cancer Center provided that opportunity.

After review of the special report, the ACS determined that it would prioritize an initiative to do what it could to make access to health care possible for the nation's socioeconomically disadvantaged populations. Additionally, the ACS National Advisory Committee on Cancer in Minorities requested that its prior work be considered sufficiently concluded and recommended that the ACS, through its traditional organizational structure, continue its efforts to be inclusive of all minority populations. It recommended a new National Advisory Committee on Cancer in the Socio-Economically Disadvantaged be appointed to (1) monitor progress of the initiative to reach and serve the socioeconomically disadvantaged, (2) provide coordination and guidance where appropriate (not to usurp the role of traditional committees), (3) provide additional new data when available, (4) support traditional committee efforts as necessary, and (5) serve as an advocate for continued growth in the involvement of minorities in all ACS activities.

Historical Overview

In 1971 President Nixon authorized a national cancer program, hailed by many as the "war on cancer." The following year the historic Howard University study

"The Alarming Increase in Cancer Mortality in the United States Black Population" was issued (Freeman May 1986).

Study after study documented the high cancer mortality rate among Black Americans compared to that for White Americans. Foremost among these were the first and second National Cancer Institute (NCI) surveys, in 1944 and 1959. Then, from 1969–71 the NCI conducted the Third National Cancer Survey in nine major areas of the United States. This was the most comprehensive survey to date (Freeman May 1986).

In 1972 a larger program, gathering data from 11 population-based registries, was begun by NCI. This was the Surveillance, Epidemiology, and End Results (SEER) Program (NCI 1973–81), a continuing project of the NCI Biometry Branch. The SEER report gave information on cancer incidence and mortality in the United Stated during the first nine years of the program, 1973–81, and updated NCI Monograph 57.

In this report were the first detailed data on the occurrence of cancer among American Indians, Hispanics, Filipinos, Chinese, and Japanese-Americans, in addition to information on Black and White Americans. Previously, data by race/ethnicity had been available only for Black and White Americans. Variations in cancer incidence and mortality among the racial and ethnic groups for whom data were available were indicated, using annual age-adjusted incidence rates for all sites.

In 1979 Harold P. Freeman, M.D., Head of the Department of Surgery at Harlem Hospital in New York and delegate-at-large member of the ACS National Board of Directors, discussed the diagnosis and treatment of cancer at Harlem Hospital at the ACS science writers seminar. He noted that half of the 165 patients with breast cancer seen consecutively at Harlem Hospital, all Black Americans and poor, had incurable disease on admission. The five-year cure rate was 20% compared with 65% in White American women (Freeman May 1986).

"Not able to pay for a private physician in a medical system stressing fee for service," Freeman said, "the poor patient with potential cancer is frequently seen first in an emergency room and referred to a clinic. Long waiting periods and complex registration procedures are common. The emergency room is geared toward treating apparently sick people. A minimally symptomatic patient is likely to be discouraged when faced by a process of diagnosis which may be perceived as being more disturbing than a painless lump. The result is often late diagnosis at an incurable state of disease" (Freeman 1987).

"By the interplay of all these factors and others, poor people with early cancer are essentially triaged off, later reappearing with advanced stages of disease resulting in death. This triaging off of the disadvantaged is given substance by an establishment that directs its major medical resources to those who can pay the price: a society which apparently views the challenge of fundamentally dealing with the problems of diagnosing and treating cancer in the poor as too enormous. This 'malignant neglect' constitutes a silent death sentence for many thousands of Americans each year," Freeman said.

Subsequently, Dr. Freeman compiled data on studies that had demonstrated the relationship between low socioeconomic status and death from cancer. These studies were presented in part at the ACS science writers seminar of 1981.

He noted that the California Tumor Registry in 1963 showed that survival rates of cancer patients admitted to city hospitals between 1942 and 1956 were significantly lower than those of patients admitted to private hospitals. The poor patients, poorer prognosis was due to their advanced stage of disease at the time of diagnosis. A study on the influence of socioeconomic factors on cancer survival noted a smaller percentage of localized tumors among the indigent. Treatment delays were more frequent among the poor, thus diagnosis was delayed until patients had advanced disease. A 1977 study of the University of Iowa Hospital records from 1940 to 1969 related economic status to survival for patients with 39 different kinds of cancer. The results showed that indigent patients had poorer survival rates than non-indigents. Nearly all the patients were white Americans. Both groups of patients were treated in a uniform way by the same clinical team, virtually eliminating the possibility that quality of care in the two groups affected the outcome. The survival of the indigent patients was at least 20% lower than that of nonindigent patients (Freeman 1987).

Freeman further pointed out that NCI estimates at that time, 1940–1970, put the five-year cancer survival rate of all Americans at 41% in contrast to a projected survival rate in Black Americans of 30%. Incidence of cancer had increased 8% in Black Americans and decreased 3% in White Americans, while cancer mortality among Black Americans had increased 26% versus only 5% for White Americans (Freeman 1987).

Freeman then asked some searching questions: Are available resources distributed to the American population in a way that obtains the best survival results? Is there a reasonable balance between the allocation of resources for cancer research and allocations for education, diagnosis and treatment of people who are candidates for having cancer now? Given that cancer incidence and mortality are considerably higher among the poor, is the American establishment willing to address this problem fundamentally?

Since 1981, more and more data has supported Freeman's conclusion that economic status is the major determinant of the disproportionately poor survival of poor and minority Americans when compared with that of higher-income Americans of all races. This, he states, is probably a major factor in cancer survival for the American people as a whole (Freeman 1987).

Conference on Cancer Among Black Americans

National attention was focused on Blacks with cancer for the first time by the 1979 ACS Conference, "Meeting the Challenge of Cancer Among Black Americans." It initiated vital commitments and programs for the ACS for which substantial funds were allocated. Many minority volunteers and staff were recruited and trained for national, division, and unit organization volunteer and staff positions.

"A major new dialogue was begun," the American Cancer Society's statement declared. "We're taking cancer prevention and detection into all the nation's neighborhoods . . . " (Horsch 1987).

To help implement these initiatives, the ACS National Board of Directors in 1979 appointed the National Advisory Committee on Cancer in Minorities, which was chaired by Dr. Lasalle D. Leffall, Jr., Past President of the ACS and Professor and Chairman of the Department of Surgery at Howard University.

One of the conference recommendations was for an ACS-sponsored national survey, "*Black American Attitudes Toward Cancer and Cancer Tests*" (Evaxx Inc. 1981). The study was based on in-home interviews with a nationwide sample of 750 Black men and women, 18 years old or older. For comparison, the findings were measured against a similar ACS-sponsored study conducted in 1978 among a sample of the general population (Horsch 1987).

Results of the survey indicated that urban Black Americans tended to be less knowledgeable than White Americans about cancer warning signals and were less apt to see a doctor when they experienced those symptoms. Of prime importance, the study showed that lower-income Black Americans (household incomes under $7,500 annually) were less likely than those with higher incomes ($15,000+ annually) to see a doctor when they experienced symptoms or to obtain physical checkups.

In addition it was found that lower-income Black American women were less likely than Black American women of higher incomes to seek Pap tests regularly and to perform monthly breast self-examinations. They were also less likely to have heard of proctoscopic examination for colorectal cancer or a mammographic examination for breast cancer.

Hispanic Workshop

The 1982 ACS workshop for Hispanic Americans (American Cancer Society, 1982b) involved nine organizations, leaders of the Hispanic community, and scientific and health professionals. A subsequent ACS study, "*A Study of Hispanics' Attitudes Concerning Cancer and Cancer Prevention*" (Clark, Martire, and Bartolomeo, Inc. 1985), indicated that Hispanic Americans were not adequately aware of most of the warning signals of cancer or of ways to reduce cancer risk. They tended not to seek early detection or treatment.

Additional findings demonstrated that a third of Hispanic Americans had annual incomes below $10,000, three of every four who were employed had limited blue-collar jobs, half had not finished high school, one-third had no medical insurance, and cost was the major reason for not seeking physical checkups or treatment.

Second National ACS Conference on Cancer in Minorities

Continuing its initiative among minority groups, the ACS convened a second National Conference in May, 1983, focusing attention on the incidence of cancer among Black Americans, Hispanic Americans, American Indians, Asian Americans, and others. With this conference, the ACS broadened its minority emphasis beyond Blacks and Hispanics to meet the challenge of cancer in all minorities—a signal step that furthered the notion of energizing all minority groups to join in the fight against cancer. This involved soliciting minority community organizations, medical professionals, health specialists, clergy, and other key leaders as advisors, volunteers, or staff (Horsch 1987).

Additionally, during the period between conferences, the Society allocated $250,000 for minority staff hiring and training. To date, that figure has grown into a $3.5 million staff development program.

In broadening the premise that poverty is a major villain in the lower survival of poor people with the disease, so overwhelming was the data on socioeconomic factors, so harrowing the human consequence that the National Advisory Committee on Cancer in Minorities in June 1986 felt compelled to address the challenge by choosing to become the National Advisory Committee on Cancer in the Socioeconomically Disadvantaged. "It is not race alone that so colors the outcome—it is deprivation, which compromises health, the comprehensible information on prevention, and risk reduction education" (Horsch 1987).

The ACS, Horsch said, had to add the factor of low socioeconomic status to "our concerns for all minorities" because "this is a human concern for all Americans but is particularly important to minority Americans because they form a disproportionate number of the poor" (Horsch 1987). Horsch further stated that during its 75-year history, the American Cancer Society has tried to educate people about cancer, to bring it out of the closet, and by so doing to maximize the use of existing knowledge by applying it to prevention, early detection, and treatment. Cancer is nondiscriminatory, as we have increasingly come to appreciate, and it has been well documented that there are some boundaries based in a general sense on differences in access to the health care system (Horsch 1987).

Research Initiatives

Research drives our other programs. Whenever we don't know the answers, we commit ourselves to further learning by means of research. The ACS research program will award over $80 million in research funding this year through our peer review committees. Most of those funds come through our regular grants and awards system, which is equivalent to the NCI RO-1 grant mechanism. Scientific advisory committees of volunteers review the grant applications, which are reviewed again by members of our research council. Funds for the most meritorious of these are then approved by the ACS Board of Directors (Horsch 1987).

About half of our committees review applications for research in clinical areas. The chemotherapy and hematology committees review applications in those disciplines, the prevention, diagnosis and treatment committee covers epidemiology, nutrition, new treatments (other than chemotherapy and immunotherapy) and diagnostic measures. The immunology and immunotherapy committee members cover both basic and clinical research in this rapidly developing area, and the psychosocial and behavioral research committee provides peer review of scientific proposals in these areas (Horsch 1987).

We welcome innovative research (not demonstration projects) on how to educate and motivate disadvantaged people about cancer, how to enable them to use existing cancer screening and other resources effectively. We recognize that the level of science is not as highly developed in these "softer" areas of research, and our reviewers will advise us to fund only the outstanding proposals. Thus the challenge is to frame questions that can be answered using rigorous means of analysis (Horsch 1987).

Start-up funds are available from our Research Development Program. These may be used to test methods and obtain sufficient pilot data for regular grant applications. Personnel awards are also available, ranging from postdoctoral fellowships to the research professor level. It happens that people working in the psychosocial and epidemiology areas rarely apply for these awards. But as salary support is usually essential to free up research time, it seems useful to mention their availability (Horsch 1987).

Finally, we have Institutional Research Grants in about 60 medical schools. These seed funds are disbursed by multidisciplinary committees to young investigators starting new projects. We encourage these institutions, and we welcome new institutions to look at opportunities for supporting investigators who are interested in questions relevant to cancer in the economically disadvantaged and psychosocial areas (Horsch 1987).

ACS Cancer Prevention Study II

The ACS Cancer Prevention Study II is a long-term, ongoing prospective study launched in 1982 to examine the habits and exposures of more than 1 million Americans (over 60,000 minorities), to learn how life-styles and environmental factors influence the development of cancer. This data is having and will have far-reaching effects on future strategies to combat cancer (ACS 1982a).

Summary

On the recommendation of the National Advisory Committee on Cancer in Minorities, the ACS Board of Directors in February 1984 committed to examine in-depth the influences of socioeconomic status on the quantity and quality of health care. The examination was to determine implications for action by the ACS relative to the risk of developing cancer, promptness in obtaining diagnosis, obstacles preventing access to available health care, the adequacy of medical care, and such other factors as may contribute to cancer incidence and lower survival rates in disadvantaged populations. The ACS, after analysis of the study and subsequent recommendations reinforced by Bureau of the Census findings and other sources on the characteristics of poverty, concludes that both cancer incidence and low survival are more related to socioeconomic status than to ethnic origin. The National Advisory Committee on Cancer in the Socio-Economically Disadvantaged is working with and through long-standing committees to coordinate strategies, methods, techniques, tools, and training that these committees and other individuals have determined are necessary to begin addressing these problems.

During this development stage, the ACS continues to support the efforts of numerous other organizations to reduce cancer incidence and mortality in the socioeconomically disadvantaged and minority populations. We are organizing a National Conference on Cancer in the Socio-Economically Disadvantaged to be held in the fall of 1989.

References

American Cancer Society, Inc: *Cancer Prevention Study II.* New York, 1982a.

American Cancer Society, Inc: *Workshop for Cancer in Hispanic Americans.* New York, 1982b.

American Cancer Society Subcommittee on Cancer in the Economically Disadvantaged: *Cancer in the Economically Disadvantaged: A Special Report.* New York, June 1986.

Clark, Martire & Bartolomeo, Inc: *A Study of Hispanics' Attitudes Concerning Cancer and Cancer Prevention,* 1985 (for the American Cancer Society, Inc.).

Evaxx, Inc: *A Study of Black Americans' Attitudes Towards Cancer and Cancer Tests,* January 1981 (for the American Cancer Society, Inc.).

Freeman HP: Socioeconomically Disadvantaged Overview, New York: American Cancer Society National Advisory Committee on Cancer in Minorities, May 1986.

Freeman HP: Because they're poor. Presentation at the Realities of Cancer in Minority Communities Symposium, April 22–25, 1987, Houston, Texas.

Funch DP: *A Report on Cancer Survival in the Economically Disadvantaged.* From the Department of Social and Preventive Medicine, State University of New York at Buffalo 1985 (for the American Cancer Society, Inc.).

Horsch K: Presentation at the Realities of Cancer in Minority Communities Symposium, April 22–25, 1987, Houston, Texas.

National Cancer Institute. *Surveillance, Epidemiology, and End Result, 1973–1981 Report.* Bethesda, MD.

32. The Role of Minority Academic Health Centers

David Satcher

We recognize now that cancer in minorities is a problem of crisis proportions that merits urgent concern and action. I shall focus on the role of minority medical schools or academic health centers in responding to this reality.

What Are These Centers?

There are only a few minority academic health centers in the country. They tend to be grouped or combined in interesting ways for varying endeavors. Some have combined to form the Association of Minority Health Professional Schools, which includes the Meharry Schools of Medicine and Dentistry, the Charles R. Drew University for Medicine and Science, the Morehouse School of Medicine, three schools of pharmacy—Florida A & M College of Pharmacy, Xavier College of Pharmacy, Texas Southern University School of Pharmacy—and one school of veterinary medicine, Tuskegee. According to 1980 data, these eight institutions together have trained more than 40% of Black physicians, 50% of Black dentists, 70% of Black pharmacists, and 85% of Black veterinarians. The goal of this association, formed in 1980, is to strengthen these institutions in their roles of expanding access to the health professions for minorities and of improving the health status of minorities in general.

Some minority academic health centers—Meharry Medical College, Charles R. Drew University for Medicine and Science, Howard University College of Medicine, and Morehouse School of Medicine—have come together to form a Cancer Control Network to promote research in Cancer control and prevention of cancer in Blacks. Additionally, an independent group of researchers interested in cancer in Blacks but working at predominantly White institutions is part of this network, whose formation was supported by the National Cancer Institute (NCI). Further, Meharry, Drew, and Morehouse make up the Cancer Control Center Consortium, an NCI-funded planning venture intended to enhance the participating institutions' research strength.

Some of us—this is perhaps the largest group—have come together as a combination known as Research Centers at Minority Institutions (RCMI), a project funded by the National Institutes of Health's Division of Research Resources to improve the research infrastructure of minority academic health centers. In addition to the historically Black colleges and universities named above, two University of Puerto Rico health professional schools, Hunter College, City College of New York, Atlanta University, and Tennessee State University participate in RCMI. These schools educate a large percentage of minority students, and most of these schools are concerned with health problems affecting minority individuals and communities.

Their General Role

Academic health centers are involved primarily in education, service, and research. We view our primary role as the education of health professionals and health scientists for the future. As a rule, everything else supports this purpose. This means that services provided at academic health centers must be exemplary and a guide to students and residents. Research is the base from which questions are asked and new knowledge is generated; without research, education and service become stale and outdated.

Because professional health education does not play for itself, academic health centers rely on service and research for funding. In recent years, along with reduced federal funding of education, the role of research and service in the funding of academic health centers has become more important (Commonwealth Fund Task Force on Academic Health Centers 1985). This has led to some confusion about the primary role of academic health centers and some concerns about the impact of clinical practice by faculty members on education and research (Petersdorf 1985).

The primary mission of academic health centers is education. When many of us were in medical schools or other professional schools, acquired immune deficiency syndrome had not been recognized as a problem. Yet today we rely on present-day health professionals for service, research, and education related to AIDS. This means that our education must have prepared us to identify and solve new problems, not only those already described when we were students. Likewise, our students today must be prepared to deal with present and future problems.

Their Uniqueness

There are 127 medical schools in the United States, among which, according to a 1987 report by the National Science Foundation, 20 received more than half of all federal funding for research during the period of 1978 to 1985. At the same time, according to a report in the *New England Journal of Medicine* (Shea and

Fullilove 1985), three of these institutions — Howard University College of Medicine, Meharry Medical College, and the Morehouse School of Medicine — had nearly one-third of all Black students in medical schools.

The role of minority medical schools is historic. In fact, until 1970, the overwhelming majority of Blacks in medicine were graduates of Meharry and Howard University. The Morehouse School of Medicine was founded in 1975 and enrolled its first class in 1978. Clearly, if it were not for the minority academic health centers, especially the schools of medicine, pharmacy, and veterinary medicine, the underrepresentation of Blacks in the health professions would be even more severe than it is today.

In addition, minority academic health centers produce health professionals who are more likely to serve minorities and practice in underserved communities. Another study in the *New England Journal of Medicine* (Keith et al. 1985), focusing on a cohort of minority and nonminority 1975 graduates of medical schools, found some interesting patterns of practice. Minority graduates were twice as likely to practice in underserved communities, and more than two-thirds of their patients belonged to minority groups. This was especially true of graduates from Howard and Meharry. The Robert Wood Johnson Foundation Report on Meharry Medical College in 1980 (unpublished) showed that 3 of 4 of a representative group of graduates over a 10-year period were practicing in underserved rural and inner-city communities.

The unique role of minority academic health centers can therefore be summed up in four statements:

• These centers educate a large percentage of minority health professionals, most of whom go on to work in underserved communities. Most of their patients will be poor and minority members.

• These centers provide credible role models for students as they develop their base of knowledge, skills, and commitment. These role models by their own existence and example say to these students, Yes, you can. You should. You must.

• These centers provide supportive environments that model institutional commitment to the underserved. Examples include Meharry Medical College's role in Mount Bayou, Mississippi, Lee County, Arkansas, and Tuskegee, Alabama, where exemplary care was provided to the poor long before federal funds were available as Medicaid or as support for community health center efforts. These institutional roles not only provide models for students but national leadership that helps shape the health care system as well (Summerville 1983).

• These centers target problems and unmet needs specific or predominant in minority communities. For example, in 1985 the Heckler/Malone Report of the U.S. Department of Health and Human Services pointed out the persistent gap in health status between Blacks and Whites in this country. Cancer was highlighted in that report along with cardiovascular disease, cirrhosis of the liver, diabetes, homicide, and substance abuse as a major cause of excessive deaths among Blacks and other minorities. The bottom line of this report, however, is that each year in this country 60,000 more Blacks die than would die if Blacks had the same age- and sex-adjusted death rates as Whites. Minority institutions view this problem as a major challenge and are committed to leading in its resolution through research, education, and service.

Research Challenges Facing Minority Academic Health Centers

Our roles and contributions in health services and education are well documented. It is also clear that we have not been as involved in research. In 1982, in fact, all historically Black colleges and universities combined (approximately 110) received less than 1% of federal funds for research. Although there are many reasons for this, it is nonetheless clear that in order to respond to the major challenges related to the health status of Blacks, we must become more involved in research. We must transform our presence, our relationships, our service, and our access in the Black community into programs that will better define questions and problems concerning the health status of Blacks and other minorities and promote strategic efforts to answer questions and solve problems.

Several clear research challenges and opportunities face us today that have definite implications for cancer control in minorities. In 1983, working through the Association of Minority Health Professional Schools, we developed the concept of Research Centers at Minority Institutions to strengthen our research infrastructure and capacity. Several minority institutions are now developing research strength through these centers, including Meharry Medical College, where we recently used RCMI support to organize neuroscience research laboratories.

Through the Cancer Control Center Consortium, we have recently submitted a proposal to NCI emphasizing research on cancer control and prevention methodologies specific to minorities. Questions related to knowledge, attitude, life-styles/behavior, and their modification, as well as access to early diagnosis and care will be addressed. This consortium was born of our perceived deficiencies and an attempt to pool our resources to become eligible for consideration as a cancer center. An innovative approach to cancer prevention and control in the Black population may well come from this consortium as a result of studying distinct communities (Nashville, Los Angeles, Chicago, Washington, D.C., and Atlanta), pooling and analyzing data from descriptive and interventional studies, and developing education and service programs based on the results.

A few of the research questions the consortium members have already identified as appropriate for their investigations are these:

—What factors account for or contribute to incidence, survival, and mortality rates of cancer in Blacks, especially as compared to those of others in this nation?

—Which approaches to behavior modification are likely to be most successful in minority communities, given problems of cultural diversity, language barriers, poverty, and discrimination?

—How do we improve access of Blacks and other minorities to appropriate information, diagnosis, and continuity of health care?

—What unique factors involved in cancers among Blacks might help explain differential survival rates and responses to therapy?

Certainly, minority academic health centers are not alone in their concern for the health status of minorities and the disproportionate impact of cancer on minorities. But it is also clear that a leadership role needs to be assumed, and that minority academic health centers are in a unique position to respond to this challenge. We will be seeking partnerships wherever possible, for we feel that it is through such partnerships that this and many other problems in this country can best be solved.

References

Commonwealth Fund: *Prescription for Change. Report of The Commonwealth Fund Task Force on Academic Health Centers*, 1985.

Keith SN, Bell RM, Swanson AG, et al: Effects of affirmative action in medical schools: A study of the class of 1975. *N Engl J Med* 1985;313:1519–1525.

National Science Foundation: *A Report to the President and Congress, Federal Support to Universities, Colleges and Selected Non-Profit Institution: FY 1985*. Washington, DC, 1987.

Petersdorf RG: Current and future directions for hospital and physician reimbursement: Effect on the academic health center. *JAMA* 1985;253:2543–2548.

Shea S, Fullilove MT: Entry of black and other minority students into U.S. medical schools: Historical perspective and recent trends. *N Engl J Med* 1985;313:933–940.

Summerville J: *Educating Black Doctors: A History of Meharry Medical College*. Birmingham: The University of Alabama Press, 1983.

U.S. Department of Health and Human Services: *National Science Foundation Report to the President and Congress*. Washington, DC, 1985.

U.S. Department of Health and Human Services: *Report of the Secretary's Task Force (DHHS) on the Status of Black and Minority Health*, vol. 1. Washington, DC, 1985.

Index